S0-CDW-871

Brinco

Brinco
The Story of
Churchill Falls

Philip Smith

McClelland and Stewart Limited

©Philip Smith, 1975

ALL RIGHTS RESERVED

ISBN: 0-7710-8184-7

The Canadian Publishers
McClelland and Stewart Limited
25 Hollinger Road, Toronto

Printed and bound in Canada
by
T. H. Best Printing Company Limited

Contents

Introduction

Summer comes late to Labrador, and the first snows of winter follow swiftly on its fleeting heels. Gaunt and empty, a place of ancient rock and rivers, of lakes and swamps and stunted, tattered trees, it has never been an easy land to live in. Few men have even tried the experiment: the earliest traces of human habitation found on the Labrador plateau go back only a thousand years. And in those comparatively recent times the men who roamed that wilderness had no tools more advanced than the chipped flints wielded by the cave-dwellers of Europe ten thousand years before.

Those who came later, the handful of Europeans who settled on the coast to be close to their Atlantic cod-fishing grounds, made no more mark on the unyielding interior of Labrador than those first inhabitants with their chipped flints. Few white travellers and not many more Indians ventured the two hundred or so miles inland to where the unchanging plateau rises abruptly to fifteen hundred feet above sea level, and no settlements took root there.

Now, in the stone heart of this harsh land, modern man has completed one of the boldest construction achievements of all time. Undeterred by the remoteness and the 50-below-zero winters, he has transported into the wilderness almost a million tons of steel and cement and sophisticated machinery manufactured in cities hundreds of miles to the south. By shaping the native rock and the debris left by retreating glaciers into a mere forty miles of strategically placed dykes, he has finished an engineering feat fortuitously begun by nature and created the third-largest reservoir in the world. And he is using the water stored in it — even though it is covered by ice for all but four months of the year — to drive a power station which is, quite simply, the largest single source of energy in the western world.

The Churchill Falls hydro-electric project was once described, perhaps slightingly, as being "drenched with superlatives." So be it — they are inseparable from its vastness. It was, for instance, the largest construction job ever tackled by a private company anywhere. Its billion-dollar cost — in those happy days before inflation added rows of noughts to virtually all such figures — dwarfed that of any previous Canadian enterprise. Its underground powerhouse, one of three huge caverns blasted out of the rock more than a thousand feet below the surface, is the largest in the world. Its eleven turbine-generators, when the orders for them were placed in the mid-sixties, were larger than any contemplated before: the rotating parts of each weigh 850 tons and stand as tall as a nine-storey building. And when they are all spinning, they generate more than seven million horse power, enough electricity to fill all the needs of three cities the size of Montreal.

Prime Minister Pierre Elliott Trudeau was therefore not being fanciful when he stood under a chill Labrador sky at the official inauguration of the project on June 16, 1972, and described Churchill Falls as "a construction achievement which will rank with any in history." On a red-carpeted dais high above the great gorge of the Churchill River, he congratulated all those who had contributed their efforts to its harnessing — "the dreamers as well as the workmen, the financiers as well as the engineers, the scientists as well as the managers." Their accomplishment, he said "begs comparison with the pyramids but with a usefulness which promises the benefits of a Nile."

We can only speculate now about the difficulties that faced the builders of the pyramids. But the almost unbelievable succession of difficulties that confronted those who conceived and carried through the Churchill Falls project was still vivid in the minds of many of those dreamers and businessmen and engineers who heard the Prime Minister's words.

Churchill Falls was the major accomplishment of Brinco Limited, a company born amid the enthusiasm of the early fifties, when it seemed that the twentieth century might yet belong to Canada. In those days, Brinco's chief asset appeared to be the mineral concession granted to it by the Newfoundland government. When, in keeping with its undertaking to foster the development of Newfoundland and Labrador, the company turned its attention to the unused water power of the Labrador plateau, it faced apparently insurmountable odds. Its plans at first seemed merely visionary. Then, as technological advances brought them within reach of realization, they fell afoul of a political controversy older than Canada itself: the long dispute between Quebec and Newfoundland over the Labrador boundary.

The years that followed were bedevilled by a series of clashes between Premiers Joey Smallwood and Jean Lesage that were probably unprecedented for their acrimony; by frustratingly prolonged negotiations to find a buyer for the power; by financial crises which several times brought the company to the verge of bankruptcy; and even by personal tragedy, when its brilliant young president and several of his most important advisers were killed in an air crash.

Somehow, Brinco and the Churchill Falls project survived, and the job was completed with unusual — possibly unique — efficiency: it was done within the allotted budget and ahead of schedule. Then came the biggest blow of all — a blow that fell because by 1974 the combination of the energy crisis and galloping inflation had changed the world to an extent that could not have been imagined during the Churchill Falls negotiations, and a new government of Newfoundland had come to question all that those dreamers and businessmen and engineers had struggled so hard to achieve.

Labrador:
"A great storehouse
of natural wealth"

First seen by a white man in
1839, Churchill Falls remained
one of the world's most rarely
seen marvels until a decade
ago, when work began to harness
their spectacular power.

Covered by the continental glacier until
six thousand years ago, the Labrador plateau
is a brooding wasteland of lakes and rock,
swamps and stunted trees. Higher at its rim
than in the centre, the plateau has been
likened to a huge saucer, with most of the
water from an area almost as large as New
Brunswick draining down the Churchill River.

The first snow falls early in Labrador, after
a brief summer made miserable for those who
work there by the depredations of the black fly.
The harsh climate, with winter temperatures
as low as 57 degrees Fahrenheit below zero,
took its toll of early travellers and prevented
the area's development until recent times.

Pilot project for Churchill Falls was the building
of a 300,000-horse power plant at Twin Falls, on
the Unknown River, part of the Churchill system.
Begun in 1960, the plant supplied power for the
iron-ore mines of western Labrador, provided a
training ground for Brinco's staff — and
power for the later construction of Churchill.

Long before any customer had been found to take
the power, Brinco had invested millions
of dollars in the Churchill project. By 1957, the
access road had reached the river and a catwalk
(top) had been erected across the rapids above
the falls. Even after the negotiations with
Quebec had broken down in 1964, the company went
ahead and completed the Brinco bridge (bottom).

Churchill Falls Underground Power Complex

A   Penstocks
B   Transformer gallery
C   Machine hall
D   Surge chamber
E   Tailrace tunnels
F   Cable shafts
G   Control and administration
    building

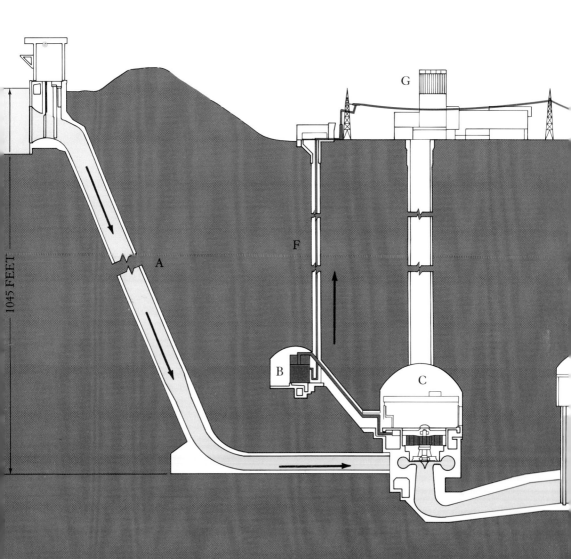

Control structures direct water step by step
from two reservoirs through man-made forebay
channel to power plant intake.

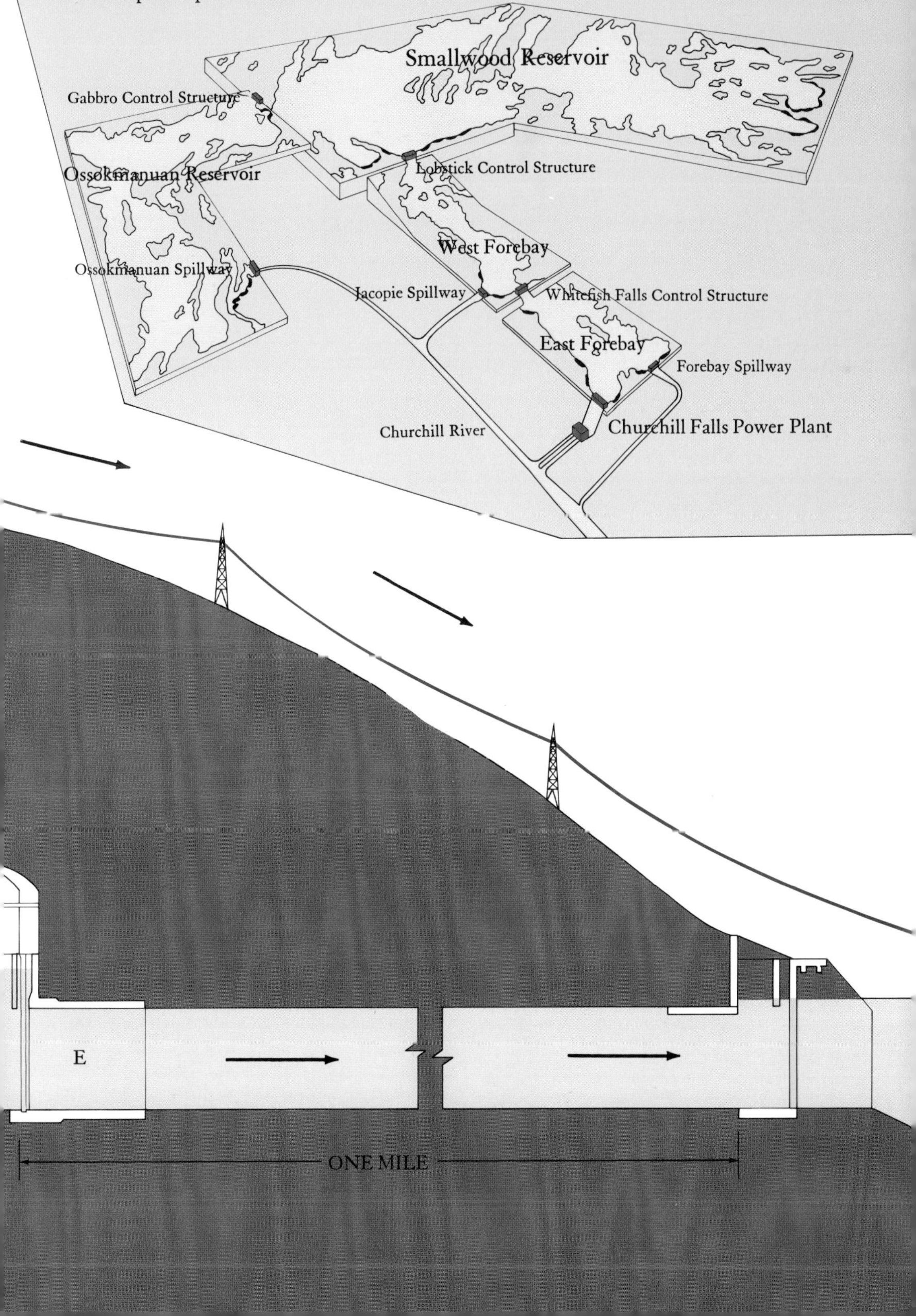

Smallwood Reservoir

Gabbro Control Structure

Ossokmanuan Reservoir

Lobstick Control Structure

West Forebay

Ossokmanuan Spillway

Jacopie Spillway

Whitefish Falls Control Structure

East Forebay

Forebay Spillway

Churchill River

Churchill Falls Power Plant

E

ONE MILE

The roar of heavy machinery seldom ceased during the years of construction at Churchill Falls. Key to the development is the Lobstick control structure (above) which, with its flanking dykes, controls the flow of water from the Smallwood Reservoir. Tailrace tunnels (facing page), which return the water to the river after it has spun the turbines, are more than a mile long, 45 feet wide, 60 feet high.

More than a thousand feet underground, steel
columns which will ultimately carry travelling
cranes are erected in the powerhouse chamber,
the biggest in the world. One of three vast
caverns hollowed out of the age-old granite,
the powerhouse is five times the size
of the concourse of Montreal's Central Station.

Giant magnets around its rim, a rotor is slowly
placed in one of the eleven turbine-generator
units installed in the Churchill Falls powerhouse.
Each unit stands as tall as a nine-storey
building and its rotating parts weigh 850 tons.

Power from Churchill Falls begins its 750-mile journey to Montreal by spanning river gorge from switchyard (at right, below). Three rows of towers carry thirty-six aluminum cables in "bundles" of four, strung simultaneously on V-shaped towers (far right) from five-ton reels. Near right: Insulators are fitted to towers used for mile-wide river crossing.

A modern town built high above the river within sight of the summit of the portage route used by explorers and trappers to carry their canoes up on to the plateau, Churchill Falls is now home to a community of about a thousand men, women and children. Houses were built on only one side of roads to make snow-clearing easier.

Concourse of the Churchill Falls town centre,
in deference to the Labrador climate, is
an indoor version of the old town square.
Named after the late Donald Gordon, president
of Brinco at a crucial stage in its fortunes,
the centre groups under one roof a hotel,
school, stores, theatre, curling rink and pool.

Brinco's first president, A. W. Southam (bottom left), arrived in St. John's
to organize company in 1953. Immediately below: Donald Gordon (facing camera at
left) and Don McParland (bow tie) enjoy relaxed moment with Premier Smallwood
at Churchill Falls sod-turning ceremony in 1967. Bottom right: Bill Mulholland
(left) and Sir Val Duncan in happy mood at 1972 board meeting at Churchill Falls.

I
The Pioneers

All those who have studied the past from the standpoint
of economics, and especially those who have studied
economic geography, are aware that, from the material
point of view, history is primarily the story of the
increasing ability of man to reach and control energy.

Allan Nevins

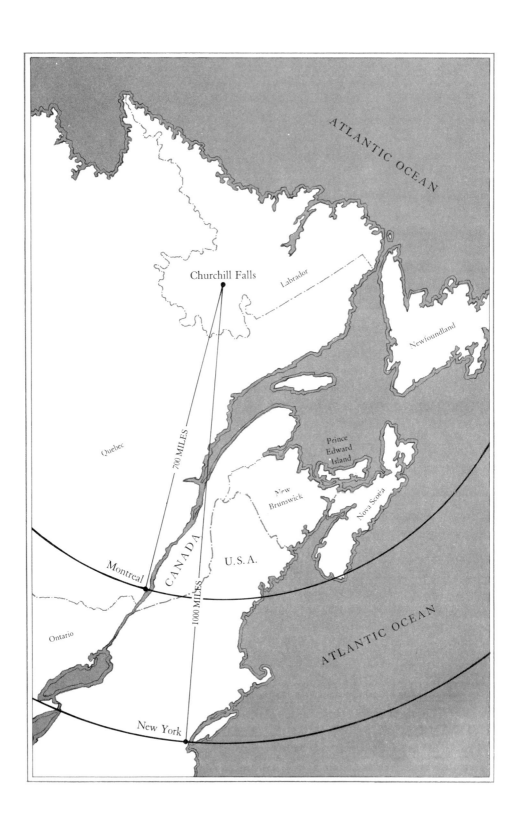

ONE

The invitation to Eldorado

The British press didn't quite know what to make of it. Hitherto, Canadian politicians visiting London had always maintained what it later became fashionable to describe as "a low profile." Mr. St. Laurent, for instance, was as dignified a prime minister as any who had ever occupied No. 10 Downing Street. But now this extraordinary little man with the beaky nose and the jutting lower lip and all the chirpy confidence of a Cockney sparrow had bounced in from Newfoundland — "a remote corner of the Empire," as he called it — and was summoning Britain to what sounded like a new Eldorado.

"I am here," said Joseph Roberts Smallwood, premier of Canada's newest province, "to offer you the biggest real estate deal of the present century." Newfoundland and Labrador, he told a press conference he summoned soon after checking into the Savoy Hotel, were the last great areas of North America open to development — "a great storehouse of natural wealth." They were British, and they wanted to remain British. And developing them could be a new challenge for Britain, "the beginning of England staging a very great industrial comeback."

But it would be a big task: "I am talking about a piece of territory about as big as England; bigger than Scotland; bigger than Wales. There is no company in all the United Kingdom big enough to do it alone, because it will cost many hundreds of millions." What was needed, the Premier explained, was a syndicate or consortium of large companies, "in the tradition of the East India Company."

Perhaps it was this echo of the days of England's imperial glory that captured the British imagination. It was August 1952, and the empire-minded had not had much to cheer about for some time. Exhausted physically and financially by two world wars, Britain had begun to liquidate her empire, and the sport of tweaking the lion's tail had spread around the world. Joey Smallwood and his invitation to renewed greatness thus made a stirring change for newspaper readers. When the reports appeared the response was remarkable: doctors, scientists, engineers, nurses and would-be explorers telephoned the Premier at the Savoy

3

offering their services. One man even called from South Africa and woke him in the middle of the night; others sent cheques and money orders to help out this remote corner of the empire which had till now been famous only for hardy fishermen and big woolly dogs that were forever pulling drowning children from the waves.

This show of public enthusiasm was gratifying to Smallwood, but it was not what he had crossed the Atlantic for. What he needed now was an entrée into the corridors of power. So, having started the ball rolling in the newspapers, he went round to explain his project to another Canadian of small stature but large influence: Lord Beaverbrook, with whom he had become friendly a couple of years earlier when he had tried, unsuccessfully, to recruit him as Chancellor of Memorial University in St. John's. It did not take him long to win over that lifelong campaigner for imperial preference. Beaverbrook picked up the telephone and called John Rupert Colville, private secretary to his old friend Winston Churchill. By 1952, Churchill was seeing very little of his old wartime colleague, not because their friendship was flagging but because Beaverbrook had by then largely retired from public life — "he had ceased to be part of the scene at 10 Downing Street," as Colville put it. So that when Beaverbrook telephoned and said. "I haven't asked the P.M. any favours for a long time, but I'd like him to see the Premier of Newfoundland," Colville guessed something unusual must be afoot. Smallwood, Beaverbrook explained, had a proposal to put to the Prime Minister which was "of remarkable importance for re-establishing Britain's economic presence in Canada."

Nearing eighty, Churchill was finding the burden of office a strain on even his sturdy constitution; bothered by advancing deafness, he had begun to ration interviews to a minimum. When Colville mentioned Beaverbrook's request he brushed it off: he was far too busy, he couldn't see this fellow from Newfoundland, whatever his business. "But, sir," Colville persisted, "Lord Beaverbrook has particularly asked that you see him." This appeal to old loyalties was too strong to resist and, reluctantly, Churchill agreed to the appointment.

He may or may not have recalled his only personal experience of Newfoundland, eleven years before. It was August 1941, and Britain, who had been standing alone against Germany until Hitler had made his fatal decision to march on Russia a couple of months earlier, needed help desperately. It could come from only one source. And so Churchill had crossed the Atlantic in great secrecy aboard the battleship *Prince of Wales* for a shipboard meeting with President Roosevelt in Placentia Bay, on the southeast coast of Newfoundland. Out of their talks came the Atlantic Charter, the declaration of the Allies' postwar aims that foreshadowed the establishment of the United Nations.

But the two leaders and their chiefs of staff were also discussing various matters of policy and strategy of more immediate concern to Britain, including her own and Russia's vital need for war materials of all kinds. Churchill had accordingly arranged for Beaverbrook, who was then his Minister of Supply, to join him in Placentia. Beaverbrook, travelling under the appropriate code name of "Newspaperman," had flown the Atlantic in an unheated bomber and arrived at Gander, but there was no very clear idea as to how he was to accomplish the last leg of his journey, the two hundred or so miles from there to Placentia.

"Get him here by air," Churchill ordered the Governor of Newfoundland, Vice-Admiral Sir Humphrey Walwyn. In reply, Sir Humphrey merely pointed to the heavy clouds pressing down on the ship's masts. It was quite obviously not flying weather and Churchill asked: "How long does it take by train?" The governor's private secretary, Colonel Sir Leonard Outerbridge, explained that if a train were available the journey would still take Beaverbrook at least eight hours. "Then get him here by road," Churchill demanded. "There is no road, sir," said Outerbridge. "Good God," growled the greatest Englishman of his time, "what a country!"

He was not the first visitor, or the last, to be less than entranced by Newfoundland's somewhat spartan amenities. For their lack of roads was only one of the desperate problems that plagued the three hundred thousand people of England's first colony in the years between the wars. Theirs had been a long and tragic descent from the days when cod was king: in Tudor England, for instance, when meat could be bought for four shillings and eightpence a hundredweight, fish was so scarce that good salt cod fetched ten times that price and fishermen counted the long journey to the Grand Banks well worth the risk. "The Newfoundland fisheries," said Lord Bacon in 1607, "are more valuable than all the mines of Peru."

The mines of Peru or of any other country are an asset only so long as there is a market for their ores. And Newfoundland fell on hard times indeed when the market for its fish collapsed. A basket of dried cod that brought $14 on the export market in the palmy days of 1918 brought only half that price ten years later; and by the early thirties it was selling for $4 and even less. Those were the days when a fisherman who earned $150 or $200 in a year considered himself fortunate, because his neighbour probably had no job at all: there were 65,000 unemployed in Newfoundland in 1933 — half the labour force. And the daily dole was a six-cent food voucher. Six cents did not buy much food even then, and diseases of malnutrition such as beri-beri, rickets and scurvy added their ravages to those of tuberculosis, the tremendous incidence of which in the early years of this century has been described as "a chronic epidemic of enormous proportions."

Living in isolated communities scattered around the island's coastline and accessible only from the sea, those who contracted these and other diseases often received no medical attention whatsover. This same isolation condemned their children to receive little or no education.

There were other factors to compound the misery. Exploitation and misrule by the mother country had played their part; so had sectarianism and political corruption among the islanders themselves. By 1932, the national debt was so large — $100 million — that the interest on it amounted to more than half the government's annual revenue; and when new loans could no longer be raised to pay the interest on earlier ones, Britain stepped in. In effect, she ruled that Newfoundlanders, bankrupt and beset by political scandals, were incapable of running their own affairs; not ready, in other words, for democracy. And so, in return for taking over their debts, Britain suspended the self-government they had enjoyed for a century and installed a six-man Commission of Government to rule them until they were once again self-supporting.

In 1934, it seemed as though that day might never come. But the island's fortunes changed with the outbreak of the Second World War. Her geographical position as the nearest North American point to Europe, commanding the approaches to the Gulf of St. Lawrence and near the main North Atlantic sea lanes, gave her tremendous strategic importance. And the alliance Churchill forged with Roosevelt in Placentia Bay brought her U.S. bases and dollars. Soon Newfoundland was not only self-supporting; she was able to give some financial assistance to Britain.

Thus, by 1945, it seemed that Britain must soon return the island to self-government. But could the wartime prosperity last? And how would the Newfoundland economy weather the probable postwar changes in world trade patterns? Might not Britain find herself once again in the unenviable position of having to rescue her ancient colony from penury? There were only two other possible courses: for the island to become part of either the United States or Canada. While some of the people might have welcomed the first choice, the United States, with her Newfoundland bases already secure, would have had little to gain from it. And while the second choice was confidently expected to appeal to Canada as a means of securing her Atlantic seaboard and "completing" Confederation, it seemed highly unlikely to appeal to Newfoundlanders.

Previous attempts to achieve union had not only failed but had left behind a legacy of dislike and distrust. The commercial and professional "establishment" in the capital, St. John's, had always opposed Confederation because it had a vested interest in the status quo and feared the impact of Canadian competition; the churches because they feared the effect of an alien, "modern" life-style on the simple island culture.

The view of the ordinary people was expressed in a number of bellicose ballads. One such, which buoyed the anti-Confederates in the election of 1869, included the verse:

Men, hurrah for our own native isle, Newfoundland —
Not a stranger shall hold one inch of her strand;
Her face turns to Britain, her back to the Gulf,
Come near at your peril, Canadian Wolf!

Notwithstanding these widespread sentiments, Britain did not simply restore self-government to the island. Instead, she announced that in 1946 an election would be held to form a national convention "to make recommendations to His Majesty's Government as to possible forms of future governments to be put before the people at a national referendum." Joe Smallwood (he adoped the diminutive "Joey" later) was elected to the convention from Gander and it was the opportunity to get into politics that he had been hankering for all his life. He was forty-five, an age at which his promising future might fairly have been said to be behind him. He had worked as a journalist, a union organizer, a pig farmer and a radio commentator and had been defeated on his only earlier attempt to win election to Parliament in 1932, in the last election before the Commission of Government extinguished free and open politics on the island.

The mood of the convention was quite plainly anti-Confederation, but Smallwood shrewdly realized that the politician who could lead Newfoundland into union with Canada — and all the economic benefits this would entail — would be a national hero. He faced apparently hopeless odds. The convention first voted down his suggestion that Canada should be approached to discover her terms for Confederation. Then, after he had extracted attractive terms from Ottawa, the convention refused to include the question of Confederation on the ballot paper. But Joey used the skills of persuasion he had learned as a journalist to appeal to the people over the heads of the convention members. And in response to a petition he organized, the British government overruled the convention and put the question to the people in the referendum.

It was defeated, though only narrowly: 44.5 per cent of the voters chose a return to responsible government, 41.1 per cent chose Confederation, and 14.3 voted to maintain the status quo. Britain had stipulated that only a clear majority would count as a victory, so the referendum had to be held again, with the losing choice, the Commission of Government, being dropped from the ballot paper. This time, July 22, 1948, 52.3 per cent of the voters chose Confederation.

And when Newfoundland formally became Canada's tenth province on March 31, 1949, it was with the Honourable Joseph R. Smallwood as premier, making him the only living Father of Confederation, an appellation that appeared to please him ever afterwards.

Now, three and a half years later, all the benefits he had promised appeared to be materializing. The combination of continued American spending on military bases and the infusion of funds from Canada — already family allowances outranked the fisheries as a source of provincial income — had given Newfoundlanders virtually full employment and a greater prosperity than they had ever known before. It was time for the next step in Smallwood's program to make this prosperity permanent, to give it a solid underpinning of industrial strength.

It was the afternoon of August 14, 1952. Soberly dressed in his customary black homburg, black pin-striped suit and bow tie, the Premier emerged from the Savoy Hotel and with admirable aplomb told the taxi driver, "Ten Downing Street, please." With him was his Attorney General, a bluff St. John's lawyer named Leslie R. Curtis. They were met at the door of No. 10 by the Prime Minister's son-in-law, Duncan Sandys, and Smallwood was shown into the Cabinet Room.

Churchill greeted him at the door, grasping in one hand the familiar cigar and a glass of what Smallwood took to be either whisky or brandy. He was in a mellow mood, having earlier in the day attended the wedding of his niece, Clarissa, to his friend and Foreign Secretary, Sir Anthony Eden, and he offered his visitor a drink and a cigar. Smallwood, who seldom in those days drank more than a small glass of sherry (his childhood had been made both poor and miserable by his father's drinking) declined both, but asked if he might smoke a cigarette.

Churchill then took him over to the oval cabinet table he used as his desk and showed him to the chair next to his own. "I have sat at this table since 1908," he said with a smile, "but not always in this chair." Then he sat down with his back to the fireplace, and the portrait above it of Sir Robert Walpole, Britain's first prime minister. Perhaps to put his visitor at ease, he recalled that he had an old friend living in retirement in St. John's — General Sir Hugh Tudor, who had ridden with him as a cavalry subaltern many years before. "Give him my best regards when you get home," he said. (Smallwood did, to the general's great pleasure. And later, when he heard that Sir Hugh had fallen on hard times, he arranged rent-free accommodation for him in a government housing development.)

The Premier had armed himself with a map of Newfoundland and Labrador and he now spread this out on the table and began to explain his scheme. He needed no notes; extolling the potential wealth of his homeland has been something of a lifelong crusade for Joey Smallwood. He sketched in the background of the pulp and paper and mining industries already established on the island, and the need for more such development. He mentioned the vast iron-ore discoveries in Labrador, which were then beginning to be developed, and the huge stands of virgin timber awaiting exploitation. He expressed his confidence that there were other virtually limitless mineral resources as yet undiscovered. And he told in glowing detail of a flight he had recently made over the mighty Hamilton River, where, it was said, millions of horse power of hydro-electric energy could be harnessed.

Churchill listened with his interest kindled, occasionally encouraging his visitor with questions. Smallwood, Jock Colville recalls, presented his case "extremely well, very straightforwardly — it was a masterly exposition of a grand design." He told Churchill it was American capital that was beginning to exploit Labrador's iron ore; but the people of Newfoundland had a tremendous pride in their British roots and did not want to see their province virtually annexed by United States' investment. He mentioned the East India Company and the Hudson's Bay Company as historic models for what he had in mind: a great consortium of private companies and capital which would explore and develop Newfoundland with government backing. He was prepared to grant such a consortium the rights to a vast area of Newfoundland and Labrador. Perhaps this exercise of British enterprise and know-how might be the means of restoring some of Britain's economic greatness.

"I like the feel of it," Churchill said eventually. "It is a great imperial concept." Then, as if to fend off the kind of criticism sometimes levelled at him in the past, he added: "And I don't mean imperialist." He would, he promised, have his people look into it and see what he could do to help.

Before leaving, Smallwood mentioned that he had with him his Attorney General, and could he introduce him? Churchill assented courteously and Curtis, who had been waiting in an anteroom with Sandys, was ushered in. The Prime Minister rose and shook his hand and the three men chatted for a little while longer. As Smallwood left, Churchill urged him to keep him informed about the progress of his mission.

In the taxi returning to the Savoy, Smallwood was elated at the reception he had received. Curtis, never one to mince words, brought him back to earth with the dour comment: "You know, he's been to that wedding. He's not going to remember a bloody word of what we've said."

But back in No. 10, Churchill had asked Colville, "Jock, whom do we know in the City?" Colville had lunched that day with his friend Edmund de Rothschild, nephew of Anthony de Rothschild, head of the British branch of the international banking family. He mentioned the celebrated name. Churchill chuckled and, in a voice more memorable for inspiring oratory than light opera, began to sing a verse from the Lord Chancellor's song in Gilbert and Sullivan's *Iolanthe*:

> The shares are a penny, and ever so many
> > are taken by Rothschild and Baring,
> And just as a few are allotted to you,
> > you awake with a shudder despairing.

Then, smiling happily to himself, he said: "Good. I know Anthony Rothschild well, and the family. They shall do it. Ring up Tony and tell him from me I would like him to see Mr. Smallwood."

Some time later that day he must also have reported his conversation to Lord Leathers, the shipping magnate who was his financial adviser and Secretary for the Co-ordination of Transport, Fuel and Power in the government, for next morning Leathers called the Premier at the Savoy and offered to come round for a chat. "No, no, of course not," Smallwood replied modestly. "I'll call on you."

And so at 2.30 that afternoon, he and Curtis once more boarded a taxi and went down to Whitehall. Leathers was at that time occupying the office Churchill had used during the war and he showed his visitors the Prime Minister's map room. He also recalled that between the wars, when Churchill was in the political wilderness, he had installed him on the boards of several of his companies. He was not, however, a great success at business. He would, said Leathers, pay no attention at all to the normal minutiae of board meetings — until he found some excuse to steer the conversation round to the menace posed by Germany and "that man Hitler." It was a pleasant conversation, and Smallwood again outlined his plan. Leathers promised to do anything he could to help.

The Premier was further encouraged by this evidence of interest in high places; but neither Churchill nor Lord Leathers had mentioned the approach to the Rothschilds and for the next few days he languished in the Savoy with little to tell the reporters who kept calling him up to ask if he had made any progress. His mission had been well-publicized even outside Britain. On August 16, for instance, the New York *Herald Tribune* said in an editorial that his proposition "seems almost tailor-made when judged in terms of Great Britain's foremost long-range problem — the inadequacy of economic resources within the British Isles." It was difficult to see how it could fail to capture the imagination of those who controlled Britain's economic future.

> Both risks and high costs are in store for Britain if she takes the offer. Her investments in Africa and the Far East have been a heavy drain . . . . Yet if the bottom of the barrel must be scraped, this would be the occasion for it. Newfoundland's resources are going to be developed. If Great Britain should not seize this opportunity to increase her present investment in Canada, others will take her place. By passing up the chance, she would risk the loss of a major opportunity to improve her long-range earnings. She would, indeed, invite a relative deterioration in her world position. These are times for large decisions. Friends of Canada and Great Britain may well hope that terms may be arranged which are within the capacity of Britain to meet and adequate to assure execution of the job in prospect.

The trouble was that Joey had not yet had the opportunity to put his terms to any of the powerful businessmen who could not only make these "large decisions" but could back them up with the large amounts of capital required. The opportunity finally came on the morning of August 19, when he received a call from Sir Eric Bowater, a tough ex-artillery officer who, after being invalided out of the army in 1917, took over the small family business founded by his grandfather and transformed it, before his death in 1962, into the world's largest newsprint manufacturer, with assets of half a billion dollars. Joey already knew Bowater, one of whose first overseas ventures had been the purchase of the pulp and paper mill at Corner Brook, Newfoundland's second largest city, in 1938; in fact the two men had discussed on several occasions the prospect of attracting other British companies to Newfoundland. Bowater knew everyone who mattered in the close little financial world of the City, to which Joey so urgently needed an introduction; and among his friends was Anthony de Rothschild.

The Premier could hardly believe his good fortune when he heard the reason for Bowater's call: was he free to lunch that day at New Court, headquarters of the British branch of the Rothschild empire since 1809? Smallwood still does not know exactly how the invitation came about, but presumably, after Colville's call, Anthony de Rothschild, aware of Bowater's interest in Newfoundland, had asked him if he knew the Premier, and could he bring him to lunch? However it happened, there could be no doubt about Joey's reaction: probably no name in the world more symbolizes wealth than "Rothschild"; he could not have wished for a more influential sponsor.

New Court in those days was an elegant stone building occupying three sides of a cobbled square off a narrow street called St. Swithin's Lane, from which it was entered through a high archway with mahogany doors that were locked at night. Inside the building, the "clerks," as all but the most senior employees were known, handled the fiscal affairs of nations as well as private companies in cramped and crowded offices which had changed little since Dickens's day. (The building was demolished in 1962 and a modern office block erected on its site.)

Bowater introduced Smallwood and Curtis to Anthony de Rothschild and his nephew Edmund in "The Room," a large, high-ceilinged office with oak panelling and two fireplaces where the partners traditionally sat at leather-topped mahogany writing-tables, separated from each other only by an expanse of ankle-deep carpet. The senior Rothschild was the great-grandson of Nathan Mayer Rothschild, founder of the British business, and Smallwood found him "a rather formidable man, correct, upright and precise." He welcomed his visitors courteously, however, and offered them a glass of sherry before lunch. This was another of New Court's many traditions: a single glass of dry sherry was all that was ever offered before lunch, even to transatlantic visitors more accustomed to martinis. And lunch began promptly at 1 p.m., when a blind would be pulled down over the glass-topped portion of the door to "The Room" as a signal that the partners had gone to the dining room and the "clerks" in the large office outside could now smoke.

Luncheon at New Court was a ceremonial as well as a gastronomic occasion. The guests were customarily rich, famous or talented — or all three — and the guest of honour always sat at the head of the table. Smallwood felt somewhat exposed in this position, but as usual was able to rise to the occasion. Once again he described the fabulous potential of Labrador. "It is probably the greatest storehouse of undeveloped natural wealth left in the world, and it's ours," he said. "It's British, and we want it to remain British. Here in London you have the headquarters of more companies than anywhere else in the world; companies that have gone out to all the remote corners of the earth, to the jungle, to the frozen wastes, and built railways and opened mines and pioneered." Britain had, he conceded, gone through a terrible war which had to some extent devitalized the nation. But the skill was still there and possibly the development of Labrador could be the beginning of England staging a great industrial comeback.

And on he went, in a fascinating outpouring of sincere enthusiasm and unabashed flattery. "My idea is this," he said. "We want you to come and develop it. We don't want you to come and sit on it; we're not interested in that — it's been sat on by time for centuries. We want to develop it and we are prepared to be generous. What we would do is begin by giving you twenty, thirty. *sixty* thousand square miles; seventy or *eighty* thousand — there's lots of it."

Over all this territory, the company accepting his offer would have the rights to explore for minerals and establish mines to develop any commercial deposits found; to cut timber; to harness rivers. In return, the government required only three undertakings: that a stated amount (say a million dollars a year) be spent on exploration; that as the exploration progressed, a percentage of the concession area would be relinquished at stated intervals unless it was being retained for development; and that suitable royalties be paid to the government on any profits realized.

It was a superb sales pitch. Luncheon at New Court invariably ended at 2 p.m., when "Mr. Anthony" would push back his chair and announce that it was time to get back to work, regardless of whether or not his guests had finished their coffee. This day, the conversation continued until three. Finally, Anthony de Rothschild told the Premier that by chance the next day's guests at New Court were to be the heads of two of Britain's leading mining companies: Lord Bessborough, of the Rio Tinto Company, and Sir Ernest Oppenheimer, of the Anglo-American Corporation of South Africa. "May I tell them what you have told me?" he asked Smallwood. "By all means," replied the Premier. It looked like another big step forward.

He could only wait now for events to take their course, except that the news of his "crusade" had prompted the calling of a special meeting of the Federation of British Industries to hear him speak two days later. In his element as always on a public platform, he returned to his theme of the potential riches of Labrador and how they could be turned to the joint advantage of Newfoundland and Britain. His speech was so well received by the assembled captains of industry that the federation later issued it as a pamphlet.

Then Smallwood left for France, West Germany, Switzerland and

Italy, continuing his search for new trade outlets and new investments. Among his party was his Director-General of Economic Development, Dr. Alfred A. Valdmanis who, before his emigration to Canada, had been Minister of Finance in the prewar Latvian government and, after fleeing the Soviet invasion of that country, a special assistant to Hjalmar Schacht, Germany's financial genius. On this trip his diplomatic contacts procured an audience for Smallwood with Pope Pius XII, but little else.

Smallwood kept in touch with London while he was away, and was delighted on September 12 to receive the news that Rothschilds planned to issue a press release disclosing that they were investigating the formation of a consortium to take up the Premier's offer.

When Anthony de Rothschild had told Bessborough and Oppenheimer about Smallwood's plan on the day after his visit to New Court, they had both expressed interest, at least in principle. Rio Tinto, which at that time consisted largely of a copper mine in Spain which was more productive of problems than profits, was about to embark on the tremendous postwar expansion which would ultimately make it one of the world's great multinational corporations, with interests on all five continents. And while Oppenheimer's empire was solidly built on South African diamonds, the great Canadian mineral boom of the 1950s was getting under way and there appeared to be no harm in Anglo-American securing a foothold in Canada.

Assured of their interest, Rothschild began a round of telephone calls, conferences and lunches with others among his circle who might have an interest, actual or potential, in Newfoundland. Sir Eric Bowater, of course, had been in from the beginning. An imperious figure, with his straight-backed military bearing, ruddy cheeks and white hair, he was to become one of the project's stoutest supporters.*

If Bowaters were to be in the consortium, no doubt their competitors, the Anglo-Newfoundland Development Company, operators of New-

*Another who helped to spread the gospel in London financial circles was Sir William Stephenson, the Winnipeg-born international industrialist who earned the sobriquet "the Quiet Canadian" in his capacity as Britain's wartime intelligence chief in the western hemisphere. After the war, Stephenson specialized in developing the economy of under-industrialized areas and for a short time served as chairman of the Newfoundland and Labrador Corporation (Nalco), a crown corporation set up by Joey in 1951 in an attempt to attract private investors to the province. In this capacity, Stephenson spoke enthusiastically about Newfoundland's potential to his many contacts in London, including the representatives of two investment banks that eventually joined the consortium.

foundland's other paper mill, should be invited to join too. So Rothschild called in Lord Rothermere, the newspaper publisher. Like Bowater, Rothermere was no stranger to Newfoundland and realized the value of the timber. He was also well aware of the potential worth of mineral concessions: the Buchans mine, discovered within the limits of Anglo-Newfoundland's timber area in the 1920s, though not large in total output, had proved to be one of the richest base-metal mines in the world. The mine was operated by an American company, but Rothermere's Anglo-Newfoundland company received about half its net profits. He, too, expressed interest.

True to his word, Lord Leathers attended some of the meetings called by de Rothschild. Remembering what Joey had told him about the Hamilton River, he suggested that a company with experience in the electric-power field should be enlisted. So de Rothschild called in his friend Sir George Nelson (later Lord Nelson of Stafford), head of the English Electric Company. And thus the idea began to gather momentum.

When Smallwood returned to London in mid-September and was told the names of the men who had expressed a desire to hear more about his proposition, he was duly impressed. There was another, and much larger, meeting at New Court, at which he outlined his plan again and answered questions. But in his conversations with Anthony de Rothschild he had begun to detect a reserve that puzzled him. The old man was quite brusque, discourteous even, to Dr. Valdmanis; almost as though he didn't trust him. Also, he asked so many questions and seemed to insist on so many conditions.

Joey always favoured the broad brush and the sweep of a large canvas over the painstaking attention to detail required of a miniaturist. One afternoon during the negotiations, he concluded reluctantly that the Rothschilds were being unreasonable, demanding altogether too much. He could, he announced, get better terms in Germany; he would return there tomorrow. And with that, he left.

The Investment Manager at New Court, R. W. C. Hobbs, an affable Londoner who for some reason was invariably called "Peter," had got along well with Joey from the moment they first shook hands. He was sorry to see him leave in this way, particularly since he suspected the reason was disappointment at the slowness of the negotiations, rather than anger. He asked "Mr. Anthony" whether there would be any objection to his trying to have another talk with the Premier. The senior partner, though he had never been wildly enthusiastic about Joey's project, had nevertheless promised Churchill, through Colville, that he would do what he could to help. He agreed to Hobbs's suggestion.

Hobbs took a taxi to the Savoy, went up to the Premier's room, and found him in pants and undershirt, packing his suitcase. He was, said Joey, off to Germany right away to offer his concession to companies there. Several German companies had already established themselves in Newfoundland in response to Valdmanis's efforts; no doubt he would get a better reception there than he had in London. Deflecting Joey Smallwood from his chosen course is akin to diverting a charging elephant with a water pistol. It is a tribute to Peter Hobbs's amiability and powers of persuasion that within half an hour he had not only convinced the Premier there had been an unfortunate misunderstanding but had extracted his promise to abandon his trip to Germany and return to New Court in the morning.

From this point on the negotiations seemed to go more smoothly. There was still much hard bargaining ahead, but on September 30, when Smallwood went to see Churchill again to report on his progress, he was able to tell him that Rothschilds and the other potential members of the consortium had agreed to send representatives to St. John's for further exploratory discussions with the Newfoundland government.

Churchill expressed his pleasure and as the Premier was leaving presented him with an autographed copy of the latest volume of his history of the Second World War, *Closing the Ring*. The old man retained his interest in the project and in 1956, when the consortium widened its membership with a private issue of two million shares, Rothschilds, through Colville, invited him to participate. He replied in a note to Colville that he would like ten thousand shares and added: "It is high time the Hamilton Falls* had a bridle."

*The great river that drains the Labrador plateau was first known to the white man as the Grand River. It was renamed the Hamilton after an early nineteenth-century governor of Newfoundland, Sir Charles Hamilton. The falls were known as Grand Falls after they were first seen by a white man in 1839. Later, perhaps to avoid confusion with the town of Grand Falls on the island of Newfoundland, they became known as Hamilton Falls. In 1965, Smallwood flew the Atlantic to attend Sir Winston's funeral and went with Edmund de Rothschild to the lying-in-state in Westminster Hall. After they had filed past the great man's bier and emerged into the wintry sunshine, de Rothschild took Smallwood's arm and said, "Mr. Premier, we have a lot of unfinished business." Smallwood appeared preoccupied and did not reply immediately. Then he murmured, "Mmm . . . yes . . . by Jove! I think I can do it. Yes — let them be called Churchill Falls." After his return to Newfoundland, both the river and the falls were officially renamed, even though a Churchill River already existed in Manitoba.

16

TWO

The Hamilton:
"Something for our grandchildren"

When Peter Hobbs arrived in Newfoundland in October 1952, he was, as the representative of Rothschilds, the head of an informal delegation hastily assembled by the prospective members of the consortium to hear about Premier Smallwood's proposal in more detail. He was met at Torbay, the airport for St. John's, by the Premier himself and introduced to Gordon F. Pushie, a Newfoundland-born journalist who had been an editor of *Time* magazine in New York before returning home to become an economic adviser to the government. The Premier, driving his own car, took Hobbs for a tour of the outskirts of St. John's and out along the coast, elaborating on his proposal as they went.

It had been a long flight for Hobbs; the big jets had not yet shrunk the Atlantic crossing to a few hours. Sandwiched between Smallwood and Pushie on the front seat, he found his eyelids drooping and his head nodding as the Premier expounded on the past, present and glorious future of Newfoundland. Finally, despite himself, Hobbs drifted off to sleep, his tired head unknowingly coming to rest on the Premier's shoulder.

Startled — he himself never needed more than a few hours' sleep a night — Joey nudged him awake. "I can see you're not going to take in much sight-seeing today," he said, as he wheeled the car around and drove Hobbs directly to the Newfoundland Hotel.

The following week was not much less tiring. There were daily meetings at which the members of the delegation were briefed on the potential resources available to the consortium by the Premier and various ministers, assisted by specialists from within their departments. The two paper companies were represented at these sessions by their men on the spot in Newfoundland: Bowaters by H. M. S. "Monty" Lewin, their vice-president and general manager, and Anglo-Newfoundland by Elliott Little, their manager. English Electric had sent over two executives from England, H. S. Carnegie and P. W. Seewer. And by this time a seventh member had been invited to join the consortium, Rio Tinto and Anglo-American having decided they needed advice from someone with Canadian mining experience.

17

The company chosen to fill this role was Frobisher Limited, the exploration arm of a Canadian holding company named Ventures Limited, which at that time bound together an unwieldy assortment of a hundred or so companies with varying fortunes that were ultimately merged into the corporate structure of one of their number, Falconbridge Nickel Mines Limited. Ventures Limited was the creation of an American named Thayer Lindsley, a lifelong bachelor who practised yoga exercises while roaming round the world building up his huge mining empire. It had had some dealings with Anglo-American in the past and had also been in partnership with Rio Tinto in a mine in Zambia. Furthermore, during the summer of 1952, Frobisher had about thirty men prospecting on two concessions it had been given in Labrador a couple of years earlier.

The partnership was thus a natural one, and Ventures was represented at the briefing sessions by one of its financial consultants, Harold H. Hemming, and its chief geologist, Dr. Duncan Derry. J. Austen Bancroft, a big, hard-driving Canadian geologist who had gone to Africa in the thirties to undertake a survey of the Northern Rhodesia copper fields, represented Anglo-American. The third mining company, Rio Tinto, appointed as its representative a professor of geology at Dalhousie University, G. Vibert Douglas, who had carried out geological mapping of the Labrador coast and knew the area well.

One of the first meetings considered the potential value of the timber rights the government proposed to grant. Lewin and Little pointed out that between them Bowaters and Anglo-Newfoundland already held the rights to all the important stands of timber on the island of Newfoundland; what remained was not sufficient to warrant the establishment of a third pulp mill. But Lewin himself had made a survey in Labrador in 1937 which he said indicated the presence in the Lake Melville area of twenty million cords of readily accessible wood suitable for pulp, "one of the finest stands of timber in North America." Later surveys carried out for the government, the representatives were told, had upgraded this estimate to thirty-nine million cords. Most of it was black spruce, which was slow-growing (it took a tree 150 years to reach forty feet) but denser than the wood on the island, so that a given number of cords would produce more pulp.

It was estimated that to be commercially feasible any development would have to aim at the harvesting of 100,000 cords annually; since one man could cut about a hundred cords in a season, a thousand men would be needed, and a townsite would have to be built for them. All in all, such an operation would cost at least $3 million. As both Lewin

18

and Little pointed out, world newsprint consumption was increasing rapidly, so that the Labrador reserves would undoubtedly become important "in the not too distant future." But there was a warning note: an attempt to develop Labrador timber a year earlier had collapsed because of the difficulty of shipping the wood out during the short ice-free navigation season.

The prospects appeared similarly uncertain when the delegates went on at a later meeting to consider mineral possibilities. True, several copper mines had operated on the island around the tuurn of the century; the Wabana mine on Bell Island in Conception Bay had since its opening in 1895 produced sixty million tons of ore averaging 51 per cent iron; and the Buchans mine, opened in the centre of the island in 1927, had produced zinc, lead, copper, gold and silver worth $182 million by the end of 1951. But elsewhere on the island such base-metal showings as had been discovered were too small to be profitable and the remoteness of much of the interior seemed likely to be a handicap to successful exploitation of any new finds.

Much less was known about the prospects in Labrador — which was still marked "Unexplored" on the map in *The Times* atlas in "The Room" at Rothschilds — except that vast iron-ore deposits had been found in the northwest, near the Quebec border, and the Iron Ore Company of Canada was building a 360-mile railroad north from Sept-Iles, on the St. Lawrence River, to get the ore out. The rights to this ore, however, had already been dispensed.

That left the water power. The Premier reminded the delegates frequently that there were limitless prospcts for this: at least 283,000 horse power at Bay d'Espoir, on the island, which might turn out to be as much as half a million horse power; and no less than ten million horse power on the Hamilton River in Labrador. Carnegie and Seewer confessed to being impressed by the hydro-electric potential of Hamilton Falls, but doubted that there would be any business for English Electric unless new mining operations were begun in the area, or new power-consuming industries could be persuaded to locate there.

There were also, as the representatives of the proposed consortium soon discovered, further complications. Rights to the areas considered to hold the most promising mineral prospects on the island had already been given out by the government. In addition to various long-term concessions that had been in existence for years, prospecting rights over two thousand or so square miles had recently been granted to Falconbridge, "a relatively large concession" to the Buchans interests, and nine thousand square miles to the government's own Newfoundland and Labrador Corporation. Nalco had in turn sub-leased large areas of this nine thousand square miles to private companies.

Moreover, the consortium representatives were dismayed to learn, Nalco held an even larger area in Labrador, amounting altogether to fourteen thousand square miles, including all rights to develop hydro-electric power on the Hamilton River.

Hobbs and the other delegates were understandably confused about exactly what it was they were being offered; the "biggest real estate deal of the present century" appeared to be hedged about with unexpected conditions. As chairman of Nalco, however, Joey made light of the difficulties. What the government had given, he seemed to suggest, it could also take away; there was a saving clause in the Nalco act providing for just such an eventuality. Also, he thought the consortium might eventually absorb Nalco — or Nalco might in time absorb any new corporation formed by the consortium. This second course hardly seemed much of an incentive to the companies who were being asked to invest their shareholders' funds in a venture that might or might not pay off. Neither, predictably enough, did the first course appeal to the private investors in Canada and the United States who held 10 per cent of Nalco shares, the other 90 per cent of the $1 million capital having been provided by the government.

When the "expeditionary force," as Hobbs once called it, returned to London, the deal was far from settled. Bancroft, in a long report on existing mineral concessions and past discoveries in Labrador, said: "Having gathered all available data, the writer is not enthusiastic about prospecting in Labrador." He also pointed out that the water rights offered would be worth very little unless the Hamilton River were included. English Electric agreed that the Hamilton might one day produce vast quantities of hydro-electric power, but felt that day was many years away; as one executive said: "That's something for our grandchildren."

There were, however, among the consortium two great enthusiasts for the scheme: Sir Eric Bowater and J. N. V. "Val" Duncan, a young barrister-turned-businessman who had lately become managing director of Rio Tinto. Bowater frequently assured anyone who would listen that "the timber alone will recoup your investment." And Duncan, perhaps because he had married a girl from British Columbia and had developed a sentimental attachment to her homeland, used to tell waverers: "After all, the few thousand you'll have to put up only amounts to the subscription for a decent American golf club."

During the next few weeks there were more discussions, with Hobbs commuting across the Atlantic, listening to government arguments in St. John's and trying to explain them to the prospective members of the consortium back in London. By now the consortium had decided that the deal would not be worth while unless the Hamilton River rights were included. It also felt that since so much of the area it was being offered had already been picked over, it should be given reasonable assurance of being granted other mineral areas if they seemed promising and had been dropped by either Nalco or other concession-holders.

By the beginning of December, the Premier seemed to be having second thoughts about granting the consortium the Hamilton rights. Once again, he flew to London, and this time he told Hobbs that the ceding of Nalco's rights to the river was the main stumbling block; he could not expect his cabinet, let alone the members of his party, to agree to that. And any such move would provide strong material for "anti-government propaganda" by the opposition.

There were other points of disagreement. The Premier had suggested that $6 million should be spent on exploration in the first five years. Bancroft and the other geologists thought this was far too much; even $300,000 a year would be more than could be wisely spent on prospecting alone, unless ore deposits were discovered that seemed promising enough to justify diamond drilling. The Premier had also suggested that the consortium ought to be able to select the areas it wished to retain for further investigation from the total area available within a year of the agreement. The geologists felt two years would be needed.

The consortium was asking for too much, Smallwood told Hobbs. Furthermore, since he had last seen him, he had been approached by a representative of the New York financial house of Harriman Ripley with an offer to buy one million of the two million unissued shares of Nalco at $5 each — five times more than their original price of $1 — on behalf of George M. Humphrey, the American steel tycoon, and Jules Timmins, the Canadian mining magnate, who had joined forces to form the Iron Ore Company of Canada. He must admit, the Premier said, that this offer seemed to have been prompted by the consortium's own interest in Newfoundland; and since he had "a very real fear" of the effects of increasing American capital investment and influence in his province he would go to almost any lengths to bring about a counter-vailing British presence. But he could not go any further than he could carry his people, through his cabinet and his party, with him.

Rather than see the talks break down, he had gone the day before to visit Lord Leathers, remembering his promise during the summer to do whatever he could to help. Lord Leathers, he said, shared his opinion that the consortium's terms were too tough, and he "might have it in mind" to talk the matter over with members of the group.

Though both men are now dead, it seems likely that Leathers did in fact telephone Anthony de Rothschild, probably more in a spirit of inquiry than remonstration. It is unlikely, however, that de Rothschild would have told him the reason for his reservations about the project and his determination to make sure that any agreement drawn up should be legally watertight; the attitude, in fact, which the puzzled Premier, who could not understand it, considered too tough.

The fact is that Anthony de Rothschild had been suspicious of the deal ever since the Premier's economic adviser, Alfred Valdmanis, had come to him secretly some months earlier and told him that, for a consideration, Rothschilds could be given the rights to a large area of southwestern Labrador containing rich iron-ore deposits. The consideration turned out to be $1 million — to be paid, of course, to Valdmanis. The area, the rights to which were later acquired by Joey's controversial friend, the American promoter John C. Doyle, eventually became the multi-million-dollar Wabush Mines development.

Furious, Anthony de Rothschild kicked Valdmanis out of his office, and it was only after the long negotiations convinced him that the Premier's offer to the consortium was a sincere one, entirely unconnected with Valdmanis's approach, that he was persuaded to go through with it.

Even then, he could hardly have been said to be the most enthusiastic of the consortium's members. On December 5, the day after his talk with Hobbs, Smallwood returned to New Court for more discussions. After outlining the conditions upon which the consortium would enter into an agreement, Anthony de Rothschild said, "Those are our terms, Mr. Premier. Do you accept them?" The Premier did, and the old man then rose from his chair and wound up the proceedings by saying: "I must now go to a meeting at St. Mary's Hospital. [He was chairman of its governing committee.] My nephew will take over."

Edmund de Rothschild, who was to become senior partner of the firm in his turn when his uncle died a few years later, took the Premier back to "The Room." He sat down at his mahogany desk, the one his great-grandfather had sat behind in 1875 when he lent the British government £4 million at a moment's notice to purchase control of the Suez Canal, and pulled toward him a lined foolscap pad. And before the end of the afternoon he and Smallwood had worked out an agreement in principle which they called "Basis of contract to be made between Newfoundland government and London group." Typed out later, its eleven clauses covered a mere two sheets of foolscap.

22

Among other things, they provided that the consortium would be granted "all water power rights not already committed in Newfoundland and Labrador and also all such rights which may revert to the government," including the Hamilton rights held by Nalco, which the Premier promised to have transferred "by Order in Council or otherwise." Smallwood also agreed that the government would "use its best endeavours to facilitate the granting by Nalco to the company, if desired, of concessions on terms not more onerous than those granted by Nalco to other concessionaires within the last few months."

On its part, the consortium consented to the Premier's timetable for the selection of its concession areas. It was to be granted mineral rights over fifty thousand square miles of Labrador and ten thousand square miles on the island of Newfoundland, which it was to choose within a year of the agreement being signed from those areas the government had not already allotted to others. Of the fifty thousand square miles selected in Labrador (which were to include the Lake Melville timber stands), ten thousand would revert to the government after one year, and a further eight thousand after each succeeding five years; the concession was to run for twenty years. A proportionate "shedding" schedule was also agreed for the island.

In return, the consortium undertook to spend at least $1,250,000 on exploration and development during each five-year period — $250,000 a year. This was less than the Premier had originally wanted, but as things were to turn out far more was spent than even he had envisaged.

Lastly, the consortium agreed to pay the government an annual rental of 10 per cent of its net earnings, after deduction of federal and provincial taxes.

It had been a good day's work, and at the end of it Edmund de Rothschild decided that an evening's relaxation was in order. He invited Joey to accompany him to the Victoria Palace to see the Crazy Gang, a manic assemblage of slapstick comedians led by the famous Bud Flanagan. It was an uproarious show in the unsophisticated tradition of the English music hall and Joey, though puzzled by some of the humour, was amused, particularly at the antics of his companion. Edmund de Rothschild, he recalled years later, "threw himself around in his chair and roared with laughter all over the theatre — you would have thought he was a madman. I was a bit embarrassed."

The story is typical of the ebullient current head of the House of Rothschild. "Eddy," as he is universally known, is a man of giant enthusiasms — not least for the magnificent garden on his 2,600-acre estate at Exbury, in southern England. This unrivalled collection of orchids, azaleas and rhododendrons was started by his father, a passionate gardener who once, addressing the suburban members of a London horticultural club, told them: "No garden, however small, should contain less than two acres of rough woodland." Hardly less dominating in Edmund de Rothschild's life has been his enthusiasm for the company he helped to found; through the years he made more than two hundred trips across the Atlantic in his zeal to see the project succeed.

With the outline of the concession now agreed, it was time for the lawyers to go to work on the final drafting. On his next visit to St. John's, Hobbs was accompanied by Hilary Scott, an eminent representative of the Rothschilds' lawyers, a firm rejoicing in the name of Slaughter and May. Scott, a tall, trim Yorkshireman who was later to become president of the Law Society and receive a knighthood, was taken aback when Hobbs introduced him to the Newfoundland Attorney General. At the mention of his firm's name, Curtis threw back his head and roared: "I don't know that I like that — we may be led like lambs to the slaughter!"

Scott smiled thinly, but during the next few weeks became more accustomed to the Attorney General's boisterous sense of humour. Eventually, the lawyers on both sides expanded the original two-page outline into a fifteen-page legal document replete with clauses and sub-clauses, henceforth to be known as the "Principal Agreement" between the government, N. M. Rothschild and Sons, and the consortium, which it had by now been decided to call the British-Newfoundland Corporation Limited. (This rapidly became shortened to the more familiar "Brinco," and in 1971 the corporation finally recognized the accepted usage and formally changed its name to Brinco Limited.)

The final version of the contract made some minor changes in the areas to be surrendered to the government at agreed intervals; changed the annual rental to be paid to the government from 10 per cent of net earnings after taxes to 8 per cent of net profits before taxes; and specified the various royalties to be imposed over and above the normal corporation tax, namely: 5 per cent on the profits of any mines resulting from the concession, $12\frac{1}{2}$ per cent on any petroleum or natural gas developments, $2 per square mile and $1 per cord on any timber cut and exported from the province, and 50 cents per horse power on any hydro-electric development.

Hobbs, for Rothschilds, and the Premier, for the province, initialled the agreement on March 11, 1953. At the same time they exchanged letters: Hobbs formally pointing out that the execution of the agreement by Brinco was conditional on the transfer to it of Nalco's Hamilton

River rights, and the Premier in effect accepting this condition, pledging the government, as before, "to use its best endeavours . . . to procure the grant on reasonable terms" of any concessions held by Nalco for which Brinco should make a formal request. In the event, the water rights were transferred by formal action of the House of Assembly: Act No. 63 of 1953, the Brinco Principal Agreement Act, given third reading on May 9, gave them to Brinco; Act No. 64, on the same date, repealed the clause that had granted them to Nalco.

That, one would have thought, should have closed the issue. But, to the corporation's discomfiture, there were to be other claimants in the years ahead.

THREE

Some early challenges are survived

The consortium did not wait for these formalities to be completed before getting down to business. One day early in February 1953, while they were still in the preliminary stages of their drafting sessions with the St. John's lawyers, Peter Hobbs and Hilary Scott went out to Torbay Airport to meet the man who had been chosen to run the new company — or rather, since it had not yet even been incorporated, to bring it into being. They were on their way to a reception at Government House and the Lieutenant-Governor had invited them to bring along the new arrival.

Any other British businessman arriving in a new country on such a mission might have considered this a command performance. But Alexander William Southam was a determined individualist with an air of lofty indifference toward convention that was to earn him a reputation as something of a starched-collar rebel. The flight, he explained, had been long and rather tiring and he felt more like a bath than a party; would Hobbs and Scott please convey his apologies to the Lieutenant-Governor, but he must go to the hotel to get a good night's sleep.

A bulky, tweedy man with a thick, clipped moustache and steeply arched eyebrows that gave him a misleadingly fierce expression, Bill Southam looked the epitome of the British "city gentleman," but he was proud of his unusually cosmopolitan background. Among his paternal forebears were a swashbuckling English schooner skipper who plied the West African trade and was, Southam suspected, probably a slaver, and a Scottish mercenary who became a Russian general. Southam's father, after going to school in England, borrowed £80 to get started in the cotton industry in Russia, made himself a millionaire as a manufacturer of cotton-mill machinery, and lost his fortune in the communist revolution.

Southam himself was born in Moscow. His mother, though she came from the Pyrenees, had Russian and German Huguenot blood; he learned French and Russian before he learned English, and though outwardly a "pukka sahib," preferred Pushkin to Kipling. When the First World

War broke out he immediately tried to enlist — unsuccessfully, since the army discovered he was only sixteen. He managed to join the infantry a year later and after a term as a bayonet-fighting instructor in France was posted to an armoured-car squadron in Russia, where his fluency in the language proved useful.

After the war, he went to Cambridge and studied economics under the celebrated John Maynard Keynes. He then worked for several oil companies and when the Second World War broke out he was managing a company extracting oil from shale deposits in Estonia. That career ended when the communists took over Estonia and Southam managed by a circuitous route to get his wife and family out to South Africa.

After holding a number of administrative jobs in the Middle East and South Africa, he joined the four-power Control Commission for Germany and Austria at the end of the war and was awarded the CBE for his part in restoring Austria's economic viability, a task in which his fluent Russian came in useful once again. It was this post that led to his appointment to head Brinco.

By 1952, his friend and superior in the Control Commission, Val Duncan, had joined Rio Tinto. He asked Southam to visit Canada to investigate and report on prospects for Rio's expansion. Southam compiled a voluminous report on Canada's economy, with particular reference to the oil industry, then beginning to hit its stride, and on the ship returning home wrote a four-page note for his friends on the outlook for closer cooperation between Canada and Britain, and the conditions U.K. immigrants might expect to find. (One passage from this, in a list of Canada's strengths, suggests that some disillusionment was in store for at least one British immigrant. The people of Canada, Southam wrote, were "robust, self-reliant, politically mature," and "not apparently unduly divided by differences of language and religion.")

Early in 1953, the seven founder members of the consortium decided that matters had advanced to the point at which the rather casual, "old boy" basis on which the affairs of the soon-to-be-born corporation had so far been conducted should be strengthened by a more formalized organization. A London Committee was set up and Lord Bessborough nominated Val Duncan to sit on it as the Rio Tinto representative. Duncan was already beginning to attract admiration for the way he had taken over the reorganization and expansion of Rio Tinto, and the other members of the committee fell in readily enough when he suggested that with his varied background and recently acquired knowledge of Canada Bill Southam would be a good choice as general manager of the new corporation.

Southam's sortie across the Atlantic, though brief, had convinced him that economic cooperation between Canada and Britain would be of mutual benefit. The idea of contributing to this, and of building his own show from the ground up, appealed to him and he accepted Duncan's offer with a sense of excitement at the challenge ahead.

And challenge it proved to be. He arrived in St. John's with no introductions and not even an official letter to certify that he had been hired to run Brinco. In fact, the circumstances of his engagement had been so informal that he had left London without even agreeing on the salary he was to receive, being told merely to draw whatever living expenses he needed from the Brinco account, which at that time consisted of a $5,000 loan from Bowaters. He was highly indignant a few months later, after the company had been incorporated and more funds had been forthcoming from Rothschilds, when an accountant from Peat, Marwick, Mitchell and Company, who had been appointed the company's auditors, complained that he was drawing expenses without authorization. An irate cable to New Court quickly elicited the required authority.

For the first few weeks he worked from his room in the Newfoundland Hotel. His wife had remained behind with the family in their London home, which proved fortunate, for during the succeeding months Southam was to live out of a suitcase, commuting between St. John's, Montreal, Toronto and Ottawa.

He soon discovered that in Labrador, with ice still in the lakes in June and the first snow returning in September, the prospecting season is a short one — perhaps ninety days in the south and even less in the north. This did not leave long for Brinco to select its fifty-thousand-square-mile concession from the seventy thousand or so square miles available. It was imperative that preparations be made to get geologists and prospectors into the field as soon as possible.

Accordingly, his first trip was to Toronto, where he was introduced to Dr. A. Paul Beavan, a consulting geologist who had worked all over Canada. A quiet, retiring man more at home in the bush than the board room, Paul Beavan had been born in Victoria and had graduated from the University of British Columbia and Queen's University before taking his Ph.D. at Princeton. The geologists Southam consulted all spoke highly of him, and by March 1 he had been hired as Exploration Manager, though the corporation still had no legal existence.

Beavan immediately began to plan his season's operations and to order the canoes, tents and other equipment and supplies his field parties would need. Recruiting geologists was not easy. The Canadian mineral boom was at its height in 1953: the uranium-staking rush began at Elliot Lake in Ontario in June of that year, and at around the same time a mining man named Michael J. Boylen discovered huge lead-zinc deposits in New Brunswick, which led to the establishment of a whole new mining area centred on Bathurst.

But Beavan's worst problem was the virtual absence of any sort of useful maps of the interior of Labrador. The eight-miles-to-the-inch topographical maps available had large blank areas on them and were all but useless for his purposes. The normal practice, which he had hoped to follow, would have been to begin with sets of mosaics made up from aerial photographs. But he found that a large part of Labrador had not yet been photographed from the air. A private company in Toronto, the Photographic Survey Corporation, was commissioned to produce one-mile-to-the-inch mosaics from such vertical photographs as did exist, but they encountered long delays in getting prints from Ottawa.

So when Beavan's first parties went into the field in June 1953, they had only a few mosaics of southern Labrador; and with no reports or annotations on them, these were really useful only for flying and plotting areas in advance. It was not until ten years later that the Topographical Survey of Canada began a large-scale mapping operation in Labrador, and the first geological map of the whole area (which drew heavily on the information gathered by Beavan and his men through the years) was not published until 1972.

The sort of survey Beavan envisaged — indeed any sort of exploration in Labrador — could be accomplished only with aircraft, using skis in winter and floats in summer. Before he returned to Newfoundland, Southam negotiated a three-year contract with Laurentian Air Services in Ottawa for the charter of two new de Havilland Beavers, at $88 an hour each for a minimum of eight hundred hours a year.

Back in St. John's, he found it increasingly impossible to work from his hotel room. There were reports to make and queries to answer from London; conferences with the Premier and other members of the government and their officials; books to keep; insurance to arrange and contracts to be drawn up for the staff Beavan was about to hire. He did not yet have even a secretary to help him. And the geologist Bancroft, passing through on a flying visit, incensed him by suggesting that he didn't need one — Brinco was still a shoestring operation and he ought to manage by himself.

Fortunately, London took a more liberal attitude. But, as Southam found when he set off looking for an office, the post-Confederation surge of governmental and business activity in St. John's had not yet been accompanied by any matching boom in new construction. One of the oldest cities in the New World, it was still largely a picturesque patch-work of weather-beaten frame houses lining hilly streets; and the prewar office buildings on its main commercial thoroughfare, Water Street, which meanders along never more than a few feet from the wharves and warehouses at the harbour's edge, were bulging at the seams.

After some discouraging days spent scouring the city for even a cubbyhole of an office, Southam thought he had found the answer. A rambling old house came on the market for $25,000 and he decided it would serve not only as office space but as dormitory quarters for himself and any transient staff members such as geologists who might be passing through the city; but when he tried to buy it he discovered it could not be used for offices because it was in an area zoned for residential use. The only other offer he had was some temporary space in the furniture section of a downtown department store.

By now, he was on friendly terms with the Premier. Smallwood at that time used to work from ten or eleven one morning until three or four the next. Southam often called on him after midnight when, free of interruptions, the Premier would be in a relaxed mood and only too pleased to discuss his plans for the province, and for Brinco. At one of these late-night sessions, Southam broached the question of his office accommodation; Joey promised expansively to solve that problem for him forthwith.

Still nothing happened. In mid-March, thanks to the intercession of Bowaters, he was given temporary quarters in the board room of a building owned by Angus Reid, grandson of the man who built the railroad across Newfoundland, founding a Water Street dynasty in the process. This at least enabled him to hire a secretary, Marion Hawco, who had been working in one of the government departments; she later made herself so indispensable that she became manager of the St. John's office.

They were still working at Reid's board-room table when the corporation was incorporated on April 17 and held its first statutory meeting five days later — an unsatisfactory arrangement which obviously could not continue. Southam was in the habit of staying at the office late making voluminous entries in his diary and writing long reports to London. And despite his obvious probity, Angus Reid was not altogether happy that a "lodger" had thus to be provided with a key to his building.

One night, Bill Southam went to see the Premier. He walked over to his desk with his hand outstretched and said, "I've come to say goodbye, Mr. Premier." Astonished, Joey asked why. "You promised to find me an office," Southam replied, "but you haven't, and no one else will rent me one."

Amused at the ploy, the Premier beamed behind his black horn rims, picked up the telephone and roused someone Southam judged from the conversation to be (a) in bed and (b) a caretaker. Having instructed this unfortunate to meet them with a key, Joey then drove Southam across town to look over a building which had been built as a soft-drink bottling plant. The deal having fallen though, like so many others through the years, the building had never been used and the government had bought it. Now it was standing empty, a cavernous place built with concrete blocks, and their voices echoed as they wandered around examining it. Southam discovered several rooms which could be used as offices and an unoccupied machine room which would hold drawing tables for the geologists. He agreed to rent it by the month. He and Miss Hawco moved in on June 1 and Brinco had its first address: 278 LeMarchant Road.

By now, Beavan had two parties in the field: two geologists and three assistants at a bush camp fifty-five miles north of Deer Lake, on the island of Newfoundland; and four geologists and three assistants establishing a base camp in Labrador, at North West River, a settlement near Goose Bay, on Lake Melville, a long inlet through which the Churchill River enters the Atlantic. As soon as the weather improved sufficiently for the Beavers to land on the lakes in the interior, the men from North West River were to split into two parties and head for southeast Labrador, working their way north during the season as the ice melted and the snow cleared.

By this time, also, the seven founder members of the consortium had invited others to join them, on the principle that a risk shared is a risk reduced, and Brinco's shareholders now numbered twenty-four companies. Most of the newcomers were either investment houses or insurance companies, but they also included such international giants as Imperial Chemical Industries, and the British subsidiary of the large Belgian company, Sogemines; a London-based group of international companies founded in Newfoundland more than a century earlier, C. T. Bowring and Company; and the Montreal investment house of W. C. Pitfield and Company, which was to become the corporation's Canadian underwriter.

On joining, each undertook to subscribe $52,100 as its share of the first five years' exploration costs. Because of Britain's strict dollar-exchange regulations, the first instalment of that commitment, $21,000, and all subsequent investments, had to be approved by the Treasury;

it is to be presumed that the fatherly interest shown in the project by Churchill and Lord Leathers helped the corporation to negotiate this preliminary hurdle.

To head the corporation and give it the right air of substance and solidity — today's word would be "image" — Edmund de Rothschild had approached a man at the pinnacle of Montreal's financial establishment, Bertie C. Gardner, chairman of the Bank of Montreal, past president of the Canadian Bankers' Association, Chancellor of McGill University, governor of the city's two leading hospitals and a member of various other community organizations. Bertie Gardner's Christian name, which in his earlier years brought him letters addressed to "Miss Gardner," was not a familiar diminutive but the surname of friends of his parents. He was born in Bristol, England, and went to work in a bank there at the age of seventeen, emigrating to Canada five years later to join a bank that was later merged with the Bank of Montreal.

After winning the M.C. in the First World War, he represented the bank for several years in Newfoundland, where he married the daughter of a senator. He had worked his way steadily up the rungs of the banking ladder and at the age of sixty-eight had just retired as president and chief executive officer when Eddy de Rothschild visited him in Montreal in February 1953.

Over lunch at Gardner's club, Eddy outlined the Brinco idea and asked him to be the corporation's first president. As Gardner recalled many years later: "I had sat on a high stool in a bank in England back in 1901 and I thought by 1953 I should take a rest. I was not anxious to take on more responsibilities, but Eddy said that if I took it on the Bank of Montreal would be the bankers."

To a lifelong banker, this proposition had a potent appeal; but Gardner was also captured, as so many others were to be in the years ahead, by what the evidence compels one to call the "mystique" of the Brinco idea, the challenge implicit in the taming of a wilderness and the harnessing of its unused resources — a challenge which at times appeared to take on a mysterious life of its own, quite independent of the financial rewards that might be expected to flow from it. He "took it on" and was president, and later chairman, of Brinco for the next six years; but he never accepted a salary, nor did he take up an option on seventy-five thousand shares offered to him a year or so later. The adventure itself, it seemed, was enough.

A man of conservative instincts, Gardner received a rude shock soon after his appointment was confirmed at the first meeting of the board of directors in St. John's on April 23. It came in a telephone call from a

Montreal lawyer, Wilbert Howard. As a director of Nalco, Howard said, he had been asked by some of the private shareholders to tell him certain facts: that Nalco had been granted rights to the water powers on the Hamilton River which had now been granted to Brinco; that this constituted confiscation of property rights; and that the minority shareholders of Nalco did not think Bertie Gardner would willingly be party to such an arrangement.

Bewildered, Gardner could only reply, quite truthfully, that he had not yet seen the agreement between the Newfoundland government and Brinco — in fact it was not formally executed until two days later, on May 21 — but that if Nalco had any representations to make they should be directed to the government. Unwilling to let him off the hook, Howard hinted darkly, "I suppose you realize that if the Newfoundland government can cancel one agreement it can also cancel another?"

It was a puzzled, and somewhat worried, president who reported this conversation to his general manager in St. John's, and he was relieved when Southam was able to tell him that the difficulties had been ironed out and that Brinco's title to the Hamilton was sound. Southam himself had been no less concerned when he heard for the first time a few weeks previously that Nalco's prior rights had been holding up ratification of the Brinco agreement by the Newfoundland House. He had gone to see the Attorney General immediately and been told that the problem was that sub-leases Nalco had granted to two U.S. mining companies carried with them the rights to establish hydro-electric developments to serve any mines resulting from their exploration. Since these concessions were about to lapse, and no mines had resulted, the problem was soon resolved. As it happened, though, an even more worrying one was to arise almost immediately.

Soon after Howard's call, Gardner was chatting with friends at a cocktail party when his counterpart at the Royal Bank of Canada, James Muir, drew him aside and casually unloaded another bombshell: that the Royal Bank owned the water rights to Muskrat Falls, thirty miles up the Hamilton River from its mouth at Lake Melville.

Back in 1901, Muir explained, the Newfoundland government had granted a timber concession in the area to a lumberman named Alfred Dickie, president of a Halifax company, the Grand River Pulp and Paper Company. The grant had included the rights to Muskrat in case Dickie needed power for a sawmill in the area. His attempt to harvest the Lake Melville timber had foundered some years later, and the bank, which lost $200,000 on the venture, had taken over the company. But the water rights had never been rescinded, and in fact the bank was still paying a nominal rent on them to the Newfoundland government every year.

Once again, Gardner put in an agitated call to Southam, and once again Southam went in to see Curtis. The news was as much of a surprise to the Newfoundland government as it had been to Gardner, but a search of the files confirmed that the old concession had never lapsed, though it was thought it could legally be held to have been superseded by subsequent legislation, namely, the granting of the Hamilton rights to Nalco and their later transfer to Brinco. Obligingly, Curtis volunteered to approach the Royal Bank himself, on behalf of the government, with an offer to repurchase the rights for, say, $10,000; and if that failed, to repossess them by legislation.

Southam immediately recognized that while this course would prove effective, it was hardly the sort of government action the new corporation would want to encourage. He suggested he should first consult the London Committee. As a memorandum written by Edmund de Rothschild said at the time: "In the last resort, Brinco can ask the Newfoundland government to abrogate . . . . This would, however, set a precedent which could enable the government to deal similarly with Brinco's rights to the Grand Falls."

This unpleasing spectre having appeared on the however-distant horizon, it was decided it would be much better for Gardner to approach his friend Muir and try to settle the matter as between gentlemen. A meeting was arranged and Gardner began by presuming tactfully that any loss the Royal Bank might have suffered in the unfortunate affair of the Grand River company must long ago have been written off; that the rights, after all, were so tenuous as to be of little value at this late date; and wouldn't twenty-five thousand shares of Brinco (then valued nominally at $1 each) be a much more satisfactory investment?

Muir naturally wanted to be helpful, but on a matter of such importance he would have to consult his fellow directors. A few days later he wrote to Gardner, reasserting "our disposition to co-operate," but adding: "It was brought out that perhaps the Muskrat Falls, due to the fact that they are the power site closest to Goose Bay and the area in which one might reasonably expect power-utilizing developments to take place, could be rather advantageously situated for the eventual purposes of Brinco and that, in the circumstances, it would not seem unreasonable that we be given 35,000 shares of the company in return for all our interests . . . ."

This outcome indeed proved reasonable and satisfactory to the London Committee, the thirty-five thousand shares were issued, and the transfer of the rights was duly regularized by a minute of the executive council of the province of Newfoundland.

These challenges to the corporation's title gave Southam some anxious moments, as did the delays he encountered initially in securing maps accurately delineating concessions already dispensed by the government to other companies. But the Premier always made light of any difficulties and clearly showed he did not intend to let what he obviously considered mere technicalities cloud the spirit of the agreement or stand in the way of the corporation's success. Joey Smallwood considered himself not only the father of Brinco but its mother as well, and his diligent assumption of his parental responsibilities sometimes embarrassed the less demonstrative Southam. He developed a habit, for instance, of reeling off the names of Brinco's shareholder companies to his audiences, totting up their total worldwide capitalization, and somehow leaving behind the impression that all these billions of dollars were about to be employed in the service of Newfoundland and Labrador.

But Joey never hesitated to press hyperbole into the service of what he considered a good cause. Introducing the Brinco bill to the House in April, he described the corporation as "the biggest combination of industrial and financial interests ever brought together in the world's history for prospecting and developing natural resources." And in listing its shareholders ("Who has not heard of the famous Prudential Life, undoubtedly the biggest insurance company on the face of the earth, whose resources run close to three thousand million dollars?") he also managed to mention at least three companies which, while admittedly "household names," did not belong to the consortium. Then, hearing that Rothschilds had the day before supplemented Southam's initial $5,000 funds with a transfer of $400,000, he anticipated events slightly and announced that "they have already spent more than $400,000 on mere exploration in this province . . . ."

After explaining the conditions upon which the concession was being granted, the Premier returned to the theme he had expounded in London. "Without vanity," he said, "I ask myself: did Newfoundland start something in England? . . . Did this offer we made, this passing over to Britain a potential empire in Newfoundland and Labrador, did it stir again the greatness that has planted the British flag so far around the world that the sun, as we know, never has a chance to set on it? Did Newfoundland, little, old and ancient, old-fashioned Newfoundland, stir the blood of those British people who count on making Britain great again?"

His rhetoric left the leader of the opposition markedly unmoved.

Malcolm Hollett, who had the thankless task of leading his three Progressive Conservative colleagues against Joey's solid Liberal phalanx of twenty-three members, wondered why "these great monied men on the other side of the Atlantic" had not sprung to Newfoundland's rescue in her hour of need before the war. He went so far (eliciting cries of "Shame" from the Premier) as to say that "the great Winston Churchill" had supported those politicians in England who had "sold us out."

As to the bill, "the very idea of this little province of one hundred and fifty or two hundred thousand square miles giving in one fell swoop sixty thousand square miles" was "a principle which most fair-minded Newfoundlanders ought to oppose." To Hollett, "the principle of this bill is a vicious one."

It was this point, of which Joey was so proud — the immense scale of his venture — that the opposition chose to pursue. One member pointed out that the area involved was "larger in size than twenty-nine of the states of the American union." Another professed to find at least one good point in the bill: "We will not have any more wrangling about alienation of lands. We will all have our homes unless these people decide they want them."

Winding up the debate, the Premier made no apologies for the size of the concession. "The magnitude and the significance" of the project were "too big . . . for the small minds of the Opposition to grasp." And, in response to the allegations that the concession was a "giveaway," he countered: "We don't give Brinco sixty thousand square miles any more than you give a man your house when you rent it to him . . . . We have given them the right, if they find anything, to develop what they find with their own money. We have given them the right to pay us taxation and royalties on anything they produce — that is how we have given away Newfoundland."

Ironically, once the House had completed its inevitable ratification of the agreement (only two members of the opposition were present to vote against it on second reading), the criticism of Brinco soon switched from its allegedly threatening gigantism to the fact that it did not seem to be doing anything; that it had no staff; that its general manager was always off gallivanting around the mainland. This, and the fact that wags around St. John's had taken to calling the company "Bingo" or "Bunco," greatly offended Southam.

Finally, after what he considered an insulting reflection on not only the corporation's integrity but his own, he telephoned Hollett in high indignation. "I suppose your remarks in Parliament are privileged," he told him, "otherwise I should sue you for slander." And he challenged the opposition leader to come round to LeMarchant Road right away to see for himself what the corporation was doing. Somewhat taken aback by this vehement reaction to his parliamentary thrust and parry, Hollett drove over. Southam greeted him coldly and spent the next two hours showing him his already bulky files of maps, surveys and reports, and lecturing him on the corporation's current activities and future plans.

Before he had finished, Hollett was mollified by Southam's patent sincerity and dedication to his task; they parted rather less acrimoniously than they had met and thereafter, however the opposition harried the Premier, there was virtually never any criticism of Brinco.

At this stage, of course, most of what Southam had to tell Hollett was concerned with the progress of the search for minerals, which the consortium's members considered to be their best hope for a return on their investment. But as the summer wore on and reports from the field indicated that all was well with the geologists. Southam turned his attention to the water rights granted in the Principal Agreement. It was clear that the Hamilton River was the jewel in that particular crown. But he could find no one in Newfoundland with any but the most generalized information about it. He met several people who had been fishing in the area, but few of them had penetrated the interior as far as Grand Falls. The Premier, who had flown over the falls, told him enthusiastically they held "millions of horse power" waiting to be tapped. But, Southam was informed, the government had no separate department devoted to water and power and such scanty information as existed about the Hamilton was buried in dusty files in various sections of the Ministry of Mines and Resources.

Southam suggested in one of his frequent letters to Peter Hobbs in London that the corporation might try to cooperate with the ministry in assembling and coordinating this information. As he put it: "Such an approach might also have a psychological value in helping to silence those who are inclined to insist that the corporation's real intention is to hoard its water power and timber assets."

FOUR

"One of the grandest spectacles in the world"

An English poet laureate, Robert Southey, once demonstrated the inadvisability, if not the utter impossibility, of trying to capture in mere words the sight and sound of a waterfall. Inspired by the comparatively modest Cataract of Lodore in the English Lake District, he unwisely ventured too near the brink and was swept away in a cascade of excruciating lines of which the following are only a brief sample:

And pouring and roaring,
And waving and raving,
And tossing and crossing,
And flowing and going,
And running and stunning,
And foaming and roaming,
And dinning and spinning,
And dropping and hopping,
And working and jerking,
And guggling and struggling . . . .

The first white man to see the much more dramatic Great Falls of Labrador was more restrained in his description of them, as befits a Scot who spent twenty-five years trading with the Indians in the service of the Hudson's Bay Company. John McLean, born on the Isle of Mull in 1799, had served in the Ottawa Valley and the wilds of what is now British Columbia when he was ordered in 1837 to the recently opened company post at Fort Chimo, on Ungava Bay. The company hoped to develop a fur trade in the unexplored interior of Labrador and McLean was told to find an overland route by which Fort Chimo could be supplied from the post at North West River, near the mouth of the Hamilton.

He set off with a party of four on January 2, 1838, and seven weeks later arrived at North West River, having accomplished one of those incredible journeys which make up so much of the history of the North — more than four hundred miles as the crow flies, and nearer to six hundred as McLean travelled. Without tents, he and his party slept beneath the stars, rolled up in their blankets in the shelter of trees where they were lucky enough to find them, burrowing into the snow when, as often, there were no trees within miles. On clear days, though occasionally suffering from frostbite, they were able to make as much as twenty miles on their snowshoes. On others, trudging knee-deep through fresh snow and stopping every few feet to manhandle their sleds, they were able to cover only a mile. Sometimes, the blizzards were so fierce they dare not travel at all and were forced to remain huddled in their blankets all day.

After two weeks' rest at the post, revelling in the luxury of a roof over their heads, they embarked on their equally arduous return journey, during which, when one of his men fell sick, McLean pushed on ahead to get help. Before he reached Fort Chimo on April 20, he ran out of food and had to eat his sled dogs to survive.

His spectacular trek convinced him that the rugged country he had crossed could never serve as a supply route for Fort Chimo from the Atlantic coast. Furthermore, his inability to live off the land (his party rarely encountered any game which might have supplemented the rations they dragged with them on their sleds) prompted him to write to the Governor of the Hudson's Bay Company predicting that there was scant prospect of establishing a profitable fur trade in the interior of Labrador.

However, despatches from an outpost such as Chimo might take two years to reach their destination in those days, and in the meantime McLean dutifully continued to try to follow his instructions. Soon after his return he heard from some passing Indians of a "Michipou," or big river, which ran from west to east some distance south of the route he had taken, eventually emptying into Esquimaux Bay, as Lake Melville was then known. So the following summer, as soon as the ice cleared from around Fort Chimo, which was not until June 24, he set off to find this big river and follow it to its mouth to discover whether canoes could navigate it in the opposite direction and thus bring supplies up from the coast.

McLean described his various journeys in a book called "Notes of a Twenty-Five Years' Service in the Hudson's Bay Territory." By the middle of August 1839, he and his companion, Erland Erlandson, were paddling peacefully down the Hamilton "when, one evening, the roar of a mighty cataract burst upon our ears, warning us that danger was at hand. We soon reached the spot, which presented to us one of the grandest spectacles in the world, but put an end to all hopes of success in our enterprise."

The sight McLean saw — the water leaping out in a cloud of spray and falling into a steep-sided gorge far below — certainly seemed an insuperable obstacle to any canoe trying to travel upstream. He wrote that the river, several hundred yards wide before it enters the rapids above the falls, "finally contracts to a breadth of about fifty yards, ere it precipitates itself over the rock which forms the fall; when, still roaring and foaming, it continues its maddened course for about a distance of thirty miles, pent up between walls of rock that rise sometimes to the height of three hundred feet on either side." (He overestimated the length of the gorge, and underestimated the height of its walls, at least toward its lower end.)

After carrying their canoes and supplies through bogs and swamps for a whole day, trying vainly to find a way down to the river below the falls, McLean and Erlandson gave up their attempt to reach North West River by this route and "with heavy hearts and weary limbs" retraced their steps. But after his return to Fort Chimo, McLean learned from an old Indian that there was in fact a portage route around the falls — up a steep gully later to be known as Big Hill, which climbs a thousand feet in little over a quarter of a mile and reaches the plateau where the town of Churchill Falls now stands.

During the next few years he made at least one successful journey to North West River by this route, and it was later used briefly by the Hudson's Bay Company to supply two posts set up in the interior, one near the present site of Schefferville, in Quebec, and the other on the shore of Lake Michikamau, largest of the hundreds of lakes now incorporated into the Churchill Falls reservoir. Neither post survived for long, because there were too few inhabitants of the interior to keep them supplied with furs.

McLean estimated that the Indian tribe inhabiting the interior of Labrador, the "Nascopies," numbered "about one hundred men able to bear arms." This was probably an underestimate, but a government count half a century later put the total number of Indians in the interior at only a thousand. The tribe is more generally known today as the Naskaupi, an uncomplimentary name meaning "uncivilized" bestowed on them by their neighbours to the south, the Montagnais. The Naskaupi, who speak a dialect of the Cree language, refer to themselves as "Nenenat," meaning "true people."

The tribe was probably forced on to the inhospitable hunting grounds of the Labrador plateau by pressure from the much more numerous Montagnais to the south and west, and their alleged traditional enemies, the Eskimos of the coast. McLean described them as "a peaceful, harmless people," but added that "they cherish the unprovoked enmity of their race towards the poor Esquimaux, whom they never fail to attack, when an opportunity offers of doing so with impunity. Our presence, however, has had the effect of establishing a more friendly intercourse between them; and to the fact that many of the Esquimaux have of late acquired fire-arms, and are not to be attacked without some risk, may be ascribed, in no small degree, the present forbearance of their enemies."

In McLean's day, and for long afterwards, the Naskaupi survived precariously by constant roaming in search of food, wandering over the interior in the short summer season and, like the Montagnais, retreating to the milder coast when the winter closed in. They caught salmon in the coastal rivers and seals on the ice of the Gulf of St. Lawrence; picked berries wherever they could; brought down ptarmigan, ducks or geese with their arrows; and speared muskrat or beaver with their long, barbed lances. Most of all, though, their existence depended on the vast caribou herds which used to travel across the interior. Caught in carefully planned ambushes, the caribou provided meat, hides for clothing and tents, bone for weapons and tools, sinews for thread.

As the caribou herds dwindled, the Naskaupi moved out of the interior to the settlements; since the opening of the iron-ore deposits in Labrador and nearby Quebec, many of them have congregated around Schefferville.

After their description by McLean,* the falls reverted to their original obscurity. Between 1866 and 1870 an Oblate missionary named Father Babel lived with the Indians in the interior, exploring stretches of the Hamilton and making what was probably the first map of the area. But it was almost the turn of the century before there was any more interest in the Labrador plateau. In 1891, several newspapers in the United States carried a report that Indians and *voyageurs* claimed the existence in the interior of Labrador of a towering waterfall fifteen hundred feet high. Intrigued by, but apparently skeptical of, this "attractive piece of geographical news," Henry G. Bryant, recording secretary of the Geographical Club of Philadelphia, recruited a friend, Professor C. A.

*John McLean resigned from the Hudson's Bay Company in 1845, when he was once again posted to the West, and settled in Guelph, Ontario, where he became first a bank manager and later clerk of the Division Court at nearby Elora. Almost forty years later, still tall and fit, he returned to the West to live with his youngest daughter in Victoria, where he died in 1890, at the age of ninety-one.

Kenaston, of Washington, D.C., and set off in search of this natural phenomenon.

Like most explorers who followed McLean, Bryant and Kenaston decided to push inland from the coast, ascending the river from Hamilton Inlet and Lake Melville, at its mouth. They arrived at North West River by sea on July 27, 1891, hoping to engage Indian guides. But when they announced their intention of travelling the 210 miles from the mouth of the river to the falls, they could find no Indians willing to go with them. As Bryant said in an account of their journey published in the *Century Magazine* in September 1892, "They believe the place to be the haunt of evil spirits, and assert that death will soon overtake the venturesome mortal who dares to look upon the mysterious cataract."

There are several versions of the old Indian legend attaching to the falls, which were known as Patses-che-wan, or "The narrow place where the water falls." Essentially, it seems, two Indian maidens were either swept over the falls while fishing from a canoe or fell in while gathering firewood too close to the brink. Death by drowning was a horrible fate for an Indian because it was believed his spirit would be trapped forever beneath the water, screaming for an escape which never came. The Indian maidens were thus condemned to live beneath the falls, endlessly processing caribou hides. As time passed, their beauty faded and it was said they would occasionally climb to the brink of the falls, their white hair streaming in the spray, and try to lure careless mortals into joining them in their servitude below.

Unable to overcome the Indians' fears, Bryant persuaded a Scots trapper named John Montague and an Eskimo named Geoffrey Ban to guide them. They left North West River on August 3 in an eighteen-foot river boat with sail, towing their sixteen-foot canoe behind them, and on the third day encountered the first of the many obstacles in their path, Muskrat Falls. It took them a day and a half, with the aid of block and tackle, to manhandle their unwieldy 500-lb. boat up the steep banks and regain the river, a hundred feet above.

For the rest of their journey, because of the swift current bearing down on them, they were seldom able to use their oars or paddles, let alone their sail. For the most part, they had to resort to the form of travel the trappers called "tracking" — towing their boats upstream by means of ropes tied to leather bands into which they could lean their shoulders. Since there are many rapids on the Hamilton, and its banks are often strewn with boulders, it was an exhausting way to go. But they pressed on, across Gull Island Lake and round Porcupine Rapids, Gull Island

Rapids* and Horseshoe Rapids until, after almost four weeks, they came to another set of rapids which they judged to be the foot of the gorge in the area of Big Hill and the portage around the falls.

Leaving Geoffrey with the boat, the other three set out carrying the canoe and a week's provisions, and after a long search found the trail and climbed up the hill on to the plateau. They were now fifteen hundred feet above sea level (which probably accounts for the garbled press report Bryant had read), on an apparently endless plain strewn with lakes and bogs and boulders. Three days travelling across a chain of six lakes, with portages between them, brought them to a point at which they could strike off across the rough, mossy ground to the south-west and reach the banks of the Hamilton near the falls, which they did on September 2.

"A single glance," wrote Bryant, "showed that we had before us one of the greatest waterfalls in the world." While Bryant made a risky descent down the sheer side of the gorge in an unsuccessful attempt to photograph the falls, Professor Kenaston tried to measure their height by the ingenious but none-too-scientific method of tossing a "heavy billet of green fir" over the edge, attached to a long length of rope he had thoughtfully provided for this purpose. He arrived at a height for the falls of 316 feet. This was considerably less than they had been led to expect, but considerably more than the falls' actual height, which is 245 feet — 85 feet higher than the Horseshoe Falls at Niagara.

No doubt to his disappointment, since priority is important to explorers, Bryant discovered as he was leaving the falls that another American party had by coincidence beaten them to the scene by a mere two weeks. Tied to a spruce tree which had been cut off about four feet from the ground he found a glass fruit bottle sealed to keep its contents dry. Inside was a paper recording the arrival at the falls of Austin Cary and Dennis Cole, two recent graduates of Bowdoin College, in the state of Maine.

Bryant added the names of his party to the bottle, thus beginning a tradition that later visitors perpetuated. When the bottle was retrieved by Brinco and presented to Joey Smallwood in 1960, it contained the names of eighty-four visitors or groups of visitors; and it is a telling

*John Montague, who hailed from the Orkneys, drowned some time later while tracking a canoe through Gull Island Rapids on a trapping expedition. His grandson, Harvey Montague, who used to be a trapper in the same area, later became a janitor at Churchill Falls. And two of *his* sons (John Montague's great-grandsons) also worked at Churchill: Ed, as project geologist, and Clayton, as a driver.

commentary on the isolation of the falls that most of them were those of surveyors and engineers sent into the area by Brinco during the preceding six years.

Cary and Cole were members of a nineteen-man scientific expedition sent to Labrador by Bowdoin College in 1891, thus initiating a long-standing connection between the area and the states of Maine and Vermont which they commemorated by naming the gorge below the falls Bowdoin Canyon and a nearby mountain and lake Mount Hyde, in honour of the president of their college. While most of the members of the expedition sailed up the coast, Cary and Cole and two colleagues, W. R. Smith and E. B. Young, pushed up the Hamilton in two fifteen-foot cedar boats, without benefit of guides.

Perhaps because of this collegiate over-confidence, one of the boats soon overturned and they lost about a quarter of their supplies. Then Young injured his hand and he and Smith turned back. Worse was to come for Carry and Cole. Forging upriver until they were stopped by what from their adventure became known as Disaster Rapids, they then left their canoe, carrying packs with only two days' supply of food. Thus unencumbered, they managed to climb out of the gorge and reach the falls. But on their return they found to their horror that they had not properly extinguished their riverside camp fire and it had spread and destroyed not only their boat but most of their supplies for the return journey.

Left with a quart of rice, three quarts of mixed meal, a little tea and some partly burned flour and rice, their clothes and boots already the worse for wear, they might have been expected to starve to death. Incredibly, they managed to walk out to Lake Melville in seventeen days, shooting an occasional squirrel or partridge with a .22 pistol which providentially escaped the flames, and fortified by a couple of food caches they stumbled across along the way.

Others who took the Labrador bush too lightly were not so fortunate, including an American magazine writer named Leonidas Hubbard who tried in 1903 to find a new route into Lake Michikamau. Since the only existing maps of Labrador were hopelessly inadequate, Hubbard was soon lost. Wearing only thin summer clothing and running short of food, with winter fast closing in, he became weak and ill and his two companions, a fellow-writer named Dillon Wallace and a Scots-Cree guide named John Elson, built a camp for him and left him behind while they headed for the coast and help. A rescue party of four trappers found his frozen body late in October.

Two years later, Wallace himself almost died on another and even longer trek across Labrador, though in that same year Hubbard's wife, who must have been both more determined and wiser than her husband, since she provided herself with four guides, managed to complete the journey he had set for himself.

These and later wanderings by amateur explorers from the United States, extending almost up to the Second World War, contributed little more than further Southey-esque effusions to the outside world's knowledge of the Labrador plateau, and in particular Grand Falls. The first real scientific information about the area was provided by a young Canadian geologist named Albert Peter Low, who deposited his name in the bottle at the falls in 1894, three years after Cary and Cole had left it there.

Low had graduated from McGill University in Montreal in 1882 and joined the Dominion Geological Survey.* In 1893 he began a criss-crossing expedition across Labrador which was eventually to last sixteen months, during which he only once received mail from the outside world. By the time he returned to Ottawa he had made detailed surveys of more than two thousand miles of rivers and lakes and collected more than two hundred rock samples.

He reached Grand Falls on May 2, 1894, and described his impressions in the report of the Geological Survey for 1895. "The noise of the fall has a stunning effect," he wrote, "and although deadened because of its inclosed situation, can be heard for more than ten miles away, as a deep, booming sound. The cloud of mist is also visible from any eminence within a radius of twenty miles."

Like McLean, Low overestimated the height of the falls — he put them at 302 feet — but his guess at their volume was closer than some estimates made many years later with the advantage of more advanced measuring techniques: he put their discharge at 50,000 cubic feet per second, "or nearly the mean volume of the Ottawa River, at Ottawa." He did not speculate at this time on a potential use for all this water, and more interest was probably aroused by his discovery in several places of "immense deposits" of iron ore. In some areas, he reported, there were so many outcrops of iron-bearing rocks that "the ores will be found in practically inexhaustible quantity."

He returned to this theme some years later, in 1907, when a committee of the Senate held a series of hearings whose proceedings were later

*Low was appointed director of the Geological Survey in 1906 and when the Federal Department of Mines was established a year later became its first deputy minister. Ill health forced his retirement in 1913 but he lived on in Ottawa until 1942.

published under the title of "Canada's Fertile Northland." Low told the committee there was "a great supply of iron" in Labrador "which will probably be valuable in the next twenty-five years." The greatest difficulty in making this iron ore commercially valuable was the problem of transportation, he said, "but there are several millions of horse-power in the Grand Falls of the Hamilton River, and in addition to mechanical horse-power it would also furnish the heat whereby by an electrical process, the reduction of the ore by electricity might be performed. Transportation might also be provided by electric power."

The fact that this never came about does not detract from Low's prescience: proposals for using Hamilton Falls power for the electrical reduction of iron ores (a process used successfully in Europe but never adopted in North America) were still being advanced in the late fifties and early sixties.

The next scientific survey of the falls was made by a French-Canadian engineer named Wilfrid Thibaudeau, who worked in Europe for three years after his graduation from Laval University in 1883 and then spent the next twenty-five years on various surveys and construction projects in western Canada, serving for a time as superintendent of public works for the Yukon Territory. In 1912, Thibaudeau surveyed the St. Maurice River for the newly formed Commission for the Management of Running Waters in Quebec, and in 1915 turned his attention to the upper basin of the Hamilton. Though copies of his report no longer seem to exist, he is credited in the early surveys commissioned by Brinco with being the first man to suggest, in a general way, the "Channel Scheme" which was eventually used to develop the falls.

It was not until 1947 that a preliminary survey of the river and falls was carried out for the Newfoundland government, by a party of four men under Commander G. H. Desbarats, a retired Royal Canadian Navy officer. Desbarats, too, was impressed by the falls' potential and reported: "Some day a use will be found for this power, pioneering men and women will move northward, and another frontier will be rolled back."

The development foreseen by Thibaudeau and Desbarats was made possible by a peculiarity of the topography of Labrador which is not apparent to a lay observer gazing at the falls; nature, in fact, was the first engineer on the Churchill Falls project. Before the last Ice Age, the rivers of Labrador ran through deep gorges worn in the granite over millions of years. Then the glaciers came and what is now the Labrador plateau was crushed under a mass of ice a mile high. As the glaciers receded, the awesome weight of the ice ground off the tops of the hills, filling up the ancient river beds with boulders and gravel and leaving

46

behind a plain which is not quite level but is lower at the centre than at its rim, like a saucer. The gouging action of the ice on this plain also created hundreds of lakes; if you fly high enough over Labrador in the summer you can see the pattern left by the retreat of the glaciers in the way the lakes generally seem to run in the same direction, as if they had been scratched out by the claws of giant bears.

The melting ice and the return of the rains filled up the lakes and new rivers formed between them. Unable to find the old channels, these rivers meandered about the plain seeking weak points on its rim through which they might escape down to the sea. Fortunately for the builders of the Churchill Falls project, the rim sprang few leaks and most of the water from the plateau ultimately came to drain through the weak spot found by the Churchill River. This weak spot was not simply the falls themselves, grand though the early travellers found their 245-foot drop to be.

Before the river was diverted, it began to run down off the plateau five miles above the falls, when it entered a series or rapids. By the time it reached the falls it had already dropped more than two hundred feet and at this point was foaming downhill in a sort of chute at an angle of forty-five degrees. The chute, and the lip of the falls, which curved upward, could be compared to a ski-jump. The action of the upcurved lip hurled the water out into space for a free fall into the churning pool below.

From there, the river turned sharply to its left and surged away down the five-mile-long Bowdoin Canyon, fortuitously providing the best vantage point for viewing the falls, from a clearing on top of a 300-foot cliff directly opposite them. Few early travellers saw the falls from this spot — dubbed "the Meadow" by Brinco employees — because it is on the far bank of the river.

At the foot of Bowdoin Canyon, where it is joined by a tributary, the Valley River, the Churchill turns sharply left again and continues to run downhill through another series of rapids in a deep gorge. In the twenty-two miles between the pool at the foot of the falls and the end of the rapids, where the trappers began their portage up Big Hill, the river drops a further 580 feet. At that point, it is thus more than a thousand feet below its original level up on the plateau.

The amount of power that can be generated by a hydro-electric plant depends not only on the volume of water available to turn the turbines (which are in essence water wheels) but on its "head": in other words, how far the water falls before it hits the blades of the turbines.

A layman looking at the falls might have assumed that to harness the river you would need a powerhouse at their base. Thibaudeau was the first to realize that if the water could be diverted before the river entered the rapids above the falls and somehow conducted back into it twenty miles downstream, the "head" would not be the mere 245 feet existing at the falls themselves but more than a thousand feet.

In its simplest outline, this is what was done at Churchill Falls: the forty miles of strategically placed dykes built with rock and glacial rubble available on the spot (there was no need for towering and expensive concrete dams) plugged the low spots in the rim of the Labrador saucer and formed a huge reservoir almost half the size of Lake Ontario. From the reservoir, the water flows through a natural canal formed in effect by raising, and thus linking, the lakes that used to make up the portage route around the falls. Then it is channelled down tunnels bored into a hill on the rim of the plateau. One thousand and forty feet below — a "head" to make an engineer's eyes shine — it spins the turbines in the underground powerhouse. From there, its work done, it rejoins the river through two mile-long tailrace tunnels near the place where the *voyageurs* and explorers and trappers used to begin their steep climb to the plateau above.

FIVE

London gives the go-ahead

This historical background, even had it been available to Bill Southam when he set about assessing the prospects for Brinco's water-power concession, would have been of little practical use to him. He needed someone technically qualified to evaluate the various ways in which the Hamilton might be developed; how much power each scheme might reasonably be expected to generate and at what cost; and who might buy the power, at what price.

Early in the summer of 1953, on one of his frequent visits to Montreal, he suggested to Bertie Gardner that the Bank of Montreal's research department might be able to supply some answers to these questions. He also had a pleasant meeting with a man he had been told in St. John's knew as much about the power business in Newfoundland as anyone: Denis Stairs, vice-president of Montreal Engineering Company, and president of one of its subsidiaries, the Newfoundland Light and Power Company. Having first visited Newfoundland in 1923, Stairs knew about Grand Falls in a general way and thought he knew where he could lay his hands on some maps of the area; he promised to see what he could find and write Southam a letter.

The bank's report, which Southam received in August, was based largely on published material and its author warned darkly in the first paragraph that the news items which had lately been appearing about Newfoundland and Labrador "tend to be romantic and visionary rather than factual." He seemed to lean toward the Horseshoe Rapids, about seventy-five miles from the river's mouth, as the most likely hydro site, but quoted a report that the Hamilton contained a total of seven million horse power — which, he pointed out, was about half of Canada's entire installed hydro-electric capacity at that time.

The problem thus became finding a user for all that potential power. The timber available in Labrador suggested a newsprint mill, but the largest mill in Canada used only about 200,000 horse power, so that a plant generating even a million horse power would serve five such mills — an obvious impossibility. Similarly, any mines that could be envisioned in Labrador would need only a few thousand horse power. An alternative could be to transmit the power south to the north shore of the Gulf of St. Lawrence, where enough new industries might be established to use it; but the author was neither very specific, nor very hopeful, about this project.

Neither was he very helpful on how much it would cost to build a hydro plant on the river: his best guess was "between $100 and $200 per horse power."

Stairs' letter, when it arrived a few days later, took the shape of a ten-page report, and it was much more encouraging. A lean, craggy-faced Haligonian with an infectious, high-pitched laugh, Denis Stairs had been a hydro engineer most of his life, though when he tried to find a job after a youthful visit to Europe in 1912 he was told that every city in Canada now had its electric supply and no more would be needed! Like others connected with the power industry in Newfoundland, he had long been aware of Grand Falls. As he recalled years later: "We all knew that it was a great big water power — quite without value because it was too far away."

The problem had always been twofold: the falls were so remote and the climate in the area was so rigorous that the idea of shipping in the men and machines and materials needed to harness them seemed utterly visionary; and even if a power plant could be built there, it would be economically impossible (if not physically impossible, given the current "state of the art" in long-distance transmission) to ship the resultant electricity out to centres of population such as Montreal, where it might be used.

But by 1953 Stairs knew of, and mentioned in his report to Southam, two developments that brought these historic problems at least within sight of solution. First, the Iron Ore Company of Canada was well on the way to completing its 360-mile railroad north from Sept-Iles on the St. Lawrence, through the wilderness of Quebec and western Labrador to Schefferville. Some seven thousand men were at present being fed and housed along its route, and were working successfully despite the rugged conditions. Since the railroad was designed to carry ten million tons of iron ore a year south from Schefferville and since it passed within a hundred or so miles of Grand Falls, its return journeys might well be used to carry north from Sept-Iles the material Brinco would need to develop the falls.

Secondly, experiments were being made in Europe with the transmission of electricity at much higher voltages than had ever been used before, which appeared likely to make it more economic to convey power over long distances. Sweden, for instance, was in a similar position to Canada: she had great potential water power in the north, many miles from her industrial centres in the south. And she had recently opened a six-hundred-mile line transmitting power at the previously unheard-of level of 380,000 volts. True, Montreal was *seven* hundred miles from Grand Falls, but this was a promising development.

In his covering letter to Southam, Stairs pointed out that in Ontario, and to a lesser degree in Quebec, the end of cheap hydro power was in sight. Ontario would soon face the prospect of generating her steadily mounting electricity needs by steam, using high-priced American or Nova Scotian coal. Quebec still had some convenient undeveloped water power, but she, too, would soon face the prospect of developing remote rivers or turning to coal. When all the cheap hydro power was used up, within perhaps ten or twenty years, it would be possible to supply both provinces from Labrador.

In this case, the Hamilton River should be developed in its own channel, beginning wth Grand Falls, where Stairs estimated the power available at four million horse power — an estimate that stood up for the following ten years, though it ultimately proved to be far below the eventual capacity of the Churchill Falls plant.

If the power were to be retained in Newfoundland, rather than exported, the large amount available could be used for only one purpose: the production of light metals, in particular aluminum, "the only industry in the world today which consumes power as a raw material in millions of horse power." In this case, it might be better to divert the Hamilton above the falls into a lesser river draining the plateau to the north, the Naskaupi. The advantage of this plan was that there were several potential dam sites along the Naskaupi where power could be developed closer to Lake Melville, which Stairs thought might be a suitable location for an aluminum smelter. However, he could foresee two main objections that might be raised to this suggestion: Lake Melville is ice-bound for seven to eight months of the year, and the market for aluminum might be fully supplied for many years to come by plants already built or proposed for other sites.

Either of these possible developments was feasible, Stairs concluded, but he could not estimate their cost. To do this would demand further engineering studies, including accurate measurements of the flows of both the Hamilton and the Naskaupi over a period of years, the preparation of contour maps of the area, and an investigation by field parties of levels at various key points around the falls.

Stairs' report strengthened Bill Southam's hand with the London Committee, whose members at this time still considered the mineral exploration to be Brinco's main order of business. Initially, when he had suggested he should hire a hydro-electric engineer to pursue the Hamilton studies or that English Electric should send over a man suitably qualified to assess the situation, he had been told to confine his research to "the collation of existing data," a task that would not require technical expertise and could be carried out by "an intelligent agent." The members of the London Committee apparently shared Bertie Gardner's opinion that to spend a lot of money investigating the Hamilton without having a customer in view for the power would be more of a gamble than an investment.

Now Southam had Stairs' view that more work was needed before even an approximate price could be set on the power, and he was under no illusion about his chances of interesting a customer without being able to quote a price. He turned to Eric Bowater, who fortuitously visited Newfoundland at around this time, and agreed to lend Brinco the part-time services of his own power engineer in Newfoundland, Eric Hinton.

Short and stooped, and plagued by the asthma that was to contribute to his death two years later, Hinton was nevertheless a wiry little man who in his youth had worked for the contractor who built the Deer Lake power station which supplies the Bowater mill at Corner Brook, and had stayed on with the operating company. By 1953, he was manager of the plant and his experience and judgment in the hydro field were much respected.

Working in the evening and at weekends, Hinton went over all the available information again. He had asked for a geologist to help him and Southam sent him Stan Roderick, one of Dr. Beavan's men whose season of field work in Labrador was now coming to a close. After a flying visit to see the falls on the ground and tireless poring over maps and aerial mosaics, trying to guess contours and levels and arrive at estimates of flows more by divination than measurement, Hinton became a missionary for the Channel Scheme. As he wistfully told a colleague at the time: "I wish I was forty years younger."

By October, six months after Brinco's formation, when the board of directors held its first meeting in Montreal, Southam had found another ally. Bertie Gardner had invited a former chairman of Ontario Hydro, T. H. Hogg, to join the board. Tommy Hogg's eminence as a hydro engineer was unchallengeable (he was said to command a fee of $1,000 a day for his services as a consultant) and when he heard Southam's explanation of what he had done so far on the Channel Scheme he gave his plans a firm vote of confidence. He had no doubt that the scheme would work, and that if the price were reasonable Ontario Hydro would jump at the chance to buy every kilowatt of power the Hamilton could produce.

Before the board meeting, Southam had been pressing London unsuccessfully for the authority to engage one or more engineering companies to carry the studies a stage further. Peter Hobbs now read out a letter which explained that English Electric, after due consideration of the reports from Canada, had changed its mind and felt it was worth while commissioning a study that might take two or three years and cost $100,000.

Hinton, who had been invited to give the board his comments, shot a startled glance at Southam. He had himself concluded that a two- or three-year survey was needed, but he had warned Southam privately it might cost $1 million or more.

Southam did not challenge the $100,000 figure, but suggested instead that perhaps Mr. Hogg had an opinion. An old hand at board meetings, Hogg had been dozing contentedly through the various reports. Someone shook him awake and the letter was read again for his benefit. Indeed, he agreed, if Brinco was serious about developing its assets, a survey should be commissioned immediately. But as for the figure mentioned, that was just about enough to fly the first field parties in to the falls — if they then turned right round and flew out again.

There was a little more discussion, during which Val Duncan also favoured a bold approach, and it was unanimously resolved that Southam should prepare preliminary plans for comprehensive studies of not only the Hamilton but of Bay d'Espoir, on the island of Newfoundland, and an estimate of how much they were likely to cost.

After promoting Southam from general manager to managing director and at long last setting his salary, his earlier suggestion that he should be paid in shares having been judged impracticable, the meeting then adjourned.

Southam did not yet have the authority he wanted to forge ahead with a full-scale study of the Hamilton, but he realized he had made a satisfying step forward. And no doubt his subtle pressure on the board had been helped along by the unexpected arrival in the wings of a man who claimed to be in touch with a group which had the not inconsiderable sum of $3 billion burning a hole in its pocket, a large chunk of which it thought could usefully be spent at Hamilton Falls. Commander R. H. "Rosie" Stokes-Rees was a former British naval officer living in Montreal who had become a vice-president of the Canadian branch of Kaiser Engineers, one of the companies owned by the U.S. millionaire Henry J.

Kaiser. He did not disclose the identity of this group so blessed by fortune, except to make clear that it was not Kaiser, but said the plan was to build a billion-dollar, 200,000-ton aluminum plant at the falls, which would call for an initial development there of one million horse power.

After a cautious display of interest in this proposal, Brinco regretfully concluded it had been founded more on Kaiser Engineers' desire to land the contract for surveying the falls and managing the ultimate construction work than on a firm project, and nothing more was heard of it. But Stokes-Rees had explained that he had been referred to Brinco by General A. G. L. McNaughton, who at that time wore the twin hats of chairman of the Canadian section of the International Joint Commission, governing U.S.—Canadian border relations, and chairman of the Canadian section of the U.S.—Canada Joint Defence Board.

This was the first indication that Ottawa was even aware of Brinco's activities, and a welcome one, since it suggested official approval of them and a willingness to help: Gardner told Southam he doubted that General McNaughton would have steered Stokes-Rees to Brinco without the knowledge of C. D. Howe, the federal Minister of Trade and Commerce and Defence Production. It was agreed that Southam should follow up immediately with a visit to McNaughton.

The general explained that the Kaiser representatives, faced with a growing power shortage in the United States, had come to him seeking a large block of hydro-electric power. He had flown over Grand Falls several times and had been keenly interested in the area for many years. Accordingly, he had persuaded the Kaiser representatives that the Hamilton was their most promising possibility, though they had originally been thinking in terms of a development in western Canada. He ended by inviting Southam to have someone examine such information about the falls as existed in federal files — an invitation he was glad to accept.

A few weeks later, Southam went to Ottawa again, this time with Bertie Gardner, who had secured an interview with Howe himself. Gardner explained that the corporation was considering commissioning a full-scale survey of the falls and Howe left no doubt that he heartily approved of this initiative. Developed hydro-electric resources in North America, he said, would soon be quite inadequate and the federal government wanted Grand Falls developed as soon as was reasonably possible. To this end, it would give the corporation any assistance within its power.

These meetings led to a policy assiduously pursued by Southam during the years that followed: that of keeping federal ministers and departmental officials informed of Brinco's progress at regular intervals; even, as it turned out, when there was pitifully little progress to report. Since the corporation later became painfully squeezed in a nutcracker of provincial sensitivities, there were strong constitutional constraints on Ottawa's ability to live up to Howe's offer of assistance. But there were to be several occasions when, either informally or through legislation, the federal government was able to intervene at crucial times to further a project which was considered from its inception to be of national importance.

More immediately, Ottawa's interest gave Bill Southam a trump card for use when, at the end of 1953, he managed to combine a Christmas visit to his family with a series of meetings with members of the London Committee. By now Hinton had told him that the magnitude of the proposed Hamilton Falls survey called for the commissioning of at least two separate engineering companies with experience in hydro-electric work. After considering various candidates, he recommended the hiring of Montreal Engineering and Shawinigan Engineering Company. Montreal Engineering, one of the companies founded by the young Max Aitken before he transferred his activities to England and became Lord Beaverbrook, was at this time owned by the late Izaak Walton Killam, a multimillionaire with a passion for anonymity. Shawinigan Engineering was a subsidiary of Shawinigan Water and Power, the largest of Quebec's private power companies.

The survey, Hinton predicted, would involve at least 150 men and several aircraft, including helicopters, and the London estimate of $100,000 as its cost seemed more than ever ludicrous. The first season's work alone might well cost $1 million, and Shawinigan thought a thorough job would take at least three years.

It fell to Southam's lot to break this news to the London Committee, and what he had been told in Ottawa apparently helped the shareholders to make up their minds to commit far more precious dollars to Brinco than they had originally envisaged. As a committee memorandum said at the time: "Clearly, an indication from this Authority [the federal government] could not be ignored and Brinco is faced with the position that (a) either Grand Falls is developed by the Corporation or (b) the power concessions might have to be abandoned to others who were prepared to carry out the task."

There was little doubt, the memorandum continued, that a $1 million survey would confirm the feasibility of generating as much as three million horse power at the falls. (Stairs had estimated four million and it is a reflection of the almost complete absence of real knowledge of the area that the many documents which survive from this era are full of conflicting figures; this, of course, is what made the full-scale survey vital.) The memorandum further pointed out that the falls were the centre of a catchment area estimated at 33,000 square miles (two-thirds the size of England) and there might be as much as seven million horse power in the entire area. A hastily conceived initial development could prejudice the ultimate realization of this extra potential; the alternative was a more thorough survey, which might cost as much as $3 million.

Within a month, the shareholders adopted the bold course and a cable went out to St. John's authorizing the full survey. The shareholders' investment had thus rapidly outgrown the subscription for even the most exclusive U.S. golf club. So it was agreed that up to six more members should be invited to join the consortium, and that all should commit themselves to an investment of $171,000 each.

The decision made, Montreal Engineering was engaged to survey the reservoir area above the falls and Shawinigan Engineering to select the location for the powerhouse. Broadly, their terms of reference were to ascertain the smallest quantity of power that could be economically developed at the falls; how long it would take to make that and progressively larger quantities available; and, the key question, how much the power would cost in each case. There was still some feeling among Brinco's shareholders that financing an expensive survey without any certainty that there would be a buyer for the power was rather putting the cart before the horse. So Southam impressed on both companies the urgency of trying to obtain before the end of 1954 "enough knowledge to enable us to talk intelligently to potential customers."

Most of the field work therefore had to be completed during the summer of 1954, and so that the short season could be used to the best advantage an advance party of four engineers was sent in at the end of February with a challenging assignment: they were to take barometric and spirit-level measurements of elevations and make a preliminary judgment on whether the general configuration of the land would permit the creation of a reservoir to regulate the combined flows of the Hamilton and Upper Naskaupi; to gather information on the height of land around the proposed reservoir so that the summer parties could concentrate their work on the critical low areas; to assess areas suitable for "dams and diversion works"; to check the elevation of the lakes along the proposed diversion channel around the falls — after all, no one yet knew if the Channel Scheme was a practicable proposition or a flight of the imagination; to measure the thickness of the ice in the various lakes; and to scout out likely sites for camps and supply routes.

For part of their three-week reconnaissance, the advance men made their base the camp at Menihek, near Schefferville, where Montreal Engineering was building the power development for the Iron Ore Company's mines. They would fly in to the falls area each day in ski-equipped Beavers, two engineers and a guide to each plane. Later, to save themselves this daily round trip of two hundred or more miles, they decided to brave the cold and establish a tent camp on Lake Michikamau. At all times the Beavers carried emergency rations and camping equipment; and whenever men were left on the ground, even for only a few hours, the vagaries of the Labrador weather were respected and they were equipped with enough supplies to make them self-sustaining for several days.

This early reconnaissance proved reassuring to the engineers planning the summer work in Montreal, since it did not turn up any evidence of unforeseen topographical features likely to upset their calculations. It also suggested an economical way of flying in the four hundred tons of supplies and equipment needed for the survey. The ice on the main lakes was found to be from twenty-eight to thirty inches thick, enough to bear the weight of ski-equipped DC-3s capable of carrying much larger loads than the bush planes it had at first thought would be used. The building materials and stores for the dozen or so camps were thus flown in before the spring break-up, permitting an early start on the survey work. This was fortunate since, apart from one balmy period of three weeks, the weather during that first season lived up to Labrador's reputation for unpredictability.

By April 1954, when the time came to take stock of Brinco's first year of operations in preparation for the annual general meeting of share holders, Southam was confident that the organization of the survey was well in hand. These early annual meetings, before any Brinco shares had been sold to the public, were cozy affairs where those attending knew each other well, and were usually conversant with everything going on within the corporation. On one celebrated occasion, Bertie Gardner, reading his speech as president (which had been thoughtfully prepared for him by Southam), stopped suddenly in mid-sentence, silently went over what he had just been saying and then surprised the gathering by adding: "I'm not at all sure I agree with that."

The first annual meeting was told that during the previous summer season the ten Brinco men exploring for minerals in Labrador had reconnoitred about 52,000 square miles. They had found indications of iron ore, ilmenite (titanium), chromium, nickel and cobalt, all of which appeared to be worth following up with prospecting. Greater foreknowledge of what to expect permitted the five men exploring Newfoundland to concentrate on a much smaller area of a thousand or so miles. On the fringe of the island's central mineral belt they had found traces of copper, silver and gold and a geological formation that suggested the possibility of occurrences of asbestos, nickel and chromite.

Naturally, it was far too early to predict whether any of these might prove commercially interesting; and, as had been expected, the mineral division had found one season too short a time to arrive at a decision on which areas of those available should be retained for further investigation. Altogether $255,000 had been spent on the first year's exploration and when the need for more time had been explained to Smallwood and the government, there had been no difficulty in having the date by which the concession area was to be chosen postponed from March 31, 1954, to the end of the year. This permitted another full season of exploration, which it was estimated would cost not more than $300,000.

While the government agreed readily enough to this extension, the all-embracing nature of Brinco's Principal Agreement led to some "teething troubles" in the early days. The first of these arose when a government contractor wanted to quarry some gravel for railroad ballast near Gambo, Joey Smallwood's birthplace, within one of Brinco's concession areas. Someone in the relevant government department decided that gravel fell within the dictionary definition of a mineral, and since Brinco had been granted the mineral rights in that area it should be consulted before a quarrying licence was granted.

The idea of a private company holding this sort of veto over local activities offended Attorney General Curtis's sense of sovereignty and it was proposed that the Principal Agreement (which had omitted to define either "minerals" or "natural resources") should be amended to include the definition of the term "minerals" used in government legislation regulating quarrying and mining, under which it meant "any naturally-occurring inorganic substance" with the crucial exception of "quarry materials, coal, oil, natural gas or salt."

Bill Southam had a reputation for knowing every one of the agreement's twenty-five complicated clauses by heart, and he defended them with the zeal of a St. Paul. He quickly assured the Premier that Brinco had no desire to get into the quarry business or to interfere with "the traditional rights of the citizens of Newfoundland to use surface materials for their local non-commercial needs." But he felt the corporation should have the right to approve such operations within its concession areas in case they turned up something more valuable which might be worth Brinco's investigation.

Also, he pointed out, the agreement had specifically granted Brinco petroleum rights in certain areas and the amendment as proposed would

58

deprive the corporation of a potential asset that the government had granted in good faith. Furthermore, any unilateral change in the terms of the agreement would not only set a dangerous precedent but would hardly be ethical.

The Premier agreed, the terms of the agreement remained unaltered, and applications for quarrying rights within its concession areas are still routinely submitted to Brinco for formal approval.

On another occasion, a couple of years later, Smallwood asked Southam to surrender the corporation's rights to gypsum deposits known to exist within its area. They had, he explained, been included in the concession "inadvertently," and he wanted to be able to offer them to a British company he was trying to persuade to buy a government-sponsored gypsum plant that was losing money. Southam took the opportunity once again to warn the Premier of the danger of tampering with the Principal Agreement. After all, he asked, what would happen if some group offered to invest large sums in exploration for, say, copper, but only if it could have the rights to all copper deposits in Newfoundland?

Joey assured Southam that he could inform his board of directors that "the Newfoundland government has no intentions during the lifetime of its Agreements with the Corporation of asking the Corporation for the return of any further rights otherwise than foreseen in the Agreements." Also, the Premier promised to give sympathetic consideration to a request Brinco planned to make for a mineral concession bordering one of its own promising areas when, as was expected to happen soon, it was relinquished by another company.

In return for these assurances, Brinco surrendered its gypsum rights, and Southam became so adept at this form of horse-trading that Curtis began to refer to him, not without admiration, as "Mr. Quid Pro Quo."

Among the other corporate growing pains with which Southam had to contend in the early days was what he considered unjustified "interference" by members of the London Committee. Since those who pay the piper have a natural tendency to call for their favourite tunes, this could equally well have been considered a normal proprietorial interest in the corporation's affairs, but Southam could never quite reconcile himself to it. And he did not even try to conceal his impatience when shareholders with no knowledge of Canada, let alone the North, asked him such questions as, "What are the streets made of in Labrador?" and, "Do they use bricks or timber for their houses?"

On one occasion, his friend Val Duncan felt obliged to warn him in a sympathetic private letter:

Eric Bowater and New Court feel that you have been a little difficult in your latest telegrams and that one or two of your phrases, e.g.
"unexpected impatience" were unnecessarily blunt. It is, of course,
very easy for New Court with a battery of bright young men to polish
their phrases from this end. [The copy of this letter which survives
in the files bears Southam's indignant comment "They don't!" scribbled in the margin.] It is equally understandable that you more or less
unaided, undoubtedly overworked and possibly despatching telegrams
in the middle of the night, do not sit down to re-polish your final
draft to ensure its inclusion in the next anthology of British Verse
and Prose! I think, however, I would be doing you a disservice as a
friend if I did not keep you in the picture as to moods at this end.

By its very nature, Brinco was peculiarly vulnerable to this type
of friction. Apart from Beavan's geologists, Southam's staff still consisted
of only an accountant and a secretary and he was far outnumbered by
the "bosses" in London. These were men of power and importance in
business, but their whole experience in prewar Britain had been one of
strong and detailed control from London over operations which may
have been scattered all over the pink parts of the map. Val Duncan was
only then beginning to break away from this traditional pattern and
starting to build up the highly autonomous management teams in different countries that now distinguish Rio Tinto-Zinc.

Between them, Duncan, with his new philosophy, and Bertie Gardner,
with his banker's caution, prevented the occasional irritations from having
any permanent effect more serious than wounded susceptibilities, and
gradually direction of the corporation's activities was transferred to Canada, a move given formal recognition when the London Committee added
a qualification to its title and became the London Advisory Committee.

The wisdom of this change — and the danger of having too many
cooks stirring what was eventually to become a rather yeasty political
broth — soon became apparent.

SIX

The search for a buyer begins

On July 21, 1954, Bill Southam flew from Montreal to Quebec City where, after cooling his heels for three hours in an anteroom, he was ushered in to see the Premier of Quebec, the Honourable and remarkable Maurice Duplessis. The interview — having regard to the climate of the times it might be more accurate to describe it as an audience — had been arranged for him by Bertie Gardner who, while not an intimate of the Premier, had met him socially on a number of occasions. Gardner's sense of propriety was often offended by the despotic Duplessis's machine-style politics but he liked the man himself; he was amused, rather than annoyed, when the Premier, in a play on his initials — B.C.G. — used to refer to him as "Before Christ Gardner."

By now, with 180 men working on the Hamilton survey, it was becoming more than ever clear that the huge quantity of power available could not be consumed within Newfoundland. Any other plan for its sale seemed likely to require Quebec's cooperation, either in the purchase of power to be used within the province, perhaps to stimulate new industries in the Sept-Iles area, or in the granting of permission for its transmission through the province to Ontario. Southam was therefore caught off stride when Duplessis began their talk by referring sarcastically to the corporation's "billion-dollar plan" to build the world's longest transmission line through Quebec to supply Ontario with millions of horse power of electricity.

Puzzled, Southam protested that the corporation's plans were by no means so far advanced. "Do you mean to say you deny this?" asked Duplessis, brandishing a newspaper clipping. To his horror, Southam then discovered for the first time that the previous day's *Toronto Star* had carried a long interview with General McNaughton expatiating on "the most daring and imaginative waterpower scheme of its kind ever envisaged by man." While the report did quote Ontario Hydro as saying it had not been approached to buy any of the energy to be produced at the falls, it contained enough details of the scheme, including a list of Brinco's shareholders, to suggest that it had been inspired from within the corporation. (McNaughton told Southam later that he had been urged to give the interview "by one of your directors from London" in the belief that it would further the corporation's fortunes.)

Southam needed all his experience of diplomacy to persuade Duplessis that he had until that moment known nothing about the interview, but after he had explained the true state of the corporation's progress the Premier appeared mollified. He said that British interest in Canada's economy, however overdue, was very welcome to the Province of Quebec. Had it been displayed sooner, Canada might not now be so dependent on the United States. He wished Newfoundland and the corporation every success, but Quebec remained, in his view, Canada's leading province: "God has given Quebec most of Canada's natural resources and the best of Canada's provincial governments."

The best, by implication, of Canada's provincial premiers then said he would welcome any reasonable proposals by Brinco so long as they were consistent with Quebec's overall long-range economic program. When Southam asked if he could have some information about this program, Duplessis responded by tapping his head and saying, "It is all in here." He did, however, assert his view that one horse power of electricity used in metal manufacturing would provide work for one man, whereas the same amount used in the pulp and paper industry would keep at least a dozen men employed.

Southam stressed that at this stage the corporation's work was purely exploratory and there could be no justification for developing the falls unless the demand for power was adequate and the political, financial and other circumstances were favourable. Hence the corporation's wish to keep M. Duplessis and his government suitably informed.

It was a cordial meeting, during which the Premier cracked numerous jokes, most of which were over Southam's head but all of which were received with great hilarity by the three cabinet ministers present, who otherwise sat in respectful silence. Particular merriment greeted the Premier when he permitted himself to wonder whether, in fact, the Hamilton River was in Newfoundland at all.

This was a disturbing portent of difficulties ahead, and Southam came away from the meeting with the impression that there was no love lost between Duplessis and his opposite numbers in Ontario and Newfoundland. "It is thus all the more important," he wrote in a memorandum describing his interview, "that the corporation should watch its step and keep a nice balance between any real or imaginary conflicting interests." It should also "build up and retain" Duplessis's goodwill, and perhaps this task should be undertaken by someone already enjoying access to him, since too close a personal contact between himself and the Quebec Premier "might be displeasing to Mr. Smallwood."

In fact, this problem was entirely academic: despite strenuous efforts by Gardner and others to arrange it, in the following five years until his death, no one from within the corporation was ever admitted to Duplessis's presence again.

Those were to be years of repeated frustrations and disappointments as attempts to find customers for the power would at first appear promising but would then collapse one after the other. Neither was there much cheer to be had from the mineral exploration: while interesting discoveries were made from time to time, none proved worth developing.

The lack of progress was all the more galling since the survey reports, received at the beginning of April 1955, not only confirmed the feasibility of the Channel Scheme but predicted that "the cost per horse power of the ultimate development will be very low." The topography of the area was "exceptionally favourable" for the creation of the huge reservoir envisaged and the reports foresaw no difficulty in siting the powerhouse underground to make use of the high head available, or in stepping up the power developed to the proposed transmission voltage of 400 kilovolts. Subject to further measurements of the water flow to be made during the 1955 season, the ultimate capacity of the scheme should be four million horse power, and the reports suggested this could be developed in four separate stages of a million horse power each. The first stage should be complete within four years of the start of construction and succeeding stages could be built as required.

Since some works required for the future stages would have to be built at the outset, the first stage would be comparatively more expensive than the later ones — $165 million for the power plant and $2.7 million for the reservoir. However, these works would not have to be provided again, so that the cost of the additional stages would be lower and the total for the whole project should not exceed $322 million for the plant and $31 million for the reservoir. In addition, there would be the cost of an access road, the transmission line, and equipment to receive the power at its destination. It was thought that $2.7 million would cover construction of the road, but there was less certainty about the cost of transmission. Brinco had two estimates prepared by separate British companies. One of these put the cost of delivering the first million horse power to Sept-Iles at $43 million; the second put it at almost twice that: $85 million. And estimates for delivering the first stage to Ontario ranged all the way up to $230 million.

These were even more heroic figures in those days than they are now, but in view of the large quantity of power available it was considered that the price per horse power would be attractive to potential consumers. Who these consumers might be had already been considered in a wide-ranging market study carried out for the corporation during 1954 by Sir Alexander Gibb and Partners, a British firm of consulting engineers.

The Gibb report, an encyclopedic survey of industrial processes and world resources running to more than two hundred closely packed pages, concentrated on what appeared to be the main problem, which was, paradoxically enough, an embarrassment of riches. The projected first stage of one million horse power, it pointed out, was equivalent to the total amount of electricity consumed at the time by the whole of Greater London; and the full scheme, four million horse power, was a quarter as much again as the total installed electrical capacity in Ontario.

There were only three potential customers in sight for such large blocks of power: Quebec, Ontario and the aluminum industry. The first of these, Quebec, was dismissed as an immediate prospect: with rivers of its own still undeveloped, it was unlikely to be interested in Grand Falls power before the 1970s. Ontario could certainly use a large quantity of power, if it could be persuaded to enter into a contract right away. Britain had begun to build its first nuclear power station, Calder Hall, and while it was too early to predict the future of nuclear-produced energy, if the Grand Falls scheme were not launched within a year or two to supply Ontario Hydro by the 1960s, the time might arrive when the province would find it more economic to turn to nuclear power stations.

This left the aluminum industry; here, too, a prompt start on the scheme was vital. The production of aluminum uses electricity in astronomical quantities. It takes eight times as much power to produce a ton of aluminum, for instance, as it does to refine a ton of iron ore. In consequence, historically it has proved economic to site aluminum smelters near a cheap, reliable source of power rather than near their sources of raw materials; hence, Sept-Iles would be an acceptable choice for the location of an aluminum smelter. But there were several potential rivals to it on the world scene.

South America and Asia had immense hydro-electric resources but were unlikely to be considered safe areas for investment by the aluminum industry. However, the projected development of 750,000 horse power on the Volta River, in West Africa, might attract an aluminum smelter. And closer to home, Thayer Lindsley's plan to develop four million horse power on the Yukon River was another potential competitor for Brinco — ironically, since Lindsley was a shareholder in the corporation, through Frobisher. Should either of these sites be chosen for the expected next round of expansion by the aluminum industry, Grand Falls would "lose its place in the queue" for many years.

The Gibb report's conclusions seemed to indicate that Brinco was on the right track. Through Tommy Hogg, the first contact had been made with Ontario; and a preliminary approach had already been made to the world's second-largest aluminum producer, the Aluminum Company of Canada — for by a fortunate coincidence its president, Ray E. Powell, was one of Bertie Gardner's best friends. As such, it was only natural that they should discuss Brinco when they lunched together at the St. James's Club or met in various other establishments favoured by the Montreal business community. Nevertheless, it came as a complete surprise to Gardner when Eric Hinton's researches disclosed that Alcan had commissioned a study of Grand Falls as a power site as long ago as 1942. This study, carried out by A. W. Lash, an engineer with the firm of H. G. Acres in Niagara Falls, suggested three possible developments for the Hamilton. One of them, in essence, was the Channel Scheme, though since Lash was able to make only a brief visit to the site he considerably underestimated the power it would produce: 1,163,000 horse power.

When Gardner asked Powell about this study, he was told that Alcan had eventually decided against Grand Falls because its remoteness seemed likely to make both construction of a plant there and transportation of materials to and from it much too expensive. Gardner suggested rather diffidently that Lash's report might be useful to Brinco and Powell agreed to send him a copy of it, though he stipulated in the covering letter: "As we put a lot of money and experience into it, I don't think it should be used to aid or comfort competitors or even prospective competitors . . . . I also hope that it will move you to reciprocate."

The usefulness of the Lash report was limited, because by the time Brinco received it, its own surveys were under way. But the corporation was only too pleased to "reciprocate"; for the next few years Bill Southam lost no opportunity to keep Alcan informed of progress, in the hope of securing it as a customer for the first block of power. The interest was perhaps more reciprocal than Brinco realized: as early as April 1954, an internal Alcan memorandum noted the possibility of Grand Falls power being transmitted to Quebec and Ontario and commented that this prospect was "intriguing to us" because of the enormous aluminum consumption it would entail — transmission lines, or "conductors," being made up largely of woven strands of aluminum.

But Brinco needed a customer before it would have any business to deal out to suppliers, and on May 1, 1955, within a month of receiving the survey reports, Southam gave Alcan "the first opportunity to consider contracting for from 800,000 to 1,000,000 horse power at Seven Islands in 1961," the price to be somewhere "between four and five mills per kilowatt-hour."*

Alcan declined this invitation in a letter that left the door to future negotiations open, and internal memoranda show that it retained a watching brief over Brinco's activities. One day in September 1956, something he heard at his club prompted Powell to dictate a brief note to an aide: "One of Alcoa's private planes is in Montreal today but the reason therefor is unknown to me. However, I can report that Mr. Gardner, at lunch, didn't have guests."

The aide did some telephoning and eventually discovered that two representatives of Alcan's U.S. competitor, the Aluminum Company of America, had indeed been in Montreal, and in fact had been taken by Brinco to see the falls.

Brinco had been put in touch with I. W. "Chief" Wilson, president of Alcoa, by C. D. Howe, to whom Southam continued to make regular visits. Gardner and Southam several times flew to Pittsburgh for talks with Wilson, who in turn introduced them to members of the wealthy Mellon family. For a time there seemed to be a chance not only that Alcoa would become a customer for power but that the Mellon interests might take up a substantial number of shares in the corporation. For Brinco, it was a heady prospect: Alcoa seemed to be contemplating building a smelter at either Sept-Iles or near the falls themselves which would require as much as two million horse power; this would be more than enough to get the development off the ground, and the tie-in with such a well-established company as Alcoa, and the Mellon interests, would virtually guarantee the successful financing of the project on Wall Street. For it was realized at the outset that the vast amount of capital needed could not be raised within Canada.

Unfortunately for these high hopes, Alcoa ultimately lost interest in the project — whether because Brinco's price was not right, or because Wilson saw the clouds gathering on the aluminum industry's horizon, was never quite clear.

*A mill is one-tenth of a cent. A kilowatt-hour represents the quantity of electricity consumed by, say, keeping ten 100-watt bulbs lit for an hour. Southam's estimated price of between .4 and .5 of a cent might appear reasonably precise, but in fact the later negotiations for the sale of the power often revolved around fractions of a mill — in other words, *hundredths* of a cent. This is perhaps not surprising when it is realized that one-hundredth of a cent, when applied to the billions of kilowatt-hours ultimately purchased, amounts to more than $3 million per year.

An earlier attempt to land a third aluminum company as a customer had already fallen through. In 1953, a London-based company, British Aluminium, was considering expanding its operations into Canada. Val Duncan had several meetings with its managing director, Geoffrey Cunliffe, but in 1955 it was decided to build the smelter at Baie Comeau, Quebec, using power supplied by an early Hydro-Quebec development, on the Bersimis River.

Powell, too, was gradually forced by circumstances to drop out of the picture. When Brinco made its first proposal, Alcan had just opened its smelter at Kitimat, in British Columbia. The demand for aluminum, however, was expected to keep on multiplying and while Powell kept an eye on Brinco's progress he was also considering the expansion of the company's capacity in the Saguenay area of Quebec.

By 1957, it was plain that the world faced a surplus of aluminum capacity, and during the next ten years the Canadian industry was depressed by the emergence of new protective trade patterns such as the European Common Market, continuing U.S. tariffs, and embargoes on imports by countries such as Australia and Mexico. Alcan contented itself by adding to its capacity in the Saguenay area in 1960, with the opening of a new power development at Chute-des-Passes, on the Peribonka River. And far from finding Hamilton Falls power necessary, it has not yet expanded Kitimat to its full capacity.

As time wore on without a customer being safely gathered into the fold, disagreements developed among Brinco's directors and advisers about the corporation's sales policy — or, as some saw it, the *lack* of a sales policy. One faction favoured the appointment of a sort of "supersalesman" to make a top-level canvass of virtually any industry, Canadian or American, that might be persuaded to transfer its operations to the North Shore of the St. Lawrence or Labrador. W. Leslie Forster, a Yorkshire-born engineer and geologist who had gravitated into the finance business and become a director of Sogemines based in Montreal, suggested that industries which had established themselves at Niagara Falls around the turn of the century now faced power shortages and mounting labour costs and might welcome the opportunity to make a new start in a new area. As early as the end of 1955, in fact, Forster complained that because of its inactivity Brinco had already "missed the bus" and the Yukon and the Congo would be developed before Hamilton Falls.

Another faction contended that it was futile to try to rush any industry into a contract; that the power would virtually sell itself when the economic time became ripe. This view not only prevailed but persisted long into the future: its apparent adoption as at least a sub-conscious tenet of faith would appear to be all that sustained the corporation through the even darker days ahead.

At any rate, no formal sales division was ever set up as such. Initially, the sales effort was in the hands of a consultant, Philip S. Gregory, an engineer who had specialized in negotiating sales contracts for Shawinigan Water and Power. Later, his duties were inherited by Eric N. Webb, a rugged New Zealander lent to Brinco temporarily by English Electric. As a young man, Webb had hauled a sled three hundred miles into the Antarctic with an expedition searching for the magnetic South Pole and he had spent most of his subsequent life building hydro-electric projects in India. He, too, was an engineer and he had more success coordinating the survey work and preliminary engineering studies than he did selling the power.

Both Gregory and Webb were "advised" from time to time by a succession of short-lived bodies with titles such as "Water-power Panel" and "Power Sales Coordinating Committee." Bill Southam himself was always more comfortable as an administrator than a promoter and he indignantly ignored hints that he, as managing director, should become the "super-salesman" some felt the corporation needed.

Early in 1955, the centre of gravity of the corporation's operations having obviously shifted from St. John's, Southam left Marion Hawco in charge of the office there and moved into new quarters in a recently completed office building at 1980 Sherbrooke Street West in Montreal. In recruiting the staff he was now beginning to build up, he was unable to offer either the salaries or, at that stage, the level of work that could attract experienced men at the top of their professions. Instead, he gathered around him a group of eager young men, often British, to whom he made only one promise: if, thanks to their efforts, Brinco grew successfully, they would grow with it. It is a tribute to him that he was not only able to create among them a morale that carried the organization through the many frustrations ahead but to inspire in them a personal loyalty that survived long after he, and most of them, had left the corporation. He did not hesitate to give them responsibility — sometimes, perhaps, rather more responsibility than either their years or training might have justified — and they were to find that versatility was no less necessary a virtue than patience.

One of the first assistants he hired, for instance, was Peter S. Marchant, a slim, reflective young man who was doing post-graduate studies in geography at McGill University. Born in Victoria, British Columbia, Marchant had served in the Royal Navy and by chance his duties at

McGill involved the study of aerial photographs of Labrador for a hush-hush Defence Research Board project. Among the first assignments Southam handed him was supervision of the construction of the access road in to the falls from the Iron Ore Company's railroad. It had been decided that to build the road right away would not only demonstrate the earnestness and feasibility of the corporation's intentions, but would give it a head start when the hoped-for customer materialized and construction of the power project began.

Marchant called first on another young man with no more qualifications for this task than he had himself. Bert Keogh, younger brother of a Newfoundland cabinet minister, had been engaged to coordinate the loading of planes flying supplies in to the survey crews from Mile 286 on the railroad during the summer of 1954. Keogh hired an Indian guide and walked in from the railroad to the falls, reconnoitring what looked like a suitable route for a road along the way. They were supported by a float-equipped Beaver which leap-frogged their tent and food from lake to lake, and, with Keogh making copious notes on topographical features along the way, they took more than a month to reach the falls.

But this inspired amateurism paid off. Montreal Engineering later confirmed the feasibility of Keogh's route and the road was built during one season, the summer of 1956, at a total cost of only $1,250,000, which was far below what had been estimated. True, it was a rough road at first; its surface was later gravelled and a dyke was built where it crossed the Atikonak River, one of the main branches of the Hamilton. But by 1957 there was not only a road in to the falls, eliminating what had always been considered one of the insuperable obstacles to their development, but the river just above the falls had been crossed by a suspension footbridge and a cableway transporter capable of carrying twenty-five-ton loads. The road, which proved immensely valuable later, became known as the "Joe Bernard Limited-Access Thruway," after the French-Canadian foreman in charge of its maintenance, who used to spend his time lovingly patrolling it at all hours of the day and night.

Southam's departure from St. John's meant that he no longer saw as much of Premier Smallwood, with whom he had developed a close and usually harmonious working relationship — though they did not always see eye to eye. During the first couple of years of the corporation's existence, for instance, Joey was continually trying to persuade Brinco to undertake various rural-electrification schemes on the island of Newfoundland. At that time, so many isolated communities were without any form of electric supply that the province's annual per capita consumption of electricity was less than half the national average. Among the forms of development Joey promised the voters in his rousing election campaigns was a prompt end to this unfortunate deprivation. As the years passed and they found themselves still cooking and heating their homes with the wood stoves their grandfathers had used, the voters began to write irate letters to St. John's.

Joey adopted the simple, if not very subtle, expedient of passing these letters over to Bill Southam, together with an avalanche of paper consisting of technical reports on available watersheds and surveys of various allegedly desirable hydro-electric schemes. Southam protested that it made no sense to dam a river to supply a handful of fishermen who would be better served by a diesel generator. Furthermore, he discovered on consulting his maps, Brinco did not even own the water rights in the area about which Joey was chiefly concerned, in northern Newfoundland. And, while Brinco wished to cooperate to the fullest extent in the development of Newfoundland, as he constantly assured the Premier, it was, after all, primarily concerned with profitable, rather than philanthropic, enterprises.

There was one area, however, where it seemed a commercially viable hydro-electric scheme might be possible: at Bay d'Espoir, a long, fjord-like inlet on the island's beautiful south coast, at the mouth of the Salmon River, one of several large rivers draining a high wilderness area inland. And so when Bill Southam had Joey to lunch at the Newfoundland Hotel on December 3, 1954 — to break the news, among other things, of his impending move to Montreal — he was also able to tell him that Brinco had decided to set up a working party consisting of three of its Newfoundland directors to investigate Bay d'Espoir's hydro-electric potential and, with an eye to possible customers for the power, the prospects for industrial growth in the area. These seemed good, since it had a deep, ice-free harbour, but the working party had been finding it impossible to get an informed assessment of the island's economic future. Southam asked the Premier if the government had an economic adviser who could be assigned to supply this information.

Somewhat morosely, Joey replied that he could think of no one who had not either left the island or gone to jail.

This was a rueful reference to the fate of Alfred Valdmanis, the economic wizard in whom Joey had placed so much faith. The prewar Latvian finance minister had been a $100-a-month adviser to the Department of Immigration in Ottawa when Smallwood hired him as an economic expert at $10,000 a year. He promised to bring Newfoundland at least one new industry in his first year and did: a cement plant built by a German company, with Newfoundland government funds. Joey raised his salary to $25,000 a year and made him Director-General of Economic Development, and in an unprecedented spending spree (more than $20 million in public funds in less than three years) Dr. Valdmanis attracted fourteen new industries to the island. Most were German-owned, and few survived, though Joey was initially so enthusiastic about Valdmanis's efforts that he predicted Newfoundlanders would one day erect a statue to him.

Alas, the little doctor left Newfoundland rather precipitately early in 1954 — and was brought back a short time later to face two charges of accepting $200,000 kickbacks from the German companies which built first the cement plant and later the gypsum plant that subsequently ran into financial difficulties. Ordering his arrest, Joey said, was "the most unpleasant duty I have ever had to perform."

The Premier's political opponents were rubbing their hands over the sensational disclosures they expected to be made in court when Valdmanis suddenly ended the trial before it had begun by pleading guilty. He was given four years' hard labour on one charge and the other was never pressed. After serving his sentence he eked out a precarious living as a financial consultant in various parts of Canada until his death in a car crash in 1970.

For a while, Valdmanis had been chairman of the government's development body, Nalco. After his disgrace, Smallwood, obviously concerned at Nalco's lack of progress and dwindling funds, tried to persuade Brinco to take it over. Lunching at New Court in October 1954, he asked Edmund de Rothschild to become its new chairman. "To make my refusal less abrupt," Eddy wrote later to Bertie Gardner, "I did suggest to him that he couldn't do better than seek an opportunity of consulting you . . . . It was not an easy proposal to deal with over the luncheon table, as you can imagine."

In reply Gardner approved of de Rothschild's action and said: "Strictly between ourselves, there was rather an unusual aroma attaching to the Company that you mention and I think at this stage it would be most unfortunate if we showed any connection with it. It might give the public a wrong impression. Already too many people are confusing Brinco with the Company that you name and I have taken great pains to point out that there is no connection whatever between us."

SEVEN

The promise of the far black hill

One summer day in 1956 a float-equipped Beaver aircraft swooped down to a lake in the barren bush country about twenty miles south of Makkovik, a tiny settlement on the east coast of Labrador. When it came to a stop, bobbing gently on the cold green water, its two passengers untied their canoe from one of its pontoons and loaded it with their tent, sleeping bags, tools and supplies. Then they said goodbye to the pilot and pushed off for a nearby gravel beach which was to be their home for the next three weeks.

One of the passengers was only a boy — seventeen-year-old Walter Kitts, who had been born in the Northern Ontario mining community of Cobalt, had just completed his first year at the province's Haileybury School of Mines and was now enjoying his first summer job as a prospector for Brinco. His companion was a fisherman and trapper from Makkovik named Edgar Anderson, older and wiser in the ways of the bush than Kitts, but a newcomer to prospecting. After they had put up their tent, they stacked their canned food and flour inside it and hung their slab of bacon from a tree to protect it from bears. Anderson then started a fire as Kitts unlimbered his fishing rod and soon provided them with their supper, a couple of plump speckled trout. Afterwards, they sat by the fire discussing their plans for the next day.

Prospecting teams always worked in pairs; two men who disregarded this rule through the years were drowned when their canoes capsized while they were alone. The partners would be landed on a lake and left there for two or three weeks, depending on the size of the area they had to explore. They were equipped with two-way radios and were supposed to check in with the base camp at North West River every evening.

Kitts and Anderson had aerial photos of their area and used them to plan each day's program. To cover as much territory as possible, they separated each morning after breakfast, striking off into the bush on compass bearings designed to bring them together for lunch, after which they would split up again and head back to camp on different routes.

One day, at lunch, they noticed that a small hill on the horizon looked quite different from the surrounding country; whereas the rest of the rock in the area was a pinkish granite, the hill stood out dark, almost black, against the sky. Kitts thought it might be diorite, a type of rock that often indicates the presence of base metals of some sort. It was obviously worth investigating, but it was so far away that they might have difficulty regaining their camp before nightfall. He and Anderson discussed this prospect and they decided to take the risk.

It was rough country, and it took them several hours to reach the foot of the hill. But as soon as they arrived Kitts realized they had made the right decision. Everywhere he looked he saw yellowish stains in the rock. Even to his inexperienced eyes, those stains spelt out a magic word: uranium.

Walter Kitts's contract paid him $300 a month, with all found; pretty good pay for a seventeen-year-old in his first summer job. It also contained a clause guaranteeing him a 7 per cent equity interest in any mine resulting from his discoveries. Drowning men are said to see their whole lives pass before their eyes with startling clarity. Kitts enjoyed the process in reverse: visions of country estates and private airplanes danced in his brain as he hurriedly chipped out a few fist-sized chunks of rock with his grub-hoe and stuffed them into his white canvas sample bag.

It was almost dark when he and Anderson got back to their camp, but before they started preparing their supper they ran the geiger-counters over their samples. Sure enough, they heard the telltale clicks that confirmed Kitts's identification.

Next morning, they set off early to revisit the black hill, this time taking their geiger-counters with them. And wherever they went on the hill they picked up strong signs of radioactivity. As Kitts recalled years later: "The counters didn't just click — they whistled!"

Brinco's chief geologist in Labrador, Murray Piloski, also whistled when he examined the black hill a few days later, having flown in to the lake in response to Kitts's guarded radio message. Piloski knew a promising uranium strike when he saw one, having worked in the Beaverlodge area of Saskatchewan during the postwar uranium boom there. He realized this was the most interesting mineral discovery Brinco had so far made in Labrador.

It came as no great surprise to him, for Piloski himself had discovered uranium-bearing pitchblende near Makkovik during Brinco's second season of exploration, in 1954. Apart from reporting his find to Ottawa, as the law required, the corporation had kept Piloski's discovery secret. For one thing, it was only what geologists call an "occurrence"; in other words, an indication that it might be worth searching in that area for a deposit — which might or might not be commercially exploitable, according to its extent and richness. Also, the corporation had no wish to alert its competitors to such an interesting prospect: it was expecting soon to inherit the rights to a neighbouring concession that was about to lapse.

In the spirit of the corporation's agreement with the Newfoundland government, Bill Southam had told Premier Smallwood about Piloski's find and explained why he preferred to make no official announcement at that stage. Even though it was the first sign of uranium in Canada east of Quebec City, Joey agreed to respect the confidence. But during the 1955 exploration season, as Brinco geologists continued to find isolated occurrences of uranium, his impatience to broadcast the news to the world began to mount. It was now three years since he had offered Britain "the biggest real estate deal of the present century" and he still had no concrete news of great developments to offer his people; neither had his other cherished development projects given him much more than promises and hope with which to stir their imagination.

Early in 1956, the government called a conference on Labrador, to be attended by all the members of Joey's cabinet, representatives of the federal government from both Ottawa and St. John's, a selection of missionaries and local residents from Labrador and — perhaps most important of all in Joey's view — representatives of the press, radio and television. Also in the audience at the Monday morning opening session was Claude K. Howse, a former Newfoundland Deputy Minister of Mines who had been appointed to represent Brinco in St. John's after Southam's transfer to Montreal.

Howse had known Smallwood for years and was well-acquainted with his "triple-expansion" oratorical style, in which he would repeat the same thought three times, each variation and embellishment of the phrasing communicating a mounting sense of expectation and excite-ment to the audiences he invariably held in the palm of his hand. He listened without surprise as the Premier sailed through a forty-five-minute paean to the incredible riches of Labrador, "God's greatest gift to Newfoundland." But he became apprehensive toward the end of the speech when Joey conspiratorially took the audience into his confidence and hinted that certain discoveries had recently been made in Labrador which would make previous discoveries, including the iron ore, "pale into insignificance."

Howse's misgivings turned into something approaching panic as the Premier pressed on. He would, he said, have a specific anouncement to make on Wednesday. And then, turning to Claude Howse with his beaming smile, he produced an appreciative ripple of laughter in the audience by saying, "Don't worry, Mr. Howse, I'm not going to say anything now."

Howse did not wait to hear any more speeches. He dashed straight back to his office and telephoned Bill Southam in Montreal. Southam's horror as he listened to his story more than matched his own. In addition to the previous reasons for maintaining secrecy about the uranium finds, there were now two other factors which made this the worst possible time for an announcement, particularly the glowing type of announcement favoured by Joey. First, the corporation was about to make a new issue of shares. True, they were to be offered only to selected investors, mostly institutional, and the public was not being invited to participate. But in Southam's view (which he knew would be fully supported by the shareholders) anything that could be construed as promotion at this time would be highly unethical, if not worse. Secondly, veiled references to a potential customer for Hamilton Falls power — always mysteriously identified only as Client "A" — had begun to creep into the corporation's confidential internal memos. Southam feared the effect any reference to uranium might have on his top-secret negotiations with this potential customer.

Howse told Southam that "quite a pitch of enthusiasm" had been built up in Newfoundland over what was expected to be one of the greatest news stories since Smallwood came to power, and it would be quite impossible to halt the announcement at this late stage.

Southam's only course, which he at once adopted, was to try to ensure that the dreaded announcement would be as accurate as he could manage to make it. An ultra-conservative, four-paragraph press release was accordingly drawn up for Howse to pass on to the Premier. This outlined the mapping and prospecting work done during 1954 and 1955 and mentioned the discoveries in restrained language, emphasizing that they were only occurrences. It added: "While no uranium ore bodies have yet been outlined, some of the showings have appreciable dimensions and occur under geological conditions considered favourable for the discovery of ore bodies."

Howse handed the statement to the Premier at noon on Wednesday. The Premier spent the afternoon reshaping it to include a reference to Frobisher, which had also found uranium occurrences in a neighbouring area, and polishing its rather austere phrasing into a form he considered more appropriate. And when he issued *his* statement at 5 p.m., it confirmed Southam's worst fears.

"I have the great honour and joy," it began, "to anounce that a great new uranium province has been discovered in Labrador." The Premier had apparently plotted the Brinco and Frobisher discoveries on the map, because he described this great new province as "a belt extending for a distance of eighty-five miles in length and consisting of approximately 680 square miles in area" — a description that certainly did not appear in the Brinco statement.

The Premier then included the substance of Southam's release without undue elaboration. But his last two paragraphs once again set Southam quivering with suppressed fury:

> Both companies are anxiously awaiting the spring break-up so that an intensive drive may be commenced to drill the known occurrences and to carry on a greatly accelerated program of prospecting and development. If this work is up to expectations it is quite likely that mining of uranium ore and processing of uranium concentrates could commence in 1957.
>
> According to the best professional advice available to me there is every reason to believe that this exciting new uranium discovery will rank in importance with the greatest names in Canadian uranium to date — Beaverlodge and Blind River.

According to the best professional advice available to Brinco these two paragraphs contained two entirely unwarranted assumptions, at least until Kitts's discovery six months later, when it began to seem as if the gift of prophecy had been added to Joey's many accomplishments. Piloski's encouraging report led to diamond drilling on the site (it is still known as Kitts) before the end of the 1956 season and during the following year. The drill results were encouraging and in the fall of 1957 equipment was moved in and a work party of about forty men spent the following winter driving an adit, or underground tunnel, into the black hill to get a close-up look at its ore. They drove in about eighteen hundred feet of tunnel, branching in two directions, and confirmed that the hill contained a relatively small but rich ore deposit. It was estimated that a ton of the ore would yield sixteen pounds of uranium oxide, which is high by North American standards, though higher-grade ores have since been found in Australia.

Amid considerable excitement, Brinco made plans to set up a subsidiary,* to be called Makkovik Mines Limited, which was to build a

---

*By this time, Dr. Beavan's mineral-exploration division had also become a separate subsidiary company, British-Newfoundland Exploration Limited, more popularly known as Brinex.

$6 million mine at Kitts to produce uranium oxide, also known as "yellow cake." By the summer of 1958, the preliminary work was almost complete: feasibility studies and financial projections had been done; the ground had been surveyed and plans had been drawn up for the mine and mill; a route had been chosen for a road in to the mine from the coast; and the federal government's hydrographic experts had picked out a dock site and confirmed that Makkovik Bay was suitable for shipping. There was only one snag.

The rest of the uranium industry in Canada at the time was receiving $10 a pound for its uranium under special price contracts with the government. These had been introduced in the early fifties when the United States and Britain were busy stockpiling uranium for military purposes, but when there was no great eagerness to supply it at the going rate of about $6 per pound. Unfortunately for the embryo Makkovik Mines, a time limit had been placed on applications for these special contracts: none was to be granted after March 1957. While Brinco knew by that date that it had an interesting uranium prospect at Kitts, it was not convinced (and certainly could not have convinced the government inspectors) that it had a potential mine. So it could not apply for a special contract, and faced the prospect of being able to market its product only at the old price of perhaps $6.20 per pound. It had been planned to produce 250 tons of ore a day (giving a daily output of 4,000 pounds of uranium oxide) and with the 300,000 tons of ore* estimated to lie in the black hill the mine would have had a life expectancy of only a little more than three years. At the old price, it was decided, the project would not be profitable. Makkovik Mines was put on ice, and Walter Kitts is still waiting for his 7 per cent interest in a uranium mine.

Brinex geologists, in a joint venture with a German company, Metallgesellschaft A.G., later outlined a much larger desposit of uranium (three million tons) about thirty-five miles southwest of Kitts. Called the Michelin deposit, after Leslie Michelin, the Labrador prospector who found it, this contains a lower-grade ore, averaging only about three and a half pounds of uranium oxide per ton. Whether either deposit eventually becomes a mine will depend on the direction the uranium market takes in the future.

The failure to launch Makkovik Mines compounded yet another of Brinco's early disappointments: the gradual collapse during 1957 of the negotiations with Client "A". The reason for the secrecy surrounding these negotiations was that Client "A" was in effect the British govern-

*This estimate was later revised downward, to 208,000 tons.

ment. Late in 1955, Bill Southam visited Sir Edwin Plowden, chairman of the United Kingdom's Atomic Energy Authority, and proposed Hamilton Falls as the site for a uranium-enrichment plant the authority was contemplating building to supply fuel for nuclear power plants. Sir Edwin was interested and the negotiations went on intermittently for more than a year, progressing to the point at which two representatives of the authority visited Montreal and were flown to Labrador to inspect the falls. Eventually, however, Britain decided to rely on domestically produced fuel.

Apart from the raw material, there are two main requirements for a uranium enrichment plant: an immense supply of electricity, and of water for cooling purposes. The Hamilton River could have provided both of these; and the one million horse power it was estimated the plant would require would have been enough to bring in the first stage of the falls' development. Also, the plan had another advantage which sharpened the disappointment when it fell through: it was thought that the whole operation could be confined to Newfoundland. For, while Brinco was sometimes embarrassed by Joey Smallwood's over-enthusiasm, it could still raise no enthusiasm whatsoever for its plans in the breast of Premier Maurice Duplessis of Quebec.

As long ago as October 11, 1955, Bertie Gardner had written to Duplessis reminding him of his meeting with Southam in July 1954: "Now more than a year has elapsed and great progress has been made so that our studies are practically complete and we are beginning to receive enquiries with regard to the sale of power. We should therefore like to inform you of developments during the past fifteen months and, with this in view, Mr. Southam and I would very much like to be favoured with an appointment with you in Quebec or, if more convenient to you, in Montreal." Two weeks later, when no reply had been received, Gardner wrote to Emile Tourigny, the Premier's *chef du cabinet,* asking his help in obtaining the appointment. Tourigny replied on November 4, that "as soon as it will be possible for me to arrange the interview asked for I will communicate with you again."

He had not done so by November 18, when Gardner wrote to him again. Several letters, and numerous telephone calls later, Tourigny promised an interview toward the end of February 1956. It never took place.

Frustrated by the wall of silence in Quebec City, Gardner and Southam realized they must try another approach, preferably through someone with that access to Duplessis which Southam had predicted might be necessary. The logical choice for this sensitive assignment was Robert

J. Beaumont, who was not only considered to be Maurice Duplessis's main confidant in the Montreal financial establishment but was a shareholder of Brinco in his capacity as chairman of Shawinigan Water and Power. (At Gardner's invitation, Shawinigan had joined the consortium, which eventually consisted of twenty-nine companies, in 1955.) The Hamilton Falls project appealed to Beaumont for two reasons: not only was there a chance that Shawinigan Engineering might secure the lucrative contract to design and manage the development, but the falls might ultimately supply Shawinigan Water and Power with the energy it needed to meet its growing requirements as Quebec's largest supplier of electricity to both industrial and domestic consumers. Shawinigan's interest in the project persisted, and when Brinco set up a subsidiary company to handle the development of the falls in 1958 — the Hamilton Falls Power Corporation — Shawinigan Engineering paid $2,250,000 for a 20 per cent interest in it.

Beaumont was confident he could help to get the project started. But, he told Gardner, they would have to tread warily in their approach to Duplessis, who had already told him he wanted to develop more hydro-electric projects in Quebec before importing power into the province from an outside source.

In preparation for the meeting with Duplessis that never materialized, Gardner had had a brief prepared setting out "three great advantages that would accrue to Quebec" from the Hamilton development. First, it would conserve Quebec's own hydro resources for "general uses which are increasing at the rate of, say, 10 per cent per annum"; secondly, there would be no need for either the province or Hydro-Québec to increase its debt load to finance the scheme; thirdly, the power would be a magnet to attract industry to Sept-Iles, which seemed destined to become "the great exchange and clearing port of Eastern Canada," thus ensuring "steadily-increasing employment and a new wealth in northeastern Quebec."

Gardner suggested that Beaumont might raise these points at his next meeting with the Premier. Beaumont demurred, saying that to press the Premier too hard at this stage might invite a flat rejection of the project, which it would be difficult, if not impossible, to reverse. Instead, he proposed to cultivate Hydro-Québec, whose president, L. E. Potvin, had recently told him privately that he was "generally in favour" of importing Hamilton Falls power, since he foresaw all accessible hydro potentials in Quebec being fully used within the next fifteen years or so. In turn, Beaumont hoped, Hydro-Québec could win over the Premier.

Beaumont saw Duplessis frequently, both in Quebec City on formal Shawinigan business and, more informally, at dinners and other social functions when the Premier was in Montreal. But for the next few years he never seemed to find the right opportunity to raise the Hamilton project with him in any but the most general way. It was not until April 1959, in fact, that he sent Duplessis a map of the falls and a one-page memorandum pointing out the benefits their development would bring to Quebec. Even then, he received no reply to his letter.

Suspicious, Bill Southam had concluded long before this that Brinco was "being led up the garden path" and ought to consider making a new attempt to break the deadlock independently of Beaumont. He speculated in an internal memorandum in June 1957, that Shawinigan was hoping to keep Hamilton Falls as "a kind of iron reserve" and that Beaumont's "alleged pressure" on Duplessis was "directed more towards the development of the remaining Quebec potentials than towards making an early use of the Hamilton."

In fairness to Beaumont, he had troubles enough of his own at that time. Most of his formal calls on Duplessis were designed to extract some sort of assurance that Shawinigan would be able to buy from Hydro-Québec the extra power it expected to need within a few years to serve its expanding market. There had not yet been any official threat of the nationalization that was to swallow up Shawinigan a few years later, but it had become clear that in future large new hydro-electric developments would be the prerogative of Hydro-Québec, rather than the dozen or so private utilities still coexisting with it in the province.

Hydro-Québec had been formed by the government in 1944 to take over Montreal Light, Heat and Power Consolidated for two officially stated reasons: that the company had failed to cooperate satisfactorily with the provincial body charged with the regulation of private utilities; and that the federal taxes it had to pay as a private corporation resulted in the people of Quebec being charged more for electricity than those in other provinces served by government-owned utilities. One of Montreal Light's assets was the Beauharnois generating station on the St. Lawrence River west of Montreal, and Hydro-Québec's first achievement was to expand its fourteen generating units to thirty-six, making it for a time the largest power station in Canada. In 1956, the provincially owned utility completed the first stage of the first project it built from scratch, on the Bersimis River, about four hundred miles east of Montreal. But then, perhaps because Quebec's long-range economic plan was still locked behind the bland forehead of Premier Duplessis, there was a period of indecision during which no one knew where Quebec's future power requirements were to come from.

This was a worrying situation for Beaumont and others like him who, faced with a demand for power that was doubling every ten years, were counting on Hydro-Québec to supply their future needs. In June 1957, Shawinigan formally asked Hydro-Québec for additional power beginning in 1961. When no answer had been received by the end of the year, Beaumont decided that Hydro-Québec's problem was worse than his own. He was eventually able to buy the power he needed from Alcan, which found itself with surplus capacity because of the slump in the aluminum market.

Hydro-Québec's apparent plight was thought within Brinco to enhance the prospects for an early start on the Hamilton project, and batches of memoranda and studies were busily turned out assessing the various options open to the province; it was known, for instance, to be surveying the Manicouagan and Outardes rivers, in the wilderness of eastern Quebec. The thrust of all these memoranda was delicately designed to demonstrate the advantages to the province of buying power from Brinco, which was confident it could start supplying it four years from the word "go," and retaining its own rivers for later development.

Unfortunately, Brinco's own efforts to win acceptance for this hypothesis were no more successful than Beaumont's had been, and some of the stratagems considered as means of advancing the cause seem in retrospect to have been pathetically ineffectual. For instance, after a staff meeting on February 14, 1958, Southam, a great believer in the beneficent influence of good food and wine, noted that he and Ron Stuart, one of his young assistants, "are looking into a program of meals to re-establish contacts, etc." Three days later, it was resolved by the twenty-fourth meeting of the Power Sales Co-ordinating Committee that "the Corporation might convene a 'top-level' conference of the Presidents of all companies who might be interested in buying Hamilton Falls power at some time within the next ten years" — a resolution that seems to show a touching faith that open covenants can always be openly arrived at.

There was considerable discussion about the advisability of mounting a concentrated public relations campaign, but as always there was the risk that any promotion of the project would antagonize Premier Duplessis. And, inevitably perhaps, the old concept of a super-salesman being engaged to market the power surfaced once again. This time it was agreed that "DM-G, under cover of an appropriate title, should try his hand at this." The initials referred to another of Southam's young English assistants, David Morgan-Grenville, who, while meticulous and resourceful in the performance of his duties, would have been the last to claim for himself either the aptitude or the inclination to be a super-salesman.*

Not surprisingly, the members of Brinco's London Advisory Committee were becoming more and more restive over the seeming stalemate in Canada, and Edmund de Rothschild decided it might help if he himself saw Duplessis in an effort to win him over. Resistant as ever to interference from London, Gardner and Southam tried to head off this initiative as tactfully as they could, fearful that an unco-ordinated approach by the effervescent Eddy might have a disastrous impact on a situation they had been trying to handle with kid gloves. Through a friend in Montreal, de Rothschild did try to arrange an interview with the Premier in June 1957, but Duplessis was apparently no more anxious to receive him than anyone else connected with Brinco; he proved to be busy with an election campaign.

Later, however, de Rothschild was introduced to Antonio Barrette, Quebec's Minister of Labour, by a young Quebec City lawyer named Marc de Goumois he had met on a transatlantic flight. Barrette, he reported later, was very much in favour of the Hamilton scheme and wanted him to see the Premier next time he was in Canada. To the relief of Gardner and Southam, this meeting did not take place either.

In April 1958, a forty-three-year-old lawyer of Irish and French-Canadian parentage named Daniel Johnson was appointed Minister of Hydraulic Resources. Since this portfolio included responsibility for Hydro-Québec, there was a good deal of agonizing within Brinco over whether someone should seek an appointment with him to try to enlist him as an ally. The pros and cons of this were debated for months and ultimately Beaumont's view won out: that Johnson was a promising young

---

*The relationship between Bill Southam and his young staff sometimes resembled that between a gruff but kindly scoutmaster and his troop. While outwardly the typical English gentleman — he had the customary upper-class public school education and a degree in economics from Cambridge — Morgan-Grenville later knocked about the oilfields of New Mexico and Louisiana as a roughneck and oil scout before joining Brinco in 1954. His great enthusiasm was a small farm he had bought in the Eastern Townships of Quebec, a far cry from the English country estate others with his upbringing might have aspired to. Southam, whose only outdoor enthusiasm was golf, visited him there one weekend to find him happily, if somewhat inelegantly, engaged in farm chores. Ushered into the old farmhouse, Southam raised his bushy eyebrows incredulously and said: "Rather *rococo*, isn't it, David?"

man who would no doubt be an asset to the province one day, but that he was not yet a power in the land; and that there was little to be gained at present from pursuing the cultivation of Hydro-Québec because that organization was completely under the thumb of Duplessis.

This assessment seemed to be borne out early in 1959 after Johnson had at last announced Quebec's future program of hydro-electric development — or at least the program as he conceived it to be. On January 26, he told an overflow dinner of the Union Nationale party at the Windsor Hotel in Montreal that Hydro-Québec planned to spend $1 billion during the coming ten years to develop the Lachine Rapids, on the St. Lawrence River at Montreal, the Ottawa River at Carillon, about forty miles from the city, and the remote Manicouagan.

Less than three weeks later, Maurice Duplessis rose in the Legislative Assembly and gave connoisseurs of the art of politics a typically deft demonstration of how an old master preserves discipline and a proper sense of fitness among his protégés. There would be no development of the Lachine Rapids, he said, because economic conditions did not justify it. Montreal had ample supplies of power, which the Carillon project would augment by 800,000 horse power.

Whatever the cause of Beaumont's reluctance to importune the Premier on Brinco's behalf, he was right about one thing: in Duplessis's fiefdom, there was room for only one seigneur; all the rest were serfs.

And occasionally, during those years, the Premier would draw aside the stage curtain just long enough to give the impatient audience a glimpse of the drama that was waiting to unfold: the real reason for his refusal to see Gardner or Southam and his reluctance to have anything at all to do with Brinco.

This became evident, for instance, in July 1957, when the directors of Brinco decided to buy a house in which the corporation's managing director could not only live but entertain guests in appropriate style. To do this, it was discovered, called for certain legal steps, notably the securing of a mortmain permit enabling the corporation to hold real estate in the province for purposes other than its principal business. Somehow, the application for this permit landed on the Premier's desk. He refused to grant it, saying that the Newfoundland government had given Brinco certain areas in Labrador which it had no right to give, since they were actually in the province of Quebec, and to grant the permit would constitute tacit acceptance by Quebec of a Labrador boundary with which it disagreed.

He returned to this theme at a meeting of the Sept-Iles Chamber of

Commerce in January 1958. Brinco was now represented in Sept-Iles by a local businessman, Georges Blouin, whose family had held land in the town before the iron-ore development transformed it from a tiny fishing village into a thriving industrial centre. Before the Premier's arrival, Blouin had done some missionary work among his friends, persuading them that new industries would be attracted to the area if they were assured of a plentiful supply of cheap power from the Hamilton.

A member of the Chamber accordingly asked the Premier whether Hamilton Falls power could be brought in to Sept-Iles. In his customary jovial manner, which softened but never quite hid the hard edge of his determination, Duplessis replied that in his opinion, Hamilton Falls should belong to Quebec. However, assuming this was not the case, his mind was open and he had not refused to permit the power to be brought into or taken across Quebec. Of course, a charge would have to be made for such permisison. He was prepared to discuss this with Brinco at any time.

Somehow, that time never arrived. But Duplessis had charted for wary mariners the tip of the iceberg which later would come uncomfortably close to sinking Brinco's plans.

EIGHT

A new plan founders in a political storm

A letter sent to prospective participants in Brinco's private share issue of 1956 made the point: "The twenty-nine original members did not join this corporation with any idea of seeing their investment yield a quick return." For the rest of the fifties, as the corporation continued to spend money with nothing to show for it except a mounting pile of reports and memoranda, the shareholders could be forgiven for wondering whether their investment would ever yield *any* returns.

More than $4 million of the original shareholders' investment had been spent by late 1955, when it was decided to raise more money with a wider share issue. Some within the corporation felt there was so much interest in its prospects that a public issue could safely be made, at perhaps as much as $6. But Bertie Gardner had been chosen to head Brinco because his reputation would inspire confidence, and central to that reputation, besides integrity, was his innate conservatism. Knowing it would be years before any dividends could be expected, and abhorring anything that smacked of "promotion," he argued, successfully, that the shares should be offered only to companies and to selected private investors whose portfolios were large and sophisticated enough to accommodate what was still essentially a speculative stock.

It was estimated that the corporation's operating expenses in the foreseeable future would amount to $1 million a year, and it was decided to raise $6 million — two million shares at $3 each. They were easily sold, and, in fact, some of the original shareholders complained that they should have been given larger allocations of the new shares. The issue, of course, broadened the ownership of Brinco considerably; so a formula was worked out beforehand to protect the prior position of the seven original members of the consortium, partly to reward them for their initial support and partly to satisfy the British Treasury, which had made dollars available only on condition that control of the corporation remain in British hands. To ensure this, two-thirds of the shares held by the original members were declared to be "Founders' shares," each of which carried ten votes, and it was resolved that henceforth only common shares (carrying one vote each) would be issued. The founder members undertook not to dispose of any of their special shares without first offering them to the rest of the consortium, through Rothschilds.

This privileged position for one group of shareholders — who had, moreover, bought their shares for only $1 — was naturally open to criticism and it was eventually abandoned in 1967. But it did ensure support for the corporation through the lean years. While an over-the-counter market in Brinco shares developed soon after the 1956 issue (some were sold for as much as $6.75 in Montreal and even higher prices were reported from Newfoundland), the founders hung on to their shares and it was not until 1958 that the first bloc changed hands, when the Suez Canal Company bought Frobisher's 250,000 shares for $1¼ million — at $5 each.

Up to this point, the corporation's largest single expenditure had been the $2½ million which the Hamilton Falls surveys ultimately cost. As the prospects for an early development of the falls receded, it was decided to spend a further $250,000 to survey Bay d'Espoir*, on the island of Newfoundland, which the corporation had been eyeing intermittently since Premier Smallwood had tried to enlist its aid in the rural electrification of the province.

The preamble to Brinco's Principal Agreement began with the phrase, "Whereas it is desirable to promote the industrial and economic development of Newfoundland and Labrador . . . ." Southam always considered the corporation to be the province's partner in that aim and Bay d'Espoir appeared to be the ideal place to demonstrate the sincerity of its purpose. Not only would a power plant there satisfy the island's growing need for electricity but the area itself seemed well-suited for industrial development. A Shawinigan Engineering survey in 1957 confirmed the feasibility of developing up to 350,000 horse power at the site in five stages of 70,000 horse power each; it was estimated that power from the first stage would cost six mills per kilowatt-hour at the site, with lower costs for subsequent stages. This was considered a sufficiently attractive price to induce new industries to locate in the Bay d'Espoir area, and further studies indicated that a good, ice-free port could be built in the neighbourhood of Swanger Cove and St. Albans, on the west shore of the bay, where there was enough level ground to permit the establishment of a new town and supporting industries.

Brinco decided to take the initiative in fostering this development

---

*Newfoundlanders almost universally pronounce it "Bay Despair" — aptly, in the light of Brinco's experience.

86

and Southam made several visits to Europe canvassing companies he thought might be interested in Bay d'Espoir's combination of cheap power, available timber and good shipping facilities. Eventually, he was able to write to Smallwood telling him interest had been evinced by several internationally known firms, which he was not yet at liberty to name, in establishing timber-consuming industries at Bay d'Espoir; indeed, there was enough interest to suggest that the first-stage development of 70,000 horse power might be undertaken soon if the project was assured of government support. And privately he hinted that one of the potential customers was considering the construction of a pulp mill.

Throughout his two decades as Premier, Joey Smallwood waged a personal crusade to attract a third paper mill to Newfoundland to supplement the activities of Bowaters and Anglo-Newfoundland. He wrote back immediately saying that if Brinco decided to proceed with a pulp and paper operation at Bay d'Espoir, the government would: assume responsibility, in collaboration with the Central Mortgage and Housing Corporation, for the creation of a new town; ensure that the new company had enough pulpwood for its operations; "take all possible steps" to have the area designated by Ottawa as a national harbour; try to gain federal assistance for a railroad running north from Bay d'Espoir to join the existing railroad across the island; and investigate the possibility of building a highway to parallel the railroad.

Soon afterwards, however, Southam discovered that in his eagerness to have a third mill built Joey was negotiating a deal with the huge U.S. company Crown Zellerbach, and was prepared to grant it timber rights on the island. This meant there would not be enough timber for Southam's main European prospect, which promptly lost interest in the project. Since he had taken Joey's letter to represent a moral obligation by the government to support the Bay d'Espoir development, Southam at first assumed that the Crown Zellerbach mill would be built there as the nucleus of the new town. To his dismay, he now learned it was destined instead for Come-by-Chance, in southeastern Newfoundland.

In the event, despite a spate of rosy announcements by the Premier, the Crown Zellerbach deal collapsed. And with it went the hopes for a new industrial area at Bay d'Espoir.

The need for more power on the island still existed, however: both Bowaters and Anglo-Newfoundland were seeking new power sources to enable them to expand their production, and the private utilities such as Newfoundland Light and Power and United Towns also needed new supplies. On February 18, 1959, Southam called on the Premier and told him

Brinco still hoped to go ahead with a power plant at Bay d'Espoir and for this purpose had decided to form a new subsidiary company, Southern Newfoundland Power and Development, in partnership with Bowaters, Anglo-Newfoundland and the Power Corporation of Canada. But transmitting the power to other centres on the island, instead of using it at the site, would add perhaps $12 million to the estimated $60 million the full development would cost, and in Brinco's view the project could not be financed without government assistance.

The Premier immediately protested that the province could not subsidize companies as wealthy as Bowaters and Anglo-Newfoundland, but Southam pointed out that the mechanism for federal assistance existed in the Atlantic Provinces Power Development Act, passed by the Progressive Conservative government in Ottawa a year earlier, which provided for federal aid for the construction of transmission lines and related equipment in the Atlantic provinces. Joey, as a confirmed Liberal, did not care for the idea of approaching Prime Minister John Diefenbaker, but he eventually allowed himself to be persuaded to send him a letter which Brinco had drafted after informally sounding out departmental officials in Ottawa.

The letter went off the next day, but before any reply was received Brinco found itself — for neither the first time nor the last — embroiled in a political storm which was not of its own making, and certainly not of its own choosing.

When the Terms of Union between Newfoundland and Canada were being drawn up in Ottawa in 1947 and 1948, it was understood that by becoming a province Newfoundland would be giving up its customs and excise duties, thus losing 60 per cent of its government revenue. It was recognized that special federal financial assistance would be needed to make up this loss, and to close the gap between the lamentably low standards of Newfoundland's public services and those of the other provinces. In view of the difficulty of deciding in advance how big these payments would have to be, Term 29 of the agreement provided for the appointment of a royal commission within eight years of Confederation "to recommend the form and scale of additional financial assistance, if any" which would be needed to enable the new province "to continue public services at the levels and standards reached subsequently to the date of Union, without resorting to taxation more burdensome, having regard to capacity to pay, than that obtaining generally in the region comprising the Maritime Provinces of Nova Scotia, New Brunswick and Prince Edward Island."

Joey began preparing for the Term 29 hearings as early as 1953, when he appointed a provincial commission to prepare Newfoundland's case. The commission handed down its report in April 1957, detailing "tragic deficiencies" in the province's public services and recommending a federal grant of $15 million a year to correct them.

The federal royal commission was appointed by the Liberal government of Louis St. Laurent in that same year, under the chairmanship of Chief Justice John B. McNair of the New Brunswick Supreme Court. Its report, in July 1959, confirmed much of what the provincial commission had said about deficiencies in the province's public services, but it also reproved Premier Smallwood for spending money that could have improved them on his various industrial ventures. It recommended that the province should receive $28½ million in federal payments to cover the period between April 1, 1957 and March 31, 1961, and "thereafter $8 million per annum."

This was only a little more than half of what Newfoundland had claimed it needed, and the opposition leader, Malcolm Hollett, joined Joey in describing the McNair report as "disappointing." But much worse was to come.

The commission had been appointed by the Liberals, but the Progressive Conservatives had taken over in Ottawa before it made its report. On March 25, 1959, while Joey was still waiting for a reply to his request for assistance with the Bay d'Espoir transmission lines, Prime Minister Diefenbaker explained how his government proposed to implement the McNair recommendations. He rejected the idea of making fixed payments over a period "of unlimited duration" and said Ottawa would provide $36½ million to Newfoundland up to March 31, 1962, and this would be "final and irrevocable settlement of the provisions of Term 29 and the contractual obligations of the union consummated in 1949."

Joey's strangled gasp could be heard all over Canada. He had helped to frame the Terms of Union and his reverence for Term 29, in particular, was as fervent as the Indian chiefs' understanding of their treaties with the Queen across the sea: it was destined to last "as long as the sun shines and water runs." Disappointing as it was, even the McNair report had recognized that, by its use of the phrase "thereafter."

The Prime Minister could hardly have resumed his seat in the Commons before Joey issued a furious denunciation of his announcement. All Newfoundlanders, he said, were stunned by Diefenbaker's "betrayal of Newfoundland and of Canada's honour." It had "plunged Newfoundland into mourning for another Canadian obligation outraged . . . ."

And so he ordered flags to half mast and all public buildings in St. John's draped in black crêpe. His anger was shared by most of his fellow Newfoundlanders.

It was the beginning of a feud between Diefenbaker and Smallwood which lasted for virtually the rest of the Prime Minister's term of office.* Within a couple of weeks, Joey carried the fight to his adversary, sailing into Ottawa under a full head of steam to give a series of press conferences in which he gleefully cast himself as David pitted against Goliath and Newfoundland as the poor little lamb savaged by that legendary "Canadian wolf."

Much as the country enjoyed the spectacle — it made Joey more of a national figure than ever before — none of it augured well for the Bay d'Espoir development. The Prime Minister's reply to Smallwood's request for assistance, dated May 22, was brief to the point of curtness. And instead of the federal subsidy Joey had hoped for, it merely offered a loan at the federal borrowing rate plus one-eighth of one per cent, repayable in equal instalments over forty years — similar terms, as Diefenbaker pointed out, to those recently granted New Brunswick for a transmission line. These terms, Joey told Brinco's Claude Howse on the day he received the letter, would cost the Newfoundland government more than $600,000 a year, and he doubted whether his cabinet would sanction them.

Bill Southam no longer had C. D. Howe as his friend at court in Ottawa, but he had made it a point to continue to keep the Progressive Conservative government and its officials informed of Brinco's activities. And through his contacts he had reason to believe that the federal government had been considering a much more generous offer to Newfoundland, which would have brought the transmission line under the umbrella of the "Roads To Resources" program, with Ottawa putting up half the cost and granting the province favoured terms for the rest. He suggested to Smallwood that Diefenbaker expected his letter to be followed by a reply asking for better terms.

Under the circumstances, Joey would not hear of this. Instead, he resolved that the provincial government would accept the offer as made and bear the initial costs of the transmission line, provided the proposed Southern Newfoundland company would take over the payments when it began to make a profit, and provided it would start building in 1959

*Joey eventually won his campaign in favour of Term 29; the Liberals reinstated the perpetual $8 million payment after they regained office in Ottawa.

so as to be able to deliver the first power before the end of 1961 to supply several new mines which were expected to be brought in by then in the Baie Verte area of north-central Newfoundland.

Unfortunately, the end of 1959 came with Southern Newfoundland still unable to put together enough firm contracts with potential customers to guarantee the financing of even the first stage of the Bay d'Espoir project. But by then Brinco had at last embarked on the negotiations which led to the development that became not only its first income-producing venture but a pilot project for the greater achievement ahead.

NINE

"A small beginning to a big venture"

The geologist A. P. Low had predicted the ultimate partnership of Labrador's iron ore and water power at the turn of the century. But the union, when it came about, was something of a shotgun marriage, solemnized only after an arduous courtship that was more acrimonious than most divorces.

In the late 1930s, Dr. J. A. Retty, a geologist working for a Canadian company called Labrador Mining and Exploration, outlined several rich iron-ore deposits on a 22,000-square-mile concession the company had been granted by the Newfoundland Commission of Government in western Labrador. Once, flying over Hamilton Falls in the Bellanca seaplane he used in his exploration, Retty joked to a companion that when he had his iron mines working and was a millionaire he would build a honeymoon hotel at the falls. But for some years it seemed no one was interested in developing any mines in Labrador. Trying to raise funds, Labrador Mining and Exploration approached the wealthy M. A. Hanna Company of Cleveland, Ohio. But the effects of the depression were still being felt and the powerful Hanna interests had plenty of iron ore; they declined to participate.

A few years later, however, Labrador Mining and Exploration's prospects caught the eye of Jules Timmins, head of Hollinger Consolidated Gold Mines, the Canadian mining empire founded by his father and uncle on the rich silver and gold deposits around Cobalt and Timmins in northern Ontario. Timmins invested heavily in more exploration and in 1942 took control of Labrador Mining and Exploration and its potentially rich concession. And once again he approached the Hanna interests which by now, with the demand for iron and steel created by the Second World War at its height, were in a more receptive frame of mind. Hanna and Hollinger joined forces to continue the exploration and in 1949 formed a partnership with five American steel companies (Republic, National, Armco, Youngstown and Wheeling) under the corporate title of the Iron Ore Company of Canada. Between them, the partners made up a substantial portion of the steel-making capacity of the United

States, thus assuring not only a market for the iron ore but a firm base for the $145 million financing needed to bring the Schefferville—Knob Lake mines into production and build the railroad from Sept-Iles to ship out the ore.

The power for the Knob Lake mines was provided by an initial 12,000 horse power development at Menihek, in a lake system fed by the Ashuanipi River, one of the two main tributaries of the Churchill. The railroad was completed and the first ore shipped out in 1954, and soon afterward advances in iron-ore processing (notably the concentration process in which the ore is crushed into a fine powder and then baked into pellets with a clay binder) caused the Iron Ore Company to take a new look at large but lower-grade ore deposits in its concession area south of Schefferville, near Wabush Lake. Since Wabush, in the extreme west of Labrador near the Quebec border, is less than 150 miles from Churchill Falls, Brinco was naturally interested in the Iron Ore Company as a potential customer for power.

It soon became apparent that the demand would not be large enough to justify the million horse power first stage of the Channel Scheme, so Brinco looked at other neighbouring rivers. In the fall of 1957, it spent $47,000 surveying the Valley River, which runs into the Churchill below the falls, and found it would be possible to build a 133,000 horse power development there in three years at a cost of $41 million.

Later, however, it was discovered that a much larger development, with a potential of 300,000 horse power, could be built at only slightly higher cost on the Unknown River, part of the system fed by the Atikonak River, the other large tributary of the Churchill. Within three miles of each other on the Unknown River there are two sets of waterfalls, Scott Falls and Thomas Falls, whose existence was substantiated only in 1929. At both these points the river divides into two branches, each containing a waterfall. Engineering studies disclosed that an earth dam above the upper falls (Scott) would create a reservoir at an elevation of 1,490 feet above sea level, giving a head of three hundred feet at a point about twelve miles from Hamilton Falls. The powerhouse was to be sited at the upper end of a steep-sided valley which, until the water began to flow through the turbines from the reservoir above, had been dry since it was plugged by glacial debris during the last Ice Age. The development was to be known by the local name for the area, Twin Falls.

It was a hot July day in 1959 when a Brinco party flew from Montreal to Cleveland to persuade the Hollinger-Hanna interests that the power for their proposed Wabush development should be supplied from Twin Falls. Bill Southam was accompanied by Victor H. Smith, an English-born accountant who had joined Brinco as its treasurer at the beginning of 1956; the corporation's financial adviser, Arthur S. Torrey, a salty New Englander who had come to Canada in the mid-twenties to write a monthly investment letter for Izaak Killam's Royal Securities and had stayed on, eventually becoming president of Pitfield's, one of Brinco's early shareholders; and Richard E. Heartz, president of both Hamilton Falls Power Corporation and Shawinigan Engineering.

They were greeted in the Hanna board room by a group that included Jules Timmins but which was quite obviously led — indeed, dominated — by George M. Humphrey, chairman of the board. A lawyer who had joined Hanna in 1917, Humphrey was a courteous and polished man whose hobby was breeding horses at his stables in Kentucky and on his plantation in Georgia. But he was also a stubborn negotiator, as tough as the iron which had been his life's work. As Secretary of the Treasury in the Eisenhower cabinet between 1953 and 1957 he fought for a balanced budget, tight money, curbs on welfare and foreign-aid spending, and tax cuts. He was now only a year away from his seventieth birthday, but he soon made it clear to the Brinco deputation that he had lost none of his fire.

Brinco, he said, had so far been "living in a dream." He and his associates could help to make that dream a reality. But Brinco's financial structure was not only "unrealistic" but "fantastic" and should be put right as soon as possible (a reference to the extra voting weight carried by the Founders' shares.) The Iron Ore Company, he went on, would need 50,000 horse power by the spring of 1962, and probably a further 100,000 horse power during the next ten years. He was prepared to put up the money necessary to develop the first 50,000 horse power at Twin Falls — a tentative figure of $17½ million was mentioned — and in return he wanted a 47 per cent voting and share interest in Brinco and an 83 per cent share of the company set up to build Twin Falls.

Flabbergasted, Southam and his colleagues, who had come expecting merely to discuss the Iron Ore Company's purchase of power from a plant Brinco intended to finance and build itself, were hardly mollified by Humphrey's magnanimous offer to let Hamilton Falls manage and operate the Twin Falls plant — if it proved capable of doing so, which he seemed to doubt — and his offer to sell surplus power to Hamilton Falls for resale to others.

Twin Falls, Humphrey said, could be "a small beginning to a big venture." (Hanna was at that time toying with two ideas that never progressed any further: entering the aluminum business, and using electricity to smelt iron ore on the spot in Labrador, either of which could have created a market for Hamilton Falls power.) He was not interested in Brinco's timber or mineral assets, and none of his money would be available for such general purposes. Neither was he interested in entering the corporation "on the mezzanine level." He wanted to be "in the front — bald-headed — row of the orchestra stalls."

He did not want the Brinco representatives to think he was holding a pistol at their heads, but if the corporation found his proposals unacceptable he would develop the power needed for Wabush at either of two potential sites across the border in Quebec: on the Pekans River, about sixty miles from Wabush, where there was an estimated maximum potential of 200,000 horse power, or at Eaton Canyon which, while it was more than two hundred miles from Wabush, could be developed up to a million horse power.

The meeting had begun a little before 11 a.m. It was still not lunch time when Humphrey suggested the Brinco party might like to discuss his proposals in private. They withdrew to another room, but all knew there was nothing to discuss at this stage: the proposals were obviously unacceptable as they stood. After lunch in the Hanna offices, there was another brief meeting, at which the atmosphere was no less oppressive than before.

The Hanna board room overlooked a baseball park where by now a game was in progress. At one point, Arthur Torrey ran a finger round the inside of his collar and out of the corner of his mouth whispered to his neighbour at the huge table, "I sure wish I was down there." The heartfelt reply — "Me, too" — reflected the tension in the room, for it came from Joe Thompson, president of both M. A. Hanna and the Iron Ore Company.

Bill Southam contented himself with the observation that Mr. Humphrey's proposals were so far-reaching that he preferred not to comment on them until they had been discussed within the corporation and with Brinco's partner in the Hamilton Falls company, Shawinigan Engineering. When, he asked politely, would Mr. Humphrey like to have a reply?

"I'd like to have had it last week," growled Humphrey. But he agreed that Brinco should take another look at Twin Falls on the ground, to be sure both sides were talking in the same terms of magnitude. This, he felt sure, would not take more than a few days and in the meantime, Brinco should "keep in touch."

It was a subdued Brinco party that left for Montreal that afternoon, but Humphrey considered he had ample justification for taking a hard line: in his eyes, Brinco had usurped rights that in fact belonged to him. He was convinced that, in taking over Labrador Mining's original concession, the Iron Ore Company had inherited the right to develop water power for its projects anywhere in Labrador. He had made his view known to Joey Smallwood soon after Brinco's formation, in September 1954, when the Premier had pulled the switch to start the water flowing through the Menihek power plant. Not only were the rights to Hamilton Falls rightfully his, he had told the Premier, but if he were granted the lease to them he would be selling the power in New York City by 1959.

Smallwood had reported this conversation to Bill Southam a few days later, saying he had been puzzled by Humphrey's claim and had asked the Attorney General's department to investigate it; and soon afterward he had assured Southam that Labrador Mining's rights had lapsed and Brinco's title to the water power was secure.

Humphrey had not let the matter rest there. A year later, Smallwood had received a visit from Jules Timmins and the executive vice-president of Hollinger-Hanna, William H. Durrell. Together they had reasserted the company's claim to any water power it might need in Labrador, which they based on Clause 37 of Act No. 41 of 1938, the legislation granting the original concession to Labrador Mining. In this clause, the government did agree to grant the company water rights; but, as Joey now pointed out, Clause 37 was subject to Clause 40, which reserved to the government the right to grant water power rights to others if they had not been specifically leased to Labrador Mining.

It was now seventeen years since the concesssion had been granted, the Premier pointed out, and Labrador Mining had never asked for the Hamilton lease. His visitors conceded the truth of this, but told Smallwood about their attempts to devise a practical method of smelting the iron ore with electricity. This process might require millions of horse power and even though it would undoubtedly take some years to perfect the technique and more to build the necessary plant, the company wanted to be assured that the power would be there when it was needed.

"Are you seriously suggesting," Joey asked, "that the power should merely lie there unused just because of a bare possibility that you might some day want to use it?"

Timmins and Durrell hastily disavowed any such intention. But, they said, their predicament remained. Joey suggested they should set out their case in writing and he would then approach Brinco about supplying their needs, which he did on October 14, 1955, in a letter saying, in part: "It would be a very great thing for Newfoundland if they smelted Labrador ore in Labrador. It would be a very great thing for them and I suppose it would be a very great thing for you." And he asked Brinco to get in touch with the Iron Ore Company.

Before doing so, Southam had thought it would be wise to ask the Premier to confirm Brinco's rights to the Hamilton in writing, which he did "categorically" in a letter dated December 2, 1955.

While Brinco would have been only too pleased to supply the power for an electric smelter, and thus get the Channel Scheme under way, the plan was eventually dropped. But the dispute over the water rights still rankled with George Humphrey four years later and some of those who were involved in the Twin Falls negotiations believe their tortuous course can only be explained by his determination, if he could not buy control of the project, to demonstrate to Smallwood that Brinco could not do the job and that the rights should be transferred — or, as he saw it, restored — to him.

A week after the Brinco deputation's first visit to Cleveland, the corporation's executive committee met to consider Humphrey's proposal and, as expected, declared it unacceptable. The committee recognized Humphrey's desire to have enough control over his power supply to ensure that it would not be interrupted. But it also realized that since the Twin Falls plant would be using water from the Hamilton system, this water would have to be recaptured later if the full potential of the Channel Scheme were to be reached; and thus, whoever controlled Twin would also, to some extent, control the Channel Scheme. Victor Smith had worked out a counter-proposal to be put to Humphrey and the committee approved it.

Humphrey visited Montreal on August 13 and listened politely as Southam outlined the counter-proposal: the Iron Ore Company could have a 20 per cent participation in Brinco for $4 a share; a 20 per cent participation in Hamilton Falls Power Corporation for $2,250,000, which equalled $10 a share, the price Shawinigan Engineering had paid for its 20 per cent holding; and 40 per cent of the subsidiary company to be set up to build Twin Falls.

In reply, Humphrey said he was prepared to reduce the 47 per cent interest he had requested in Brinco to 25 per cent, but he would not pay a premium for his shares. He wanted them at the $1 price the original shareholders had paid for them, because despite the lapse of six years since Brinco's incorporation it still "only had hopes." In addition, he wanted 30, not 20, per cent of Hamilton Falls. And he still wanted 80 per cent of Twin Falls.

Over lunch, he mellowed somewhat, and raised his offer for the Brinco shares to an average of $2. But he stressed the urgency of making a decision since he was investing $100 million at Wabush and could not delay further with "a little matter like this." If Brinco did not make up its mind soon, he would go ahead and develop his power in Quebec.

The lawyer Hilary Scott had flown over from London with Edmund de Rothschild to attend the meeting, and in his minutes afterward he wrote: "It seemed to be the general impression that the gap between the parties had narrowed, but Mr. Humphrey was still asking for too much." Nevertheless, it was agreed that de Rothschild would discuss the matter with the London shareholders.

Though it had not yet been mentioned, among the reasons why Humphrey could not be granted what he wanted was the corporation's Principal Agreement with the government of Newfoundland. While Smallwood accepted that it was logical for Brinco to establish subsidiary companies to handle its separate assets, the corporation knew it could not transfer rights given it by the government to outside companies, which in effect is what it would have been doing had it ceded control of Twin Falls to Humphrey.

Also, Humphrey was now asking that the whole of Twin's estimated 300,000 horse power should be earmarked for the Iron Ore Company, even though Bill Durrell had told Victor Smith privately that the originally mentioned amount of 150,000 horse power would take care of all the company's needs in the Wabush area for at least ten years. Furthermore, under Brinco's agreement with the government, any power plant it built was obliged to supply any customer able to enter into a valid contract, without discrimination — and another potential customer for Twin Falls power had already arrived on the scene.

This was a company called Wabush Iron which, while its plans were not as far advanced as the Iron Ore Company's, also proposed to mine iron ore in the Wabush area, on land — as though George Humphrey were not already aggrieved enough — which had once belonged to Labrador Mining and Exploration. The Labrador Mining concession had contained the same sort of "shedding" clause as Brinco's Principal Agreement, under which the company had to give up 10 per cent of its concession area every year, ultimately retaining a thousand square miles for long-term exploitation. In one of its annual surrenders, it gave up a seemingly unpromising tract of land to the east of what eventually became its operation in the Wabush area.

When the government was setting up Nalco, it included this surrendered area in its mineral concession and Nalco geologists later found iron there. At this point, John C. Doyle, a Chicago-born coal salesman who had formed a Montreal company to manufacture space heaters and barbecue grills and then secured a number of mining claims in Quebec, turned up in St. John's and went to see Joey Smallwood, seeking a mineral concession in Labrador. Doyle's buoyant personality and the nonchalant way in which he took risks that would have deterred the less sanguine must have appealed to Joey's own bullish nature, for the two later became great friends and often travelled together in Doyle's chandelier-equipped private plane in search of economic opportunities for the province. Years later, Joey described Doyle as a "tremendous promoter" but added: "There should be a law to prevent him from doing anything but promoting; he should never attempt to manage a producing company."

In September 1953, Premier Smallwood announced that Doyle's company, Canadian Javelin, and a group of associates had acquired control of Nalco by buying one and a half million shares at $5 each, a considerable advance on their original value of $1. The announcement turned out to be premature, because the deal was not completed at that time, though Doyle did manage to buy a substantial holding in Nalco (a reported 30 per cent) and in the process acquired some of Nalco's mineral and timber rights, including those to the area around Wabush. Canadian Javelin geologists continued to explore this area and eventually proved it contained immense iron-ore reserves, estimated at more than a billion tons.

Doyle then came to an agreement with Pickands Mather and Company, another Cleveland firm which from small beginnings in 1883 had grown into a large Great Lakes iron-mining and shipping complex. Pickands Mather formed a complicated international consortium* to mine five square miles of Doyle's area under a royalty arrangement with Canadian

*Pickands Mather first put together Wabush Iron Company, consisting of itself and four other American companies (Youngstown Sheet and Tube Company, Interlake Iron Corporation, Inland Steel Company, and Pittsburgh Steel Company) with the addition of an Italian company named Finsider. The actual development of the Wabush property (and the building of the new town of Wabush) was carried out by Wabush Mines, which consisted of the participants in Wabush Iron plus two

Javelin. And it was representatives of Pickands Mather who approached Brinco for power for the new development, soon after the negotiations with Humphrey had begun. They did not expect their consortium to start shipping ore until 1964 or 1965, several years after Humphrey's target date, and they expected to need only 35,000 horse power to begin with, expanding later to perhaps 66,000 horse power. But they did want an assurance that they, as well as the Iron Ore Company, would be supplied by the Twin Falls plant.

Pickands Mather's approach strengthened Brinco's hand, since at this stage George Humphrey seemed to be assuming that not only was he the only customer in sight for Twin Falls power but that Brinco could not build the plant without his money. On Thursday, August 20, a week after the Montreal meeting, Arthur Torrey hurried in to the corporation's offices on Sherbrooke Street. He had, he told Southam and Victor Smith, just received a telephone call from Humphrey, who had said his group was "at the end of its rope" and would wait only till Monday morning for a favourable answer to his proposal, though this was not to be taken as an ultimatum!

Since Humphrey presumably realized that Eddy de Rothschild had not yet had time to get the shareholders together to discuss his latest proposal (mid-August being an unpopular season for high-level business conferences in London), it sounded to Bill Southam very much like an ultimatum. He immediately telephoned St. John's and spoke to Gordon Pushie, the ex-*Time* editor who had now become Joey's Director-General of Economic Development and had been making a valiant effort to clean up the mess left behind by Valdmanis. The myopia that causes Gordon Pushie to peer benignly at the world through thick-lensed spectacles does not extend to business dealings, and by now his acute mind had become indispensable to the Premier, who had nominated him as his liaison man with Brinco when Claude Howse left to join the Iron Ore Company. Using his reporter's initiative, Pushie tracked down the Premier — no easy task since it was the day of the post-McNair election in

---

Canadian companies, the Steel Company of Canada, and Dominion Foundries and Steel, with two West German companies which later pulled out of the group: Mannesmann A. G. and Hoesch A. G. It was an unwieldy grouping, for which Pickands Mather acted as the managing agent, but, like its rival, the Iron Ore Company, it provided an assured market for the ore. And as part of the deal, the Wabush group also bought the 60 per cent of Nalco still owned by the Newfoundland government.

which Joey inflicted such a defeat on the provincial Conservatives that they took a decade to recover. And he was soon able to call Southam back and reassure him on two points: Smallwood would "stand or fall" on the principle of the Iron Ore Company and Wabush Iron selling iron ore and Brinco selling power; and he wanted to have "anyone exerting unreasonable pressure to the contrary" referred directly to him.

Thus fortified, Southam was able to mount a delaying action during the succeeding days, when Humphrey, Durrell and various other emissaries continued to press for acceptance of the Iron Ore Company's terms. No argument advanced by the Brinco side appeared to shake Humphrey's insistence on having 80 per cent of the proposed Twin Falls company. At one meeting when the subject came up, Jim Wilson, a large, genial man who had spent his lifetime in the money business and was present as a partner in Brinco's auditing firm of Peat, Marwick, objected: "But, Mr. Chairman, it seems unreasonable that the people with the asset should get only 20 per cent of the company." Humphrey replied: "Mr. Wilson, that is on the generous side of the way we make these deals." And then, amid general laughter from his side of the table, he added matter-of-factly: "We usually only give 10 per cent."

Within Brinco, various formulas for ending the impasse were discussed, including a proposal that the Twin Falls subsidiary should be controlled by the Hamilton Falls company but that Humphrey might be permitted the lion's share (even 80 per cent) of its profits, as long as he was the only consumer of power, with a proportional reduction if other customers signed up.

At about this time, while the London shareholders were considering the situation, Val Duncan, who had become increasingly interested in Canada since Rio Tinto had bought control of the Hirshhorn uranium mines in Ontario, wrote an incisive analysis of the problem. "I think," he said, "that Mr. Humphrey has made monstrous demands and it seems to me that instead of looking at the whole matter from Brinco's point of view, we are in danger of compromising between Brinco's original instincts and Mr. Humphrey's demands. This to my mind is not a desirable yardstick for negotiation. A compromise is nearly always reached in negotiation, but it must be reached between two reasonable propositions, not between one unreasonable and one reasonable proposition. I do not believe that as yet we have had any indication of a reasonable proposition from Mr. Humphrey."

The memorandum submitted that since the whole of Humphrey's projected power demand could be met from Twin Falls alone, he had no right to any shareholding in either Brinco or Hamilton Falls Power Corporation. There were "intangible advantages" to having both the Iron Ore Company and the Pickands Mather group as shareholders, but their combined holding should not be more than 10 per cent, because if other large users of power appeared as customers for the Channel Scheme they could then legitimately expect *pro rata* equity holdings and "we shall ultimately not only lose control of the Hamilton Falls, but possibly end up with a derisory interest in it."

A couple of days later, Duncan heard that Humphrey had dropped his demand for participation in Brinco, but was still insisting on his other conditions, including a 29 per cent holding in the Hamilton Falls company. In an addendum to his first memorandum, Duncan wrote: "This strikes me as a bad idea from Brinco's point of view. If Brinco is the crown, HFPCo. is the Koh-i-noor diamond, and I would be very reluctant to recommend that Mr. Humphrey should extract a sizeable portion of the diamond from the crown without any corresponding guarantees to take an equivalent percentage of the Hamilton Falls potential."

In making this latest proposal, on August 31, 1959, Humphrey had offered to pay $3,375,000 for his 29 per cent share of the Hamilton Falls company. This appeared at first sight to represent a price per share approximately the same as that paid by Shawinigan for its 20 per cent interest, and to be fairly close to Brinco's last proposal, under which he had been offered 20 per cent of the Hamilton Falls company immediately, or 15 per cent immediately with an option to increase that to 29 per cent if one of the companies in his group came up with a contract permitting a start on the Channel Scheme.

But when Victor Smith analysed it, the new offer was found to be much less favourable to Brinco than his earlier ones: since the new money would be going into the Hamilton Falls treasury instead of Brinco's, and since Brinco's holding would now drop to only 51 per cent of Hamilton Falls, it would mean that instead of receiving more than $3 million in cash, Brinco would end up with only a half-interest in that amount in Hamilton Falls — an actual cash loss of about one and a half million dollars.

Smith and Southam assumed that this was merely a technical oversight on Humphrey's part. Bill Durrell, when they consulted him about it, agreed and sent for Bill Hobbs, Humphrey's financial adviser. After going over the figures with Smith, Hobbs agreed, too, and flew back to Cleveland with the unenviable assignment of telling Humphrey he had made a mistake in his arithmetic.

Whether from pique at being caught out in an error, or because he really had intended to scale down his offer, Humphrey called Southam back on September 3 and told him he was not interested in Brinco's arithmetic: he had made his offer and he wanted it passed to the board of directors on a "take it or leave it" basis. He was not prepared to negotiate any further.

At this stage, Humphrey probably still believed he held all the trump cards, because the day before his call Premier Duplessis had flown to Schefferville secretly in an Iron Ore Company plane, ostensibly the guest of Jules Timmins, Joe Thompson and Bill Durrell on a fishing trip. Southam heard about the visit from the ever-alert Georges Blouin in Sept-Iles and immediately assumed that whether or not Duplessis would be doing any fishing, his hosts would almost certainly be fishing for a lease on either Eaton Canyon or the Pekans River, a supposition that was confirmed from other sources later.

It was time, clearly, for another meeting with Premier Smallwood, who was away in London. Arrangements were made for Southam, Smith and Pushie to meet him in New York when he passed through a couple of days hence on his way to Panama, and on Sunday, September 6, the four met for lunch in the Park-Sheraton Hotel. The Premier, who had been kept in touch with the progress of the negotiations by transatlantic telephone, confirmed an aide-memoire he had signed after a meeting at New Court before he left London. This said, in part, that "just as his neighbouring province restricts at present the importation of power from Newfoundland if it conflicts with the best interests of the province, so on the same principle, he, Mr. Smallwood, would not allow power from Eaton Canyon to enter Labrador," and "if Mr. Humphrey wished to supply power to Wabush Lake from Menihek by raising the storage level, he would inform Mr. Humphrey that the overall Newfoundland plan for power precluded this move."

Joey repeated what he had told Southam before — that having created Brinco, he had no intention of permitting "Mr. Humphrey or any other American tycoon to gobble it up." He hoped Brinco would reject Humphrey's take it or leave it offer, but emphasize its continued willingness to supply him with power on a normal contract basis. And before doing so, it might be wise to try to extract a firm commitment from the Pickands Mather group.

As it happened, the fears that Duplessis would grant the Iron Ore Company a lease to develop its power in Quebec proved groundless. He suffered a stroke soon after his arrival at Schefferville and died there on September 7. But Smallwood's assurance that he would not permit power from Quebec to be imported into Labrador encouraged Brinco to resist Humphrey's demand for control, and its hand was further strengthened on September 14 when Pickands Mather signed an agreement undertaking to buy a minimum of 25,000 horse power from Twin Falls within three years, and to pay $200,000 for the survey work and preliminary engineering design needed to get the project off the ground.

This commitment secured, Southam called Humphrey and told him the board had rejected his offer but was prepared to conclude a simple contract for the supply of power immediately, leaving the question of a possible closer collaboration until later. Humphrey remained recalcitrant. His group "wanted and intended to have" control over its power, he said, and he repeated that it had "prior rights to the Hamilton."

As the weeks passed, with more proposals and counter-proposals still failing to achieve any compromise, Joey Smallwood decided it was time he took a more direct hand in the negotiations. On December 12, 1959, he sent Humphrey what he later described as a "very savage" letter, in which he said:

> To me the situation is very clear. You have the right to take iron ore out of the Province. Others have rights to do the same. The British Newfoundland Corporation has, among other things, the right to develop the hydro resources of Labrador. The Government of Newfoundland regard you and other mining concession holders basically as miners of iron ore. The British Newfoundland Corporation are the chosen instrument of Newfoundland for the development of the hydro resources of Labrador. The position is that the Government see your relationship to the British Newfoundland Corporation as that of a possible customer . . . .
>
> During the long negotiations which have gone on concerning power, considerations other than price have come in. There has been discussion of participation by your company and others in a power development. While the British Newfoundland Corporation, if it wishes, may grant a participation, it is not obliged to do so. The Government of Newfoundland would need to be satisfied that any participation with Brinco did not in any way prejudice the rights of other consumers of power.

There was much more, in the same brusque vein, including a statement that the government intended to see that the province's own hydro resources were developed before admitting any power from outside. Discussing the letter years later, the Premier recalled: "I was rather tigerish in those days. I was so desperately anxious to get development of anything in the province, you see; I felt our backs were to the wall — we were in dire danger of being washed down the drain . . . . And then if the people coming in were to be gigantic corporations, combinations and syndicates — *gigantic* corporations — if I saw any sign that they wanted to throw their weight around, it just made me fiercely resent it . . . ."

Humphrey's resentment when he received the letter was every bit as fierce. Southam was told later that he immediately dictated a furious reply in which, among other things, he accused Smallwood of "South American methods." Apparently, cooler heads within his organization persuaded him not to send it. Smallwood's letter was not in fact acknowledged until December 24, when Humphrey's son "Bud," a vice-president of Hanna, sent the Premier a mild note, explaining that his father had become "slightly indisposed" and "therefore I am taking the liberty of acknowledging your letter." The younger Humphrey said the Hanna group appreciated the Premier's explanation of the government's policy, and, together with Wabush Iron, had presented a new proposal to Brinco "which we feel is fair," and that he understood Brinco was preparing a counter-proposal which, he promised, would be considered "very carefully and promptly."

The new proposal mentioned had originated with Hugh Hilton, chairman of the Steel Company of Canada, one of the Pickands Mather group. Hilton was a friend of Brinco's new chairman, H. Greville Smith, Bertie Gardner having retired soon after the Twin negotiations began because of a combination of advancing years and failing eyesight. Greville Smith, a Yorkshireman with an amiable manner and an engaging smile, had trained as a chemist and been posted by his company to New York in 1929. He moved to Canada in 1932, joined Canadian Industries Limited in Montreal and became its president in 1951. A bachelor with a passion for salmon-fishing and, less usual in an Englishman, baseball, he was on the board of at least a dozen companies, including the Steel Company of Canada.

Hilton's proposal to break the deadlock was that the Iron Ore Company, Wabush Mines and the Hamilton Falls company should become equal partners in the new Twin Falls company, each putting up a third of the equity and each receiving a third of the profits. Greville Smith went to Hamilton shortly before Christmas to discuss this suggestion with Hilton and representatives of Pickands Mather, but discovered that they envisaged a power price of less than $23 per horse power; at that price, Brinco considered, the ore companies would get their power at cost, the Twin Falls company would make no profit, and Brinco would receive no return on its equity. Once again, Brinco put forward a counter-proposal, seeking to retain 50 per cent of the new company and suggesting a higher price for the power. Once again it was rejected.

It may have been mere coincidence — though few thought so — that around this time both the Iron Ore Company and the Pickands Mather group began to experience inexplicable, and irritating, delays in their day-to-day dealings with departments of the Newfoundland government. At any rate, they suddenly agreed to a compromise and on January 22, 1960, Victor Smith returned from Cleveland with a draft agreement to set up the Twin Falls Power Corporation, which was incorporated within a month, on February 18. In return for Brinco's acceptance of the one-third equity principle, Humphrey dropped his demand for participation in the Hamilton Falls company and agreed that Brinco should have voting control of Twin Falls (which was achieved by making the shares issued to the Hamilton Falls company worth four votes each, whereas the ore companies' shares carry only one vote each). It was also agreed that the price to be paid for the power would give all the shareholders a fair return on their investment.

It was decided that the plant should have an initial capacity of 120,000 horse power with provision for later expansion. Its cost was estimated at $30 million. The three partners agreed to put up $2½ million each to make up the required equity of $7½ million, and Brinco had already been assured by its U.S. financial advisers, Morgan Stanley and Company, that there should be no difficulty in borrowing the remaining $22½ million by a bond issue on the U.S. market.

One of the foremost investment-banking firms on Wall Street, Morgan Stanley was founded in 1935 by a group of partners in the famous J. P Morgan company. In essence, investment bankers are marriage brokers, though the partners they bring together are businessmen who need money for development or expansion and those fortunate people — or, more commonly nowadays, companies and institutions — with large amounts of money to invest.

Morgan Stanley had handled the financing for Bowaters' expansion in to the United States in the early fifties, and it was on the recommendation of Sir Eric Bowater that two Morgan Stanley partners, John M. Young and H. Edward Vollmers, had called on Bertie Gardner as early as 1954. At the time of their call, Brinco had not yet received the results of the Hamilton Falls survey, but the project caught the imagination of Ed Vollmers, in particular, since he had trained as an engineer before entering the more rarefied world of finance. Tall and slim, with a deceptively mild manner, Vollmers was tenacious and sometimes blunt in argument.* He was also a master of the fine art of "construction" finance — which can be compared to selling dreams — with a painter's eye for the kind of picture best calculated to pry open an investor's purse. And before the Twin Falls company was even incorporated, he had persuaded Harry Haggerty, head of the investment department at the powerful Metropolitan Life Insurance Company, that it was not only a blue-chip investment but the beginning of something infinitely more exciting.

There is an old saying in the finance business that "there's nothing so nervous as a million dollars." The statement is not entirely accurate, since the degree of nervousness increases as the number of millions multiplies, but it derives from the fact that a lender about to part with money on that scale very reasonably insists on certain safeguards. He demands, for instance, a guarantee that the project he is financing will be successfully completed (even if, as often happens, it swallows up more money than was originally contemplated), and a satisfactory assurance that when completed it will be profitable enough to pay the interest on his money until the loan is repaid.

Eric Bowater once stilled the qualms of a U.S. investor who asked who would guarantee the completion of one of his ventures by raising his right hand and saying magisterially: "I, Eric Bowater, pledge my word." Most investors, however impressed they may be by the potential profitability of a project, prefer their guarantees to be both less flamboyant than that, and more enduring than the spoken word, no matter how grandiloquent its utterance; which is where the lawyers who have been waiting in the wings move out to centre stage.

Once the principals in a deal have arrived at a mutually satisfactory arrangement with the aid of their go-between, the investment banker, the lawyers are called in to translate their handshake into leakproof

*Several times during the Twin Falls negotiations he warned Brinco it was being too generous in its response to George Humphrey, and when told about the one-third equity agreement he protested angrily: "You've given away your birthright . . . when you were in the driver's seat." In fact, however, this arrangement was more favourable to Brinco than some earlier Humphrey proposals which the corporation had come close to accepting.

legal terminology which will take care of every eventuality that can possibly be foreseen; the more resourceful and persistent lawyers attempt to draw up agreements that cover all *unforeseen* eventualities as well, which is naturally more difficult and apt to introduce a certain amount of pernicketiness into the proceedings. But only when the last "i" has been dotted and the last "t" crossed and the investment banker has taken the resultant small library of documents — the "bond offering memorandum" — to a lender, does he part with his money.

It took six months for the three partners to reach the agreement in principle that resulted in the formation of the Twin Falls Power Corporation; the subsequent detailed negotiations and their enshrinement in legal documents occupied almost two years of regular meetings in Cleveland, Montreal and New York which are remembered with a shudder by many of the participants as the most difficult they have ever sat through. With one of the partners an untried, unknown quantity and the other two competing companies, each containing within itself a number of competing companies, this was probably inevitable. But the façade of gentlemanly decorum behind which business in-fighting is usually conducted often came close to crumbling under the stress. And as the wearying months of negotiations dragged on without any sign of agreement, Brinco itself almost crumbled — right into bankruptcy.

For as soon as the Twin Falls company had been incorporated, and without waiting for the financing to be completed, the corporation started work on the project to be sure of meeting the Iron Ore Company's 1962 deadline for power. Immediately the Labrador weather permitted, it began work on the $2 million job of upgrading the access road into the site from the railroad and extending it twelve miles to the Twin Falls construction camp. When the 1960 work season ended, the road was complete; an airstrip had been bulldozed out of the boulder-strewn wilderness; a steel bridge had been built across the Unknown River; and construction of the powerhouse and dams had begun.

By the end of the year, the project had eaten up almost $10 million, and Brinco had put in not only its $2½ million equity but a further $2.3 million obtained by way of a demand note from the Bank of Montreal. Yet still the arguments continued and the final agreement upon which the financing depended seemed as far away as ever.

The guarantee that the Twin Falls project would be successfully completed rested partly on the power contract and partly on the reputation of the partners. Normally, the power contract would have been a comparatively simple matter of a customer agreeing to pay a certain price for a certain quantity of power. But since the customers were also partners in Twin Falls, more interested in getting their power as cheaply as possible than in the supplying company making a profit, months were spent in haggling over how much the power would cost to produce and what sort of a return the Hamilton Falls company should receive for its investment and for managing the project. Shawinigan Engineering had been chosen to built the plant; Humphrey, as distrustful of Brinco as ever, hired Montreal Engineering to check all the estimates and the costs as the project proceeded.

Before the plant could be financed, the "Met," as Metropolitan Life is known on Wall Street, had to be satisfied that Twin Falls would sell enough electricity to make a profit. Brinco accordingly asked the Iron Ore Company and Wabush to enter into a "take-or-pay" contract, meaning that they would pay for all the energy they contracted to take whether or not they actually used it. At first sight, this seems an unlikely concession to extract from a potential buyer. But take-or-pay clauses are a common feature of contracts such as those governing the supply of raw materials and the financing of oil and gas pipelines. They rest on a simple enough principle: If company A erects a facility to meet the needs of company B, then company B cannot turn round after company A has spent all its money and say, "Sorry, fellows, but we're not going to buy your product." From the supplier's point of view, that is only elementary justice. And while the buyer probably recognizes it as such, he is never over-eager to rush into that sort of commitment, and bargaining on take-or-pay clauses tends to be prolonged.

There was still another complication in the Twin Falls negotiations. In the late fifties, and for some time thereafter, there were wide fluctuations in the relative value of the Canadian and U.S. dollars. Some U.S. investors were badly burned when the Canadian dollar, which had been worth more than its U.S. counterpart, suddenly dropped in value — at one time, to as little as 92 cents. And on their part, Canadian companies found it very expensive to buy U.S. dollars to service or repay their debts. Consequently, there was much discussion about the rate of exchange that would apply to the Twin Falls bonds. To make sure it would have enough U.S. currency to service its debt, Brinco asked that part of the power be paid for in U.S. dollars. This was logical enough, since much of the Labrador ore would be sold for U.S. dollars, and the point was eventually agreed, but again not without long debate.

Often, there were five sets of lawyers working on an agreement, representing the Iron Ore Company, Wabush, Twin Falls, Hamilton Falls and the Met. And no sooner would they manage to draft a document acceptable to all than they would get word that the agreement was not going through as planned, and the work would have to start all over again.

On the Brinco side, the brunt of the negotiations was borne by Victor Smith, who had now become a vice-president of Twin Falls as well as a director of Brinco. A pilot in Britain's Fleet Air Arm during the Second World War, Smith had spent two years in a prisoner-of-war camp, and his colleagues often thought he must have preferred it to the two years he spent on the Twin negotiations. At times in the Hanna board room he was treated with such apparent scorn that more than once Pickands Mather representatives "crossed the floor," so to speak, and made common cause with Brinco.

Neither was the skirmishing confined to the various conference rooms in which the meetings were held. Brinco's secretary, C. T. "Bud" Manning, once checked into the Newfoundland Hotel in St. John's and bumped into Charles E. Bodertha, a leading Cleveland lawyer who had been engaged by George Humphrey to protect his interests, which he did so assiduously that someone once said, "Bodertha wants to stand at the control wheel of the dam."

Manning was in St. John's to see the Premier on a matter of key importance to Brinco, so it was with some reluctance that he accepted Bodertha's invitation to dinner that evening. And he was dismayed to find when he arrived in the dining room that he was wedged in among a group of Iron Ore Company representatives at a long table from which there was no escape. Bodertha and his colleagues immediately began to pump him about the reasons for his presence in St. John's. Manning said he was not going to talk business, and if they insisted he would go and eat somewhere else. Nevertheless the probing continued and it was long after midnight before he could get away. During the next few days, he received so many inquiries and telephone calls from Bodertha and his group that he took to eating his meals at a nearby motel.

In retrospect, it seems likely that Bodertha had a shrewd idea of what Manning was doing in St. John's all along: he was there to negotiate a lease not only on the Unknown River, upon which Twin was to be built, but on the whole Upper Hamilton watershed.

Brinco had explained to Joey Smallwood that Twin was really the first stage of the Channel Scheme, and inseparable from it, and Joey had readily agreed that when the time came to grant the lease for the Twin

Falls development he would ensure that it covered the whole area.* Quite apart from the fact that Twin was Brinco's first revenue-producing venture, it thus had an even greater importance to the corporation: it appeared to settle the ownership of the Upper Hamilton beyond any further challenge.

But George Humphrey was not the type of captain to abandon ship. Bodertha was also in St. John's to see Smallwood and he took the opportunity to argue that the Premier was making a serious mistake in linking the Upper Hamilton lease with the Twin development. Though an American, Bodertha appears to have shared the mythical English traveller's belief that if the natives don't understand you first time around you should repeat yourself clearly, and rather more loudly. Natives rarely appreciate this tactic, and Bodertha emerged from Joey Smallwood's office a chastened man. As a good lawyer, though, he continued to watch over his client's interest with a vociferous attention to detail which, while it aroused admiration for his diligence, often offended those across the table from him.

As the negotiations dragged into their second year, the atmosphere of tension around 1980 Sherbrooke Street West mounted steadily, for the company was still pouring money into the project to meet the original deadline. By the time the 1961 work season opened, Brinco's loan from the Bank of Montreal had grown to $5.7 million. And its expenditures rose to more than $1 million a month during the peak summer months. In October, Bill Southam told Joey Smallwood there was "a real risk of bankruptcy" if the financing was delayed much longer. By November, more than $20 million had been spent and Brinco's loan stood at the formidable total of $12½ million. Understandably, the bank, despite its long ties with the corporation, was beginning to make restless inquiries as to

*The "rights" granted to Brinco in its Principal Agreement entitled the corporation only to explore and investigate its various assets and make plans for their development. The government reserved the right to approve plans for any development before taking the further step of granting a lease, thus giving the corporation exclusive control of the asset in question for a stated number of years. Brinco had assigned its Upper Hamilton rights to the Hamilton Falls Power Corporation soon after the new company was incorporated in 1958. The Newfoundland government granted a ninety-nine-year lease on the Upper Hamilton watershed to HFPCo. on March 13, 1961, and HFPCo. assigned a sublease on the Unknown River to Twin Falls Power Corporation on November 15, 1961.

when (and, perhaps more important, how) this money was to be paid back.

That the corporation committed itself so deeply before the financing was assured was justified as a calculated risk, based on the knowledge that the ore companies were going ahead with their mines and had no alternative source of power. But the distinction between a calculated risk and a pure gamble is often a fine one, and Morgan Stanley continually cautioned the corporation against spending so much money before the deal was closed and the Met's $22½ million was available.

After the Twin partners had reached their agreement in principle, Ed Vollmers, who was nearing retirement age, gradually handed over responsibility for shepherding the deal through its later stages to his young assistant, William D. Mulholland, who had joined Morgan Stanley a few years earlier from the Harvard Graduate School of Business Administration and rapidly earned a reputation for shrewdness and hard work. The son of a New York state government official in Albany, Mulholland attended the Christian Brothers Academy there and in 1944, as soon as he was eighteen, volunteered for the U.S. Army, only telling his family after he had enlisted, to forestall his mother's anticipated objection. Despite his youth, he became a company commander in the 342nd Infantry in the Philippines and in a spirit of adventure after the war contemplated accepting a commission in the Chinese Nationalist army — until the U.S. government ruled that anyone doing so would lose his United States citizenship.

Instead, Mulholland returned to the United States and worked as a policeman for several years to pay his way through Harvard. A quirk of fate led him to Wall Street. Originally, he wanted to be a doctor, but his marks in biology, in contrast to his other subjects, were bad. Puzzled, his instructor sat down beside him one day and asked him to describe what he saw on a microscope slide. "Ah, I thought so!" the instructor said when Mulholland complied. "You're colour-blind."

Fortunately, this affliction did not prevent him from distinguishing the colour of the balls on a pool table, for it was his talent with the cue, coupled with the good soldier's instinct for the right moment to press an advantage, which at last broke the Twin Falls log jam. Mulholland and an equally young Montreal lawyer named Jacques Courtois, representing Brinco, were attending yet another drafting session in a Morgan Stanley conference room at Two Wall Street in New York. As the lawyers once again went over the well-thumbed proofs of the final agreement, Mulholland and Courtois suddenly realized that only one or two incon-

112

sequential points remained at issue. Mulholland knew that the deal as it stood was acceptable to the Pickands Mather side, which had by now in effect made common cause with Brinco, and he had good reason to believe it was satisfactory to the Met. It could, he felt, be closed right then were it not for the Iron Ore Company's continued opposition.

But Bodertha was not at the meeting; he was represented by a junior named James E. Courtney. Mulholland knew Courtney was an able lawyer, but he also knew he had no authority to approve the final agreement and would insist on consulting his boss in Cleveland. At best this would mean a further delay, since Bodertha would certainly not approve the documents *in absentia;* at worst, it might mean the loss of an opportunity to clinch the agreement.

Excusing themselves from the meeting, Mulholland and Courtois went upstairs to Mulholland's office and called Greville Smith in Montreal. Having explained the situation, they suggested that the deal as it stood should be put to the Iron Ore Company on a "take it or leave it" basis. Would he authorize them to go ahead and have the agreement printed "for execution," that is, in its final form, on heavy paper, with spaces at the end for the various signatures?

It was hardly the orthodox procedure, and one that Greville Smith knew might provoke an unholy row. But faint-heartedness was not one of Greville Smith's characteristics and he boldly decided to take the chance.

Bill Mulholland then told Vollmers what he proposed to do. "You'll never get away with it," said the astonished Vollmers — and then joined the plot: "Don't tell me any more."

Before returning to the meeting, Mulholland despatched an assistant to the printer's with a spare copy of the agreement bearing the amendments agreed up to that time and instructions that it should be printed for execution at once. Then he and Courtois rejoined the group still minutely examining the phraseology of the agreement in the conference room, occasionally proffering a deferential objection as though they still retained an intense interest in the proceedings.

It is customary after these drafting sessions to repair to the printer's in the evening to have any amendments to the wording which have been agreed that day incorporated into the proofs. Mulholland and Courtois duly accompanied Courtney on this chore and made a show of examining the changes as they came from the printer — nervously aware the whole time of the Morgan Stanley team reading the real proofs in another office down the corridor.

To keep his customers pleasantly occupied while they waited for type to be set and proofs pulled, the printer had thoughtfully installed a pool table in a large room adjoining one of the offices. Fearful that Courtney would notice some of the other activities going on around the shop, Bill Mulholland challenged him to a game, and won handily. Stung, Courtney demanded another game, which Mulholland again won.

His competitive instincts now thoroughly aroused, Courtney challenged Courtois, a sportsman who became better known to the public some years later as president of the Montreal Canadiens. Courtois, too, won his game. And for the rest of the evening, he and Mulholland took turns beating the increasingly frustrated Courtney as the last pages of the final agreement were being printed and proofread.

Inevitably, this improvised security strategy eventually broke down. Courtney emerged from the pool room just as the printer was delivering the bound volumes of the agreement to Mulholland. Outraged, he rushed off to call Bodertha in Cleveland while Mulholland dashed downstairs and briefed a Morgan Stanley man he had waiting outside in a taxi. The taxi whisked the courier off to get the required signatures from two officers of the Met, and then to the station to catch the overnight train to Montreal, where Greville Smith added his signature with some satisfaction the next morning.

Relations between the Pickands Mather group and the Iron Ore Company at that time were strained by a dispute over whether Wabush Mines would be able to use the Iron Ore Company's railroad to Sept-Iles to ship out its ore. John Sherwin, senior partner in Pickands Mather, was in Ottawa putting his case to a hearing of the Board of Transport Commissioners, and had asked that the agreement be taken to Ottawa for him to sign personally, which he did in the hearing room, spreading the papers out on the table in front of the Iron Ore Company representatives with a considerable flourish.

Unwilling to be the last holdout, the Iron Ore Company forgave the *fait accompli* and signed a few days later. Bill Mulholland won a dollar from his boss, Ed Vollmers, who had forecast that his stratagem would never work. And shortly afterwards he was summoned to the office of the senior partner in Morgan Stanley, Henry S. Morgan, who beamed at him happily and invited him to become a partner in the firm.

The Twin Falls financing was closed on December 7, 1961, and the Met handed over its cheque for $15 million, the first instalment of its $22½ million, no doubt to the great relief of the Bank of Montreal. The plant began delivering power six months later, and by that time the operation was such a success that it had already been agreed to double its capacity to provide for the ore companies' expansion, by adding two more units, for which the Met put up a further $20 million. Later still, in 1967, it was decided to add a fifth unit to complete the 300,000 horse power installation.

As a pilot project, Twin Falls was a triumph for Brinco. It demonstrated that large power stations could be built and operated in the severe Labrador climate; it provided a training ground for staff and labour; and it supplied the power for construction of the main Churchill Falls development later.

Above all, it was built on time and within budget, so that, as well as bringing in Brinco's first income, it gave it something more than a paper reputation to take to the lenders when the time came for the infinitely larger Churchill Falls financing. At last, the corporation was no longer "living in a dream."

II
The Politicians

I have never known an important issue in Canadian politics which has not been deeply influenced and sometimes determined in its results by factors of the most purely personal kind.

John W. Dafoe

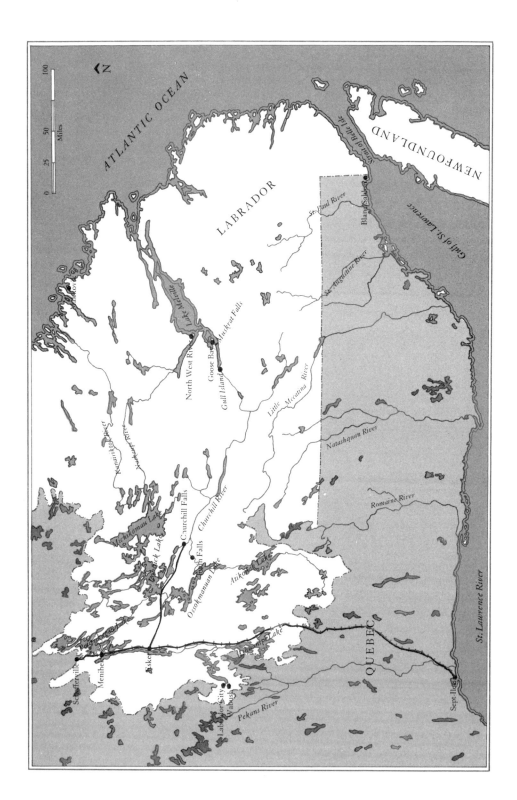

TEN

A billion-dollar real estate proposition

The death of Maurice Duplessis symbolized the end of an era in Quebec. During his sixteen-year domination of the province he had held the Heights of Abraham against a tide of change he seemed unable to recognize, let alone accept. He stood not merely for the hallowed causes of provincial autonomy and the French language, which have always transcended party boundaries in Quebec, but for the preservation of a church-oriented, rural way of life which the growing industrialization of the province and the drift to the cities had already made obsolete.

There were widespread hopes that his successor, Paul Sauvé, who seemed to be more outward-looking and less shackled to a vanished past than Duplessis, would remove the brakes on the province's evolution and introduce the reforms and adjustments needed to make the new society work more efficiently and more equitably. For the past five years Duplessis had refused to discuss Brinco's plans. Sauvé indeed proved more amenable: he received Greville Smith, Bill Southam and Victor Smith six weeks after his appointment. The meeting lasted more than an hour and the conversation ranged over such subjects as federal-provincial tax-sharing arrangements and the development of Quebec's natural resources. The possible development of Hamilton Falls was "mentioned but not detailed," since this was considered to be only a "get-acquainted" call. Sauvé made "a passing reference" to Quebec's traditional objections to the Quebec-Labrador boundary but on the whole, Southam noted afterward, "his attitude to us was very friendly and reflected genuine interest in Brinco's work and plans."

Unfortunately for Brinco's revived hopes, Sauvé died suddenly a couple of months later. He was succeeded by Antonio Barrette, but the loss of two leaders in so short a time caused such an upheaval within the Union Nationale party that the Brinco management decided to delay any further approach to the Premier until after the provincial election it was now obvious must be held soon. Eddy de Rothschild, though — as enthusiastic as ever — remembered his friendly meeting with Barrette

119

earlier and proposed to invite him on a fishing trip to Twin Falls, where the construction work was just getting under way. Bill Southam protested that Joey Smallwood might not like this, since he had not yet been invited to visit the falls himself.

The provincial election of June 22, 1960, made this rather nice point of protocol merely academic: Jean Lesage's Liberals, riding the crest of the new ferment in Quebec, swept the Union Nationale from office, increasing their membership in the House from seventeen to fifty, a clear majority of five over all the other parties.

This appeared to be the best news Brinco had had since its formation. As the minutes of a London Advisory Committee meeting held next day put it: "Mr. Lesage's victory for the Liberal party may well mean a difference in approach by the Quebec authorities to Brinco. Mr. Lesage is well known to be pro-Brinco and keen to develop the Hamilton River for power for Quebec."

The basis for this optimistic assessment was the fact that Lesage, who had left federal politics to lead the Quebec Liberals, had first been briefed on Brinco's plans for Hamilton Falls in April 1954, when he was Minister of Northern Affairs and Natural Resources in Ottawa; he had been kept informed of progress through the years and had appeared to share the general view in federal government circles that the development of the falls was a project of national importance. Also, as a fellow Liberal, he was considered to be a friend of Joey Smallwood; and he had said during his election campaign that if he became premier he would seek negotiations with Newfoundland for the joint development of the falls — a proffered collaboration that Joey immediately said would be "warmly welcome."

The two premiers first discussed the Hamilton when they met during a federal-provincial conference in Ottawa five weeks after Lesage's victory. Both recall that first meeting as a friendly one. Lesage had visited Newfoundland often as a federal minister, had found Joey to be "a very popular chap who knew his way around" and had formed what he later called an "active sympathy" for him. Joey's views were reflected in a remark he made to a reporter: Lesage, he said, was "like a breath of fresh air for Quebec."

Since the conference was held so soon after Lesage's election he had many more pressing matters than the Hamilton on his mind and his talk with Smallwood was "very general." Hydro-Québec's plans for the development of the Manicouagan and Outardes watershed in northeastern Quebec had by this time advanced to the stage at which Lesage felt he was committed to the project. He thought, however, that when it was completed Quebec might want to draw on Labrador for some of its further power requirements and he agreed to meet Joey later to discuss the Hamilton in more detail.

But the iceberg that Maurice Duplessis had charted was still floating about in the sea lanes: a reporter asked Lesage after the meeting if the Quebec-Labrador border would be a problem in the future negotiations. Lesage replied: "There is a problem to be solved."

Just how intractable this problem was to prove during the next few years had not yet become apparent, and Lesage did not mention it when, in response to their request for an interview, he entertained Greville Smith and Bill Southam to lunch at the Windsor Hotel in Montreal on February 18, 1961. In preparation for the meeting, the Brinco staff had updated the various memoranda and aide-memoires prepared through the years to underline the advantages to Quebec of buying Hamilton Falls power.

Estimates of Quebec's future power needs at this time varied, but all of them, in the light of experience during the succeeding ten years, fell short of the rate of growth that actually occurred. Between 1950 and 1960, the consumption of electricity in the province had increased at a compounded yearly rate of a little over 5 per cent. The Gordon Commission forecast in the mid-fifties that the power requirements of Canada as a whole would grow at the rate of about 7 per cent a year between 1955 and 1980. In fact, by 1969 the growth rate had reached almost 8 per cent, which meant that the demand for electric power was doubling every ten years.

Using an ultra-conservative growth-rate estimate of $4\frac{1}{2}$ per cent, Tim Hobson, the Hamilton Falls company's power engineer, calculated that Quebec would face a severe power shortage by 1969, even after the completion of all projects already under way (including the Manic complex) and any new ones that might be undertaken on other undeveloped rivers so far surveyed.

Greville Smith and Southam pointed this out to the Premier and explained the work so far done on the Hamilton project. It could, they said, supply Quebec with four million horse power, beginning in 1965 if a commitment were made early in 1961, at a lower cost than anything Hydro-Québec could provide from projects within the province. Privately, it was felt within Brinco that the price differential would be such that the province would be wise to postpone the Manic development in favour of Hamilton Falls, but Greville Smith and Southam thought it impolitic to mention this to the Premier at their first meeting. Instead, they pointed out that the low cost of the power would enable Hydro-Québec to sell any quantity surplus to the province's needs at a good profit: to Ontario, for instance.*

Among the other advantages of the Hamilton Falls scheme put forward over the lunch table were that, since it would be financed by private capital, Quebec would not have to borrow hundreds of millions of dollars for power development at a time when the government urgently needed money to improve the province's education, health and other social services; it would provide jobs for Quebec workers and opportunities for Quebec suppliers and manufacturers; and it would enable the province to hold other potential sites for economic hydro-electric developments in reserve. Furthermore, an abundant supply of cheap power at tidewater around Sept-Iles could attract new industries to the growing North Shore area of the province. And (perhaps the most compelling argument in the circumstances) the development of Hamilton Falls power for use in Quebec would recognize the geographical facts and override the political boundary that Quebec had traditionally opposed, making the whole area one economic entity.

It was a good case, and Lesage seemed impressed. He said Premier Smallwood had recently assured him that Newfoundland would permit Hamilton Falls power to be exported to Quebec and acknowledged that one reason for his interest in the scheme was that it would relieve his government of a major portion of the heavy capital expenditure it faced. He did not think, however, that Quebec would have any surplus power to export, and he certainly did not favour any plan to "leapfrog" power across the province into Ontario.

He told his guests he had been informed that Manic power could be delivered to Sept-Iles at a cost of four mills per kilowatt-hour, and seemed taken aback that Brinco's estimate for its own power delivered at the provincial boundary was higher than that: 4.6 mills. But he readily

---

*Tommy Hogg, a valued Brinco adviser in the early days, died in 1958 and his successor as chairman of Ontario Hydro, Dr. Richard L. Hearn, replaced him on the Brinco board. Through Hearn, Brinco continued to receive assurances of Ontario Hydro's interest in Hamilton power if it could be brought through Quebec. In the late fifties, the corporation carried out various studies aimed at solving the problem of taking the power from Labrador to the Ontario-Quebec border across high-voltage transmission lines carrying direct current instead of the more common alternating current. Long-distance D.C. transmission, though now more advanced, was then in its early development stages.

122

agreed that such matters should be left to the experts. He suggested that Brinco get in touch immediately with the man he had recently installed as president of Hydro-Québec, Jean-Claude Lessard, a former Ottawa civil servant and vice-president of the St. Lawrence Seaway Authority.

After eight years of alternating hope and disappointment, events now began to move with heartening speed for Brinco. Greville Smith and Southam saw Lessard three days after their lunch with the Premier and put forward their case again. Lessard confessed that he was still unfamiliar with Hydro-Québec and did not understand the technical terminology of the power business. His main interest was economic: would it pay Hydro-Québec to buy Brinco's power? In the hope of finding an answer to that question, he proposed a meeting between his engineers and their Brinco counterparts.

This took place two weeks later. The Hydro-Québec engineers questioned some of Brinco's technical assumptions but seemed satisfied with the answers and quickly passed on to a discussion of costs. Peter Marchant, by now manager of the corporation's water-power division, said Brinco estimated that the first million horse power would cost $235 million delivered at the provincial boundary; the main attraction of the scheme was that succeeding stages would be much cheaper, and the full four million horse power potential would cost less than $500 million. At this stage, Brinco did not attempt to quote a mill rate for the power, but Marchant said it was proposed to finance 70 per cent of the $235 million cost by first mortgage bonds at an interest rate of 5¾ per cent, with the remaining 30 per cent of the cost being equity, on which a return of 6 per cent after tax would be required. On the basis of these figures, and taking into account such factors as depreciation and tax, Hydro-Québec's assistant planning engineer, Ray Hango, did a quick calculation on his notepad and came up with a price for the power of 3.85 mills per kilowatt-hour.

At this time, the Manic scheme was thought to have a potential of eight million horse power, twice the current estimate for Hamilton Falls. But the estimated cost of its development was $2 billion — four times the estimate for the Hamilton. And Dale Farnham, Hydro-Québec's chief engineer, admitted that to take advantage of the full head of one thousand feet between the upper waters of the Manic system and sea level it would be necessary to build several separate developments (ultimately there will be seven), instead of one, as at Hamilton Falls.

It is tempting, if fruitless, to speculate on what might have happened had Brinco not been deterred by the political complications from approaching Hydro-Québec formally at a much earlier stage in its investigation of the Hamilton scheme. Hydro-Québec did not commission its surveys of the Manic system until 1955, by which time Brinco had the first results of the Hamilton surveys. The preliminary construction work at Manic did not begin until the fall of 1959, when Premier Sauvé authorized a start on an access road. And the project was still not committed fully at the time of Brinco's first meeting with Hydro-Québec. In fact, the Brinco deputation thought that Leo Roy, Hydro-Québec's general manager, was considering postponing Manic in favour of the Hamilton.

Roy said the Quebec government would have to decide by April 1 or soon after which power projects should be undertaken in the province. Hydro-Québec had to submit its estimates and recommendations before then, so could Brinco make them a formal offer containing a firm price for the power within the next two weeks?

Faced with this unaccustomed note of urgency, the Brinco staff rose to the occasion and plunged into a round of further talks with the Hydro-Québec engineers and a review of the estimates with Shawinigan Engineering. And on March 23, 1961, the Hamilton Falls Power Corporation sent a two-page letter to Leo Roy offering to make a million horse power available at the provincial border from October 15, 1965, under a twenty-five-year contract. This would be achieved by installing five generator units of 275,000 horse power each — one being a spare to guarantee that the million horse-power output would not be interrupted.

The price suggested was 3.5 mills per kilowatt-hour at the power plant. No estimate was made for transmission costs because it had not yet been decided where Hydro-Québec would take delivery of the power. The letter also offered Hydro-Québec an option on a second million horse power at 2.6 mills per kilowatt-hour.

Brinco's experts considered these attractive prices and settled back to await Quebec's response, reasonably confident that at long last their cherished Channel Scheme was about to get off the drawing boards. But the air of optimistic expectancy around 1980 Sherbrooke Street West was shattered on May 12, when Leo Roy telephoned Phil Gregory, Brinco's power-sales consultant, and told him he was drafting a letter to say that the corporation's offer was not going to be accepted "under present economic conditions." It had created a great deal of interest and he had been instructed to "keep the door open, not to close it entirely."

But the privately owned utilities supplied by Hydro-Québec now seemed to need less power than they had previously estimated (the country had been going through a slowdown in business activity) and Hydro-Québec had decided to meet its forecast requirements by developing the first two and a half million horse power at Manic.

"Is our price too high?" Gregory asked. Roy said it was not. Hydro-Québec's studies had shown that the lower cost of generating Hamilton Falls power compensated for the higher cost entailed in its transmission over a long distance, so that its price in Montreal would be the same as Manic's — and Manic was preferred.

Gregory asked if there was anything Brinco could do to try to change the decision. "Well," replied Roy, "if the government would relieve us of our obligations on the Manicouagan that might make a difference."

Taking this hint, and after consulting Bill Southam, Gregory wrote the same day to George C. Marler, leader of the Quebec Senate and a Liberal party stalwart, in the hope that he would intercede with Lesage to change the decision. After advancing various arguments in favour of the Hamilton over Manic, his letter said there appeared to be two main reasons for Hydro-Québec's refusal of the Brinco offer: its forecast of future power requirements, and its commitment to Manic. Gregory added: "As to the economic forecast, I can only say that from many years' experience I know that, recession or not, the power demand grows steadily. At worst the rate of growth slows down for a year or two . . . . With regard to the commitments of Hydro on the Manicouagan it does seem that the advantages to the government of being able to postpone raising about two hundred million dollars for ten years or so should go a long way to compensate for any embarrassment caused by the delay in building one or even two powerhouses."

Southam also addressed himself to the problem of Hydro-Québec's apparent fear of buying more power than it could use, suggesting in an internal memorandum that any surplus could be sold to Ontario, and adding, in a rather florid foray into backstage diplomacy:

> If Hydro-Québec and/or the government of Quebec shy away from an inter-provincial deal, Mr. Smallwood might be induced to say to Mr. Lesage something like this: "I, the Premier of Newfoundland, am prepared to commit (virtually forever) half of a unique provincial potential for the good of Eastern Canada. I appeal to you, the Premier of Quebec, to share the benefit that will accrue to your province with Ontario and, by strengthening your reputation as a good Canadian, pave the way for your eventual leadership of the National Liberal party." We in Brinco,

whilst falling over backwards to make it Mr. Lesage's project and giving him and Mr. Smallwood all the credit, could on an "old-boy" basis prepare the ground by talking to [Ontario Hydro].

This ingenious strategy does not seem to have been tried, and Gregory's letter to Marler did nothing to change the decision. But Brinco kept on trying. A few weeks later, hearing that Premier Lesage was planning a trip to Sept-Iles and Schefferville, Southam wrote to him inviting him to drop in at the Twin Falls airstrip and see Hamilton Falls for himself. Lesage declined the invitation because, he said, his itinerary was already arranged. Then Southam discovered that he would be travelling in an Iron Ore Company aircraft and called Sept-Iles to see if the program could not be rearranged to permit the Premier an hour or two in Labrador.

The Twin Falls negotiations were still in an acrimonious phase and he was told without ceremony that the Twin airstrip was out of bounds to Iron Ore Company aircraft because the rocks with which it was allegedly strewn were deemed to constitute a serious hazard. Southam put in a hurried call to Twin Falls and all available men were assigned to a clean-up job on the airstrip — at a cost of several thousand dollars. But on the appointed day, even though a Brinco welcoming party was assembled, the plane carrying the Premier flew over without landing.

Brinco was more successful late in July when it managed, with the help of Joey Smallwood, to arrange a visit to the Falls by a man who was rapidly emerging as the most influential figure in the Lesage government: René Lévesque. As a popular television commentator whose expressive shrug and tense, fugitive smile were familiar to English as well as French Quebecers, Lévesque had helped Lesage to win the election and had been entrusted with two portfolios, those of Public Works and Hydraulic Resources. In both he faced a massive job of cleaning up the aftermath of the previous government's discredited system of distributing construction contracts. Hydro-Québec in those days had been powerless to resist political influence in its letting of contracts and it was thanks to Lévesque and the changes he made that it began to exert its own control and establish its present international reputation for efficiency and innovation.

Lévesque had been interested in the economics of the power industry since his school days in the Gaspé peninsula, when he had supported a group of nationalists, L'Action Liberale Nationale, which broke away from the prewar Liberal government with publicly owned power as one of the planks in its platform. He had not yet put forward his policy of nationalization of the private power companies or openly espoused separatism, but he had announced soon after the government took office that private companies would not in future be permitted to expand their operations.

While it did not promise to be an easy task, Bill Southam realized Brinco must try to win Lévesque's confidence. On a visit to St. John's, he told Smallwood of the unsuccessful attempt to show Lesage the falls and added that Lévesque, too, was now about to make a flying visit to the Sept-Iles—Schefferville area as guest of the Iron Ore Company. Joey immediately picked up the phone, called Lévesque in Quebec City and in his easy, bantering way invited him to take the opportunity to see the falls as a guest of the Newfoundland government. "Sure, Joey," Lévesque replied, "if you want me to make like a tourist in your province, I don't mind."

Smallwood assigned Gordon Pushie to constitute a one-man welcoming committee and on the Saturday morning that Lévesque was expected he was waiting at Twin Falls. Once again, the Iron Ore Company seemed reluctant to include Twin on the itinerary and Pushie tried vainly in telephone calls to its office at Sept-Iles to discover what time the Minister was due. At lunch, he heard a plane fly over and realized with a sinking feeling that it was coming in to land and he, the official welcoming committee, was twenty minutes away from the airstrip. Luckily, however, Roy Cavender, manager of the guest house Brinco had by now built at Hamilton Falls, happened to be passing the airstrip when Lévesque arrived and with commendable presence of mind appointed himself official greeter and drove him to Twin.

After he had taken a look around Twin, Lévesque seemed reluctant to accompany Pushie to Hamilton Falls, perhaps because Earl Farnam, his Iron Ore Company host, kept looking at his watch and reminding him they were due in Schefferville at 2 p.m. But when Pushie exercised his reportorial initiative and "borrowed" a helicopter owned by one of the Twin contractors, he agreed to make the trip. The helicopter landed them on the "grassy meadow" opposite the falls and Lévesque spent some time admiring McLean's "mighty cataract" before they strolled down the path to the Brinco guest house, a modest cabin with camp cots and grey blankets in fishing-camp style.

There, in an atmosphere lightened by suitable refreshments — the manager's report afterwards said "Quebec government officials apparently have a preference for gin" — Tim Hobson explained the Hamilton project to Lévesque and his party with the aid of maps and engineering drawings he had pinned up on the walls the night before. Lévesque seemed interested, and despite continual reminders about the welcoming party waiting at Schefferville, insisted on hearing all of Hobson's presentation, occasionally stepping outside the cabin to gaze at the river gorge and the cloud of spray rising above the falls. When he finally took his leave, in great good humour, it was already past four o'clock.

The Brinco party considered he had been impressed with both the efficiency of the Twin Falls construction job and the possibilities of the Hamilton, and Lévesque confirmed this to the author years later. "You could see at once . . . , " he said, reaching in the air for a suitable phrase and coming down with ". . . the awe-ful potential." He went on: "It stared you in the face that it was one of the most incredibly feasible sites in the world. In a sense it would have been criminal not to have developed it. But the question was: was it compatible with Hydro's own development? Could it be dovetailed with our own potential and would it be a paying proposition for Quebec?"

There was, of course, that other big question, and he had lost no time raising it back in 1961, when he returned from his inspection of the north country. Uncertainty over the Labrador border, he told reporters, was stalling the development of a large section of Quebec territory rich in iron, copper, zinc and nickel, and the border should be re-negotiated. "These lines are idiotic," he said, "and have never been recognized by anyone. It's time Quebec and Newfoundland stopped gazing at each other across the frontier like a couple of porcelain dogs. This problem must be settled once and for all and the first move would seem to be for the two interested parties to get together."

Joey Smallwood for once had no comment to make to reporters. But unknown to the outside world, he and Jean Lesage had already discussed these "idiotic" lines at some length and were at that moment considering a solution to the problem which, had it been agreed, would not only have made headlines but might have raised some thorny constitutional questions for Ottawa — the proposal being that Newfoundland should sell the whole of Labrador to Quebec, for no less than a billion dollars.

ELEVEN

London looks around for a "big brother"

The dispute over the boundary between Quebec and Labrador, and the bitter emotions it aroused on both sides, can be traced back to the early days of the rivalry between France and England for supremacy in North America. The French, Portuguese and Spanish fishermen who were already sharing the Newfoundland cod grounds with the English in 1583, when Sir Humphrey Gilbert claimed possession of the island for Elizabeth I, appeared to take English sovereignty for granted. But in 1662, possibly by secret agreement between Charles II and Louis XIV, a French force fortified Placentia, on the southeast coast of Newfoundland, and laid claim to the southern, western and northern coasts of the island. Four years later, d'Iberville captured and destroyed St. John's, and though he later withdrew, the city was raided by French forces again in 1705 and 1708.

The Treaty of Utrecht in 1713 declared Newfoundland to be the property of the English crown but also granted France fishing rights along a large part of the island's north and west shores, from which the French immediately ejected British settlers.

In 1762, another French force captured St. John's and though it was soon expelled again by the English, the Treaty of Paris in 1763 confirmed France's fishing rights on the "French Shore," as it came to be known. And for more than a century British ships made sure that no Newfoundlander encroached on French rights, a strange situation which understandably created great bitterness among the settlers.

The Treaty of Paris also recognized British possession of the whole of Canada, including Quebec. Newfoundland's jurisdiction was to include "all the coast of Labrador from the entrance of Hudson Straits to the St. John's river, which discharges itself into the sea nearly opposite the west end of the island of Anticosti . . . ." Quebec complained that this took in an area along the north shore of the Gulf of St. Lawrence which had been considered part of Quebec and settled, if sparsely, by French fishermen whose operations would now be subjected to "regulations inconsistent with the nature of such fisheries." The point was accepted and in 1774 the "coast" of Labrador was annexed to Quebec.

Since Quebec was not interested in the cod fisheries off the east coast of Labrador, which had now begun to be settled by British and Newfoundland fishermen, and in any case was unable to administer them because of their remoteness from Quebec City, this decision was soon considered to have been a blunder and the "coast" changed hands again, being returned to Newfoundland by the Newfoundland Act of 1809.

In response to renewed Quebec protests against the adverse effect of this ruling on its fisheries, the British North America Act of 1825 attempted to solve the problem by separating the Quebec fisheries from the rest of the "coast." A line was drawn northward from Blanc Sablon, at the western end of the Strait of Belle Isle, to the 52nd parallel, and the strip of land west of Blanc Sablon and south of the parallel was incorporated into Quebec.

No doubt because Labrador was not yet even explored, let alone occupied, nothing was said about the inland border between eastern Quebec and western Labrador. Quebec assumed that "coast" meant a strip of land following the shoreline and extending a mile inland, which would have placed the eastern border of Quebec (and hence, also, of Canada) just a mile from the Atlantic. Newfoundland contended that "coast" meant all the land north of the 52nd parallel and inland from the Atlantic as far as the height of land separating those rivers draining into the Atlantic from those flowing west through Quebec. This not only made for an extremely sinuous border line but placed the western extremity of Labrador more than four hundred miles inland from the ocean.

Since John McLean had yet to begin his travels through the interior of Labrador, the problem was not an immediate one and the 1825 ruling seems to have solved it temporarily. It did not surface again until the turn of the century, and one wonders whether Low's discovery of iron ore near the Hamilton a few years earlier had anything to do with the timing of its re-emergence.

At any rate, on December 5, 1902, the Deputy Minister of Lands, Mines and Fisheries of Quebec, J. E. Taché, penned a stern letter to Mr. Alfred Dickie in Lower Stewiacke, Nova Scotia — that same Mr. Dickie whose Grand River Pulp and Paper Company had been granted the rights to Muskrat Falls which Bertie Gardner bought from the Royal Bank so many years later. Referring to Dickie's concession from the Newfoundland government to cut timber in the neighbourhood of Lake Melville, near the Atlantic coast, Taché pointed out that "all the territory south of River Hamilton belongs to the Province of Quebec" and "any timber cut upon said territory without a license from this Department should therefore be considered as cut in violation of the law."

Dickie's reply said he was surprised to hear of Quebec's claim and protested that he was certainly "not stealing anything." The Quebec government, he suggested, should take up the matter with the Newfoundland government. Instead, Quebec took it up with Ottawa, where the federal Minister of Justice concluded that "even upon an interpretation of the legislation most favourable to the Colony of Newfoundland, nothing can be included within the Newfoundland Labrador but coast and islands . . . and 'coast' cannot be possibly so interpreted as to include the territory through which the Hamilton river flows . . . ."

Canada thereupon referred the question to the Secretary of State for the Colonies in London, Joseph Chamberlain, who in turn referred it to Newfoundland which, as was to be expected, rejected Quebec's claim. In 1904, Ottawa once again wrote to London, forwarding Quebec's request that the matter be adjudicated by the Judicial Committee of the Privy Council. London agreed that this seemed to be the best course but the mills of bureaucracy evidently ground even more slowly in those days than now: many years went by before the parties could agree on the precise wording of the question which should be put to the Privy Council.

Before the issue went to their Lordships, Quebec and Newfoundland made a last attempt to settle it between themselves; in December 1924, delegations led by the Newfoundland Prime Minister, Walter S. Monroe, and his Quebec counterpart, Alexandre Taschereau, sat down to talk things over in Montreal. The Newfoundland ministers, as chronically short of funds as ever, had been wondering whether they could not only save the heavy cost of the litigation but at the same time solve their financial problems by selling Labrador to Quebec. A figure of $110 million had been mentioned unofficially: $100 million for Newfoundland and the rest to satisfy the claims of any entrepreneurs who might find concessions granted to them by Newfoundland wiped out by the new dispensation.

In the event, Monroe named a much lower figure — only $30 million — but there was no serious discussion of the price, the talks apparently foundering on Taschereau's insistence that any settlement must resolve all dispute by extending Quebec's sovereignty right to the Atlantic. Monroe countered in a letter shortly after his return to St. John's that Newfoundland could not accept this condition without a firm guarantee that Newfoundlanders would continue to enjoy their traditional fishing rights, including that of landing on the coast to cut wood. Taschereau replied that he thought this question could be settled satisfactorily, but he seems not to have taken the suggested price seriously, since he asked if Monroe could inform him, "even in a very confidential way," of the minimum price he would accept for the territory.

Monroe wrote reaffirming the $30 million figure, which was what he would ask "if the property belonged to me personally." He added: "It is, of course, like selling 'a pig in a bag,' for we none of us know the true value of this great area." Quite obviously, Taschereau didn't. His letter rejecting the offer crossed another from Monroe bringing it down to $15 million, which Taschereau still considered "excessive." There was nothing more for it but to let the Privy Council decide.

The case was heard in 1926. The question it had finally been agreed should be considered was: "What is the location and definition of the boundary between Canada and Newfoundland in the Labrador Peninsula under the Statutes, Orders-in-Council and Proclamations?" Newfoundland was represented by a battery of legal luminaries led by the eminent Sir John Simon, K.C. The case for Canada, and thus Quebec, was put by a Scot, H. P. MacMillan, K.C., leading a team which included a distinguished Quebec lawyer, Aimé Geoffrion. The documentary evidence alone ran to eight printed volumes totalling several thousand pages and two atlases containing more than fifty maps each; and the oral submissions lasted four weeks.

Newfoundland claimed that the effect of all the various decrees concerned with Labrador through the years had been to give Newfoundland jurisdiction over the interior. Sir John Simon cited references going back to biblical times to bolster his contention that the term "coast" should be interpreted to mean a territory or country, as in the Gold Coast or the Coast of Coromandel. In essence, Canada claimed that "coast" meant no more than what ordinary people would take it to mean — in other words, the shoreline.

On March 1, 1927, the Privy Council ruled in favour of Newfoundland, holding that the boundary followed the 52nd parallel westward from a point north of Blanc Sablon to the Romaine River, which rises in Labrador and flows south through Quebec to the St. Lawrence; from there northward, along the west bank of the Romaine to its source; and from there west and north along the crest of the height of land separating those rivers which flow west and those that drain east into the Atlantic, all the way up to Cape Chidley, on the east side of Ungava Bay.

The effect of this tortuous line, which to this day has not been properly surveyed, was to make the whole Hamilton watershed, and its rich iron deposits, appear on the map like a huge bulge into Quebec territory, and Quebec was furious. Charles Lanctot, the province's Deputy Attorney General, said next day that "the Privy Council has sacrificed Quebec territory to important British interests," and successive governments refused to accept the decision as final. For years, maps in Quebec government departments showed Labrador as part of Quebec, with footnotes saying, "The frontier is not indicated, for good reason." From time to time attempts were made to reopen the issue; a motion for "the return of Labrador to Quebec" created great enthusiasm in the Quebec Legislative Assembly in 1943 and the matter was again raised with Ottawa.

Two of the main objections to the decision, which were still being voiced forty years later, were: that the wording of the question the Privy Council was asked to answer virtually conceded the case to Newfoundland, since it implied that there was in fact a boundary to be delineated when actually Quebec claimed its rights extended all the way to the Atlantic; and that two of the five judges who sat on the case should have been disqualified because they had a vested interest in its outcome as ministers of the British government, which had a financial stake in Newfoundland. As late as 1968, a Quebec writer named Roger Bedard alleged in a series of articles carried by the Montreal newspaper *Le Devoir* and later published as a book that "Justice was only blind in one eye in the Labrador case: the other remained firmly fixed on British interests."

Soon after the controversial decision was handed down, Canada had another opportunity to solve the problem by buying Labrador. In 1931, the Newfoundland Prime Minister, Sir Richard Squires, sent a deputation to Ottawa offering to sell the whole territory if Canada would pay off Newfoundland's national debt of $87 million, make a further payment of $13 million direct to the Newfoundland government, and set aside $10 million to settle any claims by concessionaires dispossessed by the transfer of the territory to Canada — a total price of $110 million.

R. B. Bennett, the Canadian Prime Minister, wrote to Squires on October 14, 1931, saying: "I regret, under present economic and financial conditions, it is not feasible for us to favourably consider your proposal. If circumstances were more propitious a committee of the Cabinet would have been appointed to consider the whole situation, but until there is a general improvement in world conditions no good purpose would be served by considering in detail a proposal which we are not prepared to accept in principle."

The admission of Newfoundland to Confederation in 1949 might have been thought to constitute legal recognition by Canada of the 1927 boundary but, like so many of his compatriots, Premier Duplessis could not bear to give up Quebec's claim. When Joey Smallwood was in London for the coronation of Queen Elizabeth II in 1953 he met Onesime Gagnon, Quebec's Finance Minister, who told him Duplessis wished to discuss the border question. After his return to Canada, Smallwood told Bill Southam about this approach and said he thought Duplessis's intention was merely to straighten out the difficult contours on the frontier; he did not consider there was any intention of encroaching on Labrador and so he had written to the Quebec Premier agreeing to a meeting and asking him to suggest a suitable time and place.

Duplessis's reply was non-committal and Smallwood heard no more for three years. By this time it was clear that Quebec's objection to the boundary was one of the roadblocks in the way of the Hamilton Falls development, so on December 13, 1956, Smallwood wrote to Duplessis again, suggesting that a dinner he was about to attend in Quebec City in honour of the Prime Minister, Louis St. Laurent, would give them a chance to meet and discuss the border question without attracting undue attention. In a move that was by no means general practice in Canada then, he took the trouble to have his letter translated into French by a Memorial University professor, and he closed it with a rather flowery effusion: "I hope that this finds you in good health, and I assure you of my cordial goodwill toward so great and colorful a Canadian statesman whom it has been my privilege to meet on a number of occasions."*

*This passage rebounded on the Premier in 1962. The Progressive Conservative party had nominated a catering supervisor named Wolfred Nelson for a Labrador riding in a pending federal election. Joey promptly condemned the nomination as "a scandalous piece of conduct" because, he alleged, Nelson, who came from Quebec, had worked for Duplessis's Union Nationale, "the most infamously corrupt political machine to exist anywhere in the world since the days of Boss Tweed and Tammany Hall." Nelson responded by appearing on a television program, denying he had ever worked for the Duplessis machine and holding up for the cameras a photostatic copy of Joey's letter and its fulsome last pharagraph. The Premier had to publish the letter, saying he had been "trying to protect Newfoundland's interests with one of the most colorful, but at the same time, difficult, political personalities that Canada has ever seen." Some might call his letter "soapy" but "dealing with Mr. Duplessis was always like walking on egg-shells."

The two premiers duly met in Duplessis's suite in the Château Frontenac in February 1957, and Joey told Southam afterward that Duplessis had been "charming and friendly" and had regretted Taschereau's failure to buy Labrador when he had the chance. The meeting ended with them each agreeing to nominate a trusted official to hold preliminary discussions on how the exact location of the border might be established. On his return to St. John's, Smallwood twice wrote proposing his Deputy Minister of Mines, Fred Gover, as his nominee, but he heard no more from Duplessis and Gover never went to Quebec.

Against this background, Smallwood was not surprised when Jean Lesage appeared to seize on the Hamilton Falls project as an opportunity to settle the boundary dispute. And while there was ample precedent for the idea of resolving the issue by the sale of Labrador to Quebec, it is not clear how the proposal arose on this occasion. In conversations with the author, Lesage recalled that he himself brought it up; René Lévesque said he was "one of those who raised the delicacy of the thing being in Labrador" and had suggested "Why don't we buy the whole thing from them?"; and Smallwood thought he might have said something like, "Jean, instead of our going on about that boundary thing forever, why don't you buy Labrador from us — we'll sell it to you at a bargain."

Smallwood now denies that he made the offer seriously: "It was from the lips out, with me." Lesage recalls that when he first made the proposal he was "half-joking," but that it was later discussed seriously. Lévesque recalls feeling that while the sale might have been possible before the iron-ore development in Labrador and the full appreciation of Hamilton Falls' potential, it was doubtful that it was a serious proposition in 1961.

However the proposal arose, Smallwood and Lesage discussed the possible sale on several occasions during the summer of 1961. It was considered at three private talks they had when both were in Charlottetown in August for a federal-provincial conference, and Lesage recalls discussing "ways and means by which it might be done" at a meeting in the Queen Elizabeth Hotel in Montreal. And each mentioned the idea to others, apparently seriously.

Smallwood also discussed it in a telephone call to René Lévesque from his office in St. John's on July 20, in the presence of Bill Southam. From the memorandum Southam wrote later, it is plain that postwar inflation had taken its toll: "A figure of $1 billion was mentioned as the price for Labrador, payment to be spread over 100 years, an arrangement that Mr.

Smallwood told me afterwards should bring a minimum of $30 million to Newfoundland annually. Replying to Mr. Lévesque's questions, Mr. Smallwood described his offer not as firm but as quite serious. Replying to mine, he implied that it was as good a way as any to interest Mr. Lévesque and could in any case be a thought worth pursuing."

Southam noted that one reason Smallwood gave Lévesque for selling Labrador was that it was beyond Newfoundland's resources to develop such a large area. He also said Newfoundlanders showed no interest in working in the interior of Labrador,* and that it would benefit Canada if Labrador were developed and colonized by Quebecers, who had a flair for taming the wilderness. Lévesque voiced a reservation at this, saying Quebecers, too, liked to get home to their families.

Southam was in St. John's again on August 30 and this time Smallwood told him he had discussed the proposed sale with members of his cabinet, who had strongly opposed it. In Southam's presence again, the premier called Lesage and told him he could not go through with the deal. Lesage agreed that it was probably "politically impossible." Instead, Joey suggested ,"two of Canada's Liberal provinces should collaborate to develop Labrador," beginning with the development of Hamilton Falls. According to Smallwood, Lesage liked this idea.

After a few questions about the kind of collaboration Joey had in mind — a tentative suggestion was a new company with its equity divided equally between Brinco and Hydro-Québec — Lesage promised to give the proposal "serious and immediate consideration" and to get in touch with Joey again.

At a lunch meeting with the Premier a few days earlier, Greville Smith had been pleased to see that Lesage showed goodwill toward Brinco. But the Premier's contention that power from the Hamilton would be much more expensive than that from Manic (7 mills as against 4.25 mills) both surprised and puzzled him. It is still a mystery why Hydro-Québec's initial estimate of the cost of Hamilton power was so wide of the mark. Greville Smith could only assume that the Quebec calculations had been

*The labour turnover on Labrador construction jobs, at least in the early days, was high, some Newfoundlanders being accustomed to taking time off from their jobs for such traditional activities as cutting wood for the winter and providing their families with food by hunting and fishing. Smallwood lamented this tendency several times. Once, in the hearing of the author, he complained that workers in Labrador had "a deep-seated conviction that they are heroes," and despite the fact that they were given good pay and conditions, "They think you should elevate them to the peerage — to the peerage."

136

founded on "an altogether excessive duplication of the facilities for transmission or in write-off over a relatively (and unnecessarily) short period." Whatever the reason, the Hydro-Québec estimate was more than double the eventual price of the Hamilton power, even though construction costs at that time were far lower than when the plant was ultimately built; and it would be five more years before Brinco could convince Quebec that power from Hamilton Falls was an unrivalled bargain.

Lesage's host at this lunch was an old friend from his days in Ottawa, Robert H. Winters, who had been a rising young minister until the wrath of John Diefenbaker had wrought the destruction of the Liberal government in 1957. Winters had then returned to the business world and had been asked to take an interest in Brinco by virtue of his position as president of Rio Algom Mines, Rio Tinto's Canadian subsidiary.

By 1961, the London shareholders had become more concerned than ever at the stalemate in Brinco's affairs. Greville Smith having let it be known privately that he doubted Brinco's ability to raise the money and carry out the Hamilton Falls project alone, the shareholders had been casting around for a "big brother" for the corporation, some company with a more substantial organization and reputation which could not only provide efficient management for the eventual construction job but whose name would inspire confidence in potential investors.

Both Eric Bowater and Val Duncan had been approached to take Brinco under their wings and occasionally over a friendly dinner each would deferentially try to persuade the other to shoulder the responsibility. Bowater was already past the age at which most men retire, and had in fact only another year to live. Duncan was much younger and his rapid worldwide expansion of Rio Tinto was becoming one of the City of London's golden success stories. His Canadian activities had also marked him out as a man to watch on this side of the Atlantic. Starting out with a small exploration company in 1953, he later bought the rich uranium properties owned by the Toronto and New York financier Joseph Hirshhorn, and by 1959 had built Rio's Canadian subsidiary into the largest single producer of uranium in North America.

At a meeting of Brinco's executive committee on June 28, 1961, Duncan said that while it had not been his idea that Rio Tinto should take a hand in the development of the Hamilton Falls Power Corporation, if invited to do so he would be "very willing" to consider "whether we could play a useful role." He had been warned that Bill Southam and at least one of the other directors might be "rather antipathetic" to this idea, but the meeting welcomed his offer. In a note dictated afterward, he said:

"I made a point of spending an hour or so after the meeting with Bill Southam thinking out loud with him. I think he and the others will probably go along with the idea that Rio Tinto should be the project managers, with almost certainly Shawinigan as the design and consulting engineers, for the Channel Scheme."

This would involve Rio in overseeing all aspects of the project — including not only its actual construction but its costs, the preparation of documents for the finance houses, the terms for Shawinigan's services and the calling of tenders from manufacturers and contractors — in return for a fee which would probably be a percentage of the total cost. But Duncan assured Southam that "if Rio Tinto became project managers then in my view Mr. Winters would naturally give prior consideration to taking over any of the Brinco employees who were regarded by us as suitable for the job."

The note continued: "I think everyone would go along with the idea that Rio Tinto should back its judgment on this project by taking substantial equity participation, and if the profits are good in prospect I think we could contemplate this with equanimity for this project is big league business, the biggest in Canada — like a mine with inexhaustible resources."

At this stage, Duncan seems not to have been prepared for an idea which, while it did not come up at the executive committee meeting, had been mentioned to him privately the previous evening. Hilary Scott, who was in Montreal for a meeting of the board of directors, threw out the suggestion that Rio Tinto might take over Brinco, and asked Duncan for his views. "I replied that my mind had not previously run on the idea of making a takeover bid for our friends and that therefore my reply would be very much off the cuff. I then said that if everybody felt it a good idea we should certainly examine the possibility . . . ." That, however, was to be a matter for the future.

When he returned to London, Duncan wrote to Winters asking him to arrange a meeting with Greville Smith and have some of his senior staff check the work and estimates already done on the Hamilton Falls scheme, without mentioning at this stage the prospect of Rio eventually becoming project managers. After meeting Greville Smith and familiarizing himself with the project, Winters wrote to Lesage and invited him to lunch.

Tall, athletic and invariably tanned, Bob Winters was the sort of man who dominated any room he entered. The son of a Lunenberg fishing captain, he had a career that almost carried him to the Prime Minister's office. After taking his B.A. at Mt. Allison University, he waited on tables to pay his way through the Massachusetts Institute of Technology, where he earned an M.Sc. in the communications branch of electrical engineering. He joined Northern Electric in Montreal in 1934 and at the end of the Second World War was a lieutenant-colonel in the Royal Canadian Electrical and Mechanical Engineers. He won the Lunenburg seat in the federal election of 1945 and soon came under the approving eye of C. D. Howe. He was made Minister of Reconstruction and Supply in 1948 and was Minister of Public Works when the Liberals were defeated in 1957. Howe wanted him to stay on in opposition but Winters preferred Val Duncan's offer to head Rio's activities in Canada. By 1961, he was not only president of Rio Algom but a director of numerous other companies and the personification of a dynamic business leader. While he had a reputation for picking bright young subordinates and giving them their heads, he was often preoccupied and aloof with those who worked for him. But no one questioned his almost strait-laced integrity and his burning energy. As one of his associates put it: "Bob was blessed with an excellent set of glands."

Fortuitously, he also had two other assets which he and everyone else thought fitted him to be the "honest broker" for the Hamilton Falls project: through the years in Ottawa he had become friendly with Joey Smallwood, who once said of him wistfully: "Most men respect a big-built man"; also he had entered Parliament on the same day as Jean Lesage and matched steps with him up the political ladder. The next few years, however, were to test these friendships sorely.

TWELVE

A buyer enters the field

Smallwood and Lesage met again on December 19, 1961, in a room at the Château Frontenac hotel in Quebec City. The idea of the sale of Labrador to Quebec was now dead, but they discussed, in general terms, the suggestion that the two provinces should collaborate on the development of Hamilton Falls. It is almost certain, though neither now remembers this meeting in detail, that they also returned to the question of adequately delineating the border, if not actually adjusting it by an exchange of territory, since both premiers agree in retrospect that in the early days of their talks there was a proposal that Newfoundland should receive a piece of Quebec territory in the north, near Schefferville, in return for granting Quebec an area of similar size in the south. At this stage, the proposal was still only a vague one; it became more specific later.

Joey told Southam his meeting with Lesage was "most useful." Lesage also seemed satisfied with its outcome because he suggested that Brinco should reopen its discussions with Hydro-Québec. He appears to have believed at this time that Smallwood had agreed, at least in principle, that Hydro-Québec should acquire 50 per cent of the Hamilton Falls rights and form a joint company, perhaps with Brinco, to carry out the project. But Joey in later years likened the idea of a partnership between Quebec and Newfoundland to a union between "one elephant — one rabbit." He told the author: "Our blood would turn cold at the thought of finding ourselves in partnership with Quebec. It was unthinkable — we would have been eaten alive."

Nevertheless, Brinco believed it was Joey's proposal, and that the premiers were in agreement on it. In a letter to Eddy de Rothschild, Greville Smith said: "I have grave doubts of the practicability of Mr. Smallwood's ideas — sound though they may be — on a joint development . . . ." And an internal memorandum considering how the proposal might be translated into practice began: "The implication of the Lesage-Smallwood agreement is that 50 per cent of the Hamilton Falls rights will have to be made over to Quebec . . ."

The problem was a complicated one. Brinco doubted whether Hamilton Falls Power Corporation and Hydro-Québec could join forces on the project, since Hamilton Falls would be subject to federal corporation tax and Hydro-Québec, as a provincially owned agency, would not. In that case, would a new partnership have to be formed, and would Hamilton Falls be included in it? Or would the partnership have to be between Hydro-Québec and some similar agency owned by the Newfoundland government? In that case, would Brinco be compensated for the millions of dollars it had already spent — and if so, by whom? At the very least (since the corporation was unaware of the misunderstanding at the political level) it seemed definite that Brinco was about to lose half its main asset. All in all, it was not an enticing prospect.

Since neither Bob Winters, who had now joined the board of directors, nor anyone else could discover just what the premiers had in mind, Bill Southam resolved to sound out René Lévesque. He had seen Lévesque the previous November for the first time and had come away with the impression, less than accurate as it turned out, that he was in favour of the Hamilton project, no doubt partly as a result of his visit to the falls. Now Southam wrote to him saying that before Brinco followed up the Premier's invitation to resume the talks with Hydro-Québec, "you might like to see one of us first."

Lévesque's reply was brief and distinctly cool: "We do indeed hope to have something to discuss in the not too distant future. Depending   on quite a few factors, however. May I ask you to be as patient as we are!"

A few days later Lévesque sent a chill through the Montreal business world with a speech to the Electrical Club of Montreal in which he urged nationalization of the province's private power industry because it was "chaotic, aberrant, wasteful and uneconomic." Hydro-Québec, he claimed, was the only organization that could "bring order into the present mess." His audience (or at least the goodly portion of it employed in some capacity in that "mess") listened with mounting misgivings as he continued: "Some who are attracted to Adam Smith principles or to Victorian beliefs may cry that this may bring socialism or even communism. However, let me proclaim again my deep faith that there is ample room in our spacious economy for both private and public enterprise. Each can do some jobs better than the other, but electricity is one where the state can obviously do better than the other, which has had its opportunities to prove itself but has failed."

With his sights set on this objective, it was clear that Lévesque would henceforth have little aid or comfort to offer Brinco. He admitted as much when he finally did grant Southam an interview some months later. He was determined to nationalize Shawinigan Water and Power, he said, and it was thus impossible for either the government or Hydro-Québec to negotiate in the interim with a company that was partly owned by Shawinigan. Southam objected that Brinco's partner in the Hamilton Falls Power Corporation was Shawinigan Engineering, not Shawinigan Water and Power. Lévesque shrugged and said the public was hardly likely to draw such fine distinctions.

Southam also went to see Jean-Claude Lessard in the large new building recently erected for Hydro-Québec on Dorchester Boulevard. Lessard accepted his compliments on his new quarters gracefully but had little encouragement for him. Mr. Lesage, he said, had many more important problems on his plate than power developments. At the technical level, obviously, Brinco was making no more headway than a ship in dry dock.

But the Quebec cabinet was far from unanimous on the nationalization issue and Lesage kept the Hamilton Falls pot boiling at the political level. He invited Smallwood to join him in Bermuda, where he was planning an Easter holiday, for a weekend of private talks. Southam, reporting this projected meeting in a letter to Bob Winters, said Smallwood had told him "recent telephone calls between the two premiers had indicated that Mr. Lesage might be ready to clinch simultaneously two outstanding matters: the Quebec-Labrador boundary and an inter-provincial development of the Channel Scheme. Mr. Smallwood hoped to be able to make enough concessions within the 'height of land' definition of the boundary to meet Mr. Lesage's political needs."

At the last moment, Joey cancelled his trip, saying he had to remain in Newfoundland to welcome the electioneering leader of the federal opposition, Lester B. Pearson. The meeting was rearranged for May 21 in Quebec City, and judging from subsequent developments both premiers this time believed they had reached agreement. No formal statement was issued but Joey was expansive with reporters afterward. Quebec and Newfoundland, he said, "could very well be the first link in a cross-Canada power grid,"* and "the highest ambition of Newfoundlanders is

*The idea of a national power grid linking all provinces was being pushed by the Progressive Conservative government early in 1962. "I can visualize," said Prime Minister Diefenbaker, "a national energy grid anchored at one end on the Hamilton River in Newfoundland and at the other by the Columbia and the Taku." Brinco welcomed the proposal as another factor in the Hamilton's favour but the idea was ahead of its time. Lesage turned it down; power, he said, was a provincial responsibility.

to be partners with Quebec." The Brinco site was "ready for commencement, whoever carries it out" — a statement that can hardly have aroused great enthusiasm within Brinco, though he did once again refer to the corporation as his "chosen instrument."

Lesage was certainly under the impression an agreement had been reached. Three days after his meeting with Smallwood he telephoned Bob Winters and told him that, while some members of the cabinet might have qualms, he, Lévesque and George Marler were prepared to defer Hydro-Québec's plans for the Outardes River in favour of the Hamilton development. Winters dictated a note after the call in which he said:

> He says he anticipates a new Authority with representation from Brinco and Quebec Hydro. I asked him if he had any ideas about the form of the new Authority. He said he didn't and would welcome it if we would endeavour to think this through and present it to him. He said he was setting up a team to settle the matter of the border between Labrador and Quebec with Mr. Smallwood. I told him that on the basis of my conversations with Mr. Smallwood, he would find him quite amenable to proposals. In this regard he mentioned certain head waters which will come to Quebec and in which Brinco has rights. He told me he would require Brinco to waive these rights so that they could fall to the province of Quebec. I didn't recognize the names of the rivers and wasn't quite clear as to what he had in mind. Presumably they are the head waters which lie very close to the border and which Mr. Lesage expects will be within the Province of Quebec once the border is settled . . . .

This was the first open mention of a proposal that was to be discussed in various forms over the next four years. It concerned five rivers which rise in Labrador and flow south through Quebec to the St. Lawrence: the Romaine, Natashquan, Little Mecatina, St. Augustine and St. Paul. Together they have a power potential of perhaps three million horse power, but they cannot be developed by either province alone. Quebec cannot develop them without controlling their headwaters and creating reservoirs in Labrador; and Newfoundland cannot develop them by controlling only the headwaters. It seems to have been René Lévesque who first suggested what apeared to be a logical solution: since the height of land forms the Labrador boundary for most of its length, why not extend that principle to the whole border, including its only straight section, where it follows the 52nd parallel? This would place the headwaters in

Quebec territory, permitting Quebec to develop the rivers, and Newfoundland could be compensated by an equal amount of territory in the north.

Joey Smallwood has always stoutly denied that he ever agreed to give up an inch of Newfoundland soil during his negotiations with Lesage. But he does not deny that the question was discussed on many occasions, and it is clear that on several of those occasions Jean Lesage thought Joey was prepared to agree to an exchange of territory. This seems to have been one of them; but the May 21 meeting was followed by a strange silence. No "team" was set up to discuss the boundary and in fact the whole Hamilton project appeared to have been put on the shelf.

The reason was not long in surfacing: Lévesque's determination to nationalize the private power companies provoked a bitter controversy within the Quebec government and throughout the summer of 1962 Lesage had his hands full trying to avert a disastrous split in the Liberal party. The more conservative Quebec ministers viewed the diminutive Minister of Natural Resources as a wild-eyed leftist. Lévesque countered that there was nothing revolutionary about the idea of a state-owned power industry, pointing out that Tory Ontario had had one since the early years of the century. He claimed 90 per cent of the voters would support him and threatened to resign if nationalization was not adopted as party policy. And if he resigned, it was clear that he would not fade from the political scene and return meekly to his television career. After months of backstage debate, Lévesque won his point and in September Lesage called a provincial election with nationalization the central plank of the party's platform.

While this incidental impediment to its plans was being resolved, Brinco could do nothing but mark time and tend to its "housekeeping." It had been realized early in the year that, whatever delays bedevilled the Channel Scheme, the corporation would soon need more working capital for its other activities. The first stage of the Twin Falls project was nearing completion and the decision to double its capacity to 240,000 horse power meant that the Hamilton Falls company had to find $1,250,000 as its share of the new equity required. Also, Dr. Beavan's geologists by now believed they had a commercial deposit of copper at Whales Back Pond, on the Baie Verte peninsula in northern Newfoundland. Local residents had mined copper at Whales Back as long ago as 1885, but the primitive methods of those days had left the main ore body undisturbed and the Brinex geologists considered it their best opportunity to develop a producing mine since the negotiations for exploiting the Labrador uranium finds had collapsed. But more money was needed for underground exploration and, if this confirmed the geologists' hopes, for construction of a mine and mill.

It was estimated that more than $3 million in new capital was required, and the question arose whether this should be raised by Brinco, as the parent company, or by the two subsidiaries concerned, Hamilton Falls Power Corporation and Brinex. Since the Hamilton Falls company's only assured income in the foreseeable future was the money it would eventually receive in royalties and dividends from Twin Falls, it was considered unlikely that the public would want to invest in it, except perhaps as a speculative promotion based on the ultimate hope of the Channel Scheme going ahead. Also, public participation in Hamilton Falls, it was felt, would not only dilute the current shareholders' interest but would complicate the future financing of the Channel Scheme and any corporate restructuring which might become necessary.

As for the mine financing, Brinex was still wholly owned by Brinco, but the Whales Back exploration had been carried out as a joint venture between Brinex and the Anglo-American Corporation of South Africa.* If these two partners formed a separate company to build and run the mine, there would be no place in it for private investors. Worse still, Brinex, which had now spent $3,300,000 on mineral exploration since 1953 without earning a cent in return, would not be able to deduct that sum for tax purposes from the eventual earnings of Whales Back.

Taking all these considerations into account, it was decided that Brinco should raise all the capital required itself; so in July 1962, there was a rights issue, with shareholders being offered three common shares for each ten Founders' or common shares they held. While the price at which they were set, $1.50, reflected the uncertainty still plaguing the corporation's plans, more than two million shares were sold without difficulty, augmenting the Brinco treasury by $3.1 million.

In November, both Lesage and Smallwood were returned to office within a few days of each other and Brinco once again took up the torch

---

*By mid-1975, in addition to its own activities, Brinex had carried out forty-eight joint ventures in Newfoundland and Labrador with a total of thirty-two different exploration companies, the idea being not only to spread the cost of exploration but to take advantage of other companies' technical expertise. Brinex originally had a 60 per cent interest in the Whales Back venture; Anglo-American later decided against further expansion into Canada and sold its 40 per cent interest to Brinex at cost, making the Whales Back mine, which went into production in 1965, a wholly owned Brinex operation.

for the Hamilton Falls project, buoyed this time by a new development: a change in policy by the Conservative government in Ottawa which in retrospect can be seen to have had a crucial influence on the future negotiations.

In 1907, when the hydro-electric power industry was still in its infancy, federal legislation had decreed that surplus power could be exported from Canada under licences supposed to be renewed every year, a condition designed to ensure that power considered surplus at the time it was sold could be recaptured if it were needed at home. Over the years, some suppliers entered into long-term contracts with United States customers without including recapture clauses. During the twenties, a number of U.S. companies which had come to rely on Canadian supplies aroused great indignation by refusing to give up their power when asked to do so because it was needed in Canada. This led to a virtual prohibition of new power exports which lasted for many years.

In 1957, the Gordon Commission, set up by the Liberals, recommended a less rigid power-export policy. So, not long afterward, did the Borden Commission, appointed by the Progressive Conservatives. The Borden Commission also suggested the establishment of a National Energy Board to coordinate policy and foster the development of adequate supplies of all forms of power within Canada. The board was created by the Diefenbaker government in 1959 and although its mandate permitted it to sanction the export of surplus power for periods of up to twenty-five years, this provision had still not been implemented three years later.

By the middle of 1962, the Conservatives' plan for a national power grid had run into heavy weather. Even more formidable than the technical problems involved were the problems of federal-provincial protocol: Jean Lesage's reluctance to participate "under the tutelage" of Ottawa was matched on the other side of the country. "You can't discuss a grid system," said British Columbia's prickly Premier W.A.C. Bennett, "without having some power to go on the grid." Bennett had plenty of power — millions of horse power — swirling untapped down the Peace and Columbia rivers; and he wanted to develop it for sale in the United States. If he could get permission to do this, he let it be known, he would reserve some of the output for John Diefenbaker's cherished grid.

Ottawa at that time was anxious to attract U.S. dollars into Canada. It also felt the need for some sort of imagination-firing construction project to prime the national economic pump, as the Distant Early Warning radar line, the St. Lawrence Seaway and the Trans-Canada pipeline had done during the fifties. In addition to the Peace and the Columbia, the

146

Hamilton was crying out for development in Labrador and the Nelson in Manitoba — to say nothing of the Yukon up there in the far north.

The government resolved to change the policy which had persisted for more than fifty years. "The development and use of Canada's resources of energy must be a central feature of the program for national economic growth . . .," said the speech from the throne at the opening of Parliament in September 1962. "My ministers have come to the conclusion that large-scale, long-term contracts for the export of power surplus to Canada's needs, present and potential, should now be encouraged in order to expedite the development of major power projects in Canada which are too large to be supported by the domestic market. Such exports can also strengthen our balance of payments."

Brief though it was, this passage revived Brinco's flagging hopes. The energy crisis had not yet burst into the headlines as it was to do in 1973, but as early as 1958 the corporation had been told by engineers working for an Italian company installing transmission lines for Alcan's Chute-des-Passes development that New York power companies were worried about the state's growing shortage of electricity. Then in 1961, J. Hartness Beardsley, a Maine engineer who had been hired two years earlier to take charge of the Twin Falls project, learned through friends in the industry that the New England states, already linked in an informal grid to exchange power at times of shortage, were also concerned about their future supplies and were prepared to consider taking at least a million horse power from Brinco.

Neither approach was followed up because Brinco could raise the financing to develop the falls only on the security of contracts lasting long enough to repay the bonds, and despite the National Energy Board Act of 1959 Ottawa had not yet begun to grant long-term export permits. Now the speech from the throne appeared to change the picture completely. If Lesage had been reluctant to negotiate a deal because Quebec had ample power sources of her own, perhaps he would agree to Hamilton Falls power passing through the province for export, an arrangement Ottawa seemed to believe would benefit the country's balance of payments. And if he objected to the idea of the power crossing the province "in a sealed tube" — a phrase once used by Lévesque when he rejected Southam's suggestion that Ontario would be a willing customer — surely he would be attracted by the prospect that Quebec might buy the power at the Labrador border and sell it at a profit in the United States?

The time was not yet ripe to put this to Lesage, who was still on the election trail, but Arthur Torrey, Brinco's financial adviser, was a good friend of Wallace McCutcheon, the influential Bay Street figure Diefenbaker had just named to the Senate and appointed Minister without Portfolio to serve as a link with the business world. Torrey quickly arranged to visit Ottawa and in a cordial meeting with McCutcheon was assured that the government earnestly wished to increase the flow of U.S. dollars into Canada and would do whatever it could to assist Brinco's cause; in particular, there would be no difficulty with export permits. Torrey told McCutcheon Brinco might find it necessary to enter into contracts extending over more than twenty-five years, and came away with the impression that if so, the government would not stand in the way.

Torrey immediately reported this conversation to Ed Vollmers, who realized at once that the prospect of importing cheap power from Canada would almost certainly appeal to one of Morgan Stanley's clients, the huge Consolidated Edison Company of New York. Vollmers mentioned this possibility to Bill Southam, who apologized that his hands were tied: he had promised to negotiate only with Hydro-Québec and could not authorize an approach to anyone else. But if Vollmers on his own initiative decided to make such an approach . . .

So Vollmers called Harland C. Forbes, chairman of Consolidated Edison, and explained the situation to him. When he began to talk in terms of the four million horse power available at Hamilton Falls, and its low cost, he had no difficulty in enlisting Forbes's enthusiastic attention, and his acceptance of the fiction that it was he, Forbes, who was making the approach to Brinco.

"Con Ed," as the company is familiarly known to the millions of New Yorkers who never cease to deplore its propensity for tearing up their streets, supplies both electricity and gas to most of New York City and suburban Westchester County. This large but geographically highly concentrated market presents the company with unique problems, high among them being the difficulty of siting new generating plants in such a crowded area, and a load that is almost grotesquely unbalanced. All electrical utilities face this problem: they must install enough generating capacity and equipment to cope with each day's peak load, and simply grin and bear the uneconomic state of affairs that results in much of their capacity going unused for most of the time. Con Ed's situation is far worse than most, since its customers are largely skyscraper office blocks and high-rise apartment buildings, with little or no sustaining industrial consumers. Its night-time load is thus only a fraction of what it must generate during peak hours.

148

When Ed Vollmers called Harland Forbes, Con Ed was considering two costly projects designed to meet its future electricity needs, both of which were beginning to encounter public opposition. One was a $175 million nuclear power station, the largest ever planned in the United States up to that time, which it proposed to site in the thickly-populated borough of Queens. The other was a $115 million plan to build an artificial reservoir a thousand feet above the Hudson River in the hills near West Point, fifty miles north of New York City, to help to cope with its peak-hour supply problem.

The plan was to pump water from the Hudson up into the reservoir every night and then to release it at peak daytime periods to drive six turbines generating 1,350,000 kilowatts of power, more than the output of the famous Hoover Dam. This might sound to the layman like a self-defeating proposition, in that pumping the water uphill could be expected to consume more electricity than it would generate coming down next day. But what made the scheme attractive was that the water would be pumped uphill with electricity generated by steam plants in New York City which normally stood idle overnight. The reservoir would thus in effect be a giant storage battery enabling Con Ed to make more efficient use of its equipment.

On the basis of what Ed Vollmers told him on the telephone and at a carefully prepared meeting later, Harland Forbes thought Hamilton Falls might well be able to supply him with cheaper power than either of his own contemplated projects could, and he readily agreed to "request" a meeting with Brinco representatives, which took place over lunch in a private room at the Union Club in New York on November 15. Bill Southam outlined the background of the Channel Scheme and its political complications; Vollmers, Mulholland and Victor Smith explained its estimated cost and how it was proposed to finance it; and after lunch Tim Hobson unrolled his maps and charts and briefed Forbes, who was himself an electrical engineer, on the engineering details.

Forbes was impressed, and in a forthright way that surprised and delighted his guests, who had become accustomed to responses ranging from flat rejection to hedging and promises to consider, said he would buy all the power that could be economically developed at the falls and transmitted to the New York—Quebec border, provided the price was right. And judging from the estimates he had just heard, Forbes figured that this should be no more than four mills per kilowatt-hour. Southam thought that figure might be somewhat low. He also warned

Forbes that Brinco could only sell, in the words of the speech from the throne, "power surplus to Canada's needs, present and potential." Forbes appreciated this, but said that if it would help, Con Ed would contract in advance to surrender stated quantities of power at agreed intervals.

The Brinco party returned to Montreal in high spirits. The importance of the potential Con Ed deal could not be over-emphasized: it promised a neat solution to two major problems. First, it had seemed until now that Quebec could not immediately absorb the whole of the Hamilton Falls potential, which meant that the project would have to be built in stages over a long period, at a consequent higher capital cost. With Con Ed prepared to buy all the power, or anything left over after meeting Quebec's needs, the whole development could be carried out in one operation, at a saving of millions of dollars. Second, the memory of the arduous Twin Falls negotiations was still fresh in everyone's minds and it was realized that the foreign-exchange problem would bulk large in the eventual attempt to persuade U.S. lenders to part with the huge sum of money needed to build the plant. Brinco would have to convince the potential lenders that, whatever political or economic conditions might hold in the future, and regardless of any exchange restrictions that might be imposed, it would always be able to obtain the U.S. currency needed to service its bonds. It would also have to protect itself against any decline in the value of the Canadian dollar or perhaps go broke buying U.S. dollars to repay its debt. If Con Ed could be sold a sufficient proportion of the power produced, its payments would create a built-in supply of U.S. dollars, protecting Brinco against currency-exchange losses and reassuring potential lenders.

Back in Montreal, Southam arranged to visit Joey Smallwood to give him the good news, which he did two days after the provincial election on November 19. The Premier reacted enthusiastically to this offer from such a "gigantic" customer: "Sell them every horse power you have," he said, "provided Canada can get it back when it's needed." He also thought the new development would at last persuade Jean Lesage, whose "procrastination" he could not understand, to agree to the deal. He would talk to Lesage again, if Brinco would give him "a piece of paper" spelling out the details of the Con Ed offer.

This meeting took place on December 18 in Quebec City and the mood in which Joey approached it can be gauged from his bantering exchange with reporters when he arrived at the airport the night before. He had come, he said, to visit "the greatest Canadian in Canada today." His forecast was that Lester Pearson would soon be replacing John

Diefenbaker as Prime Minister, and after Pearson had held office for about ten years he would be succeeded in his turn by that other good Liberal, Jean Lesage. Joey therefore wanted to put in his word early so that when the time came Mr. Lesage would give him a good job as a Canadian ambassador, preferably to Jamaica. They would doubtless discuss "a lot of other things," but it would be up to Mr. Lesage as host to make a statement afterward.

The recipient of this unsolicited tribute was apparently not amused. When reporters asked him whether he would be making a statement after the meeting he said he could not guarantee it because he did not know what subjects were to be discussed. Furthermore, he had told Mr. Smallwood he would be busy all day and could only see him for dinner.

Lesage's irritation, if such it was, must have evaporated during the day because the meeting itself, over dinner at the Garrison Club, seems to have been friendly enough. Joey gave Lesage Brinco's "piece of paper" and judged him to be "intensely interested" in the new situation created by Con Ed's advent on the scene. The possibility of the two provinces jointly carrying out the development came up again but Lesage appeared to have lost his enthusiasm for this. He said his government could not contemplate any further capital expenditures for another year or two. (One reason for this would soon become public.) Joey hastened to point out that the Brinco—Con Ed project could be launched "without costing Quebec a cent."

At this time, the proposal was that Brinco should build the transmission line across Quebec to Rouse's Point, on the New York border, paying Quebec a rental fee, and enter into a long-term contract to sell Con Ed all the power not required by Quebec or Newfoundland. On this occasion, Lesage did not insist on Quebec providing the transmission line. But Joey assured him that Quebec would "remain the boss" over its Quebec section anyway, and would be given an option to acquire it if this was ultimately thought desirable.

Lesage raised no objection to the deal as Joey outlined it, but asked that Brinco should send him more details of its "economics," including the approximate capital cost of the power plant, together with the price of the power at the plant, at the provincial border, at Chaudière, south of Quebec City, and at Rouse's Point. When Joey urged him to discuss the proposal with representatives of Brinco and Con Ed in person, he replied, "Not yet." Well then, said Joey, perhaps it would be helpful if Brinco discussed it with René Lévesque? Lesage again demurred, saying he would handle the matter himself for the time being, in his capacity as Premier and Minister of Finance.

Once again, the two premiers seemed to be in general agreement and Lesage walked his guest back to the Château Frontenac after dinner. It was a crisp winter evening and they were sufficiently relaxed to pause briefly and lean on the boards and watch a group of boys playing hockey on an outdoor rink. The apparent amity was shattered only a few days later.

On Friday, December 29, 1962, Jean Lesage announced an offer by Hydro-Québec to buy all the shares of Shawinigan Water and Power and seven other private power companies in the province. "This is not an offer made with a view to bargaining," he said. It was designed "to avoid the long delays any other method of settlement would inevitably entail," and shareholders who refused it would have their holdings expropriated. In total, the takeover would cost almost $600 million.

The government believed the prices offered for the shares were reasonable, Lesage said, and shareholders of Shawinigan Water and Power would also be offered rights to buy shares in a new company which would incorporate those Shawinigan subsidiaries not being nationalized, including Shawinigan Engineering Company. However, Shawinigan Engineering would be required to sell Hydro-Québec its 20 per cent holding in Hamilton Falls Power Corporation for $2,275,000. (Shawinigan Engineering had paid $2,250,000 for its 225,000 Hamilton Falls shares.)

Joey Smallwood was at the Americana Hotel in New York on his way to Japan with John Doyle, who was still trying to find customers for the rest of his Labrador iron ore, and he heard nothing about Lesage's announcement until Bill Southam called him on the Saturday morning. When Southam told him that Hydro-Québec was henceforth to be a 20 per cent partner in Hamilton Falls, Joey exploded.

That type of collaboration, he said, had never been envisaged in his talks with Lesage, who had not even given him a hint of his intention at their meeting just before Christmas. He would call Attorney General Curtis in St. John's to see if there was any message for him, and if not would try to get hold of Lesage himself.

Having satisfied himself there were no messages for him in St. John's, Smallwood then telephoned Lesage. "I turned on him like a dog," Joey told the author, still burning years later at what he considered "a goddam dirty trick." At least, he protested, Lesage could have consulted him about his plan beforehand.

Lesage explained in vain that he had taken extraordinary precautions to prevent speculation: at 3 p.m. the previous afternoon, he said, he had met with René Lévesque and all the commissioners of Hydro-Québec in the cabinet room, and after informing them of the announcement he proposed to make had forbidden anyone to leave the room. The whole cabinet had joined them there at 5 p.m. and no one had left the room until the reporters were ushered in for the announcement at 6 p.m., after all stock markets across the country had closed for the long New Year's weekend.

If anything, this reflection on his capacity for keeping secrets angered Smallwood more. "What would you do," he demanded, "or what would your government and your House do, if suddenly you found that the government of Newfoundland had bought a huge slice of one of your basic natural resources? Not a company — but the government of Newfoundland! You are the government of Quebec and you've just bought a big slice of our natural resources."

The telephone call, Smallwood told Southam later in the day, lasted forty-five minutes. Lesage had said he considered Hydro-Québec's purchase of the Hamilton Falls shares "a logical step towards the joint development of Labrador," and had expected Smallwood to be pleased by it; after all, it was a token of his determination to hasten the development of the falls and perhaps the premiers could best forestall the risk of further misunderstanding by coming to a prompt agreement "to pass from words to action."

Mollified by this conciliatory approach, Smallwood agreed that there was nothing he would like better and took the opportunity to mention another advantage of the Con Ed deal he had forgotten to bring up earlier: that with the Hamilton Falls transmission line linking their systems, Quebec and Con Ed would be able to exchange power in emergencies or at peak periods. For instance, Con Ed, whose heaviest load was in the summer, when New Yorkers' air-conditioners were working full blast, could take surplus power from Hydro-Québec then, returning it during the winter when the Quebec load was heaviest.

Lesage saw the benefit of this, repeated that he was looking forward to hearing more about the deal from Brinco, and Joey left for Japan satisfied that at last his grand design for the falls was taking shape.

Brinco, too, luxuriated in the same impression. Bob Winters saw both premiers separately early in the New Year and wrote to Ed Vollmers afterward: "All are anxious to have the project go forward, and I see no major obstacles at the moment."

Indeed, so confident was the atmosphere within Brinco that in February Southam's assistant, David Morgan-Grenville, drafted a press release for both premiers to issue simultaneously. "Premiers Lesage and Smallwood," it began, "today announced their joint sponsorship of a development at Hamilton Falls in Labrador." Brinco and Con Ed, it continued, had reached "a provisional agreement" under which Con Ed would buy any power surplus to Canada's needs. Premier Smallwood "confirmed that Brinco, as the chosen instrument of the Newfoundland government, would be responsible for the power project. It would also be responsible for transmission within Newfoundland/Labrador." By now, Lesage had apparently had second thoughts about the Quebec section of the line: "Mr. Lesage stated that Hydro-Québec would be responsible for transmission of Hamilton power within Quebec. It would also participate in any power sales arrangements made between Brinco and Consolidated Edison."

The copy of this statement that survives in Brinco's files bears a scribbled note in the angular handwriting of Bob Winters: "NOT to be released."

THIRTEEN

New hands at the helm

The original surveys upon which the Hamilton Falls cost estimates had been based were now eight years old. With the pieces of the jigsaw puzzle apparently falling into place at last and both Jean Lesage and Harland Forbes pressing for more information about the project's "economics," it seemed time for a new study to arrive at a more precise offering price for the power. Coincidentally, at around this time the Niagara Falls engineering firm of H. G. Acres and Company, which had surveyed Hamilton Falls for Alcan twenty years earlier, was coming to the end of several hydro-electric projects it had been building and was casting around for new business. Hugh Rynard, its representative in Montreal, had met Peter Marchant and through him obtained an interview with Bill Southam.

It did not take Rynard long to convince Southam that Acres was ideally qualified to carry out the new study. Founded between the wars by a former Ontario Hydro engineer, it had not only built up an international reputation in the hydro-electric field but had carried out many of Hydro-Québec's early developments, including one of the first feasibility studies for the Manic project. One of its partners, Ron Clinch, had just completed an exhaustive study of the whole Hydro-Québec system, so that the Acres staff had the most up-to-date knowledge of the province's power market and its requirements. In February 1963, for a fee of $65,000, Acres was commissioned to review the previous Hamilton studies in the light of this knowledge and the other new developments which had occurred in the hydro-electric field since the mid-fifties, and to prepare a new estimate of how much power the development could produce, and its cost, assuming it was built in one continuous operation instead of in stages, as originally envisaged.

Impressed by Brinco with the need for urgency, Acres took men off other jobs and put them to work with the idea of producing a draft report within two months. One engineer was assigned to the basement of 1980 Sherbrooke Street, where he spent weeks sifting through the bulging files accumulated about the falls since 1953, passing on anything he considered worthwhile to the engineering team set up to evaluate the project in Niagara Falls. A draft of Acres' conclusions was ready in May, which enabled Bill Mulholland and his assistants at Morgan Stanley to begin the complicated calculations involved in the financing of the project. But the final report was delayed until September to permit more field work during the summer season. This included establishing levels at key points around the proposed reservoir to check previous survey work; digging "borrow pits" in places where dykes were envisaged, to assess the quantity and type of the glacial "till" from which they would largely be built; and bulldozing holes in the boulder fields with which Labrador is strewn to see how far down the dyke-builders would have to go to establish firm foundations.

Acres had one great advantage over the engineers who conducted the first surveys: the accurate measurements of the river's flow which had been instituted in 1955 and continued ever since. By themselves, nine years' records would not normally be enough to predict the river's flow over a long term. But Acres compared them with figures for the flow of the nearby Outardes, which had been kept for more than forty years, and found enough similarity to justify the prediction that Brinco could count on a "firm flow" of at least 45,000 cubic feet per second at the falls, and could probably expect as much as 49,000 cubic feet per second. (The remarkable A. P. Low had guessed 50,000 at the turn of the century.)

This probable flow of 49,000 c.f.s., Acres pointed out, was less than the total flow at Niagara; but since the head at Hamilton Falls was more than a thousand feet, against Niagara's three hundred, the Hamilton Falls plant would produce six million horse power — more than Niagara's total installed capacity. This tremendous output was half as much again as the four million horse power estimated in the original reports and the project, Acres said, "will thus have a greater installed capacity than any hydro-electric development in North America — existing or under construction — and will rank among the great hydro-electric developments of the world." Clearly, Hamilton Falls was even more "big-league business" than ever.

Against this, the report indirectly underlined an unpleasant fact of which Brinco was only too conscious: because of inflation and the mounting cost of labour and materials, each year's delay in launching the project was pushing up the eventual bill to ever more astronomical levels. Acres now estimated the cost of building the plant and reservoir at $454 million, not counting such expensive but indispensable extras as financing charges and interest payments during the five-year construction period. This was a formidable increase on the original estimate of $353 million. Building the transmission line to the border was expected to add a further $91 million to that, making a total of $545 million. With financing and other charges included, the project was now expected to cost a minimum of $627 million.

Nevertheless, the Acres report added: "Although it was not within the scope of our work to estimate the cost of energy . . . this development may well be the lowest-cost undeveloped hydro-electric power site in North America."

This heartening assurance, and the new cost estimate, were not available to Southam, of course, when he sent Lesage early in 1963 the additional information he had requested about the Hamilton Falls "economics." But the Premier seemed satisfied and for a time it looked as if all the difficulties had been resolved.

On April 17, Joey Smallwood flew from St. John's to Wabush on the inaugural flight of a new service instituted by Newfoundland's own Eastern Provincial Airways and in high good humour told a VIP luncheon in the Sir Wilfred Grenfell Hotel that he expected a start to be made "this year" on "the biggest hydro development the world has ever seen." Without benefit of the Acres report, he said the project would cost one and a half billion dollars. But, as he had been saying for two or three years, it would eventually drive the subways of New York and streetcars and factories all over Ontario, Quebec and New England. And it was "not ten or even five years away." The begining of construction, he repeated, was expected "this year."

Perhaps nudged by Joey's exuberance, Lesage told the Quebec House on April 30 that Quebec would buy Hamilton Falls power "at the Newfoundland-Quebec border" if the project was agreed upon by Brinco, Hydro-Québec and Con Ed. Consequently, Hydro-Québec would not be a mere transmitter of the power but would own it, and after using some of it for Quebec's needs, would export the rest to the United States, "in accordance with Quebec and Canadian laws." Asked by an opposition member if any progress had been made on a settlement of the border dispute, the Premier replied: "Mr. Speaker, it is not in the public interest that I should answer that question at this time."

During the next few days, Brinco shares, which had been trading over the counter at $3 a month earlier, climbed to $4.75.

A week later, Lesage was in London and bumped into Eddy de

Rothschild at a party. In a letter to Bob Winters, de Rothschild described the Premier as being "in exuberant form" and added: "He came up to me three times and once put his arm round my shoulder, saying 'Eddy, we are going great places, great places, my friend.'"

Later in the letter, de Rothschild wondered if it might be a good idea for him to see Lesage when he visited Canada in June for a meeting of Brinco's executive committee. With the stepped-up tempo of the negotiations, it had been decided the time had come for Rio to take the lead in the management of Brinco. Greville Smith, realizing that "the problems are political rather than technical," had expressed his willingness to stand down. And on the urging of Ed Vollmers, in particular, Winters had been persuaded to take over. De Rothschild's letter went on to say he would like to tell Lesage "that you have agreed to head up the whole project. He has expressed such admiration for you to people in the Brinco picture that it would be pleasant to ask him if he did not think we had found the best man for the job. Apart from that I should confine myself to generalities, telling him that we see it as a Canadian-run venture with no more than help from this side."

On this occasion there was no objection to de Rothschild's intervening personally and he had "a most cordial interview" with Lesage on June 12, during which the Premier "gave whole-hearted approval" to his news. "In fact he said that Mr. Winters was the only man capable of the job," de Rothschild wrote later. They discussed various aspects of the project, including Quebec's desire for representation on the boards of both Brinco and Hamilton Falls Power Corporation, and de Rothschild added that the Premier "realized the full implication of all the work that would be involved for Quebec . . . . He talked about the 11 per cent unemployment and the need for secondary industries. He was fully cognizant of how useful cheap power could be."

At that time, while assuring him that the power would indeed be "cheap," Brinco had not yet quoted a mill rate to Lesage. But in a meeting with Jean-Claude Lessard on July 2, Winters told him it was felt the power could be delivered to the Labrador-Quebec border "at around three mills." He could not be more precise, he explained, until the Morgan Stanley experts had completed their calculations on the cost of the financing. The huge scale of the project, and the fact that the mill rate for the power was to remain unchanged throughout the life of the contract, no matter how costs rose, made these calculations almost incredibly complex. The main problem was the number of simultaneous equations that had to be solved. It was impossible, for instance, to arrive at a firm estimate of the total cost of the project without knowing what rate of interest would have to be paid on the bonds — and vice versa. The physical cost of constructing the reservoir, power plant and transmission line would be affected by how long the job took, and the effect of the escalation of costs during the construction period. Then there was the annual operating cost of the plant to be estimated far into the future, and the taxes, royalties and rentals that would have to be paid.

At that time, no one had yet managed to evolve a computer program capable of handling all these interdependent equations and the calculations had to be done "by hand," on rotary-drum calculating machines which made such a clatter that they were walled off in a separate room at Morgan Stanley. And each time one of the variables changed (if a new term was proposed for the contract, say, or the prevailing interest rate on bonds changed) its effect on all others had to be laboriously reworked. Jim Smith, Bill Mulholland's lieutenant, estimated that it took four man-days to prepare one set of calculations, and four machines were reserved for the Hamilton work during this period.

Much of this work was designed to arrive at the most profitable capital structure for the project. While businesses are sometimes plagued by under-capitalization, its opposite, over-capitalization, can be ruinously expensive in interest charges which must be paid throughout the life of the bonds. The objective was to keep the long-term bond debt as low as possible and supplement it with bank loans which could be paid off as soon as revenue began to come in.

The effect of this consideration on the engineering plans demonstrated the close interrelationship of all aspects of the project. The Acres report had recommended the installation of ten 600,000 horse power turbine-generator units — larger than anything yet in use in the world but not, in Acres' view, "beyond the state of the art" — in one continuous construction operation. But Morgan Stanley now felt the amount of bond money which would have to be borrowed (and hence the interest to be paid) could be reduced by installing six units during the first two years of construction and then pausing for a year before installing the rest. The revenue earned by the first six units during the year's pause could then be applied to the cost of the second stage of the construction, reducing the project's total indebtedness. Discussions on various such phased sequences continued for the next few years, and each time a new one was suggested the complex financial calculations had to be undertaken anew.

When Winters explained this to Jean-Claude Lessard at their July meeting, Lessard said Hydro-Québec would prefer to see the whole project developed at the earliest possible date, rather than on a "pay-as-you-go" basis, but he agreed that Brinco must be guided by its financial advisers. On the whole, Winters considered, "the meeting was congenial and constructive" and he was "impressed with the urgency Hydro-Québec now attaches to this project."

A few days after this meeting there occurred an event which, while it was totally unrelated to the Hamilton Falls project, heaped coals on Joey Smallwood's already smouldering resentment of Jean Lesage. On July 11, Lesage told the Quebec Legislature that Wabush Iron had started to build a $50 million plant to pelletize its Labrador iron ore at Pointe Noire, on the Quebec coast near Sept-Iles.

On the face of it, this seemed a straightforward commercial decision, since the pelletizing process uses large quantities of bunker "C" oil, bentonite (a type of clay from Wyoming especially suited to binding the pellets) and sundry other materials, all of which it would have been costly to ship inland to Wabush; and a plant at tidewater had obvious advantages for shipping out the processed pellets to the Great Lakes or Europe. Indeed, the Iron Ore Company had also proposed originally to site its pelletizing plant at Sept-Iles, but it had run into such intimidating opposition from Smallwood that it had capitulated and built it at Labrador City.

Wabush Iron did not capitulate. In fact, according to Smallwood's explanation at the time, it had made "a firm, unalterable and final decision" to build its plant at Pointe Noire or not in Canada at all. Rather than see Canada lose a potential source of employment, Joey had given in and come to "a very satisfactory agreement" under which Wabush returned to the Newfoundland government, without charge, its controlling interest (600,000 shares) in Nalco.* "We lost the pellet plant and employment for over two hundred men," Joey said, "but I am quite sure that Newfoundland gets the best of the bargain."

They were brave words, but it was one of the bitterest disappointments of his career and it rankled, the more so since he had been confident enough to announce publicly that the ore would be taken from Labrador for processing "only over my dead body." Daniel Johnson, who had by now proved himself an adroit leader of Quebec's Union Nationale opposition, could hardly be said to have poured oil on the troubled waters when he recalled this statement in the House and asked Lesage solicitously, "Is he dead?"

*The government later sold control of Nalco to John Doyle's Canadian Javelin.

160

The whole episode deeply offended Smallwood and he was to blame Lesage for it ever afterward. He was not even mollified by the fact that Lesage used the occasion to repeat in the House that it had been "agreed in principle" that Hydro-Québec would buy all the Hamilton Falls power not required by Newfoundland.

It was during this same month, July 1963, that Bob Winters took over as chairman and chief executive officer of Brinco and the terms of the arrangement by which Rio Algom assumed the management of the corporation were agreed. Rio Algom undertook to supply senior staff and technical assistance to bring the Hamilton Falls project into operation; to ensure "the proper execution of engineering design and construction"; to assist with the financing; and to handle the negotiations with the governments of Canada, Quebec and Newfoundland, Hydro-Québec, Con Ed and any other potential customers. The fee for these services was set at $1 million a year for the first six years and half that sum for four more years, out of which Rio Algom was to pay Winters' salary and those of any other senior staff seconded to Brinco. In addition, Rio Algom bought 185,000 shares of Brinco at $3 (the market price at the time the arrangement was first agreed in principle) and 75,000 shares of Hamilton Falls Power Corporation at $20 (double the original price), with an option to buy a further 75,000 shares before 1972 at a price which was to increase by 10 per cent a year compounded.

Though this arrangement had been thoroughly discussed informally and by the executive committee for some time before it was presented to the board, some of the directors felt it was too generous and had been sprung on them without sufficient warning. Jacques Georges-Picot, chairman of the Suez Canal Company and a shareholder of both Brinco and Rio Tinto-Zinc,* objected that while the agreement was quite specific about Rio Algom's fee, it was much more vague about "where the responsibilities of that company begin and where they finish." When the situation was explained to him in more detail later, Georges-Picot dropped his opposition, but Esmond Baring, of Anglo-American, resigned from the board in protest and his company withdrew from the consortium.

Most of the shareholders, and Morgan Stanley, which had been pushing for the change, were glad to see Brinco taken under the wing of the "big brother" they felt it had needed all along; and in retrospect

---

*Rio Tinto adopted this new name when it merged with the Consolidated Zinc Corporation in 1962.

it can be seen that the agreement was an essential stage in the corporation's development. Henceforth, Val Duncan's incisive business mind was to be more than ever at Brinco's service, and Winters immediately began to move in vigorous young executives with the kind of technical experience that could not help but strengthen the corporation's still comparatively small staff.

Such a far-reaching change, of course, could not be accomplished without some resentment and bruised feelings. It was expecting a lot of a man with even Winters' energy to run Rio Algom in Toronto and Brinco in Montreal, and since he kept his home and main office in Toronto, he was often little more than a visitor to 1980 Sherbrooke Street. The news that he was coming to Montreal would be signalled by a flurry of preparations among the Brinco staff. On the appointed day, Winters would fly in early from Toronto and, anxious to make every second of his visit count, would hold a working breakfast at the Ritz-Carlton with those members of the staff who had reports to make to him. Though the thought probably never crossed Winters' mind, other staff members often felt themselves excluded from these get-togethers and thus from the inner councils of the corporation. And when he did reach the office, he would often plunge into a furious round of dictating letters and making long-distance telephone calls; after all, he was not merely a businessman but a nationally known public figure. Whereas Southam's young men had always been able to walk in on him and chat about their problems, Winters was a much more remote figure and they now found they must have an appointment to see him. These appointments were not always easy to arrange: Victor Smith tried unsuccessfully to obtain one for six months before departing for greener pastures.

The man Winters brought with him to supervise the technical aspects of the project was a complete contrast. A jaunty young mining engineer, Donald J. McParland was as informal as Winters was austere. A friendly and considerate boss who liked to party with his staff after hours, he nevertheless expected them to work as hard and as efficiently on the job as he did himself, which was no easy achievement. He could be stubborn when he knew he was right (and sometimes when it turned out he was wrong) but he admitted mistakes cheerfully and did not harbour grudges. And he had an extraordinary capacity for inspiring trust, affection and, above all, admiration for his brilliance among those outside as well as inside Brinco.

The Hamilton Falls negotiations were so complex and prolonged, and they involved so many people, that it would be naive to ascribe their

162

success to any one man. But all those concerned with them agree that if one man can be said to have been indispensable it was Don McParland.

An earlier Canadian construction genius, Sir William Van Horne, once said: "Poker is not a game but an education." That was certainly true for McParland. The son of an insurance agent, he was born in North Bay, Ontario, but grew up in the Quebec mining town of Noranda and used his poker winnings to help pay his way through the University of Toronto, graduating with honours in mechanical engineering in 1952. His thesis, prophetically enough, examined the rapid postwar expansion of Quebec, said one reason for it was a plentiful supply of power — the cheapest on the continent because it was almost all hydraulic — and forecast that Quebec need have no fear of future power scarcities because of the presence nearby of Grand Falls, "one of the largest undeveloped power sites in the world."

McParland's first job was as master mechanic at a gold mine in Val d'Or, Quebec, and in 1955, after helping to build a copper mine in Murdochville, on the Gaspé coast, he joined the Rio group as plant engineer for the Quirke and Nordic uranium mines in the area that eventually became the northern Ontario town of Elliot Lake. He was still only three years out of university, a slight, bespectacled young man with a toothy grin whose outward appearance gave no hint of his toughness and capacity for leadership.

One memorable night, returning from a meeting in Toronto, he sat up on the train sympathizing with a contractor who was angrily journeying to Elliot Lake to berate "some young whippersnapper of an engineer" who had been complaining about his company's inadequate performance of its duties. When the contractor walked into McParland's office next day and recognized the "young whippersnapper" sitting coolly at his desk, he could only mutter, "I guess I blew it, didn't I?"

McParland's talent for taking charge of things developed quickly and a year later he was moved into Rio's Toronto headquarters as chief engineer, responsible for designing all the company's mines. Here, too, he shone and Val Duncan was soon flying him around the world as a troubleshooter on Rio Tinto's mining operations in such countries as Australia and South Africa. By 1963, he was the natural choice to take charge of the Hamilton Falls engineering.

But when he arrived at Brinco, with the title of Vice-President (Technical), he knew so little about hydro-electric engineering that Tim Hobson had to find him a "glossary of electric utility terms" and write him memos explaining the terminology used in the negotiations with Hydro-Québec. McParland pitched in and read everything he could get his hands on about the hydro-electric business and within a few months was able to hold his own in technical discussions with the Acres and Hydro-Québec engineers.

And before he even assumed his new duties he had given considerable thought to the organization that would be needed to handle the staggering volume of work entailed in the Hamilton project. Obviously, he could not hope to build up a large enough staff to cope with it all himself; even if he could have recruited enough men with the knowledge and experience required, he would have had nothing for them to do when the job came to an end. So he began to call on engineering companies, assessing their qualifications to manage the project, under Brinco's general supervision. Acres, he was soon convinced, was the best company he could get to do the engineering design. But he considered the project too big for one company to handle alone; besides, he wanted to draw on as large a pool of talent as he could find.

In his consulting role for Rio Tinto McParland had held a watching brief over the design and construction of the big Palabora copper mine in South Africa and had been impressed by the efficiency of one of the companies handling it, the Bechtel Corporation of San Francisco. Founded in 1898 when Warren A. Bechtel, a Kansas farm boy, hired out with his team of mules to help build a railroad through what was then known as Indian Territory and is now Oklahoma, the Bechtel organization had prospered under three generations of the same family and become one of the world's foremost engineering and construction firms. With a professional staff of more than seventeen thousand (many of them Canadians), the company by its seventy-fifth anniversary had undertaken contracts in ninety-one countries.

Bob Winters was already acquainted with Sidney M. Blair, an Albertan engineer who in 1949 had founded the Canadian branch of the company, Canadian Bechtel, after a distinguished career in the oil industry. He helped to develop a process for extracting oil from the Athabasca tar sands in the early twenties and spent the war years in England coordinating the supply of high-octane aviation spirit for the British Air Ministry. In addition to building chemical plants, oil refineries and pipelines all over Canada, Canadian Bechtel had managed the construction of the Iron Ore Company's mining operation in Labrador, and its experience of the terrain would clearly be an asset to Brinco. Winters approached Blair early in the summer of 1963 and asked him if

Bechtel would be prepared to join forces with Acres on the Hamilton job.

Steve Bechtel, Jr., Warren's grandson, who had recently succeeded his father as president of the company, was enthusiastic when he heard Winters' proposal, since it promised to be one of the biggest jobs even Bechtel had ever undertaken. Winters arranged for him to meet C. Norman Simpson, president of Acres, and after familiarizing themselves with each other's organizations in an exchange of visits between San Francisco and Niagara Falls, the two companies agreed in the fall of 1963 to become partners in a joint venture operation which ultimately became known as Acres Canadian Bechtel of Churchill Falls. It was agreed that in general Acres would be responsible for the design and engineering of the development and Bechtel for managing its construction, though in practice these functions often overlapped and the employees of the two companies assigned to the joint venture worked closely as a team.

The man chosen to take overall charge of the venture was Bechtel's senior vice-president and most experienced power engineer, John R. Kiely, who had joined the company in 1942 to run its Los Angeles shipyard. Henceforth, no detail of either the planning or the execution of the Hamilton project was to escape Kiely's penetrating eye, and on his frequent visits to the site in later years he used to leave younger men reeling in his wake as he stalked up hill and down dale inspecting the work. (He was a lifelong mountaineer and skiing enthusiast and even after his retirement, though confessing that he was "past the age for any difficult rock work," he took two of his sons to the Alps to climb the Matterhorn and was annoyed when heavy snow confined them to a lower peak.)

Bechtel's first assignment, even before the joint venture was set up, was to prepare an independent check of Acres' estimate of the capital cost of the development. Encouragingly, when this was submitted late in the fall it turned out to be very close to the Acres figure. By now, the nucleus of the Acres Canadian Bechtel organization was taking shape in 1980 Sherbrooke Street West under the man Kiely had appointed as its general manager, his own assistant, Fred E. Ressegieu. A retired U.S. Army Corps of Engineers colonel, Ressegieu had supervised several major projects for Bechtel, including the construction of ICBM sites. Slight and dark-haired, he was a quiet, sensitive man with a great gift for organization and a happy faculty for bringing people together which, while he ran a taut ship and could lay down the law in truly military style when aroused, was to prove invaluable in welding ACB into a cohesive team. Though he was older and more reserved than McParland, the two men quickly earned each other's respect and became firm friends.

The late summer of 1963, while McParland was still familiarizing himself with his new duties, was a hectic time for Brinco, and it seemed as though the long-frustrated Channel Scheme was under way at last. Jean-Claude Lessard had told Winters that Hydro-Québec needed a new source of power by June 1968. (The Manic 5 project, with its towering dam, key to the other developments on the Manic River, was in its early stages but was not expected to start supplying power before 1970.) If Brinco could not give him a definite assurance that the Hamilton was going ahead by October 1, Lessard said, he would have to begin construction of an alternative source, probably on the Outardes — in which case the Hamilton scheme might be posponed indefinitely.

Confident that agreement was near, Brinco followed the bold (or, according to your point of view, foolhardy) precedent set during the Twin Falls negotiations, and began spending more money without waiting for a formal commitment. Already, more than $6 million had been spent on the project without any guarantee that it would go ahead. Now, to pave the way for the start of major construction, the corporation let a contract for the erection of a bridge across the river above the falls and began preparations to complete the access road from there to the proposed site of the powerhouse, twelve miles further on. And David Morgan-Grenville began a series of meetings with Yvon deGuise, general manager of operations and sales at Hydro-Québec, to ascertain the technical points Quebec would expect to be covered in the power contract.

During August, the Brinco staff hammered out a twenty-two point "letter of intent" — in effect, a draft contract to be submitted to Hydro-Québec for its approval. Much of the technical input for this was provided by Ron Clinch, of Acres, an Englishman who had come to Canada in 1950 after some years building power stations in the north of Scotland. In the frequent absences of Bob Winters, Brinco was being virtually run at this time by another Englishman, John Kirwan-Taylor, whose elegant appearance and pink-cheeked, almost ascetic features scarcely suggested his background as a former English international rugby player and Second World War paratroop officer. A quantity surveyor by training who had become Bowaters' financial director, Kirwan-Taylor had worked on the financing of that company's expansion into the

166

United States, in cooperation with Morgan Stanley. As the Hamilton negotiations had begun to warm up, Ed Vollmers had urged that he be seconded to Brinco temporarily to take charge of its financial affairs.

Work on the letter went on over the Labour Day weekend and on September 5 it was submitted to deGuise. Thus began, though fortunately no one realized it at the time, a marathon series of negotiating sessions that was to continue almost without interruption for the succeeding three years, during which the letter was drafted, amended, expanded and redrafted dozens of times.

McParland, with Ron Clinch as his technical adviser, soon entered the negotiations, and gave an early indication of his decisive *modus operandi*. Under the method of payment for the power proposed initially, Hydro-Québec would have paid the full price only for "firm" power, which Acres had estimated as being based on a river flow of 45,000 cubic feet per second. Any extra energy supplied would have brought a lower price. McParland consequently ruled that henceforth the only figure Brinco would use in the negotiations would be the 49,000 cubic feet per second Acres had predicted as the "probable" flow. That, he said, was the best estimate, and by mentioning any lower figure the Brinco negotiators would be admitting that their best estimate could be wrong.

Many aspects of the deal, including the method of payment, would be completely changed during the incredibly laborious negotiations, and Hydro-Québec's comments on Brinco's first draft indicated the intricacy of the problems ahead. For the Hamilton project to be successfully financed, the U.S. lenders would have to be satisfied that Brinco's earnings over the life of the contract would be sufficient to service the bonds. While Quebec's power needs might fluctuate from time to time, Brinco could not afford fluctuating earnings, so a take-or-pay clause was written into the draft, committing Hydro-Québec to pay for an agreed minimum quantity of power, whether or not it took delivery of that much at any one time. This idea seemed to come as a surprise to the Hydro-Québec officials, and at one meeting Edmond Lemieux, general manager of finance and accounting, observed sardonically that Brinco apparently wanted Hydro-Québec to pay for the power "even if the whole plant is blown up." The clause was deleted from the draft until it could be further defined.

Another clause in Brinco's draft proposed, as an aid to the financing, to make the Hamilton Falls company a party to the contract between Hydro-Québec and Con Ed for the resale of the power. (At that time, it was envisaged that Con Ed would buy almost half the total amount purchased by Quebec, and there was some discussion whether the contract should be for thirty or fifty years.) The Hydro-Québec officials questioned whether any reference to Con Ed belonged in a contract concerning only Hydro-Québec and Hamilton Falls, and this clause, too, was deleted pending further negotiations. But it was understood that Hydro would arrange for Hamilton Falls to receive at least part of its payment in the U.S. dollars which would be paid by Con Ed.

During the almost daily meetings in September, there was also considerable exploration of such technical matters as the transmission and how the Hamilton Falls plant could be made compatible with the Hydro-Québec system. And concern was expressed over the legal implications of various clauses in the letter: someone pointed out, for instance, that one phrase seemed to make it possible for Newfoundland to tax Quebec.

Mercifully, there was never any disagreement about one aspect of the deal that was still very much a sore point at the political level. DeGuise and his colleagues had been warned not to permit the word "border" to find its way into any of the documents. The first draft of the letter produced within Brinco spoke of the power being delivered "at a point on the boundary between Labrador/Newfoundland and Quebec." Before the document ever left the office someone had second thoughts and this was changed to "a point to be agreed." And Brinco fell in readily with deGuise's suggestion that the words "approximately 130 miles from the Hamilton Falls site" should be added to that phrase. In later drafts, this became "110 miles," and still later the delivery point began to be stipulated as "Point A" — it being left to higher authority to decide exactly where in that barren wilderness "Point A" existed.

One other point, the most crucial of all, was also left to higher authority: in those early drafts of the letter of intent the price Quebec would pay for the power was invariably expressed simply as "X mills per kilowatt-hour." It was understood that the value of this unknown quantity, "X", would be settled between Bob Winters and Jean Lesage. But first, Winters had some pressing business with Joey Smallwood. Quebec's takeover of Shawinigan Engineering's 20 per cent share of Hamilton Falls, besides angering Smallwood, had embarrassed him in his legislature, where the opposition seized on it to needle him with the demand that Newfoundland should have at least an equivalent interest in the company. Smallwood accordingly told Brinco the government wanted

20 per cent of the Hamilton Falls shares, at $10, the price originally paid by Shawinigan. With Rio Algom now holding an option on 10 per cent of Hamilton Falls, Brinco's interest had dropped to 70 per cent, and the corporation did not want to let it fall below that level. And besides, as Winters told Joey, the shares were now worth far more than their original price, in view of the $1 million annual income that would shortly be coming in from Twin Falls and all the money spent on the Hamilton project so far. Rio Algom, he pointed out, was paying $20 for its shares. Smallwood was adamant.

Winters first tried to solve the problem by persuading Jean Lesage to sell Quebec's shares back to Brinco for $20 each — a handsome profit. Wasn't there, he suggested, a potentially serious conflict of interest in the fact that Hydro-Québec, as a partner in Hamilton Falls, would be entering into a contract to buy power from itself? Lesage did not seem concerned by this argument, but to accommodate Smallwood he agreed to give up 5 per cent of his shares, which Brinco could then sell to Newfoundland. Winters flew to St. John's to offer Joey the 5 per cent shareholding on September 24, armed with various calculations designed to show that Newfoundland had little to gain by a heavy investment in Hamilton Falls.

At the same meeting, he raised the question of the 8 per cent royalty Brinco was obliged to pay the province under its Principal Agreement. This applied only to those portions of any asset which were owned by Brinco. For instance, when Shawinigan had bought in to Hamilton Falls, Joey had agreed that henceforth the royalty would be 8 per cent of Brinco's 80 per cent share of the company's profits. With Rio now joining Hamilton Falls, it seemed the royalty would be paid only on 70 per cent of the company's profits.

Brinco was concerned, Winters said, that the admission of any new partner into Hamilton Falls in the future would dilute the province's revenue even further. But if Newfoundland would be satisfied with a 5 per cent holding in Hamilton Falls, Brinco would voluntarily put a "floor" under the royalty to guarantee that it would not be reduced any further: in other words, Brinco would undertake to pay the 8 per cent on 70 per cent of Hamilton Falls' profits in perpetuity. Joey accepted the bargain, but continued to insist he would pay only $10 for the shares.

Winters returned to Montreal well pleased with the agreement, only to discover that his satisfaction was not shared by his financial advisers, who recognized that he had committed Brinco to pay out money it might not, for one reason or another, be taking in. For instance, if any more partners were admitted to Hamilton Falls, Brinco's share of the profits would be less than 70 per cent. Furthermore, it was quite conceivable that in certain situations the Hamilton Falls profits might not be passed "upstairs" to Brinco but retained within the subsidiary's accounts, leaving Brinco to pay the royalty on profits it was not receiving.

The problem was ultimately solved by transferring the responsibility for paying the royalty to the Hamilton Falls company itself and committing it to pay the 8 per cent on 100 per cent of its profits before taxes. Since this arrangement, which was accepted by Joey, promised to dilute the other shareholders' profits, they were compensated by a free issue of new shares in proportion to their holdings.

After his meeting with Winters, Joey Smallwood, as optimistic as ever, told reporters that "the biggest hydro-electric development in the history of the world" awaited only formal approval. A "definite plan" for the project had been "made in detail on a tentative basis," and he expected it to be approved within the next two or three weeks. Construction, he hoped, would begin "next spring."

His statement appeared to surprise Lesage, who told a press conference next day he was unaware of any decision to go ahead with the project and had not yet received an engineering study promised him by Brinco.

Nevertheless, rumours of an agreement persisted and on October 19 the *Financial Post* reported: "By next spring, construction should be under way to harness the power potential of Hamilton Falls. It will be a project of empire-building proportions."

Ten days later, Winters paid another visit to Lesage in Quebec City. The Premier once again asked about the price of the power. Winters replied that "because of certain variables which still remain to be solved," he could not be any more specific than before but he still hoped the price would be "in the vicinity of three mills." The premier repeated the need for a quick decision and Winters "told him that we are already proceeding as though there were in fact agreements and that engineering plans and specifications are already in the process of being developed. He seemed pleased about this."

By November 25, reassured by Bechtel's check of Acres' estimate, Winters was at last able to be specific. He wrote to Jean-Claude Lessard proposing that up to the commissioning of the fourth turbine-generator unit the price of the power should be four mills per kilowatt-hour; from then until the commissioning of the seventh unit, it should be three and a quarter mills; and thereafter for the expected thirty-five years of the contract, three mills.

Brinco had reason to believe these prices would prove acceptable to Hydro-Québec. John Kirwan-Taylor attended many of the early meetings on the letter of intent, and at one of them, he reported to Winters, "one of the Hydro-Québec people referred to an annual power bill of $96 million. This coincides with our original thinking of three mills per kilowatt-hour . . . ."

FOURTEEN

The price comes down — but the axe falls

It was Joey Smallwood's custom, with the start of each new year, to give the Rotary Club of St. John's a pep talk which Newfoundlanders came to look forward to as their own "state of the union" message. On these occasions, he would permit his oratorical gifts full flight in a virtuoso performance designed to inspire the Rotarians to twelve more months of ceaseless endeavour in the cause to which he assumed they were as deeply dedicated as he himself: the furtherance of Newfoundland's prosperity.

On January 9, 1964, the Premier excelled himself. Offering the assembled businessmen "an eye-witness report from the front of the Newfoundland revolution," he declared: "I've just come from the very barricades." After recapitulating the tremendous advances made in the province's public services in the previous five years and predicting an imminent start on a third paper mill at Come-by-Chance, he expressed his confidence that John Doyle would soon find a Japanese customer for his remaining iron-ore deposits, which would mean a new $300 million development for Labrador.

Then, of course, there was Hamilton Falls. "Some time soon," he said, "probably next week, I will meet with someone, somewhere, and we will issue a simple announcement signalling the start of the greatest hydro development the world has ever seen." Then, after hinting at other developments in Labrador "about which I can't speak at this time," he added: "Within ten years from now the Minister of Finance will take in, in cash, each year out of Labrador developments, more than from all the rest of the province combined. There are still people who do not appreciate what a great gift God gave us in the northeast corner of North America."

Urging his businessmen listeners to take a stake in "this great empire in the building," he thundered: "Unless we have the courage, imagination and patriotism, Labrador will become part of some other region of Canada which shall be nameless."

There followed a novel suggestion as to how a man could apparently combine his patriotism with a prudent regard for his future: the Premier advised his audience to buy Brinco shares. "If a man could afford to put $35,000 in cash into 5,000 Brinco shares," he said, "he could lock them away and forget them. I am confident that these shares will one day go to $100 or $150 each. A man's children and grandchildren could live in luxury for the rest of their lives."

The audience lost no time taking the Premier's advice: before the afternoon was out St. John's brokers reported a run on Brinco shares, and by the time the Toronto Stock Exchange closed they had jumped a full dollar, to $7.60. The price fell back a little during the next few days, but on January 13 it shot up again from $7.25 to $8.50 bid and $8.60 asked. The volume of trading (on the over-the-counter market, since the shares were not yet listed) was described as "tremendous."

By now, the financial pages were suggesting that the reason for the rise might be Con Ed's growing desire to import Hamilton power because of the difficulties it was encountering in assuring its future power requirements. A public outcry had forced it to withdraw its application to build a nuclear power station in Queens, though Harland Forbes ascribed the abandonment of the project to "present prospects of securing large amounts of hydro-electric power from Canada." And its plan for the pumped-storage plant on the Hudson River was also under heavy fire from conservationists.

But behind the scenes some technical obstacles to the proposed resale had emerged. During 1963, after Brinco had brought Con Ed and Hydro-Québec together, engineers of the two corporations had carried out extensive studies of each other's systems, investigating ways in which they might be linked. Because of their size, designing a "tie" between them promised to be no simple matter. For technical reasons, a trans-mission line quite adequate to deliver the power to the New York border was not considered adequate to link the two systems without the risk of an imbalance between them causing a breakdown in one or the other. To use a mechanical analogy: if one big truck were towing another with a thin rope, the "tie" might well function satisfactorily as long as both were moving along at the same speed. But if the rear truck suddenly put on its brakes or hit a bad bump the sudden strain on the rope would certainly snap it. In the same way, a sudden variation of load on either system, with a tie of the size envisaged, would have been likely to trip one or both systems out of action. To construct an adequate tie with the alternating-current transmission lines used by both corporations appeared to demand so many lines as to be uneconomic. The only alternative — a direct-current "clutch" with the ability to "slip" and thus balance the respective loads — also seemed expensive enough to threaten the deal's economics. In addition to this problem of system stability, Con Ed faced heavy costs and legal difficulties in purchasing a right-of-way to conduct the power from the border to New York City.

As discussion of these complications dragged on, Brinco began to develop qualms over the large amounts of money it was spending at the site. The 1963 work had cost more than $1 million and on January 30, Winters wrote to Lessard expressing his anxiety and pointing out that if Brinco were to continue pressing ahead to meet Hydro-Québec's 1968 deadline for the power, it faced an additional expenditure during 1964 of $25 million, to pay for such essential work as the design and development of the turbines and generators and to build a transmission line from Twin Falls to the Hamilton Falls site to provide power for the main construction job.

"We intend to borrow this money from the banks," Winters wrote, "and we believe we will have no difficulty in doing so against our own credit supplemented by an appropriate letter from you." In this context, "appropriate" meant that Lessard's letter would state Hydro-Québec's intention to buy "at agreed rates, power in the amount and on the schedule we have already discussed."

Winters had shown the draft of his letter to Lessard before it was sent, and Lessard had already prepared the reply for which Winters asked. But when he submitted it to Lesage for approval the Premier ordered him to hold it up until the whole deal could be discussed at a cabinet meeting set for March 3 — a month hence.

The nervousness at 1980 Sherbrooke Street mounted when this development was communicated to Winters by Lessard, and it was reflected in a letter Kirwan-Taylor immediately wrote to Ed Vollmers at Morgan Stanley. Anticipating that Quebec would want a lower price than three mills, Kirwan-Taylor wrote:

> For our own private and confidential purposes, I think we should know at what mill-rate figures the project (a) ceases to be an economic venture; and (b) could no longer be financed on any reasonable basis.
>
> I realize that this is not the usual or industrial approach to the problem. We should only be concerned with producing power and energy at a competitive price and then selling it to consumers on a

174

better basis than they could obtain power from any other source. But unfortunately that approach does not seem to commend itself to certain influences in Quebec.

Secondly, we may have to consider our position if Con Ed is no longer in the deal. I know this possibility means an entire re-appraisal of the whole situation, and no one appreciates more than I do the disadvantages to Brinco of trying to do the finance without having Con Ed in . . . .

This prospect had arisen because Con Ed was still holding out for a price of four mills for the power at the international border. Because of the differential between the Canadian and U.S. dollar, this worked out to 4.43 mills in Canadian funds. But Hydro-Québec had estimated the cost of transmitting the power from Point "A" to the international border at 1.6 mills, which would make the cost of the power at the border 4.6 mills if it accepted Brinco's price of three mills. Privately, Brinco suspected that Lessard's engineers were over-estimating the cost of the Quebec section of the transmission line, but obviously the province would not sell the power to Con Ed at a loss.

By this time, Premier Lesage had set up a separate committee to supplement Hydro-Québec's own studies of Brinco's asking price, and the cost estimates upon which it was based. In addition to Yvon deGuise and Edmond Lemieux of Hydro, this consisted of three men who had served on the committee which had planned the takeover of the private power companies: Michel Bélanger, Assistant Deputy Minister of Natural Resources, who had been an economist in the federal Department of Finance for six years before being recruited into the Quebec government during Lesage's "quiet revolution"*; Douglas H. Fullerton, an investment consultant who, though born in Newfoundland, grew up in Montreal and had been involved with the Quebec reform movement; and Roger Letourneau, a Quebec City lawyer and adviser to the Premier.

The committee met Winters for the first time in January 1964, and Fullerton, in particular, resented the fact that he "looked down his nose at us" and made it plain he preferred to deal with the Premier directly. After comparing the cost estimates given them by Winters with Brinco's

---

*As director of planning in the Department of Natural Resources, Bélanger had visited Hamilton Falls with Lévesque in 1961. He later held a variety of important posts in the Quebec civil service, including the secretaryship of the Treasury Board. In 1972, he was named president of the Montreal and Canadian stock exchanges.

projected earnings, the committee decided that the three-mill price was too high. "Our reaction was that Quebec was being robbed," Fullerton recalls bluntly. But, he pointed out to his colleagues, the gap between the two parties was more than accounted for by the federal corporation tax Hamilton Falls would have to pay as a private utility. Accordingly, he drew up a memorandum proposing that the falls be developed by a crown corporation jointly owned by Quebec and Newfoundland, which would be exempt from federal tax.

This idea was considered by the Quebec cabinet early in February. Lesage, of course, had already contemplated some form of joint development of the falls. The suggestion also appealed to René Lévesque and Eric Kierans, the Minister of Revenue. Kierans had been asked by Lévesque some months earlier to look into the deal and, hearing this, Winters had sought an interview with him. Stonewalling, Kierans took Winters to lunch at his club in Quebec City and asked him to write to him giving more details of the scheme. When he examined the figures, he concluded that the price Brinco was asking was "ridiculous."

There was, accordingly, a fair degree of unanimity on the Quebec side when Lessard wrote to Winters again on February 13, saying he had now seen the preliminary report of the Prime Minister's committee. "The findings . . . confirm our view that a price of three mills per kilowatt-hour for Hamilton Falls power would be too high to allow Hydro-Québec a sufficient margin to cover transmission costs and risks," he wrote. "The committee has also pointed out that if the project were carried out by a government-owned corporation the price would be appreciably reduced, and has estimated that of the suggested three-mill price, federal income tax and return on shareholders' equity would exceed one mill per kilowatt-hour . . . ."

This last proposition was clearly a grave threat to Brinco's existence. Winters immediately got in touch with his old friend Walter Gordon, the federal Minister of Finance.

In those days, while provincially owned utilities paid no federal corporation tax, the government levied a 48 per cent tax on private utilities, but rebated approximately half of it to the province in which the company operated. There had been opposition to this tax in those provinces with privately owned utilities, since it obviously worked to make power there more expensive than in the provinces which had nationalized their utilities. Indeed, the tax was considered by many to be an invitation to nationalization.

Winters raised this point with Gordon. "Having in mind the justi-

176

fiable pride Canada takes in its private enterprise economy," he wrote to Lessard later, "I suggested that it would be anomalous to discriminate against Hamilton Falls, which is being developed by private enterprise for and with the cooperation of governments. Moreover, practically the whole of the power from Hamilton Falls is to be sold to Hydro-Québec, which is a crown corporation exempt from federal taxes . . . . "

The federal government had always seemed to want the Hamilton Falls scheme to go ahead. Winters came away from his talk with Gordon reasonably confident that something would be done to improve the tax position — so confident, in fact, that in this same letter to Lessard, dated February 19, he lowered Brinco's asking price for the power to 2.85 mills. At this figure, only two-tenths of one-tenth of a cent separated Hydro-Québec and Con Ed, which Winters felt was close enough to ensure the bargain being struck.

The spectre of a government takeover still disturbed him, however, and on February 13 he had dictated an "urgent and confidential" letter to Joey Smallwood, saying that Lesage was "most anxious" to see him. He wrote:

Jean would, of course, like to talk about the border, but I believe even more important is that he would like to consider with you some basis for developing Hamilton Falls as a joint operation between the Quebec and Newfoundland governments so as to avoid the Federal corporation tax . . . . Jean asked me if I thought you would agree. I told him I thought not; that the rights had been assigned by you to Brinco and that I felt you would be of the mind that as you have designated Brinco as your chosen instrument in this field, you would be strongly disinclined to change that now . . . . I fear that the Quebec government has been giving too much attention to the amount of money they believe Brinco is apt to earn, rather than whether or not Hydro-Québec can get a better deal from Brinco . . . than they can get from anywhere else . . . . We are now so close together in our negotiations that it would be a tragedy if they broke down . . . . Jean, who I believe by himself is always reasonable about these matters, stated that if the two governments decided to do the project together, they would, of course, buy out the shares and reimburse Brinco for monies expended on its efforts to date. That, however, would add very substantially to the cost of the project and that in itself is a pretty serious consideration . . . .

177

Discovering that Smallwood was in England, Winters sent the letter to Eddy de Rothschild, who tracked the Premier down to his favourite Savoy Hotel and had it delivered by hand, with a covering note saying it was "supremely urgent" that he see Winters, who was about to arrive in London on his way to South Africa on Rio business. Winters left Montreal on February 17 after a Brinco board meeting which Don McParland described in his desk diary as "rather gloomy." (A companion entry quoted Kirwan-Taylor and Bill Mulholland as saying René Lévesque had been "difficult" at a meeting that morning.)

Winters and Joey met in the Savoy on February 18 and talked from midnight to 3 a.m. Winters made it plain that he did not conceive his destiny to be the stewardship of a nationalized company. He repeated his view that the project should stand or fall on its merits: namely, whether Hydro-Québec could get cheaper power from anywhere else. And he seconded Joey's opinion that the merits of the case had nothing to do with a determination of the Labrador boundary.

It was a pleasant, if somewhat anxious, meeting and Winters left for Africa with no suspicion of the crisis he was to encounter on his return to Canada.

When Joey returned to St. John's, he called Lesage and agreed to fly to Montreal to see him on Sunday, March 1. The two premiers met privately in a suite at the Queen Elizabeth Hotel. No doubt Lesage believed that this time he was in the driver's seat, that the Hamilton could never be developed without Quebec's cooperation. Perhaps he was unaware of how much he had offended Smallwood in recent months: Quebec's takeover of the Shawinigan shares and Wabush's decision to build its pelletizing plant at Pointe Noire were still bitter memories for Joey, and despite his jocular remarks about seeking an ambassadorship on his last visit to Quebec City he had felt unforgiveably slighted by Lesage's offhand comment to reporters that he was too busy to see his visitor until dinner time.

At any rate, the terms Lesage now put forward for a Hamilton development made scant concession to Joey's susceptibilities. In retrospect, Lesage views them as merely a new compilation, a summary almost, of matters they had discussed on previous occasions. Joey claims to have been shocked by them. He recorded them in his diary as follows:

1. Brinco out.
2. Que. and Nfld. jointly to develop Falls.
3. Border to be changed.

4. Nfld. to absorb 4,000 Quebecers.

5. Quebec materials.

Apropos of Lesage's first point, Joey's feeling that he was both father and mother to Brinco has already been recorded; in later years, he also told the author that while he often threatened to nationalize the corporation, he was never serious: partly because "little Newfoundland" could not have afforded to do so, and partly because he knew it would have ruined the province's reputation with international bankers. His feeling that a partnership with Quebec would inevitably have been one-sided has also been mentioned, and by now he had been made well aware that any hint of his willingness to yield Labrador territory to Quebec would place him in political peril at home. Lesage's last two points, which carried similarly dangerous political implications for Smallwood, hardly needed to be spelled out: while Brinco had a contractual obligation to give Newfoundland preference in labour and materials, it was obvious that the province's resources in both these fields would be inadequate for a project of the size and technicality of Hamilton Falls. In fact, of the 219 men on site that month, 142 hailed from Quebec and only 67 of the rest were from Newfoundland.

Recording his reaction to Lesage's proposals in his diary, Joey restricted himself to the brief sentence: "I said NO." Presumably he said much more — none of it complimentary and much of it doubtless inflammatory.

Lesage was still angry when he telephoned Brinco two days later and in the absence of Bob Winters spoke to Kirwan-Taylor. Sunday's meeting, he said, had been "completely unsuccessful." Mr. Smallwood had been "completely unreasonable" and he would not see him again. But he would like to see Bob Winters and could meet him in Montreal the following weekend.

As soon as the Premier had hung up, Kirwan-Taylor placed transatlantic telephone calls to Winters in South Africa and Eddy de Rothschild in London. Winters just as promptly called both premiers and managed to arrange to meet them in Montreal on Sunday, March 8 — but separately, since Lesage still refused to see Smallwood.

Winters spent much of that Sunday shuttling back and forth between the Ritz-Carlton Hotel, where Smallwood waited in the Brinco suite, and the Windsor, a few blocks away, where Lesage was staying. Kirwan-Taylor, who stood by with Joey, recalls that he was "curiously subdued" and "seemed genuinely hurt" at the things Lesage had said since their meeting.

After hearing from each premier his account of the previous week's disastrous meeting, Winters began to exercise the charm and diplomacy all had expected him to need as chairman of Brinco, trying to wean his twin conversations away from personalities and back to the undoubted benefits to both sides of an agreement on the falls. Eventually, Lesage was persuaded to give way on all his points ("to drop those foolish demands," Joey's diary put it) except the third: a change in the border. And even on this, he said he would be satisfied at that stage with Smallwood's promise that "something would be done."

Winters headed back to the Ritz this time in rising spirits and there evolved with Smallwood the wording of the following statement, which he wrote out and the Premier signed:

> If all other aspects are agreed and resolved, Mr. Smallwood will strive earnestly to introduce a resolution into the Newfoundland legislature agreeing to an exchange of territory along the lines Mr. Lesage suggested to Mr. Smallwood about a year ago — i.e., control of the head waters of rivers emptying into the Gulf of St. Lawrence in exchange for roughly equivalent territory along the north-south border north of Schefferville.

When Joey had signed the statement, Winters read it on the telephone to Lesage and then to Prime Minister Pearson, Walter Gordon and Jack Pickersgill, the ex-Manitoban who represented Newfoundland energetically in the federal cabinet for many years. Winters told Lesage and Pearson he thought resolutions would have to be introduced into both provincial legislatures and that the federal government would then have to enact some covering legislation. Pearson agreed to take whatever steps became necessary. Winters also stressed to Lesage, who agreed with him, that it would not be reasonable to expect Smallwood to introduce the resolution "before the other aspects of the deal are agreed."

On March 19, both premiers made new statements in their respective legislatures. "Negotiations . . . are proceeding smoothly," Smallwood said, "and we all look for a start of this vast development in the present year. Newfoundland will be proud to share with our neighbouring province of Quebec in this greatest of all Canada's power projects." He also announced a plan (as much news to Brinco as it was to the people of Newfoundland) to harness two million horse power on the Lower Hamilton and transmit it via the Strait of Belle Isle and across the island

180

to the south shore of Newfoundland, where it would attract "large and important industrial users of electric power for the manufacture of chemicals, fertilizers, aluminum and other products," making possible the development of a new all-weather port on the Atlantic seaboard.

Lesage's statement was perhaps not quite so optimistic. "All are agreed," he said, "that the development of Hamilton Falls is greatly to be desired . . . . On the other hand, such an undertaking is as complex as it is immense, and obviously gives rise to many difficult financial, political, economic and technical problems. The main preoccupation of our representatives is to ensure that Hydro-Québec will be able to obtain this abundant supply of electricity at the lowest possible rate . . . ."

The guarded nature of Lesage's statement prompted the *Telegram* in Toronto to headline its report of it: "Is Brinco Power Deal Floundering?" And in Montreal, the *Gazette* opened its account with: "Premier Lesage yesterday served notice that Quebec will only participate in the development of the Hamilton Falls power project on its own terms."

Such statements, coming on top of rumours that Hydro-Québec's negotiations with Con Ed had been broken off, depressed the price of Brinco shares, which had reached a top of $8.80 on January 21, to $6.

Further evidence that other aspects of the deal were still far from settled reached Bob Winters in a brusque letter from Jean-Claude Lessard dated March 19 — the same day Lesage made his statement. "Regarding the question of the mill rate," this said, "you state that in the mutual interest . . . a fair and reasonable mill rate should be established . . . . All of us at Hydro are convinced that the mill rate which you proposed in your letter of February 19th, 1964, is not 'fair and reasonable.' . . . I am authorized to inform you that Hydro-Québec has decided to meet its demands for 1968 without any power from Hamilton Falls Power Corporation."

Winters had arranged to have dinner with Lessard on March 23 but when he received this letter he decided there was little point in prolonging the negotiations. He called Lessard and told him so, but Lessard persuaded him to keep the date, and then reported Winters' gloom to Lesage. The Premier telephoned Winters and urged him not to be pessimistic, saying that the project should go forward and couldn't Brinco bring down its price to permit a spread of 1.8 mills, between Hydro-Québec's buying price and its sale price to Con Ed? Winters agreed to come down to 2.75 mills, but doubted he could go below that and still finance the project. However, when he got off the phone he called Bill Mulholland and asked him to rework the figures to see if he could come down to 2.65 — which would be only .02 mills away from Lesage's figure.

In a note for the files later, Winters described his dinner with Lessard as "pleasant and congenial" and added: "He is most unhappy about the line he has been obliged to take in their negotiations with us and mentioned that several times he has been on the point of resigning. He told me that the letter he wrote and finally signed on March 19 was far milder than the letter Mr. Lévesque wished him to sign in the first instance. He told me that Quebec needs the Hamilton Falls power and while he did not say so specifically, I gathered he felt 2.75 was a fair and reasonable price."

Lessard was no doubt influenced by the fact that his chief engineer, Dale Farnham, had told him a year or so earlier that Hydro-Québec's break-even point for Hamilton power would be about three mills at the border, and that at 2.85 mills the deal would be attractive to Quebec. Within the Quebec councils, however — as Winters suspected — the argument now revolved around how much profit Brinco could be expected to make, rather than whether the power would be a bargain for Quebec, and the committee had concluded the company would be making a killing.

Neither Lesage nor Lévesque could afford to ignore the committee's verdict: both were well aware of the political repercussions they would face if, having nationalized Quebec's private power companies, the government now concluded a deal which put excessive profits into the coffers of another private company. The prospect of Brinco's shares soaring to $100 might have pleased Joey Smallwood; it would have appalled Lesage and Lévesque. That would have been altogether too close an echo of the scandal over the reaping of quick profits in natural gas shares which helped to topple the Duplessis government, and in fact Lesage made it clear to all his ministers that he would fire anyone who bought a single Brinco share.

The outlook for an agreement was also clouded by more personal considerations. René Lévesque had little respect for Bob Winters and no liking whatsoever for the way he seemed to assume that he and Lesage could work out a deal privately on an "old boy" basis, without reference to the Minister for Natural Resources. (Actually, the policy that Winters should deal directly with Lesage was initiated by the Premier himself at the outset of the negotiations and Winters, while he was aware that it might be resented, felt powerless to change it.) Neither did Lévesque have much time for Lessard — he was inclined to dismiss him as a mere "Ottawa mandarin" — and he often wondered whether Lessard's apparent readiness to agree to Brinco's terms was not simply a consequence of his chumminess with Winters.

The chumminess certainly existed, and Winters' reply to Lessard's letter of March 19 was roughed out between them over the same dinner at which Lessard expressed his unhappiness at the course of the negotiations. In essence, it said that while Hydro-Québec now did not need Hamilton power in 1968, Winters presumed it would want it in 1969, but that Brinco could not continue to spend money on construction without receiving a letter of intent "within the course of the next few days". (The rate at which Brinco was spending money had now become a sore point between Morgan Stanley and the corporation.)

Soon afterwards, Winters received a phone call from Walter Gordon, who said he expected to see Lesage and Smallwood at the federal-provincial conference due to open in Quebec City on March 31 and was wondering about the current status of the negotiations. Winters told him "one good development" was that "we had effected a rapprochement between Messrs. Smallwood and Lesage," though there was still no agreement on the price of the power. Winters' note on their talk quoted Gordon as saying that in view of the difficulties Brinco had been experiencing he had been expecting Winters to come and see him to propose that Brinco should sell the power to the federal government and that the federal government should build the transmission line across Quebec to the New York border.

"I told him," Winters wrote, "that Quebecers would never tolerate such action even though the federal government has overriding power to act accordingly. He said the federal government could build any structure it wished anywhere but I nevertheless was bound to remind him that this was an impractical approach."

Winters mentioned Gordon's suggestion to Joey Smallwood in a later telephone call and "he too dismissed it out of hand, saying that he would be opposed to such action in Quebec just as he would oppose it vigorously if it were contemplated for Newfoundland."

Joey also dismissed — probably again out of hand — another hardly less surprising suggestion made to Winters, this time by Lesage: that Newfoundland might lower the price of the power to Quebec by turning over to the Hamilton Falls company part of the corporation tax rebate it would receive from the federal government when the plant was in production. As Winters had expected, Joey figured Newfoundland was doing Quebec enough favours without subsidizing its power.

In Bob Winters' view, there could be no better forum than a federal-provincial conference for the announcement of a piece of imaginative and constructive provincial cooperation which he now considered long overdue. As the premiers and their entourages were gathering in Quebec City he wired Smallwood saying:

> This might be a most appropriate occasion for you and Jean to make a joint announcement about intentions re Hamilton Falls power stop Believe it would add substance to whatever results conference might achieve.

No such announcement materialized, but on the first evening of the conference, in a private talk, Lévesque tried to persuade Smallwood to "take the best men — the engineers" from Brinco, nationalize it and "do it yourself." This, he said, would make for cheaper power and more revenue for Newfoundland's treasury. Joey's response, Lévesque said later, was "strictly negative." Next day, during a recess in the conference, Lesage, Lévesque, Smallwood and Attorney General Curtis retired to a small anteroom behind the throne in the assembly chamber. There, gathered around a map, they discussed the proposal to adjust the Labrador boundary and give Quebec the headwaters of the five rivers flowing south into the St. Lawrence.*

In the light of later events, this seems to have been yet another of those occasions on which the premiers thought they had come to an agreement without either being completely aware of the other's position. That night, at a large though private dinner attended by all the delegations, Lesage surprised Smallwood by "talking openly of the border" and expressing his confidence that the Hamilton scheme would go ahead. Joey telephoned Winters after the dinner and told him things looked hopeful. Describing their conversation in a letter to Lessard next day, Winters said: "I understand . . . Quebec and Newfoundland reached general agreement yesterday respecting the boundary and that Mr. Lesage said within the hearing of all the other Premiers and Mr. Pearson that there was very little now between Hydro-Québec and Brinco and that he was confident a deal would be concluded at an early date. I

---

*While they were so occupied they heard a noise outside and went to the window, to see a crowd of students demonstrating in favour of separatism. Joey recalls Lévesque saying: "My own son is down there — and if I were his age I'd probably be there too." Years later, Lévesque told the author it was in 1964 that he first realized an independent Quebec was "viable."

184

understand the statement was received with considerable approval by the audience."

Hardly had he returned home than Smallwood received a portent that storm clouds were gathering around Canada's easternmost province. Charles S. Devine, the Independent member for Labrador West, asked him in the House of Assembly for an assurance that no part of Newfoundland would be ceded to Quebec. The Premier outlined the history of the Labrador boundary dispute and pointed out that Quebec regarded the Privy Council ruling as "a foul betrayal of justice" and Newfoundlanders in Labrador as "usurpers, interlopers, invaders." Asserting that "this is a time for statesmanship," he hoped neither he nor his government would be found lacking in this "great quality." And, he ended, "as soon as any matter of import is discussed," he would inform the House.

Unfortunately the next issue of *Time* magazine beat him to the punch. In an article bearing every evidence of authority, it said "agreement in principle" had been reached on "a tentative settlement" of the Labrador border dispute which would "give Quebec a substantial chunk of Labrador."

The Premier rose in the House on April 13 to describe the article as a "mixture of correct and incorrect statements." He admitted that he and Lesage had discussed an exchange of territory but said: "No agreement has been made to change the boundary; no agreement, no bargain, no deal, no commitment. In my conversations with Premier Lesage I made it abundantly clear that Newfoundland's policy was to treat the Hamilton Falls development project and the Labrador boundary as two separate things, completely unconnected. It is, therefore, quite incorrect when the magazine says that anything in the nature of a bargain has been made between Premier Lesage and me . . . ."

What had emerged from the discussions was "the thought — and it is no more than a thought" that Newfoundland might give Quebec an area of about eleven thousand square miles encompassing the headwaters of the five rivers flowing south into the St. Lawrence in return for eleven thousand square miles of Quebec territory in the north.

This [he went on] is merely the thought that we have discussed. I have given no commitment beyond the promise to bring the matter before the House of Assembly. Only the House of Assembly has the authority to say yes or no to the suggestion of an exchange of territory. If the House of Assembly considered it, and it were not overwhelmingly carried, my feeling is that the matter should then be referred to the people of Newfoundland. This could be done in either one of two ways: a general election or a secret-ballot referendum. I wish to make it absolutely clear that there is no power capable of forcing Newfoundland to agree to any change in the boundary. Newfoundlanders would react violently to any suggestion of force* or compulsion, and would not take kindly even to a proposal to bargain a change in the boundary for the development of Hamilton Falls. It is pleasant to report that Premier Lesage fully understands and appreciates our feeling in this matter . . . .

The *Evening Telegram* in St. John's, which had described Smallwood's reply to Devine's question the week before as "evasive," now expressed itself as relieved that no bargain had been made. Of Quebec's apparent desire to link a border settlement with the Hamilton Falls development, it asked: "Is this bargaining or blackmail?" and wondered what kind of precedent an exchange of territory would establish: "Would it mean that in future the same hard 'bargain' could be struck by any other province (especially the richer, stronger ones) whose cooperation was essential in the development of Canada's natural resources?"

All in all, the *Telegram* concluded, the episode appeared to have weakened Newfoundland's position "at a time when it needed to be most strong . . . . We do not believe we have heard the end of this matter."

The last statement, at least, was well-founded. On April 22, Premier Lesage told the Quebec House he intended to present a resolution on the border during the current sitting or at the next session of the House. The territorial exchange, he said, would require approval not only from the Quebec and Newfoundland governments but from Ottawa and, because of the Privy Council decision, the British Parliament as well.

---

*This reference to the use of force is interesting as an indication of the strength of Newfoundlanders' feelings in the Labrador dispute. One of Smallwood's close advisers told the author he once overheard the Premier say to Lesage on the telephone: "What are you going to do, Jean — send in the troops? It's the only way you'll get it." And a venerable member of the Newfoundland opposition once told the House he had carried arms in the First World War and would do so again to protect Labrador. Jean Lesage was quoted as saying after his defeat in 1966: "You could recover the territory if you want to declare war as Hitler did. The only method would have been to commit an act of aggression."

186

Asked by reporters later if his statement meant that a deal had now definitely been worked out between the two provinces, he replied simply, "No."

Neither, in fact, were those "other aspects" of the deal any closer to being definitely worked out. A meeting between Brinco and Hydro-Québec had been called for April 7, at which Winters thought final agreement would be reached on the letter of intent. Lessard cancelled the meeting without explanation the day before, and Don McParland noted in his desk diary: "RHW rather upset. Everything fouled up now."

Winters immediately wrote to Lesage saying it was impossible to carry the project any further without additional financing. Since April 1963, when Quebec had expressed serious interest in buying Hamilton power, the Hamilton Falls company had spent more than $4 million on the project, and this would have grown to $5 million by the middle of April — over and above the $6.4 million spent *before* April 1963.

"The seriousness of the problem," he said, "prompts me to ask you if as a means of keeping the project alive at this stage you would consider authorizing Hydro-Québec, as virtually the sole customer, to provide a matching amount of money." Thus by June 30 both parties to the proposed contract would have spent about $5 million each since the negotiations began. If the project materialized, Hydro-Québec's $5 million would be regarded as an advance payment for the shares it planned to buy as part of the $35 million equity financing contemplated for later in the year. If, on the other hand, the negotiations broke down, the $5 million would be forfeited and both parties would have suffered comparable losses.

Three days later, Winters staggered under a new blow. Brinco's latest estimate of the cost of the project was now $671 million. In a letter dated April 10, Lessard said Hydro-Québec considered a more realistic figure to be $605 million, give or take 10 per cent. And on that basis, "we believe that a price of two mills per kilowatt-hour . . . would provide a fair and reasonable return on your investment . . . ."

The arrival of King Herod himself at a convention of mothers could not have caused more consternation than this letter did at 1980 Sherbrooke Street. But Bob Winters was nothing if not game. On April 13, he wrote virtually identical letters to both Lesage and Lessard. "The suggested price deeply disturbed me," he told Lesage, in a considerable understatement of his outraged reaction to Lessard's letter. "It is significantly below any rate we have previously discussed, and indeed substantially below the limit that would provide a reasonable return on the investment . . . ." However, if Hydro-Québec's estimate of the capital cost proved to be correct, he could lower the price to 2.65 mills.

Lessard's letter had also contained two proposals which would have substantially increased Hydro-Québec's percentage holding in the Hamilton Falls company: an offer to lend the company $80 million at an interest rate of 6 per cent, "which might take the form of junior securities," and another offer to buy $36 million worth of new Hamilton Falls shares. Winters welcomed these offers as an indication that Hydro-Québec was prepared to advance the matching funds he had requested. He told Lesage: "I am leaving today for New York and London but will be back on Friday. In the meantime, I will assume that the immediate advance of $5 million by Hydro-Québec . . . will enable the project to proceed for the time being at an orderly rate . . . . I am instructing our officials to be ready to enter into negotiations with your 'team' at once."

Later that same day, a Monday, Kirwan-Taylor met Hydro-Québec officials and they drafted an agreement committing Hydro to advance the $5 million to Hamilton Falls as an interest-free loan, convertible later into shares. But by Thursday there was apparently some doubt that the transaction would go through, because Winters cabled Lesage from London:

> Having regard my position vis-a-vis my board and the banks pending receipt of letter from Hydro-Québec regarding advance payments could you telegraph your personal assurance to my Montreal office that there will be agreement in substantially the terms discussed between our two committees last Monday regards.

Lesage's reply, received at Brinco on the Friday morning, was utterly non-committal:

> At the request of Mr. Winters I am sending you this telegram stop I must tell you that I will have to explain the situation to Mr. Winters in replying to his personal and confidential letter to me dated April 13th.

After calling Val Duncan in London, Bill Mulholland in New York and some of the corporation's key directors, Kirwan-Taylor and Don McParland drove out to Montreal airport to meet Winters' plane. They had booked a room at the Aeroport-Hilton and on the way there they broke the news of Lesage's telegram. As soon as they got into the room Winters phoned the Premier, who confirmed his fears and told him he was writing to him that same day. Another call, to Lessard, proved equally discouraging and, grim-faced, Winters told McParland to shut down all work on the site and set in motion negotiations to cancel the contracts which had been let for materials and equipment. Winters then continued on his way to Toronto. McParland went back to 1980 Sherbrooke Street, called in Fred Ressegieu and a few other key men and broke the bad news to them.

As the Hamilton Falls company took stock of the situation during the next few days, it was discovered that it had $450,000 cash in hand and was awaiting Newfoundland's payment of $750,000 for its allotment of shares, making a total of $1,200,000 — of which more than $1 million was owed to Brinco for advances made to it previously. In the expectation that agreement would soon be reached, it had committed itself to contracts worth at least $2 million during the next few months and was planning to spend approximately $450,000 a week on the project during the coming summer season. Even if all work ceased immediately, it was estimated that cancellation of the contracts would cost at least $600,000.

In the event, the faith that the project would ultimately go ahead lingered mysteriously on, and while most of the contracts were cancelled some work continued, though at the much-reduced cost of $300,000 a month. The bridge over the river, for instance, was deemed so important that it was completed; and some other vital work was undertaken at the site that season, including further exploratory diamond-drilling of the rock in which the powerhouse was to be built.

The Acres Canadian Bechtel team which had been busy with the preliminary planning and engineering design was dispersed, but not entirely disbanded, the various managers and engineers returning to their parent organizations but in places from which they could be quickly retrieved if the project was given the green light. Fred Ressegieu stayed on in the Brinco office, his salary shared by Brinco and ACB, and in effect became part of McParland's staff. The manager of engineering, Gray Thomson, a Scot who had begun his career as a seventeen-year-old apprentice surveyor in a coal mine, took his five project engineers over to Hugh Rynard's hitherto one-man office and formed Acres Quebec Limited. The manager of the crucial scheduling and estimating department, Dick Phillips, a Bechtel man from California, moved over to Canadian Bechtel's Montreal office, but like Thomson and anyone else whose specialist knowledge McParland needed from time to time, remained on call for Brinco assignments.

Lesage's reply to the suggestion that Hydro should match the company's expenditure, when it was received, said he had given it "serious and even anxious consideration," but "it is absolutely impossible for me to authorize Hydro-Québec to commit itself in any way before the negotiations are completed." And he left no doubt that the negotiations would not be completed until Brinco met his price: "I must point out that I will obviously have to make full disclosure in the Legislative Assembly of the basis on which any agreement is arrived at." For this reason, "negotiations cannot be continued otherwise than in accordance with the letter which Jean-Claude Lessard is sending you today."

Lessard's letter confirmed the refusal to match Brinco's expenditure of risk capital and adroitly harpooned Winters with one of his own phrases: "On a project of the order of hundreds of millions of dollars, risk expenditures of $5 million would appear far from disproportionate, especially in the light of your reference in your letter of February 19th, 1964, to 'the justifiable pride Canada takes in its private enterprise economy.' . . ."

The letter also reproved Hamilton Falls for not supplying enough information on its costs and added: "When you have supplied us with detailed year by year pro forma income statements and balance sheets, based on a capital cost of $605 million . . . at our suggested price of two mills and at the price of 2.65 mills you are now willing to accept . . . together with a specific list of the assumptions used in programming the tabulation, we will then be in a position to consider suitable interim financing arrangements . . . ."

In reply, Winters offered a reproof of his own. Hydro-Québec, he said, was applying one set of conditions to its negotiations with Brinco and another to its negotiations with Con Ed, which had so far been conducted solely in the light of the price at which Con Ed could get power elsewhere and not on the basis of Hydro's costs which, "quite properly," Con Ed had not sought to discover. Moreover, Winters went on, the two-mill price suggested would give Quebec a mark-up of 2.4 mills between its buying and selling price, a higher return than Hamilton Falls would receive on a much larger capital outlay. More constructively, perhaps, he asked if Lessard would agree to the establishment of a committee unconnected with either side "to review our financial program alongside yours . . . and determine what the relative returns should be." Lessard agreed, and Arnold Hart, president of the Bank of Montreal, and Douglas Chapman, of the investment firm of A. E. Ames and Company, agreed to examine the figures.

Soon afterwards, Winters lunched with René Lévesque — an occasion he described as "not brilliantly productive" — and it was agreed that Lesage's committee should visit New York for a thorough briefing on Brinco's calculations at the office of Morgan Stanley, where Bill Mulholland and his battery of assistants had been working far into the night to provide the information for which Lessard had asked.

By now, the Hamilton calculations were occupying so much time at Morgan Stanley that two of Mulholland's assistants, Jim Smith and Bob Greenhill, had been assigned to a cram course at a computer school and, with the aid of IBM specialists, had worked out an ingenious program enabling the calculations to be handled by a 7094 computer, the largest then in use outside the defence establishment. While this speeded up matters, the calculations themselves had lost none of their complexity, and it fell to Mulholland's lot to explain them to Lesage's committee and field their many questions. Even though he had lived with the figures now for many months, he remembers the experience as the most gruelling two days he ever spent. As one of the architects of the now-abandoned policy that Hydro-Québec had no right to know Brinco's costs, Ed Vollmers viewed the proceedings with barely concealed impatience. On the Quebec side, his mood was matched by Douglas Fullerton, perhaps the most implacable opponent of the Brinco proposals, who recalls: "We had just pulled off the biggest and most successful nationalization operation on the continent and we were fairly cocky about our ability to examine facts."

By the end of the second day it was fairly clear that there was still no agreement on the figures, and Mulholland and Bélanger shared a chuckle that afternoon when René Lévesque telephoned to tell Bélanger: "Don't give in to anything those guys want."

At around this time, the idea that the federal government might build the transmission line across Quebec was revived and there was discussion in Ottawa as to whether the Prime Minister should write to Lesage on the subject. After consultation with Joey, Jack Pickersgill drafted a letter in which, he suggested, Pearson should say he was "greatly disturbed" at the possible abandonment of the Hamilton Falls scheme, since it was "important to the economic and financial progress of the country as a whole," and should offer to build the line with or without the partnership of Hydro-Québec. "We would not seek," the draft said, "to do this under the constitution by declaring the line a work for the general advantage of Canada, but only by agreement with the government of Quebec."

Shown the draft for his comment, Gordon Robertson, Clerk to the Privy Council and Secretary to the Cabinet, objected to this last sentence in particular. "It seems to me," he wrote, "that at this stage, this reminder that the federal government could take constitutional power for this work would be regarded as a threat; moreover, it is a device the government might eventually have to turn to as a last resort and therefore should not be given away in advance . . . ." Also, Robertson said, the letter as a whole implied that Pearson was taking Smallwood's side and trying to put pressure on Lesage. Pearson apparently agreed, because it was never sent.

By now Bob Winters had suspected that what he viewed as "delaying tactics" by Quebec were designed to strengthen Hydro-Québec's bargaining position by putting the Hamilton Falls company into a dangerously exposed financial position. While he may have been mistaken in this assumption, there was no doubt about the company's precarious situation. More precisely, in the words of Sir Mark Turner, one of its financial advisers since the beginning, it was "nearly bust."

A director of Kleinwort Benson, a firm of merchant bankers which was among Brinco's twenty-nine original shareholders, Sir Mark was knighted for his wartime services to Britain in the Ministry of Economic Warfare and other government agencies, including the Control Commission for Germany and Austria, where he had become a friend of Val Duncan. It was Turner, in fact, who, as managing director, had hired Duncan at Rio Tinto. Perhaps the best testimonial to his financial acumen is the list of more than thirty major companies in Britain and overseas of which he is a director.

The crisis in Brinco's fortunes had led to Turner being summoned to Montreal and his examination of the Hamilton Falls company's accounts soon disclosed just how parlous its position was. He concluded that if the company could borrow enough on its shares in Twin Falls to meet the more than $1 million it now faced in various cancellation fees, and if it suspended payment of its management fee to Rio (which it did in June) "there is just enough left in the kitty to cover operating expenses for four months."

Turner had attended some of the early financial discussions with Hydro-Québec but had decided his presence might be more of an irritant than an asset after an unfortunate meeting with René Lévesque. Leading a Brinco delegation which also included Bill Mulholland and Kirwan-Taylor, he had worked for two days preparing his notes for what he intended to be a brief opening speech. He never got a chance to deliver it. Lévesque, who made it clear later he thought it incongruous that, in a French-speaking province of Canada, he should be faced by two Englishmen and an American, began the meeting by saying: "The only matter we're prepared to discuss is the terms on which we take over the company." His sails suddenly deprived of all wind, Turner tried to restore the discussion to a more seemly course, but Lévesque refused to consider the deal as it then stood. "In that case," Turner asked, "will you give us way-leave to transmit the power through Quebec to the border?"

Lévesque said the pylons would never stand up. Surprised at this injection of technical matters into what he had thought would be a financial discussion, Turner asked: "You mean it wouldn't be possible to transport the power that distance?" Lévesque replied: "No — the people of Quebec would not allow the pylons to go across Quebec."

Henceforth, Turner decided, he had better leave the negotiations to those with more knowledge of local conditions.

Lévesque gave a frank indication of his views at around this time to an interviewer from the *Atlantic Advocate*:

All this nice, beautiful talk about private enterprise developing new empires demands some examination, particularly when there is no risk at all, and all they are trying to do is make as much profit as possible on as little equity as possible . . . . The argument is about how much profit is legitimate, because it is basically a public utility that is being developed. It is a question of how much profit is permissible on the equity or on the complete capital expenditure. This is something which is obviously rather hard to sell politically except in Newfoundland. It is against the normal trend of political thought everywhere that private entrepreneurs, promoters, if you like, should make a profit out of public utilities . . . . We don't want any scandal about this. This has to go through the Quebec Legislature. We have an opposition; and if you think back, remember what happened to a government of Canada over the pipeline debate . . . . We already have the problem of having a private enterprise to deal with which has a rather medieval set-up in that Brinco concession. It is none of our business, except that we are dealing with that sort of enterprise established on principles unacceptable practically everywhere in Canada, and *certainly* in Quebec . . . .

During May, aware that Lesage's committee would soon be reporting to the Premier, Brinco decided to prepare yet another report in a last attempt to demonstrate that its financial projections were reasonable. Prepared by Mulholland and Kirwan-Taylor, this time with the assistance of Robert Dale-Harris, a well-known Toronto accountant, this was sent to Lesage at the beginning of June. It submitted that a price of 2.75 mills, on a capital cost now estimated at $662 million, "is not only advantageous to Hydro-Québec but also will produce no more than a fair and reasonable profit . . . ."

After a study of rates of return in the United States and Canada, it said, "it is concluded that in Canada a fair rate of return for a utility already in operation and able to obtain rate adjustments is between $6\frac{1}{2}$ and $7\frac{1}{2}$ per cent." The projected price of 2.75 mills would give Hamilton Falls a rate of return of approximately 6.85 per cent "under the most favourable circumstances," but Hamilton Falls "would be in a unique position for a utility in that its return would be subject to a ceiling but not a floor. While other utilities' service rates are determined after their costs are known, Hamilton Falls Power Corporation's price will be determined in advance, and the risks attendant upon constructing and financing this large power project over a period of eight years in a remote area will largely fall on its shareholders . . . ."

It is an old principle of the finance game that those who take the risk also take whatever killing there may be, but this latest submission apparently left Lesage unmoved. He invited Winters to visit him in Quebec City on June 29 and when Winters was ushered in to his office he began by saying that the prospects did not look very good. Reading from the report of his committee, which had recommended after its visit to New York that the price should be between 2.4 and 2.5 mills, the Premier said the price would have to be 2.4 mills delivered on the Quebec side of the provincial boundary, an apparent departure from the previously agreed Point "A" which Winters feared would have unfavourable tax implications for the company, and possibly Newfoundland. Hydro-Québec's equity in the Hamilton Falls company would have to be increased to 25 per cent, at $10 a share (Winters considered the shares were now worth $30), and there were several other conditions the company would have to meet.

"At that stage," Winters wrote in his account of the interview, "he stopped and observed that I did not seem very interested. I told him that what he had just related certainly did not excite my interest and that I was obliged to tell him quite frankly that Brinco could not accept such terms and that if they were being offered as an ultimatum there could be no deal."

194

To back up his words, Winters showed Lesage figures which he said demonstrated the impossibility of the company's accepting the Quebec price — it would mean a deficit over the life of the contract of more than $80 million. The Premier replied that the cabinet had specifically instructed him not to increase the offer.

So Winters began to pick up his papers and prepare to leave, warning Lesage that he would be identified with the failure of one of the most imaginative and important projects in North America. Lesage seemed reluctant to end the conversation and asked whether Brinco could reduce its price if the province were to guarantee any over-run of expenses above the capital cost estimate. Winters asked if Bill Mulholland could join them, and the three continued their discussion of various formulas by which the price might be reduced.

At one stage, Mulholland asked the Premier if, instead of insisting on a fixed price for the power for the life of the contract, he would agree to assure the company a guaranteed rate of return on its investment, with periodic price increases if the return fell below the agreed percentage. Lesage said he was willing to accept that principle. Winters promised to have the terms studied and report back to him on July 2.

Three days later, at a full-dress meeting in Morgan Stanley's offices, it was decided that if the province met certain of the conditions suggested by Lesage, including the provision of an over-run guarantee, Brinco could safely bring down its price to an average of 2.65 mills. Winters phoned Lesage on July 2 and gave him that figure. (Unaccountably, the idea of the province guaranteeing the company a minimum rate of return seemed to get lost in the later negotiations, even though it was an important departure from the lines along which the deal had always previously been discussed; had it been adopted, it might have removed the greatest barrier to an agreement.)

The axe fell at last on July 8. Lesage called Winters at 5:30 p.m. and told him he had very bad news: the cabinet had unanimously concluded it could not accept Brinco's latest offer. He was about to make a statement in the House and wanted to read it to Winters first. He had, he said, already broken the news to Smallwood, and Lessard was at that moment calling Harland Forbes of Con Ed.

Winters listened in silence as the statement was read to him, Lesage asking him to note particularly his reference to the fact that large hydro projects were now usually developed under public ownership. When he had finished, Winters told him that on the basis of Quebec's performance so far, he was not surprised at the news. But he was bitterly disappointed.

Brinco was, after all, offering the power at a price cheaper than Hydro-Québec could produce it for itself.

Lesage insisted that the door was still open and that if Brinco would accept the terms he offered on June 29 the province would sign an agreement at once. "I told him we couldn't negotiate in that atmosphere," Winters wrote later, "and that in fact I didn't regard that process as being one of negotiation at all."

Morgan Stanley had realized by now, and Bill Mulholland had told Winters, that Brinco and Hydro-Québec were actually discussing different sets of figures under the mistaken assumption that they were the same. Because the calculations had been built up from different bases, Brinco's 2.65 mills equalled 2.55 mills in the Quebec calculations, so that Winters could safely come down a further one-tenth of a mill without making any real difference to the deal. Whether because he was tired of bargaining or because he thought it would be useless to try again at that late stage, Winters did not attempt to put forward a new offer.

Lesage said he would always be glad to see Winters and still valued their friendship, as he hoped Winters did. Then he went into the House, reviewed the background to the deal in four brief sentences and added: ". . . after lengthy examination and studies, we have to state that it is, at present, impossible to arrive at an agreement."

FIFTEEN

Joey tries the long way round

The gloom this announcement brought to the Brinco offices at 1980 Sherbrooke Street was shared by the public: Brinco stock, which had closed at $6 the day before, opened at $4.50 on the day after Lesage's statement. It dropped a further 25 cents before the panic eased but rallied to $5 by the end of the afternoon.

Only one man was undismayed. Back in February, Joey Smallwood, doubting Winters' optimism that an agreement could be worked out with Quebec, had been seized by a plan that was as daring as it was unexpected. If the output of Hamilton Falls could not be taken to the United States through Quebec, he decided, he would take it there through Newfoundland, Nova Scotia and New Brunswick, supplying those provinces with cheap power along the way. He asked Brinco to look into it.

This new route quickly became known as the "Anglo-Saxon route," though Brinco always referred to it, more diplomatically, as the "Atlantic route." It was about 750 miles longer than the route through Quebec. Worse still, it included two stretches which would have to be bridged by submarine cables: fifteen miles under the Strait of Belle Isle and seventy-five miles under Cabot Strait. The underwater transmission of power is much more difficult and expensive than its transmission by overhead lines and Brinco undertook the task assigned to it by Joey without enthusiasm. But after its own engineers had given the plan a preliminary examination — and while the negotiations with Quebec were still going on — it commissioned a feasibility study of the new route by a British firm of engineering consultants, Preece, Cardew and Rider, recommended by Smallwood as "the greatest independent authority in the world" in the field of submarine transmission.

This was not the only assignment Brinco carried out for Joey during the early months of 1964: Don McParland was heavily involved at around that time with preparations for the start of construction on another project the Premier had long held dear. It was now five years since the corporation had decided to set up Southern Newfoundland Power and

Development to develop Bay d'Espoir, but all its efforts to find enough customers to make the scheme a commercial proposition had failed. In the fall of 1963, Smallwood told Winters he thought he could get a $20 million federal grant for the project if it were carried out by the government or a crown corporation. Accordingly, he proposed to appoint George Hobbs, a Newfoundland engineer then working for Bowaters in Tennessee, as chairman of a provincial power commission which would build the Bay d'Espoir development and ultimately take over the main responsibility for supplying all power on the island.

Winters objected that if this action were interpreted as a government takeover of private interests it might cause difficulty when the time came to finance the Hamilton Falls project. He suggested instead that Bay d'Espoir should be a joint venture between the government and Brinco. As the negotiations progressed, it became plain that the federal grant would not be available to a private company, so Winters offered to give up the rights to Bay d'Espoir in return for the rights to develop the Lower Hamilton. When he mentioned this quid pro quo in Montreal, however, Bill Southam pointed out drily that the Lower Hamilton rights were already included in the corporation's Principal Agreement with the government.

At a later stage in the discussions, Joey proposed to repeal Clause 9 of the Principal Agreement (the one dealing with water rights) to avoid a potential situation in which the government's own power commission might have to apply to Brinco for rights to develop water power on the island of Newfoundland. By now Bill Southam had reached retirement age and returned to England. He left in the spring of 1964, his duties having gradually been taken over by the new men Winters had brought in. But the vigilance with which he had guarded the agreement through the years had left its mark on the organization and it was realized that the repeal of Clause 9 would have the effect of taking the Lower Hamilton rights away from Brinco also, since the lease it had been granted applied only to the Upper Hamilton. With the help of a letter from Eddy de Rothschild recalling the circumstances in which the agreement was drawn up, Joey was persuaded that it was neither desirable nor necessary to amend it.

Eventually it was agreed that the government should buy all Southern Newfoundland's rights and assets, including its surveys and preliminary engineering work, for $476,918 — the company's investment in the Bay d'Espoir project since its inception — and Brinco was hired to assist the Newfoundland and Labrador Power Commission to carry out the project. Early in 1964, at McParland's suggestion, Shawinigan Engineering and Montreal Engineering formed a joint-venture company, Shawmont, to carry out the actual construction. And McParland seconded some of his senior engineers to supervise the work on behalf of the commission.

The first stage of the development, 300,000 horse power, was completed in 1967 at a cost of $87 million, $20 million of which was an outright grant from the Atlantic Development Board and $4 million a low-interest loan from the same source. The project, expanded later to 600,000 horse power, finally realized Joey's dream of rural electrification: since 1964, the commission has more than tripled Newfoundland's generating capacity, built fifteen hundred miles of transmission lines and created an island-wide power grid And by 1972, more than 99 per cent of the island's people had access to electric power.

Joey's experience with his cherished Atlantic route proved far less happy, and it led to a series of public exchanges which, while they may have entertained newspaper readers, did little to promote the inter-provincial amity for which Winters was striving. At first, Brinco carried on its study of the new route in the utmost secrecy, to avoid complicating the negotiations with Quebec. But late in April, in an apparently unguarded moment, Bob Winters told reporters that Hamilton Falls power did not have to be transmitted through Quebec to reach the United States. Smallwood was asked about this in the Newfoundland House of Assembly and confirmed that an alternative route, through Newfoundland, was feasible.

His statement brought a prompt riposte from René Lévesque: any such idea, he told a weekend gathering of students in Montreal, was "preposterous" and "ridiculously impractical." And to back up his assertion, he recalled Hydro-Québec's experience in 1962 with four underwater cables laid beneath the St. Lawrence to take Bersimis power to the Gaspé coast. One by one the cables broke down, Quebec had to wait months for a cable ship to be sent from Europe to lift them and they were eventually abandoned. "We lost $15 million," Lévesque said. Furthermore, Smallwood was not a party to the negotiations between Hydro-Québec and Brinco, but merely the "concessionaire" of resources which Brinco wanted to develop

Joey, as anyone who knew him could have predicted, came out of his corner swinging. It was not his intention, he assured the House, to "bandy words" with Réne Lévesque; but the Minister of Natural Resources of the province of Quebec "should stop wearing anything on his head because he talks a lot through it." The power belonged to

Newfoundland and it was Brinco that was the "concessionaire." Brinco, in fact, "doesn't move a little finger without consent and close collaboration with the provincial government." Nor did Lévesque appear to know that electricity was at that moment being carried by submarine cable from England to France, from Sweden to Denmark, and from Sweden to the island of Gottland, sixty-two miles away. "The government of Newfoundland," in short, "disagrees completely with Mr. Lévesque in his contention that the power must go through Quebec."

Joey's confidence seemed justified when the preliminary Preece, Cardew report in June provided what Winters described as "grounds for encouragement." On the strength of this report, Smallwood urged that a "full and definitive" study be commissioned and asked if Brinco wished to finance it alone or jointly with the Newfoundland government. Winters replied that in view of Brinco's position with Quebec and other customers (the negotiations had not yet broken down) it would be better if the report were financed solely by the government, to which Joey agreed.

In July, when Lesage announced the breakdown — or, as he preferred to call it later, the "interruption" — in the negotiations, Joey was out of the country on holiday, so to Winters' relief there was no renewal of the battle of the headlines. Winters wrote to Lesage two days after his announcement, saying he was "acutely disappointed" by it and adding: "You mentioned that the only difference between us relates to price and as it is such a small difference I was rather puzzled as to what impelled you to make a statement in the Legislature at this time rather than continuing our negotiations . . . ."

Lesage responded on July 13: "I did not say that the only difference between us relates to price and that all the other measures are agreed upon. I said that the difference about the price is so important that the very fact of its not being settled has convinced a unanimous Cabinet that a thorough study of the other aspects of your counter-proposal would have to be made . . . ." Two days later, asked by an opposition member in the Legislature to disclose the reasons other than price which prevented an agreement, he replied that it was "not in the public interest to reveal them."

If those other reasons remained enveloped in mystery, the Premier had by this time reaffirmed the price gap still separating the two sides. At a party in a private room at Blue Bonnets race track one evening he ran into Kirwan-Taylor and told him to tell Winters that Brinco would have to come "right down" in its price. Dropping his hand from shoulder height to his knees, he said in a voice loud enough for other guests to hear that 2.40 was the most Quebec would pay. In his note reporting the conversation to Winters, Kirwan-Taylor remarked drily: "It was very hot and Mr. Lesage looked as if he felt the heat."

Still trying to find ways to arrive at a price acceptable to Quebec, Winters went to see Walter Gordon in Ottawa immediately after the breakdown and revived his suggestion that Brinco should be declared a tax-free corporation. Gordon doubted this would be possible but reiterated the federal government's desire to see the deal go through, to improve the country's unemployment situation and its balance of payments. He said Ottawa would be willing to extend the period for which the power might be exported if this would reduce Brinco's costs by enabling it to enter into a longer-term contract, thus giving it more time to repay its bonds. Bill Mulholland, who had gone to Ottawa with Winters, calculated this would bring the price down by a tenth of a mill.

Winters tried unsuccessfully for three consecutive days to reach Lesage on the telephone to make this offer, and to suggest other potential ways of reducing the price, such as the use of direct-current transmission. (Hydro-Québec favoured the more usual alternating current.*) Unable to speak to the Premier, he first wired him, again without result, and then wrote to him, on July 21. When he had still not received a reply, he wrote again on July 28, saying, "I have been wondering whether as a result of my letter of July 21 you are contemplating further discussions . . . ." Lesage replied on July 30, explaining that the House had been sitting "from morning to midnight" and he had also had to prepare for a federal-provincial conference about to open in Jasper. Accordingly, he would not be able to consider Winters' proposals before August 10.

"It seems clear," Winters wrote to Gordon, "that Lesage's repeated statements that the door is open are virtually meaningless. I say this because of the fact that while he knows we are trying to reach him with modified offers, he is apparently not anxious to receive them."

---

*Brinco and Hydro-Québec engineers examined the relative merits of A.C. versus D.C. transmission over a period of several years. Direct-current transmission is cheaper over long distances, but it also has several disadvantages. For instance, costly equipment is needed at each end of the line to convert the current from and to the normal alternating current, and without such terminal equipment it is not possible to take off current at intermediate points along the line. The eventual decision to feed the Churchill power into the Quebec grid, rather than pipe it directly from Churchill to Montreal, governed the ultimate choice of alternating current.

Winters now turned to the Prime Minister in the hope that he could suggest some way of ending the stalemate.

The most logical route from every point of view [he wrote Pearson on July 29] is through Quebec. If we could arrange a right-of-way, Ontario and New York would take the power, I believe, at once. From memory it seems to me that we have been faced with this situation more than once, wherein large sources of energy were available on the one hand with hungry but distant markets on the other and great problems in bringing the two together. I have a hazy recollection that in one pipeline case, Saskatchewan was reluctant to grant permission to carry gas from Alberta to eastern markets across its territory. I have forgotten how this was resolved but some accommodation was arranged. Then too we had the celebrated case of the Trans-Canada Pipe Line where the government had to take a hand in bringing the energy to the markets. I wonder if there is any feasible way whereby this power might be brought across Quebec . . . I am sure the project . . . would mean enough to Canada to warrant any thought that might be given to it and if any suggestions occur to you as to what the next step might be, I would welcome the opportunity of discussing them with you.

Winters elaborated on this thinly veiled suggestion, which confronted Ottawa with a potentially explosive constitutional question, in a later letter dated September 10. Saying he was convinced the next approach should be to seek a right-of-way through Quebec, he added:

I have refrained from putting this question to Jean Lesage because I don't believe that constitutionally it is his prerogative to deal with it and I don't wish to invite a turn-down. The tactics of the approach are something on which I would like to have the benefit of your views and judgment. Iron ore from Labrador passes through Quebec via rail to the markets of the world. Power in the form of coal from Nova Scotia passes through Quebec to Ontario by rail and water. There are myriads of other examples of commodities and power in one form or another moving between and across provinces by highway, rail, pipe line, water and wire. The B.N.A. Act guarantees the "free" admission of articles of growth, produce or manufacture from province to province and I presume this could include power. Under the circumstances I should think the Quebec government would regard it as quite normal for power to be transmitted from Hamilton

Falls to, say, the state of New York. However, we cannot count on that sort of normal reaction from Quebec in the light of statements that have already been made by Mr. Lévesque and others to the effect that they will not provide a right-of-way if they do not choose to use the power . . . . After you have had an opportunity of turning this over in your mind, would you mind having your office let me know when I might discuss it briefly with you?

Pearson's advisers appear to have thought Winters' interpretation of the constitution might well be correct, but no doubt they shuddered at the thought of it being put to the test: Pearson consistently avoided any federal action that could be interpreted as interference in Quebec's affairs and whenever he was drawn into the Hamilton Falls dispute he seems to have tried to adopt a position of friendly neutrality. At any rate, there is no reply to Winters' letter in either his own files or Brinco's.

Neither could the Prime Minister accede to Brinco's request for special tax consideration, even though when he approached Pearson about this Winters suggested that since there were only about half a dozen privately owned electrical utilities left in the country, and the revenue they paid to the federal government was consequently small, the tax exemption should be granted to them all. In Brinco's case, he said, this would enable the price of the power to be reduced by .5 or .6 of a mill — more than enough to meet Lesage's objections.

"I have been discussing this matter with Walter Gordon and his boys," Pearson wrote on August 27, "but I am afraid it is impossible, for reasons which I am sure you will understand, to undertake at this time to change our tax policy . . . . Any change would have to be general in its application or we would be in trouble, particularly as Manning [Premier E. C. Manning of Alberta] wrote to us some months ago asking us to make the same tax change and I told him why we could not do it at this time."

Indefatigable though he had demonstrated himself to be, Winters now realized there was nothing more he could do for the time being and retired for a brief respite to his summer cottage at Mahone Bay, Nova Scotia. Even if Lesage had shown a disposition to continue bargaining, which he had not,* Smallwood, his enthusiasm for the Atlantic route waxing stronger by the week, had ordered him not to resume

*Lévesque admitted to the author that the "breakdown" was "a sort of ultimatum: we said 'Let's shelve it, maybe for a long time — but make it very clear we're not interested in those terms.'"

negotiations with Quebec pending receipt of the final Preece, Cardew report.

Strictly speaking, the Premier had no authority to issue such an "order": Brinco's Principal Agreement did not saddle it with the responsibility of either consulting the Premier or following his instructions in the normal conduct of its business. But Winters did not bother to resist the pressure, in view of his latest indirect contact with Lesage, through two of Brinco's directors who knew him well: Senator Maurice Bourget and André Monast, a Quebec City lawyer and staunch Liberal party supporter.

When Bourget and Monast called on him as a sort of unofficial deputation, Lesage said he was still waiting for an acceptable offer from Brinco. Asked what he would consider acceptable, he replied that it would have to be the price at which a public enterprise, not subject to federal taxes, could deliver the power: in other words, two mills. Bourget and Monast asked if he was using his bargaining position to settle the border dispute. No, replied the Premier, that problem had already been settled with Smallwood. He was then asked if he would give Brinco a right-of-way for the power and he replied, "very emphatically," that he would never agree to that.

The Premier said his advisers, Letourneau and Fullerton, had warned him that at 2.65 mills Brinco would be making a "killing." And he closed the interview on an unpromising note: "Two sixty-five mills is unacceptable; two fifty-five mills is unacceptable; I would not agree to pay two point five; make us an offer."

The stalemate naturally aggravated Brinco's crucial financial problems. By now, despite the shutdown of work on the site, more than $10 million had been spent on the project. Hamilton Falls, as Sir Mark Turner had said, was "nearly bust," and Brinco itself was no better off. To maintain its position in the Hamilton Falls company, it had invested a total of $6¼ million in two 1964 Hamilton Falls share issues, which left it owing the Bank of Montreal $4½ million on a demand loan. In addition, it had to find $6½ million to finance the Whales Back mine and pay Brinex's exploration costs for the coming year.

The various courses open were summarized in July by Michael F. Nicholson, a Rio financial specialist Winters had appointed vice-president and general manager of Brinco after Kirwan-Taylor's return to England: none of them, he wrote, was attractive and "it is a matter of selecting the best of a bad lot."

It is a telling commentary on the widespread conviction that the

Hamilton River's immense power potential simply could not be permitted to remain unharnessed in the middle of the twentieth century that in October — at a time when there seemed to be no prospect of the power being sold — Brinco was able to raise more than $8.25 million with a rights offering at $3 per share. In addition to buying a little more time, this new capital enabled Brinco to pay off its bank loan and advance $1.5 million to Brinex for Whales Back. The rest of the money needed to bring the mine into production, $4.8 million, was again advanced by the Bank of Montreal; but at least this time the bank had the assurance that the loan would be paid off by the mine's earnings. The prospect of Brinco itself having any earnings seemed a remote one in the fall of 1964 — to everyone except Joey Smallwood.

On November 26, Smallwood turned up in Montreal and told Bob Winters excitedly that he had just come from New York, where he had been given the main conclusions of the Preece, Cardew study, which would be available in its final form about two weeks hence. It showed, he said, that the Atlantic route was feasible, both technically and economically, and that from now on Newfoundland need no longer depend on Quebec's cooperation to get the Hamilton scheme moving.

Joey had told Winters earlier, and had repeated to Eddy de Rothschild in London, that Quebec politicians were "sick" and indeed that Quebecers generally were "a sick people" — an unwelcome hint of storms ahead which prompted Winters to write to Gordon Pushie in St. John's: "I don't know whether we can do anything to prevent the Premier from burning his bridges completely with Quebec. I have told him on various occasions that we must bear in mind that the time might come when he will have to go back to Quebec and seek their cooperation. With this in mind I hope we can all use our best efforts to have him moderate his statements."

It was a forlorn hope. After his meeting with Winters, Joey summoned the reporters and gleefully put the torch to the bridges — shaky as they were — that Winters had laboured so hard to build.

Newfoundland, he said, beaming with triumph, had at last "escaped the clutches of Quebec." The negotiations for the sale of the power had been "painful, prolonged, delayed and protracted," but he was grateful to Lesage because their collapse had forced Newfoundland to examine other ways of taking the power to New York and the New England states. Now, five months later, he had his answer and the door was finally and completely closed to Quebec: "Hamilton power is not the prisoner of Quebec and has not got to go through Quebec."

The price of the power, he said, had not been the only reason for the breakdown of the negotiations: Quebec had wanted Brinco nationalized so that it could sell the power to Con Ed and make "twice to three times more out of Hamilton Falls than Newfoundland would have made." Furthermore, he had told Lesage that Quebec's purchase of 20 per cent of the Hamilton Falls company was "an outrage" against Newfoundland, but even with those shares, "Quebec can't influence any decision by Brinco."

When reporters contacted him for his reaction to Joey's outburst, Lesage said Newfoundland could not develop the falls without Brinco's cooperation. "Mr. Smallwood," he said, "can entertain all the lovely plans he likes. He can do nothing without Brinco because Hamilton Falls do not belong just to him." And he added that it was "absolutely false" that the negotiations had been broken off completely.

Stung to even greater bitterness by this response, Joey countered by "exposing" the five conditions Lesage had sought at their March 1 meeting and adding: "I rejected them contemptuously." Newfoundland, however, was not adopting an anti-Quebec policy: "We are not turning our back on anyone. We're turning our faces toward something — toward Newfoundland, Nova Scotia, Prince Edward Island and New Brunswick."

Lesage called Winters next day and said he was putting the finishing touches to another statement in reply to Joey's latest eruption. Winters persuaded him to take a "statesmanlike" approach and his statement turned out to be more restrained than that of the day before. He said Quebec had only suggested nationalization to make the power cheaper and, since the province would have to postpone power projects of its own if it took Hamilton power, his requests for the use of Quebec labour and materials were "normal." He had only raised the question of the border because it was "a problem that should have been discussed." Quebec, he said, had "gone out of its way to consider all the facts coolly and seriously" and it still held the door open for negotiations.

Joey considered this statement "more moderate" but repeated that there were no negotiations in progress with Quebec — and there would be none. "It appears from Mr. Lesage's statements," he said, "that he now bitterly regrets driving Newfoundland to the course we have followed." The project would start in the spring with no help from Quebec whatsoever and Brinco would build it. Winters, he said, would pitch into the project with a will: "You can take it from me that he will go through with it now with every bit of drive and every bit of strength and energy that he has . . . ."

His assumption was almost pathetically mistaken, and Winters must have squirmed when he read it, for he had been assured right at the outset of the Atlantic route studies that the problems presented by its underwater sections were "fantastic." Harry Mathews, director of engineering for English Electric, had reported to him in February that the cable costs would be "prodigious" and that the route was "really too far beyond the present state of human knowledge."

A meeting in Toronto on December 14 at which Joey introduced the final Preece, Cardew report did nothing to reassure either Winters or Don McParland and the Acres Canadian Bechtel engineers who were present. The Atlantic route, the meeting was told, would be 1,710 miles long and the cost of the transmission line alone would be $940 million, almost double the estimated cost of building the power plant itself. The six cables which would be needed to cross Cabot Strait would weigh more than seven thousand tons each and since they should not be jointed, a ten-thousand-ton cable ship would have to be built to lay them. Nothing was said about the difficulty of raising them if they were damaged, but the report admitted that they would be longer, and expected to carry more power, than any cables yet built in the world and that therefore a period of perhaps two years should be allowed for their development. (Eddy de Rothschild, who was also at the meeting, had been told by one of his friends in England that the British cable manufacturers were "fighting rather shy" of the cables: they thought a special factory would have to be built to manufacture them, a process expected to take seven years.)

Quite apart from these technical difficulties, there was the question of the price of the power, which the report estimated at 5.01 mills per kilowatt-hour at the two proposed terminals of the line, in New York and Boston. With Con Ed refusing to pay more than four mills to Hydro-Québec, Winters considered this figure to be the Atlantic route's *coup de grâce* and it was without conviction that he promised Joey he would have the report studied. As he wrote to Val Duncan after the meeting: "I am bound to tell you privately and in the greatest confidence that I do not believe the project can be implemented . . . . There are so many uncertainties about it that I don't believe customers will commit themselves to long-term contracts."

He added that he thought Quebec was anxious to reopen negotiations "and I believe we can find ways and means of doing this without Quebec suffering too much loss of face. Jean Lesage even went so far this morning as to say he would be willing to try to get together with Joe Smallwood. Our problem, therefore, will be with Joe."

Smallwood was certainly in no mood yet to resume his talks with Quebec: he was still bubbling with enthusiasm for the new route. Ever since the summer, he had been having talks with state officials and utility executives in New England, and with Dillon Read and Company, a Wall Street investment house and competitor of Morgan Stanley. One of the problems of the Atlantic route would have been the securing of a right-of-way for the transmission line through thickly populated areas of New England; without the powers of expropriation possessed by state governments this would have been prohibitively expensive. Dillon Read believed this problem could be overcome if the line were built by a publicly owned corporation. Furthermore, it had retained a law firm specializing in municipal taxation which had delivered an opinion that if power was drawn off the line by municipalities and power commissions along the way, the corporation would not be liable for federal tax on either its bonds or its income.

Peter Flanigan, a Dillon Read man who later became one of President Nixon's White House aides, paid several visits to St. John's, and also saw Lester Pearson at least once, trying to persuade Joey to nationalize the project, in which case, he said, Dillon Read would have no difficulty financing a publicly owned corporation to build and operate the transmission line.

Though he has said he was never serious about his repeated threats to nationalize Brinco, the Premier certainly came closer to it on this occasion than on any other. Bill Mulholland, who was by now as much of an enthusiast for Hamilton Falls as Joey himself, was once furious to hear on the grapevine that Eddy de Rothschild had been invited to St. John's to discuss terms for the corporation's nationalization. After a number of animated transatlantic telephone calls, Eddy cabled Joey and apologized for not being able to make the trip owing to an attack of flu.

Recalling his hopes for the Atlantic route, Smallwood told the author he eventually abandoned them because "it involved me ratting on Brinco and I didn't feel like ratting. I was not prepared to commit infanticide." Even had he been, the last nail was driven into the route's coffin at a meeting in Boston on February 2, 1965. Joey had flown in with Gordon Pushie to meet his potential customers: executives of a group of privately owned New England utilities whose systems were interconnected in a sort of informal grid to balance their power load as much as possible at peak periods and in emergencies. After a Preece, Cardew engineer had explained the project, Robert Brandt, vice-president of the New England Power Company, the largest in the area, summed up the prevailing sentiment by describing the scheme as "optimistic . . . considering the state of the art." He and his colleagues, he added, were looking at it "with a grain of salt," and "it must show a clear-cut advantage to us, not [be] merely a break-even deal."

Under questioning, the Preece, Cardew engineer had to admit that the Quebec route was shorter and preferable and the meeting broke up with the implication that if Joey could deliver the power cheaper than they could produce it themselves, the companies might be interested. But he could not count on them for participation, even in the building of the line. With that, all prospect of financing the alternative route vanished.

As for the Atlantic provinces, whose requirements Joey had also hoped to satisfy, their attitude was best summed up by Daniel A. Riley, chairman of the New Brunswick Power Commission. "There were too many question-marks," he said.

After the Boston meeting, Pushie recalls, "Joe was 'down' for about forty-eight hours — which was twenty-four hours longer than he was usually down about anything." But the Premier had faced daunting odds before and overcome them; he clung to the hope that somehow he could still pull off the Atlantic route.

Winters, however, was more than ever convinced that the Hamilton could not be developed without Quebec's cooperation, so on February 1 he carried his campaign for relief from federal tax a stage further. Addressing the Toronto branch of the Canadian Club, he said that under Canada's free enterprise system the government's role was "to create a salubrious climate through incentives and otherwise" in which private enterprise could operate vigorously and constructively to provide employment opportunities and produce benefits for the whole nation. "If a field can be developed to public advantage by private initiative," he went on, "it seems to me it should be encouraged to do so, not only because it fits the Canadian pattern of philosophy but, perhaps of more practical importance, it prevents the burden of capital cost from falling on the taxpayers."

But in the field of hydro-electric power, public ownership seemed to be favoured over private enterprise, as evidenced by the tax situation.

"If the government were to put public and private ownership on the same footing in this regard," he said, "there would be fewer expropriations and the Hamilton Falls project would doubtless now be a reality. [It] does not require assistance from governments. In fact the development of the project by private enterprise can save the taxpayers many hundreds of millions of dollars, benefit consumers and bring a staunch flow of U.S. currency to Canada to help our balance of payments . . . ."

By now, Brinco's various financial advisers, who had been considering how to approach Ottawa with a politically acceptable solution to the problem for some months, had evolved a plan which they hoped would stand more chance of success than a mere request that Brinco be exempted from tax. Since Alberta and Nova Scotia, which both had private utilities, had also made representations on the inequity of the tax, Brinco presented a proposal to Ottawa which it was thought could form the basis of legislation with general application and yet not cost the government too much revenue.

Because the Hamilton Falls scheme seemed to be unique, in that virtually all the power produced would be sold to Hydro-Québec, it suggested that the federal government might rebate all, instead of only half, the corporation taxes levied on those private utilities which sold 90 per cent or more of their output to tax-exempt provincially owned utilities or power commissions. In Brinco's case, since the extra rebate would presumably go to the province in which the commission buying the power operated, this would mean that Newfoundland and Quebec would each receive an equal share of the corporation tax paid by Brinco — which would have the effect of reducing the price to be paid for the power by Hydro-Québec.

A hint that Ottawa might be considering this proposal favourably came on March 8, when the *Financial Post* reported "growing indications" that Walter Gordon would announce the removal of the tax on private utilities in his April budget.

Whether or not he had been given this assurance, Winters had already told Lesage he expected Brinco's tax position to be eased and Lesage had agreed that if there was a prospect of a lower price being offered he was prepared to resume negotiations, provided Winters could reconcile Joey to Quebec's re-entering the picture.

It was probably one of the most difficult telephone calls he ever made, but Winters duly told Joey on February 22 that he seriously doubted whether the Atlantic route could ever be financed. He was, however, sure a deal could still be made with Quebec.

Joey could hardly have been expected to make such an about-turn on the spur of the moment. As he told Pushie gloomily after Winters' call: "I'll have to resign if a deal is made with Quebec." Two days later, he called Winters back and told him he was now thinking of developing just enough power for Newfoundland's own needs (which was obviously impractical, since back in 1954 it had been realized that it would be uneconomic to develop less than a million horse power at the falls; and the total horse power eventually installed at Bay d'Espoir was only 600,000 — no more than is developed by one generator unit at Churchill Falls today).

On February 26, Smallwood talked the situation over with Pearson and Walter Gordon at the Prime Minister's house in Ottawa. Both told him they were anxious to see the falls developed, for the benefit of eastern Canada as a whole, and urged him to patch up his differences with Lesage. Afterward, Smallwood agreed to see Bob Winters in St. John's two weeks hence.

Winters spent a nerve-wracking morning on March 10 explaining to Joey and his cabinet just why the negotiations with Quebec must be resumed if the falls were going to be developed at all. Eventually a face-saving formula was hammered out which Joey presented to the House that afternoon: the Lower Hamilton, he said, would now be developed at the same time as the main scheme instead of later, and its estimated three million horse power would be transmitted to Newfoundland under the Strait of Belle Isle. As for Hamilton Falls, he explained that "Brinco, bearing in mind and sharing the Newfoundland government's strong desire that Labrador power be made available to sister provinces of Canada, including Nova Scotia, Prince Edward Island, New Brunswick, Quebec and Ontario, will commence immediate investigations of the most economic way to transmit Labrador power to those five provinces."

Just in case anyone got the wrong idea, Joey underlined the fact that "the government impressed upon Mr. Winters, and he agreed thoroughly with us, that Newfoundland, as the prime owner of the power, must now and always have first claim on it; and that Newfoundland's interest is and must always be paramount." He was pleased to say, he added, that the government and Brinco were "in perfect agreement," a sentiment with which Mr. Winters, who had been invited to address the House himself, graciously, and doubtless with profound inner relief, concurred.

As it turned out, there was some dispute later over exactly what they had agreed, but for the moment the retreat had been accomplished in as orderly a fashion as could have been expected.

Winters had a long-standing date to address the Electrical Club of Montreal on March 24. He now inserted into the prepared text of his speech, which was otherwise a technical description of the Hamilton project, a passage which said:

> As a result of recent developments involving statesmanship by provincial leaders I believe we are now in a position to re-examine the several routes on their merits and, I hope, select the one that will best serve the common interest. Mr. Lesage has consistently said the door is open for further discussions. I have told him Brinco would like to avail itself of his invitation and I hope we can all negotiate . . . in a spirit of purposeful cooperation which will bring this great Canadian endeavour to a successful conclusion in the near future.

SIXTEEN

A "double-cross"—and a compromise

"It was recognized by those present that the meeting constituted a renewal of talks . . . ." So began Mike Nicholson's minutes of a meeting held at the Hydro-Québec offices on March 30, 1965. Premier Lesage had deliberately made a distinction between "talks" and "negotiations" when he announced in the House a few days earlier that Brinco and Hydro-Québec officials were about to get together again.

The Brinco delegation at the renewed talks consisted of Winters and Nicholson, with Bill Mulholland representing Morgan Stanley. (McParland was away on Rio business in Australia.) Hydro-Québec was represented by Jean-Claude Lessard, Ed Lemieux and one of its commissioners, Jean-Paul Gignac. A dark, shock-haired young man of mercurial temperament, Gignac was a friend of Réné Lévesque and he would play an important role in the tortuous "talks" that still lay ahead.

Winters had prepared himself with a sheaf of notes which he read at the start of the meeting. He gathered, he said, that since Quebec had gone ahead with the Manic/Outardes development it would now not need Churchill Falls power (Joey had recently changed the name) until 1972 at the earliest. If development began in 1965, the power could be on stream by 1970, which was when Con Ed had indicated it would need it. And Con Ed was prepared to buy all that could be produced until Quebec was ready to take up its own share. If Hydro-Québec wished to build the transmission line, Churchill Falls (Labrador) Corporation (as it was henceforth to be known) would pay a rental fee for it; if not Churchill Falls would be quite willing to build the line itself. And for economy's sake, it was thought the transmission should be by direct current.

Winters went on at length, discussing various routes the transmission line might take, until Gignac broke in to say that instead of Churchill Falls selling the power to Con Ed, Hydro-Québec would prefer to buy the total output from the outset and deal with potential customers itself. Winters protested that this brought the talks back to the basis on which they had previously been held, and that Premier Smallwood had agreed to their resumption only on condition that Brinco would deal with the customers and some of the power would go to Ontario and the Atlantic provinces. Also, the contract with Con Ed was an important ingredient of Brinco's financing plans.

Gignac, who was by now doing most of the talking for Quebec, then asked whether Brinco could offer a lower mill rate than before. Winters said he was quite sure the federal government was ready to remove the corporation tax and this saving would be passed on to Quebec to reduce the 2.65 mill price he had already offered. But, he asked Gignac, if Brinco did bring down its price, would Quebec immediately press for a further reduction? Gignac said the Premier's committee had agreed on a price which was below 2.45 mills.

On these two crucial points, it was obvious that more bargaining was in store. Pointing out that it was now eighteen months since the original letter of intent had been drafted, Winters said Brinco was revising its capital-cost estimate in the light of current conditions. When that was done, he would submit four sets of mill rates: for both A.C. and D.C. transmission, with and without federal tax. In turn, Hydro-Québec promised to compare the cost of D.C. transmission with the A.C. it preferred and the meeting broke up.

In effect, it had done nothing but reopen lines of communication, but the news that talks were being resumed prompted heavy buying of Brinco shares during a week when the market was otherwise quiet. By April 5, more than 350,000 shares had changed hands and their price had advanced to $6.75, up more than a dollar from the $5.50 at which they had traded when they were finally listed on the Montreal Stock Exchange in February.

On Saturday, April 24, Bob Winters drove out to Toronto airport to meet Jean Lesage, who was to present the National Newspaper Awards at a dinner that evening in the Royal York Hotel. They drove to Winters' house in Forest Hill and there had "a splendid visit."

The day before, Bill Mulholland had flown in to Toronto to arm Winters with the latest Morgan Stanley financial projections, which indicated that Lesage could be offered a price of 2.50 mills at Point "A", using A.C. transmission; and if the tax rebate went through the price could be as low as 2.2 mills. Winters did not mention this new possibility to Lesage. He suggested they relate their discussion to the price of 2.65 mills which was on the table when the negotiations were suspended.

After reviewing the recent meeting with Hydro-Québec officials,

214

upon which the Premier had obviously been briefed, Winters reminded him of the conditions which had enabled him to quote this price: the power would be sold in Newfoundland, to avoid Quebec sales tax; Quebec would guarantee any borrowing necessary to finance an over-run on the capital cost; there would be an agreed "floor" on the rate of return; and Quebec would guarantee any bank loans needed to carry on construction between the signature of the letter of intent and the major financing — which, of course, would depend on the firm contract that would follow agreement on the letter of intent.

Winters said the price would be lower if the contract was for longer than twenty-five years and if the federal government rebated the corporation tax. He hoped Ottawa would agree to both these measures but it would help if Lesage could discuss them with the Prime Minister when he saw him, as arranged, on May 3. Lesage agreed to do this, and also to see Joey Smallwood to try to heal the breach between them. "On the whole," Winters wrote afterward, "I thought the meeting was excellent. I am convinced Mr. Lesage himself wants to see the project implemented. He told me he thought he could carry with him those of his cabinet who had other views and he said in this regard the removal of the corporation tax would be the determining factor."

Winters spent the rest of the weekend in a mood of cheerful optimism, only to have his peace of mind shattered once again on Monday evening, when Smallwood called him from London to say he had been asked by reporters to comment on a statement by Lesage that his talks with Winters had been fruitless and the negotiations had been broken off. Aghast, Winters asked Joey to say nothing until he could find out what had gone wrong.

He telephoned Lesage next morning and recorded his explanation as follows: "He said he had made the minimum comment: when asked if he and I had reached agreement, he said 'No.' In reply to the question as to whether another meeting was scheduled between us, he said 'No.' He told me he said nothing more. However, the reporters read much more into what he said and my own feeling is he did say considerably more than he reported to me."

In this assumption, Winters seems to have been correct: in Montreal, both the *Gazette* and *Le Devoir* quoted Lesage as saying reporters could draw their own conclusions from his two answers, and the *Gazette* further quoted him as saying his talks with Winters had resulted in "no progress." At any rate, the conclusion the reporters drew was that the talks had once more broken down.

The news could not have come at a worse time for Brinco share-holders: only the day before, Walter Gordon had made his budget speech without including the expected announcement on the removal of corporation tax from private utilities. Brinco shares, which had been trading heavily for a month now, to the mystification of the Brinco management, touched $7.50 on Monday, before the budget speech. By Wednesday afternoon they were down to $5.50.

Lesage referred to the heavy trading in another call to Winters the next day, saying "it wouldn't hurt the speculators to take a knock." Winters found this attitude "very disturbing" and said in a letter to Jack Pickersgill the same day: "I personally do not own a single share of Brinco either directly or indirectly but we do have about 12,000 shareholders and we have a responsibility to them. Knowing the stock responds so violently to either good or bad news I think a sense of responsibility in public statements is necessary. If these statements were made by private individuals rather than government officials we could expect the stock exchange to conduct an investigation."

Winters now wrote to Lester Pearson. "The public must be sick and tired of all this on-again off-again uncertainty," he said, and the best way to end it, "in the national interest," would be for Pearson to invite both premiers and himself to a meeting to thrash out their differences.

There is no record that Pearson ever did discuss the Churchill project with both premiers together, but he did raise it with Lesage at their meeting on May 3, and with Smallwood at lunch the next day. So far, Joey had preserved a golden silence on Lesage's statement the week before. And when he arrived in Ottawa on May 3 he contented himself with telling reporters that Pearson and Lesage would be discussing the Churchill project that evening. Strangely, since the Quebec press had already carried speculation to that effect, this angered Lesage. He called Winters and told him that "unless we could keep Joe Smallwood from 'talking,' Brinco couldn't make a deal with Hydro-Québec." His attitude threatened to crack the serene façade Winters had so far managed to preserve: "I told him that I couldn't give any such undertaking; that too much talking had been done by both sides and that as a result the project was already in jeopardy." Recognizing the danger signals, Lesage hastened to remind Winters that they were friends. And, he added, he saw no reason why Brinco and Hydro-Québec should not come to an agreement "within three weeks at the outside." First, though, he must have some definite price figures.

Then Lesage proceeded to impose another strain on his good friend's

John McLean:
The first white man to see the falls

John McLean was a trader for
the Hudson's Bay Company
based at Fort Chimo, Quebec,
when he came across the falls
in 1839 during one of his
remarkable journeys across
the Labrador plateau.

Initialling the agreement in principle with the Newfoundland
government that led to the formation of Brinco, on March 11, 1953,
R. W. C. Hobbs, of N. M. Rothschild and Sons, sits on Premier
Smallwood's right. Back row, left to right: R. A. Clark, of the British
legal firm Slaughter and May; H. M. S. Lewin, of Bowaters;
Dr. Fred Rowe, Newfoundland's Minister of Mines and Resources
at the time; and Attorney General Leslie R. Curtis.

Premier Maurice Duplessis of
Quebec (centre) shares a joke
with Joey Smallwood in
Sept-Iles at 1954 opening
of the Q.N.S. & L. Railway,
one of the developments that
made Churchill Falls possible.
Extreme right: Bill Southam.

First chairman of Brinco,
the late Bertie C. Gardner,
was a former president
of the Bank of Montreal,
beginning company's long
association with the bank.

Bill Southam (in field clothes at left) soon
established a close working relationship with Joey
Smallwood (right). On this early visit to a Brinex
exploration site, they were photographed with
Dr. A. Paul Beavan, first president of Brinex.

Opposite: Edmund de Rothschild, whose enthusiasm
helped to build Brinco, and Lord Tweedsmuir (left)
on an early visit to falls. Below: Eric Hinton
conducted pioneer surveys for "Channel Scheme."

H. Greville Smith (left) was chairman of Brinco
during the long negotiations that led to the
building of Twin Falls. In this 1962 photograph,
he explains the project to Premier Smallwood.

Robert H. Winters (at left with Governor General Vanier in ceremony at York University, of which he was Chancellor) was chairman of Brinco during the first phase of the negotiations with Quebec.

Henry Borden (centre, below), who succeeded Winters as chairman, lines up with Governor General Michener and project manager Dick Boivin (left) in Churchill Falls messhall.

Donald J. McParland, escorting Prime Minister
Trudeau on his 1968 visit to the Churchill Falls
construction site, was a successful young mining
engineer when he joined Brinco in 1963. His
brilliance soon carried him to the presidency.

Supplies are unloaded at Sept-Iles dock (top) for
1954 survey that first established the feasibility
of the Channel Scheme. Below: Beside cabin at
Sona Lake in 1955 are early staffers (L to R):
Stan Roderick, Eamonn McCormack, Alan Graves.

Joey Smallwood is only one of many who
have enjoyed fishing in Churchill area
since Brinco built the first access
road (below) at a cost of $1¼ million.
Facing page: Miners drive tunnel into
hill (top) during exploration of Kitts
uranium deposit in Labrador. Below:
Among Brinco's activities on island
of Newfoundland was the Whales Back
copper mine, on Baie Verte peninsula.

No sooner had Twin Falls plant come on stream in
1962 than work began to double its production.
Above: New penstocks are installed. Facing page, at
top: Culmination of years of effort, contract with
Hydro-Québec is signed in 1969. From left: Yvon
deGuise and Jean-Claude Lessard of Hydro; Don
McParland and Eric Lambert of Brinco. In bottom
picture: Premier Smallwood presents a replica of
his celebrated gold shovel to Brinco president
Donald Gordon at sod-turning ceremony in 1967.

Transportation of material to site posed challenge for Churchill Falls planners. In 1969, a three-month airlift was mounted (right) when a strike closed the railroad. Below: This huge transporter built to truck in 224-ton transformers was 200 feet long and powered by two 700-h.p. diesel tractors.

Bill Mulholland (left in top picture) chats with
Harold Snyder (right) and Yvon deGuise on terrace
of McParland House, overlooking river. Below:
Dick Boivin (left), Harry Macdonell show intake
structure to Governor General Michener in 1971.

At 1972 inauguration of Churchill Falls,
Prime Minister Trudeau places a cylinder
containing historic project documents
in a Labrador boulder bearing plaque
commemorating the occasion. Premiers
Bourassa of Quebec and Frank Moores of
Newfoundland look on at right.

Right: R. D. Mulholland, a former
president of the Bank of Montreal,
was chairman of Brinco during the
negotiations for the return of
Churchill Falls to Newfoundland.

patience: he said it would be necessary to have a realignment of the Labrador border. "I told him it was not possible for me to bring this about," Winters wrote, "and that it could be done only by arrangements between him and Mr. Smallwood. I asked him if this was essential as a prelude to an agreement and he replied 'absolutely essential,'" but that once Brinco and Hydro-Québec had reached agreement in principle, he himself would negotiate this arrangement with Newfoundland."

Jack Pickersgill reported to Winters afterward that Pearson and Smallwood got along well at their luncheon meeting. But Smallwood then called a press conference and the battle of the headlines began again. He appeared on national television that evening explaining that Brinco now planned to transmit the power through Quebec on D.C. transmission lines built either by itself or Hydro-Québec. "There is no question," he emphasized, "of permitting all of the power moving out of Labrador to be sold to Hydro-Québec, with Hydro-Québec's reselling it to Brinco's customers."

Lesage had been preparing to call Smallwood to suggest that they meet to resolve their differences until he saw this interview on television. It was now his turn to summon the reporters. He told them it was "an absolute condition" for continued negotiations that Hydro-Québec buy all the power. "Never under any conditions," he repeated, "will we let others build a transmission line across Quebec . . . and never will we agree to simply rent out the transmission facilities."

Bob Winters had a strong conviction that the only appropriate repository for dirty linen was a laundry, and the more private and inconspicuous the laundry the better. But in response to insistent questions from reporters he swallowed hard and issued a statement saying: 'I am sure that whatever differences there may be between Newfoundland and Quebec . . . can be resolved very quickly if Mr. Smallwood and Mr. Lesage would meet together to discuss them in the friendly and constructive atmosphere that has characterized their relations in the past."

His suggestion received what could hardly be called a friendly and constructive reception. In Quebec City, Jean Lesage said he was "not ready" to meet Smallwood and added: "I can only negotiate with people who know how to keep quiet." And from St. John's, Smallwood called Winters "to denounce Mr. Lesage again and to say he would never yield from his position; that he was now embarked on a program toward nationalization and that the Dillon Read officials from New York were with him . . . ."

Winters could only reply that there had been "far too much rigidity on both sides," leaving Brinco little or no room to manoeuvre, and that he proposed to work toward an agreement with Hydro-Québec and then leave it to the premiers to judge it on its merits.

Once again, Brinco took Joey's nationalization threat to be a real danger and asked its lawyers to prepare an opinion on the various courses he might adopt and how they might be countered; serious consideration was even given to moving the corporation's head office out of St. John's to forestall him.

In contrast to all this ferment at the political level, the talks with Hydro-Québec were now beginning to look more promising. Brinco had made its latest proposal on Monday, May 3, after a hectic weekend typical of many that were to be put in over the next few years.

Don McParland, now vice-president and general manager of Churchill Falls, spent the Saturday morning on an engineering assignment he had been neglecting in the recent flurry of work: fixing his four children's bikes and tricycles. What he had planned as a relaxed weekend with his family ended abruptly just after lunch, when the phone rang and he discovered that Bob Winters was at Montreal airport and wanted to talk to him urgently. He jumped in his car and drove to the airport, where Winters told him they had to have a letter incorporating their proposal in Jean-Claude Lessard's hands by 9 a.m. Monday and handed him a batch of notes for him to discuss with Bill Mulholland, who was flying in to Montreal that evening.

While Winters flew back to Toronto, McParland headed for the office, called his secretary, Noella Poulin, and asked her to come in later in the evening, then began to go over Winters' notes. He broke off at 6 p.m., went home for a hurried supper and, after taking a brief look at the eggs in a robin's nest the excited children had found, was back in the office by 6:45 working on the letter to Lessard. Noella left for home at 11 p.m., having typed the first draft. McParland waited on for Mulholland, who arrived at 11:30. Between them, they revised the draft until 3:15 a.m., when McParland took Mulholland home for a drink and put him up in the spare room.

They were back in the office by 9:30 a.m. on Sunday, by which time Noella had typed out the revised draft they had left her overnight. They amended this once more after a telephone conference with Winters. Then they caught the 2 p.m. flight to Toronto and by 3:45 were going over the draft with Winters at his home. Mulholland had included in it Morgan Stanley's recommended price for the power: 2.50 mills, coming down by .25 mills if the tax adjustment went through. Winters, presumably to give himself some room for last-minute bargaining, changed the price to 2.55 and deleted the reference to the possible .25 reduction. Then he read the letter to Smallwood and Pickersgill on the phone, after which his secretary, Mary Paquet, retyped it once again.

By 9 p.m., McParland was back in the office in Montreal, where he ran off ten copies of the letter on the duplicating machine and addressed envelopes for them, including two to Joey Smallwood — one to be left at the Queen Elizabeth Hotel and the other to be sent to the Château Laurier in Ottawa, where he was expected next day. It was 1 a.m. on Monday by the time he got home again for a nightcap with his wife, Connie, who had patiently waited up for him.

The letter he delivered to Lessard next morning contained two proposals. The first, the one preferred by Smallwood, suggested that if Hydro-Québec was not ready to take power when the plant came on stream in 1970, Churchill Falls would finance and build a direct-current transmission line from the falls to the Quebec—New York border to supply power "to those customers in Canada and in the United States who have indicated their desire to purchase this power"; Quebec would be given an option to take power later and, if it so desired, to purchase the transmission line. Under the second proposal, if Quebec wanted power from the outset, Churchill Falls was prepared to deliver it by A.C. transmission to Point "A" and discuss the transmission and resale arrangements further. The letter also suggested a forty-year term for the contract — longer if Quebec wished.

Lessard had previously set up a call to Lesage's office and while he and Ed Lemieux questioned McParland about details of Brinco's proposals, the letter was dictated to Quebec City. Their questions, McParland told Winters afterward, seemed designed to clarify Brinco's proposals rather than challenge them, and when he left after about an hour and a half Lemieux said he hoped their meeting "might lead to us seeing more of each other."

Both sides got together again for a day-long session on the Wednesday during which, even though the battle of the headlines had broken out again in Ottawa, Quebec City and St. John's, the atmosphere remained amicable. It appeared to McParland that while Quebec still had reservations about the price of the power, and Lemieux wanted any potential tax saving taken off the mill rate rather than paid as a lump-sum rebate, the various points at issue were being discussed in a constructive spirit which seemed to indicate that Hydro-Québec was at last anxious to reach agreement.

The progress continued during the following week, with agreement being reached on several technical points. Also, McParland was able to convince Hydro-Québec easily enough that even after Brinco had satisfied its obligation to give preference to Newfoundland labour and materials there would still be plenty of opportunity for Quebec participation in the project. On May 11 there was a further step forward: Winters wrote to Hydro-Québec again, this time disclosing the figure he had deleted from the earlier proposal, saying that if the tax rebate went through Brinco would bring the price of the power down by .25 mills to 2.30 mills per kilowatt-hour.

By now, the major stumbling blocks to the agreement appeared to have been narrowed down to two: Lesage's insistence that the Labrador border would have to be changed, and Joey's refusal to permit Quebec to buy all the power and control its transmission and resale. Both these problems, it was realized, would have to be solved at a higher level. But McParland, Bud Manning and the rest of Brinco's senior executives had put their heads together and now thought they could see some possible solutions to them.

On May 12, Winters, a director of the Canadian Imperial Bank of Commerce, sat next to Lesage at a dinner given to celebrate the first directors' meeting the bank had held in Quebec City,* and took the opportunity to outline these possible solutions to him. By the end of the evening, Lesage had promised to call Joey after a cabinet meeting scheduled for the following week, to suggest a new meeting at which they would try to resolve their differences.

Two days later, Winters wrote to Joey to report progress, saying: "I think we have reached the point of agreement with Hydro-Québec on the technical and commercial aspects of the Hamilton Falls project. In doing so, we have not sacrificed any of the profitability which we planned for Brinco at the time of the break-off last July . . . . It has been a cardinal principle throughout that Newfoundland's power requirements

---

*Earlier, during cocktails, Eric Kierans told Winters he considered Brinco to be an unnecessary "middle man" in the deal; that Quebec and Newfoundland could easily develop the falls together — a suggestion he had made publicly on several occasions. Winters bridled and their conversation became so heated that other guests moved away nervously. Finally, Winters said disgustedly: "Eric, I thought you were one of us." Kierans has never been able to understand his remark: "Whether he meant that I was a St. James Street type or that I was English-speaking and not French-speaking."

will have first priority. You will therefore be assured of an abundance of low-cost power . . . ."

In the search for a solution to the transmission problem, Brinco had realized that if the Churchill output was fed into the Quebec system at Point "A", as Hydro-Québec preferred, it would be difficult to determine where the power ultimately sold to Con Ed at the other end of the grid had originated. In his letter to Joey, Winters said: "It has virtually been decided to revert to the concept whereby the power comes into the Hydro-Québec system via A.C. Just where it will be converted into D.C. remains to be determined." In fact, he suggested, it might be better not to convert it into D.C. at all, for a number of reasons: connection to the Quebec grid would lessen the risk to Con Ed of the long transmission route, since the capacity of Quebec's system would be available as back-up generation; and the tie-in between the two grids — rather than having Churchill power delivered directly to the border — would enable New York and Quebec to exchange power at peak periods and in emergencies. The same advantage would also be available to Newfoundland, since if the power were piped into the Quebec system at Point "A" it could also flow in the other direction in an emergency such as a breakdown of the Bay d'Espoir plant.

Churchill Falls would continue to control the resale of the power to Con Ed as a party to the ultimate contract, which would not only inspire confidence in the potential lenders but provide the company with dollar exchange to service its debts. But as a practical matter it was essential that Quebec also be a party to the contract, since Con Ed and any other customers such as Ontario and the Atlantic provinces, which Quebec was anxious to serve, would insist on having rights to enforce Hydro-Québec's performance of its undertakings.

Having thus sketched in the intricate nature of the arrangements that still remained to be made, Winters told Joey he could expect a call from Lesage on May 18, "to discuss subjects over and above the mundane and technical matters on which Hydro-Québec and Brinco have been negotiating. I hope you can arrange an actual get-together at a neutral point, say Moncton, and see fit to make a joint announcement then. If you wish it, I will be glad to draft something or otherwise help in any way I can."

Winters could hardly have expected Smallwood to be overjoyed by these tidings, but he was probably unprepared for the extent of the fury they unleashed. Joey considered himself the victim of "a perfect double-cross" and noted in his diary: "Sounds like a sell-out." And he immediately fired off a six-page reply to Winters which fairly rang with reproach. "I am astonished and bitterly disappointed," he said, accusing Winters of not keeping him properly informed of the trend the talks had taken, which was by no means the one he and Winters had agreed on at their March 10 meeting, but one introducing "radically and fundamentally different ideas." At that meeting, he recalled, they had agreed that while Quebec might want to build the transmission line itself, or purchase it later, "the essential thing was not so much the question of title to the D.C. line, but rather the fact that there should be a D.C. line," and that the power going over it and the profits from its resale to Ontario, Con Ed and the Atlantic provinces should belong to Churchill Falls. This principle now seemed to have been forgotten.

As for the call Winters had told him to expect from Lesage, he said: "It seems to me that the 'subjects' alluded to in your letter would probably include the question of the boundary. I think that it would be advisable for you to notify him that if this is so it would be much better if he did not telephone me or make any other approach to me."

Winters called Smallwood immediately he received this letter and indignantly denied his allegations. And he followed up with a letter of his own for the record, dated May 19, in which he pointed out that he had in fact put Joey's proposal to Quebec, and that Joey had approved the letter beforehand and been given a copy of it on the same day as it was delivered. He went on:

> But, as you well know, negotiations seldom follow a hard and rigid line on any one point. If they are to culminate in success, I presume there must be a measure of flexibility and, although emphasis on various points have [sic] altered during the course of our negotiations, I persisted throughout both with Jean Lesage and with Hydro-Québec on asserting the attitude of the Newfoundland government toward the resale of power. As I pointed out to you, this was a relatively straightforward concept when we were talking about D.C. transmission from the Falls to the customers, but in this regard the concept became less precise and more difficult to maintain when the weight of opinion seemed to swing back toward A.C. last week . . . .

> In my discussions with Jean Lesage I have urged him not to press the matter of the boundary. I told him I thought that ways and means could be worked out on an amicable basis to develop the rivers in question without a change in the boundary. In this I had in mind my conversation with you. I would be very surprised indeed if Jean con-

tinued to press this issue to the point of disrupting negotiations .... I am convinced that we can reach agreement with Hydro-Québec. Whether the project will develop, however, depends to a very great degree upon the measure of mutuality that can be reached between you and Jean Lesage ....

During the next few days, Winters exercised all his formidable powers of diplomacy in an apparently successful effort to promote that "mutuality." Lesage eventually made a conciliatory telephone call to Joey suggesting they get together for the secret meeting Winters had suggested. Others, such as Jack Pickersgill, added their appeals for conciliation and by May 28 Winters was able to write to Eddy de Rothschild saying, "I am pleased to be able to inform you that for the moment harmony prevails between Messrs. Lesage, Smallwood and me. Joe seems to have got over the unhappy frame of mind he was in at the time of your last visit with us .... At my request Jean Lesage has phoned [him] on two occasions and Joe responded very well indeed ...."

Winters and McParland visited St. John's on June 1 and 2 and apparently succeeded in allaying Smallwood's fears that Quebec, by reselling the power to Con Ed, would make more on the deal than Brinco itself. They also discussed the compromise which had emerged as a possible solution to the border dispute, namely that without actually agreeing to a change in the border (which Joey was now more than ever convinced would be political suicide) Newfoundland should give Quebec perpetual rights to flood Labrador territory to create the reservoirs needed to develop the Romaine and the other four rivers flowing south into Quebec. In return, Newfoundland would receive part of the power generated — perhaps 10 per cent — and a corridor through Quebec which it could use to build a transmission line to take Lower Churchill power under the Strait of Belle Isle to Newfoundland.

Originally there was also a proposal that the corridor should give Newfoundland access to an ice-free port on the Gulf of St. Lawrence, in Quebec territory, west of Blanc Sablon, on the existing border. Gordon Pushie had gone as far as flying over the area at treetop level in a forestry department Canso water-bomber, reconnoitring a possible route for a road running south from Goose Bay to the Quebec coast, the idea being to open Goose Bay itself and the eastern part of Labrador to year-round operation.

The suggested compromise revived Joey's flagging spirits; it was, he decided, something he could live with. Before Winters and McParland left St. John's, he called Lesage and, in the words of his diary, "suggested swap of rights — headwaters in return for use of port and transmission rights." Lesage had already been given a hint by Winters of the form the compromise solution might take, and by now both he and Lévesque fully realized the depth of the opposition within Newfoundland to any change in the border. When Joey proposed that they get together in the secret meeting Winters had suggested, he agreed and a date was made for June in Montreal.

When Winters paused at Montreal airport on his way home to Toronto the same day, he called Lessard, who told him the Quebec cabinet had approved the deal in principle and he had a letter of intent ready to be sent to Brinco if the premiers' meeting proved successful.

While no news of these encouraging developments was divulged to the press, word apparently leaked out that the situation had taken a turn for the better, because Brinco shares traded heavily for the rest of the week and the price rose again to $7. The renewed activity worried Winters, who asked Arthur Torrey to see if he could find out what was behind it. Torrey could discover only that much of the trading originated in Newfoundland. Winters was not the only one to note the activity: Daniel Johnson asked in the House for an investigation by the Quebec Securities Commission into "the relationship between the statements and efforts of the principal actors in these negotiations and the activities as well as fluctuations of the stock market."

Joey flew into Montreal secretly on June 7 and Lesage and Lessard joined him in his hotel room. "Apparently we agreed on everything," Joey noted in his diary later. The same evening, Jack Pickersgill drafted a letter for him which was delivered to Lester Pearson next day. "The Premier of Quebec and I had a long discussion on this great project today," the letter said, "and we found ourselves in complete agreement on all points." They had reached an understanding on the development of the five southward-flowing rivers and "made still other cooperative arrangements for the development of the area which should be of great advantage to both provinces and to the whole of Canada."

In the same letter, Joey renewed his request to the Prime Minister that the federal government should "withdraw from the taxation of the production and distribution of electric power in favor of the Provinces," thus removing "the last major obstacle" to an immediate start on the construction work.

Further evidence that the two premiers had at last reached agreement came the day after their meeting, when Hydro-Québec delivered to

224

Brinco five copies of a new letter of intent covering "all the major points that have been discussed in the last few weeks."

On June 10, Winters wrote to Lesage saying: "The majority of the paragraphs in the letter of intent are agreeable to us without change. There are also several other important principles embodied which are a matter of gratification to us in that they will be of assistance in the financing . . . There are, however, as might have been expected, a number of important points on which we will need to have further negotiations with a view to obtaining modifications." The tone of his letter reflected his confidence that these other points could be resolved to the satisfaction of both sides with little difficulty.

The letter added that Joey Smallwood had called him after the June 7 meeting and told him how pleased he was: "He is delighted to be in harmony with you again and I am sure this is a good development, not only for Brinco, but for the country . . . . This, I think, can be a fitting anniversary for our entry into public life twenty years ago tomorrow . . . ."

Next day, at Smallwood's request, the forty-fourth meeting of Brinco's board of directors approved a motion surrendering "all the company's right, title and interest" to the five rivers and their watersheds, subject to the agreement between the two governments being consummated. Winters reported to the meeting that in its latest letter of intent Hydro-Québec had now agreed to many of the "cardinal principles" of the Churchill Falls deal, including the price of the power, "subject to certain tax qualifications which could not yet be resolved." Some other points remained to be agreed — he listed fourteen of them, mostly technicalities — but with his assurance that no difficulty was foreseen in working these out, the board authorized the corporation's officials to sign the letter of intent.

Winters then left for Europe on other business, in the belief that he had the agreement all but signed. On his return, anxious not to lose the momentum he thought had finally been achieved, he wrote to both Lesage and Smallwood enclosing the draft of a press statement he suggested all three of them should release a few days hence. This spoke of "a good measure of agreement" having been reached and added: "It is the hope of all of us that work can start this year . . . ."

It was never issued; on the same day Yvon deGuise told McParland Lesage had issued instructions that the letter of intent was not to be signed until Hydro-Québec had a U.S. customer's signature on a contract, and that Hydro was discouraged by the slow pace of the negotiations with Con Ed.

Winters sensed immediately that failure of the talks with Con Ed would threaten all his hard-won progress, so he wrote to Lesage on July 14 saying that even if no U.S. customer materialized, Brinco would be prepared to finance and develop the project on its own. This would probably mean an increase in the mill rate, but he did not think it would amount to more than one-tenth of a mill.

There was better news on July 21 when Walter Gordon announced at a federal-provincial conference in Ottawa that the federal government planned to introduce an amendment to the Public Utilities Income Tax Transfer Act, under which it would increase to 95 per cent the rebate to the provinces of the corporation taxes levied on private power companies, including those distributing gas or steam as well as electricity. (Five per cent of the tax would be retained to offset the 20 per cent income tax credit available to the companies' shareholders.) It was hoped that the provinces would pass on the extra rebate to the companies so that they could bring down the price of their power.

While Gordon made it clear that the legislation would apply to all provinces, he did not try to hide the government's hope that it would help to get the Churchill Falls scheme under way. "There is no single project we would rather see started," he said. "It will make a tremendous difference to the economic development of the Atlantic area." Perhaps because the measure had been requested by provinces with Liberal, Conservative and Social Credit governments, there was little or no op-position to it. The *Montreal Star* summed up the general feeling when it described it as "highly constructive." Certainly in retrospect it was the most important contribution Ottawa was able to make to the ful-fillment of Joey's dream, and without it the falls might never have been developed.

The day after Gordon's announcement, Jean Lesage told reporters that "only the fine print" now separated Hydro-Québec and Brinco, and on July 29 Winters wrote to Lessard filling in the most crucial of the "fine print" clauses: assuming that Newfoundland passed on the extra tax rebate to the company, as Premier Smallwood had promised to do, Brinco would bring down the price of the power to 2.25 mills per kilowatt-hour in alternating current at Point "A". The corporation, Winters added, was now ready to sign the letter of intent.

All was still reassuringly quiet on the political front, and in the fall Michel Bélanger and Louis-Philippe Pigeon, legal adviser to the Quebec cabinet, arrived in St. John's to discuss the wording of the agreement on the five rivers with Les Curtis, the Attorney General, and his deputy, Cyril Greene. Curtis told the author years later: "We had no difficulty reaching a gentleman's agreement." But still the letter of intent remained unsigned. And now Bob Winters received a higher call.

Lester Pearson had called a federal election for November and he promised Winters a cabinet post if he would return to politics. Perhaps Winters considered he had done all he could to foster the Churchill Falls project and that the signing of the letter of intent was now only an imminent formality; or perhaps he was influenced by the fact that Lester Pearson, now sixty-eight years old, had told him he was tired and the party would soon be needing a new leader.* At any rate, even though Val Duncan tried to persuade him to stay with Rio, he entered the political lists again. When he announced his candidacy in September, a cartoon published in the *Western Star* of Corner Brook showed him in peaked cap and fisherman's sweater, a kit bag on his shoulder, reporting purposefully aboard a sinking fishing boat. The beleagured skipper, Lester Pearson, up to his waist in water and trying ineffectually to bail it out with a tin can, was quoted as greeting him with: "Glad to have you aboard — how are you at manning a pump?"

The Liberal ship, as it turned out, was not so leaky after all and on November 8, 1965, the electors of the Toronto riding of York West, evidently feeling Bob Winters would make a welcome addition to her crew, elected him to Parliament with a healthy majority over his Progressive Conservative opponent.

*Winters stood for the leadership after Pearson's retirement in 1968 and was defeated by Pierre Elliott Trudeau, prominent among whose supporters was Joey Smallwood. Winters returned to the business world and died of a massive heart attack while playing tennis on a visit to California in October 1969. He was fifty-nine.

SEVENTEEN

The knife at the throat

During the evening rush hour on November 9, 1965, the city of New York, parts of nine northeastern states and much of Ontario and Quebec were blacked out by the biggest power failure in history. The failure was not Con Ed's fault — it originated in an Ontario Hydro station at Niagara Falls — but the chaos it caused and the time it took to restore service cast a revealing light on the difficulties the company faced in adequately supplying power to North America's largest city: two airports were closed, hospitals were deprived of vital supplies, 600,000 passengers were stranded in subway trains and many more in elevators, traffic jams blocked streets for miles, television stations went off the air and movie houses closed.

Harland Forbes informed his millions of irate customers next day that the pumped-storage plant the company was hoping to build on the Hudson, while it could not have prevented the breakdown, would have enabled the power to be restored much more quickly. But the plant had now been held up for two years by (as Forbes referred to them scornfully) "groups who felt it might injure the scenery."

No doubt unwittingly, New York conservationists were thus partly to blame for yet another delay in a far larger project of which they had probably never heard. During the summer of 1965, the points at issue between Con Ed and Hydro-Québec appeared to have been narrowed down to the technical arrangements for the delivery of the power. "I believe the price they could pay would be acceptable to Hydro-Québec," Winters assured Joey Smallwood in a letter on September 9. In the early days of the negotiations, this had always been in the neighbourhood of four mills, but Ed Vollmers recalls that he and Bob Winters once visited Harland Forbes at his summer cottage in Maine, and that Forbes told them he would be willing to pay 5.2 mills. Forbes, however, was due to retire at the end of the year and his enthusiasm for the deal does not seem to have been matched by others within the Con Ed organization, who continued to talk in terms of four mills.

There was another complication: because of the continued delay in signing the letter of intent, plans now called for full construction to start at the beginning of 1966, so that the first power would be available in 1971. Quebec now did not expect to need it until 1973 or 1974, but Winters had continued to press Hydro to match the money Brinco was spending to meet its target date. In turn, Hydro had been trying to persuade *its* customer, Con Ed, to share these costs.

Toward the end of the year, Forbes told both Winters and Hydro-Québec he could not do this. Like Hydro, he did not expect to need the power in 1971, though he said that as a favour to Winters he could absorb it by closing down some obsolescent steam plants before the dates on which it was planned to do so. He did not see, however, why he should have to pay for the privilege of doing a friend a favour.

Worse was in store. In December, Con Ed submitted its second letter of intent to Hydro-Québec. (Its first had been delivered in February, 1964.) In it, Forbes told Lessard Con Ed reserved the right to cancel the whole deal up to October 1966, if it encountered any difficulties in obtaining permits for the transmission line. Also, he said, he could make no firm commitment until his company had secured approval for its pumped-storage plant on the Hudson, which was not expected before the fall of 1966.*

Hydro-Québec was less disturbed than Brinco by this latest delay, partly because it did not view the Churchill project with the same urgency but also because by this time another potential U.S. customer for the power had appeared on the scene. Philip H. Hoff, the Democratic governor of the State of Vermont and a vocal critic of the thirty-nine private utility companies which supplied New England with electricity, had approached Quebec with what seemed an attractive proposition. He proposed to set up a private, non-profit corporation to import as much as two million kilowatts of Churchill power to the United States. This was vastly more than Vermont itself could use but Hoff planned to sell at least 80 per cent of it to the other New England utilities. And the main feature of his scheme was that the corporation should issue

---

*Though the Federal Power Commission originally granted Con Ed's permit for the plant in 1963, conservationist groups fought a number of actions against it in both the New York State Court of Appeals and the U.S. Supreme Court, and the company's right to build it was not confirmed until ten years later, early in 1973, when it was announced that the plant would be in operation in 1979 or 1980.

$400 million worth of tax-exempt bonds, most of which would be handed over to Hydro-Québec as a prepayment for the power.

On the Brinco side there was only one man who seemed neither disappointed nor unduly concerned at the prospect of the Con Ed negotiations collapsing. That, strangely enough, was Henry Borden, who had been chosen to succeed Winters as chairman and chief executive officer of Brinco. Borden had never believed that the Con Ed deal had a chance: as chairman of the royal commission which had recommended the formation of the National Energy Board almost ten years earlier, he had been convinced all along that the board could never sanction the export of Churchill power to the United States while power-hungry Ontario was having to install expensive nuclear generating capacity.*

A lawyer who, like Winters, hailed from Nova Scotia, Borden had joined the Brinco board in 1963 at Winters' invitation. But he was surprised when he was asked by Val Duncan to become its chairman and accepted the post reluctantly because, despite his many company directorships, he already considered himself retired and was enjoying editing the speeches of his uncle the former prime minister Sir Robert Borden, on his farm at King, north of Toronto.

Borden had resigned not long before after almost twenty years as president of Brazilian Traction, Light and Power, a Toronto-based company operating transportation and utility companies in South America. He agreed to take on the new job, but only until the letter of intent was signed, when it was understood someone would be found to succeed him. Duncan, who was now giving more time than ever to Brinco affairs, became chairman of the executive committee at the same time, and soon afterward Don McParland was made president of Churchill Falls.

When Borden took over at the beginning of 1966, the negotiations on the letter of intent overshadowed all the corporation's other activities. Twin Falls had by now become a routine operation; the plant had just completed its first year of production without some sort of construction work going on, bringing Brinco its first income, and the company had begun to retire its bonds. The Bay d'Espoir development was proceeding smoothly under the guidance of Churchill Falls engineers. The

---

*In fact, Ottawa did not seem opposed to the principle of the deal. Walter Gordon, for instance, had assured Bill Mulholland he foresaw no difficulty in securing an extension of the twenty-five-year term for power exports if it proved necessary for the Churchill financing.

Whales Back mine had been opened three months earlier by Joey Small-wood and in November its first copper concentrates had been shipped to Noranda Mines in Quebec for smelting. The mine, which had cost $8 million to build, was now employing 120 men, almost all of them Newfoundlanders. Brinex continued to explore Labrador for minerals (at a cost of $422,000 during 1965), and more uranium and copper prospects had been discovered. The timber, which Eric Bowater had counted on to recoup the Founder shareholders' investment, remained a disappointment. Despite several surveys through the years, and approaches from various potential customers, both North American and European, its development was still not felt to be an economic proposition.

After Bob Winters' departure, in an attempt to impart a new momentum to the negotiations, Brinco made a major change of course. On January 11, 1966, Duncan, Borden and McParland entertained Lessard and deGuise to lunch in the Mount Royal Club in Montreal, and Duncan told them that in future Brinco would confine its negotiating to Hydro-Québec and leave the Hydro officials to handle any matters that required intervention at the political level. The new policy obviously pleased Lessard and deGuise, and Duncan came away from the meeting convinced they really wanted to work out a satisfactory deal.

The early negotiations on the letter of intent had resembled nothing so much as a Geneva peace conference. Winters and Lessard would open the proceedings by making formal speeches and then their various aides would take turns gravely elaborating on their leaders' presentations. Understandably, little was achieved in this way, and the Hydro officials resented the fact that when any matter of substance arose Winters usually communicated directly with Jean Lesage. Jean-Paul Gignac, in particular, clashed with Winters at one of their first meetings, when he got the impression (mistakenly, as it turned out) that Winters planned to order the generating equipment from English Electric. Quebec firms, he protested, were well able to build generators and turbines and they would do so if he had any say in the matter.

As McParland took over the main weight of the negotiations, the atmosphere changed. He was among the first to realize that Brinco could only make headway by frankly disclosing all its financial calculations to Hydro-Québec, and his candid, cards-on-the-table manner, his grasp of the technical details, and his engaging personality, rapidly won the Hydro officials' confidence. McParland's mother was of French-Canadian descent, and while she spoke English to her family and McParland's command of the French language would not have impressed the Academie Française, he had grown up in a Quebec town and in spirit he could meet the Quebec engineers on their own ground. He soon established a rapport with them which, in some cases, ripened into a warm friendship. Gignac, particularly, found him a refreshing change from Winters and often, when some particularly difficult point arose to stall the negotiations, he and McParland would meet for a congenial lunch or dinner at the Beaver Club and at the next negotiating session the difficulty would seem to have melted way. Ultimately, while the bargaining remained tough, the two sides became more like partners seeking a joint objective than opponents intent on scoring points off each other.

When they lunched together at the beginning of 1966, Duncan told Lessard that since Con Ed would not commit itself and did not seem to need the power by 1971, it was unreasonable of Brinco to expect Hydro-Québec to match its expenditures to meet the 1971 deadline. Instead, he offered to go ahead with a modified program (he had cut McParland's budget the day before from $9½ million to $4 million) if Hydro-Québec would sign a letter of intent right away, even one containing escape clauses: he called it "a letter of intent with holes." This would enable Hydro-Québec to apply to Ottawa for an export permit, a procedure expected to take some months, and Churchill Falls to build up its project organization and field program gradually, while initiating negotiations for the major financing.

He was, Duncan said, going to see Premier Smallwood the next day. Did Lessard agree with his suggestion, and could he tell Smallwood so? Lessard replied that he thought the program made sense and he had no objection to Duncan's making his view known to Smallwood. In the meantime, he would set up a new round of meetings to put the finishing touches to the letter.

Duncan, Borden and McParland flew to St. John's on January 12. For some time now, Joey had been unable to understand what was holding things up; after all, he had agreed to the five-river settlement months ago and had been led to believe all other aspects of the deal were satisfactory. Duncan now explained the "letter of intent with holes" idea and said that once the hurdle represented by the signature of the letter was surmounted the various "holes" could easily be plugged in further talks. Joey approved this plan of campaign, but once again warned his visitors that "if we have to nationalize we will."

During the next few weeks, Brinco's changed policy appeared to be bearing gratifying fruit. The meetings Lessard had set up went smoothly, and were given new urgency by an important development within Hydro-Québec. With the Con Ed negotiations apparently stalled, the Hydro officials had initiated an internal study of their own future power requirements. To their surprise, this disclosed that not only could Hydro-Québec eventually take all the Churchill Falls output itself — but that it would begin needing it in 1972, unless it set out immediately to develop new power sources of its own, at the cost of heavy capital borrowings.

This study, and the realization that the deal no longer depended on finding a U.S. customer for some of the power, naturally changed Hydro's attitude to the Churchill project and on February 9, McParland received a new letter of intent approved by the full commission. As Brinco had requested, it increased to $100 million the amount Hydro-Québec was prepared to guarantee if Brinco found it necessary to float a loan to finance an over-run in construction costs. By raising the mill rate to 2.45 it also tacitly admitted that Quebec had been at least partly to blame for the repeated delays in reaching an agreement, during which the rising cost of labour and materials, and of borrowing money, had steadily pushed up the estimated final bill for the project.

Two days later, the directors of both Brinco and Churchill Falls authorized the signing of the letter and soon afterward McParland and deGuise got together over lunch to settle a few minor amendments to its wording and review a press release to announce the signing. Then on February 22, Lessard wrote to Lesage enclosing a copy of the letter of intent and asking permission to sign it.

At this point, when an air of euphoria might have been expected to be settling over 1980 Sherbrooke Street, yet another crisis suddenly erupted in Newfoundland. Months before, when the company was expecting Ottawa to announce the extra rebate of corporation taxes, Bob Winters had supplied Joey Smallwood with a forecast of how much money Newfoundland would receive from Churchill during the lifetime of the contract. Within Brinco there had been a strenuous argument about how the benefits of the tax relief should be passed on to Hydro-Québec. Winters' financial advisers were virtually unanimous in their belief that this was a matter for the two provincial governments to work out between themselves. But Hydro-Québec, wanting no official dealings with another province, was holding out for the extra rebate to be paid to the company, and reflected in a lower mill rate for the power. During one of his more difficult negotiating sessions at Hydro, Winters agreed to this. When he told Bill Mulholland what he had done, Mulholland threw up his hands and told him the effect of his agreement would be to give Newfoundland less than he had promised Smallwood it would receive; and if he could not persuade Joey to accept the new situation, he would have a company that would not make any money.

It is not clear now how this news was broken to Joey, but he apparently realized that Winters could not go back on his word to Hydro-Québec without jeopardizing the whole project and so magnanimously agreed to let him off the hook if an acceptable formula for doing so could be worked out. The Premier had appointed J. Douglas Fraser, a St. John's accountant he had employed as a consultant on other government business, to discuss various tax matters with Brinco, including a request made by Winters early in July 1965.

In a letter to the Premier, Winters had pointed out that the draft letter of intent contained a clause protecting Churchill Falls against any new or increased Quebec taxes, a provision included since Churchill Falls would be selling virtually all its output at a fixed price for forty years, with no opportunity to increase its mill rate to compensate for such additional expenses as rising labour costs or the tax increases which might normally be expected over such a long period. To satisfy the lenders who would be financing the project that the company would not one day be bankrupted by unforeseen expenses, Winters wrote, it would be necessary for Newfoundland to give a similar assurance. Joey had agreed that this was reasonable, so toward the end of 1965 Mulholland and Fraser closeted themselves in the Ritz-Carlton Hotel for two days of brow-furrowing effort which eventually resulted in the draft of a letter for the Premier to sign embodying this assurance and also accepting the new situation caused by Winters' concession to Hydro-Québec.

Henry Borden sent the draft to St. John's for the Premier's signature on February 11, 1966; but it appeared that the Premier, who was away, had not briefed his colleagues on the undertakings he had given. At any rate, the letter seemed to take the cabinet by surprise and an anxious Gordon Pushie called Brinco to say that vociferous objections were being voiced to it. Bud Manning flew off to St. John's post haste to explain Brinco's case and found the critics of the letter headed by Les Curtis, the Attorney General, who had in the past complained that Joey was being too generous to Brinco.

Curtis angrily told Manning the letter amounted to "blackmail." There was absolutely no justification for freezing taxes on any company, he claimed, and for the government to hand over the rebated federal tax to Churchill Falls would merely be fattening the shareholders' dividends. Manning explained that the tax rebate would not in fact be returned to the shareholders but would be used to lower the price of the power, as the Premier had agreed. Another objection raised was that according to the wording of the letter, Newfoundland would receive slightly less money from the rebate than it would have done had Ottawa not introduced the new legislation. This had certainly not been intended and after a phone call to Bill Mulholland in New York Manning was able to rephrase the letter so that Newfoundland's share of the tax remained the same.

With the help of Fraser, Manning spent a busy three days meeting various other objections before the matter was resolved to everyone's satisfaction. And when he returned to Montreal on March 2 it was with the letter, bearing Joey's signature, in his briefcase.

This unpleasantness disposed of, Smallwood called McParland a few days later for a progress report. McParland was able to tell him that Louis-Philippe Pigeon, the Quebec cabinet's legal adviser, had approved the letter of intent and it was ready for the cabinet's consideration. This, however, might be delayed because Jean Lesage was tied up in laborious negotiations in an attempt to head off a threatened strike by the province's civil servants. Reporting his talk with Smallwood to Borden later, McParland wrote:

> The Premier said that he had set a deadline in his mind at the end of January and had moved the deadline to the end of February, because it seemed we were making progress. However, he asserted very firmly that the absolute final irrevocable date in his mind was the end of March, and that he had alternative plans should we be unable to deliver the goods by that time and that it was his fond hope and fervent prayer that we would come through etc. etc . . . . I explained that it was beyond our control to schedule the agenda for the Quebec cabinet . . . . The general tone of the discussion was friendly and not too hectoring.

Within a few days, McParland learned that the Quebec cabinet had discussed the proposed agreement, but that the press statement he and deGuise had been preparing to announce its signing was still premature: the cabinet had questioned a number of points in the letter and referred it back to Hydro-Québec.

Up to this time, the wording of the letter had been largely drawn up by the engineers on both sides. Lesage now asked his personal legal adviser, Yves Pratte, a Quebec City lawyer who would later become chairman of Air Canada, and Michel Bélanger, by now Deputy Minister of Industry and Commerce, to go over it, discuss the details of the proposed contract with both sides and make sure that the letter was legally unassailable. And so the round of negotiating sessions began again, this time at an even more intensive pitch than before.

Pratte was a veteran of labour negotiations, which have a tendency to go on all night, and he seemed to have an inexhaustible fund of energy. Still busy with his law practice and various other government affairs in Quebec City, he would rush to the airport after a full day's work and arrive in Montreal early in the evening ready for another session on the letter of intent. At the age of sixty-five, Henry Borden did not care much for meetings that went on until two or three in the morning, and more than once their conclusion found him stretched out sleeping peacefully on a sofa.

During March and April, the Brinco and Hydro-Québec negotiators went over all the ground they had covered in the previous two and a half years, explained to Pratte and Bélanger the agreements they had arrived at and the rationale for them: the price of the power, which the Hydro officials were now satisfied was by far the cheapest they could obtain anywhere; the extent of Hydro-Québec's control over the project; the guarantees Hydro must give to ensure its successful financing; and the safeguards Hydro would receive in return. Pratte challenged some concepts and changed the wording of the letter here and there and by April 21 it was once again ready for submission to the cabinet.

And once again, incredibly enough, all that work led only to yet another disappointment: the company now learned it could expect no action on the letter before a provincial election Lesage had called for early June. Jean-Paul Gignac, though, assured McParland that the cabinet would approve the letter at its first meeting after the election.

Joey Smallwood's end-of-March deadline had come and gone but McParland had managed to restrain his impatience with encouraging telephone calls reporting progress on the letter of intent. And on April 29 Henry Borden flew to St. John's to pass on the assurance the company had been given. The Premier "dressed him down" for the delay but agreed to do nothing until after the election.

On Sunday, June 5, Don McParland voted in his home riding of Westmount and then flew to Toronto for a meeting at the Rio Algom office next day. He stayed at the house Rio maintained for its executives, where his fellow guests were Val Duncan and Sam Harris, a director of Rio Algom and one of the leading corporation lawyers in New

236

York. Harris, who had been an American prosecutor at the Nuremberg war crimes trials, had been invited to join the Brinco board by Bob Winters several years earlier and McParland had come to value his shrewd advice at critical moments.

Duncan, McParland and Harris watched a late-night telecast on the Quebec election results with a keener interest, probably, than anyone else in Toronto, and afterward McParland called his wife, Connie, in Montreal. "Do you know that big tree in the yard here?" he asked her. Mystified, she agreed that she did. "I'm going to get a rope and hang myself from it," said Don. "I'm not going through all this again with a new government."

For to the astonishment of virtually everyone except perhaps himself, Daniel Johnson had led his Union Nationale party to victory over Lesage's Liberals by the narrow margin of fifty-six seats to fifty-one.

This unexpected development brought Bill Mulholland winging in from New York on Monday morning, and Duncan, McParland, Harris and Mulholland held a day-long strategy session to discuss the implications of the change of government. McParland telephoned Robert Boyd, general manager of Hydro-Québec, who had been assigned by Gignac to head the Hydro team in the later stages of the letter-of-intent negotiations. Boyd, who was to have a powerful influence on the ultimate agreement, told him the commission could do nothing about the letter but sit tight until the new government had been formed. Gignac, in another call, gave McParland better news: René Lévesque, who had in recent months been convinced by Hydro-Québec that the province must have the Churchill power, had promised to see Johnson and impress on him the urgency of coming to an agreement.

In the afternoon, McParland telephoned Smallwood and told him Brinco had decided it could only continue to deal with Hydro-Québec, counting on the Hydro officials to handle whatever dealings were necessary with the new government. Joey agreed with this course of action and volunteered that he knew Johnson. The previous summer, hearing that the Quebec opposition leader was on holiday in Newfoundland with his two sons, he had invited them to call on him and they had had a pleasant meeting which he thought might bode well for their future relationship.

The meeting in the Rio Algom office now turned its attention to the latest version of the letter of intent, about which it soon emerged that Bill Mulholland had some serious reservations. Most disturbingly, he told McParland he could give no assurance that the project could be financed on the basis contemplated in the letter — a warning he had already given

Val Duncan in London in April. The company was still a long way from nailing down a deal that the lenders would consider leakproof enough to justify their backing, yet it was going ahead as though the money was already in the till. Mulholland remembered only too well the perilously exposed position Brinco had lived through during the Twin Falls negotiations; now he scented the same air of impending financial disaster developing.

For one thing, though the financing prospects would undoubtedly be improved by the sale of some of the power in the United States, neither the company nor Hydro-Québec was doing anything to land a U.S. customer. It was now fairly clear that Con Ed, under the management which succeeded Harland Forbes, had lost interest in the deal,* and the negotiations between Hydro-Québec and the Vermont group were marking time. Governor Hoff's scheme, in fact, had become a highly contentious issue in New England, and the state House of Representatives had rejected it in March, feeling it did not provide for adequate regulation of the corporation Hoff proposed to establish, and objecting to the huge advance payment envisaged to Quebec. Senator Frederick J. Fayette, who had successfully piloted the governor's proposal through the state Senate before its rejection by the House, had then revived it in a different form and was negotiating with Hydro-Québec on behalf of a private corporation formed by officials of various small municipal and cooperative utilities in Vermont. This scheme aroused vigorous opposition from the private utilities which supplied 80 per cent of Vermont's needs, and from the rest of the private power companies in New England, which saw it as a mere attempt to interpose a new power broker between consumers and a potential source of supply.

Bill Mulholland had been in touch for some time now with representatives of the New England power companies. Back in January, when he had concluded that the Con Ed deal was all but a dead letter, he had asked Ed Vollmers whether the New England companies might be interested in buying some of the Churchill power. Vollmers had for many years been a financial adviser to the Connecticut Light and Power Company and was a close friend of its chairman, Sherman Knapp. He arranged for Mulholland to meet Knapp and Howard J. Cadwell,

*Though not completely, for six years later, in 1972, Con Ed agreed to buy surplus power from Hydro-Québec during the summer months for twenty years, beginning in 1977. Average annual payment for the 800,000 kilowatts involved was expected to be $25 million, a price that works out to eight mills per kilowatt-hour.

238

chairman of Western Massachusetts Electric Company, who were indeed interested — so much so that two other large New England utilities, the New England Electric System and Boston Edison, were brought into the talks.

Initially, thinking it might help to solve Con Ed's difficulties, the New England representatives offered to buy the power Con Ed would be unable to use at night if its pumped-storage plant failed to win approval. To their surprise, Con Ed rejected their offer. The New England companies, however, assured Mulholland that they would be interested in discussing the matter further with Hydro-Québec. And they made it clear they had no intention of cooperating in Fayette's scheme.

In view of this background, Mulholland told Duncan and McParland during his criticism of the proposed letter of intent that it was very important for Hydro-Québec to open negotiations with the New England group. Privately, he did not believe a U.S. customer was an absolute essential for the deal. But putting together a marketable bond issue is a little like assembling a jigsaw puzzle, and the more pieces there are available to build up an attractive picture, the better the chances of success. Selling part of the power in the United States offered two solid advantages. First, the realization that Quebec would need all the Churchill power as fast as it could be brought on stream took time to crystallize within Hydro, so the presence of a U.S. customer at that stage seemed to improve the chances of the plant being built in one continuous operation, with consequent large financial savings. And second, the U.S. dollars received in payment would help to surmount the currency-exchange hurdle. So, as a prudent tactician intent on assembling as many plus factors in his favour as he could, Mulholland sought to imbue his hearers with the conviction that a U.S. sale was vital.

But he felt bound to warn them that the letter of intent was couched in terms more appropriate to a definitive agreement than was warranted by the circumstances. It failed to indicate that the obligations the company was about to assume were subject to the success of the financing. The company was on the threshold of entering into an important commitment for which it would probably be held morally — if not legally — responsible. And if it was unable to carry out its commitments, the record provided little comfort by way of saving clauses or indications that it had ever warned Hydro-Québec of the possible difficulties still to be overcome.

Furthermore, the company's plan to start spending large sums on construction immediately after the letter of intent was signed would tend to place it in a vulnerable position if the definitive power contract and the major financing which depended on it were for some reason delayed. In the circumstances, the company should take steps to minimize its risks and to protect itself by insisting that these risks be recognized and the obligations of the parties to the contract defined.

All in all, Mulholland warned, entering into a letter of intent on the terms proposed, when so many risks remained, could expose the company to censure and lack of confidence, if not to large financial losses and "political and legal sanctions."

These were perhaps rather larger "holes" in the letter of intent than the Brinco management had intended, but once again the confidence that the magnitude and general desirability of the project would ultimately triumph over all difficulties reasserted itself. As McParland noted in his diary later, "all ended in good accord." And after his return to Montreal next day he told Fred Ressegieu and his right-hand man within Churchill Falls, Harold Snyder, a taciturn but extremely thorough engineer he had brought with him from Rio, that the target date for the resumption of work on the site was still the end of June.

This was surprising optimism. As leader of the opposition for almost five years, Daniel Johnson had appeared to be a fiery ultra-nationalist, if not an outright separatist. He had publicly endorsed the "two nations" concept of Canada which so frightened English Quebecers, and indeed the rest of the country; he had published a book on this subject with the ambiguous but threatening title *Equality or Independence*; he had said Quebec must control 100 per cent of personal and corporate income taxes; and three days after his election, when a reporter asked him if his new government would recognize the border between Labrador and Quebec he answered simply, "No."

But in power, rather than opposition, Johnson was to show himself to be far more pragmatic and much more moderate than his previous statements had suggested. He had often criticized, even ridiculed, Lesage for placing too much reliance on the young technocrats who had flocked into the civil service during the "quiet revolution," but he continued to make use of their advice. And he left the Hydro team which had been negotiating with Brinco intact. In fact, a few days after the new premier took office, Gignac went to see him and offered his resignation as a commissioner of Hydro-Québec, since he had been appointed by the previous government. Johnson left no doubt that he needed continuity in the negotiations and asked Gignac, who had stressed the importance of reaching an agreement with Brinco quickly, to stay on.

Early in July, at one of its regular Monday meetings, the full commission of Hydro-Québec passed an unusually strong resolution and sent it to Johnson, urging him to approve the letter of intent as soon as possible. But it was some time before the Premier could give more than passing attention to the details of the agreement, because soon after taking over the government he was faced with two damaging strikes: one, by hospital workers, virtually closed all the province's main hospitals for three weeks; the other, by construction workers on one of Hydro-Québec's own projects, threatened to disrupt the commission's schedule for ensuring the province's future power supplies.

Instead, the Premier asked two of his close advisers to investigate the proposed deal: Jean-Louis Lévesque, one of Quebec's leading financiers, and Roland Giroux, his partner in the investment house of Beaubien, Lévesque and Company. Jean Lesage, when he was premier, had occasionally sought Giroux's advice on financial matters, though as his own Minister of Finance he tended to handle most fiscal affairs himself. Johnson freely admitted his lack of expertise in the financial field and when he took office virtually insisted that Giroux, his friend for many years, become his financial adviser.

After familiarizing himself with the status of the negotiations between Brinco and Hydro-Québec, Giroux made a proposal that horrified the Brinco high command: before the letter of intent could be signed, he said, Brinco must secure signed guarantees from Canadian banks for $100 million, to finance the construction work pending signature of the firm contract and to establish that the project could be financed. Brinco felt this was putting the cart before the horse and that the $13 million it had already spent on the project should be enough to demonstrate its serious intentions.

Jean-Louis Lévesque had served on Henry Borden's royal commission and the two were friends of long standing; Arthur Torrey also knew Lévesque well. After some hurried telephone calls, a meeting was arranged with Giroux, and Val Duncan, who had flown over from London to cope with this latest crisis, explained that it was impossible for Brinco to produce a guarantee of that magnitude at that time. After some discussion, Giroux agreed that the guarantee would be acceptable when the firm contract was signed, rather than with the letter of intent. As things were to turn out, far more than the suggested $100 million would be spent on the project before the contract was finally signed.

Johnson now asked Yves Pratte to "vet" the letter of intent yet again to make sure the deal was a good one for Quebec and that there was nothing in its wording that might rebound to his political embarrassment. The letter eventually filled twenty-one typewritten sheets of foolscap and many of its provisions were so intricate that they defy accurate summary: indeed, some clauses were so technical that they could be fully understood only by the engineers who had drawn up the agreement. In essence, however, Churchill Falls undertook to supply Hydro-Québec with 32.2 billion kilowatt-hours of energy per year, the price at that time being quoted as 2.50 mills during construction, decreasing in stages to 2.10 mills at the end of the forty-year contract.

The price quoted in the letter was subject to a number of variations. Since Hydro-Québec's estimate of what it would cost to build the plant was still lower than Brinco's, an average of the two figures was struck and it was agreed that both sides would share either the savings, if the final cost turned out to be lower than that figure, or the extra costs (up to an agreed maximum of $800 million) if it turned out to be higher. A complicated formula was worked out to relate these sums to the mill rate.

Also, as the negotiations had dragged on through the years, the cost of borrowing money had kept on rising. Each time the interest rate Churchill Falls would have to pay on its first mortgage bonds changed, the complicated calculations needed to arrive at the final cost of the project, and thus the price of the power, had to be reworked. To simplify matters, it was decided to leave this fluctuating interest factor out of the calculations and base them on the rate ruling at the time Brinco had made its first firm offer to Hydro-Québec: 5½ per cent. And it was agreed that the mill rate would be increased by the fraction of .075 mills for each quarter of a per cent that the cost of borrowing rose above that figure. This was an important point, since each rise of ¼ per cent in the interest rate represented an extra payment of $25 million over the life of the bonds.

In the original letter, there was a clause on which Yves Pratte dug in his heels: he absolutely refused to sanction the corporation's exemption from future tax increases. He did, however, agree with Henry Borden, who pointed out that if Brinco found Quebec taxes too burdensome it would have every right to avoid them altogether by moving its offices out of the province.

Throughout most of the negotiations, of course, it had been envisaged that Hydro-Québec would pay for part of the power in the U.S. dollars received from the resale to Con Ed. With no arrangements for a resale specified in the letter of intent, the Brinco negotiators tried to persuade

Hydro-Québec to shoulder all the exchange risk. This was another point on which Yves Pratte dug in his heels, but it was ultimately agreed that both sides would share either the losses or the profits arising from fluctuations in the exchange rate up to 3 per cent, after which Hydro would take it all.

Under Clause 25 of the letter, Hydro-Québec agreed to guarantee the repayment (up to $100 million) of any extra money Churchill Falls had to borrow to complete the project if its cost ran over the amount raised in its initial financing. Another clause bound Churchill Falls to permit Hydro-Québec to step in and "implement the project" if it seemed that Churchill Falls would not be able to put the first two turbine-generator units on stream within five years of the start of construction. Churchill Falls agreed to give Hydro-Québec free access to the construction site and the right to audit its books to ensure that the project was being carried out economically. It also bound itself not to sell any securities without prior consultation with Hydro-Québec, if the interest rate was at a level which required Hydro to make supplementary payments to the company.

Another clause of the letter gave preference to "Quebec labour, personnel and services and to materials and equipment manufactured in Quebec," though it specified that this was subject to the company's prior obligations to Newfoundland. There were other, more technical clauses covering such things as the design of the transmission line and its compatibility with Hydro-Québec's system, but these caused few difficulties during what ultimately, to everyone's relief, turned out to be the last, exhausting, re-examination of the letter.

Even while Pratte was still holding his almost daily late-night sessions on the letter, Premier Johnson, in his subtle way, appeared to be preparing the ground for his government's acceptance of the deal; on August 2 he told a press conference that a final agreement had been reached just before the June election and it would have been signed immediately by the Liberal government had it been returned to power. Lesage promptly denied this statement. "Intensive" negotiations had been going on before the election, he said, and he had been told they were going well. But he had not been able to see or study the text of the agreement because he was too busy with the election.

The issue broke into the headlines again at the end of August, when Johnson was quoted in Montreal newspapers as saying the cabinet would probably approve the deal within a few days. The Premier said next day he had been "misunderstood" and the government was still studying the project, which the previous government had been close to approving in principle.

Apparently in reply to this statement, Jean Lesage rose in the House on August 31 in an attempt to set the record straight — and provoked the most astonishing rejoinder by Joey Smallwood in all their many exchanges. He had believed, Lesage said, that it was impossible for Quebec to sign an agreement to buy power from Churchill Falls without first coming to an agreement on the Quebec-Labrador boundary. So before the June 5 election his government had been engaged in secret negotiations with Newfoundland to settle the boundary, and his legal adviser, Mr. Pigeon, had had talks on the matter with the Newfoundland Attorney General. The results he added, were "not satisfactory."

Joey exploded. "If Mr. Lesage is correctly quoted," he said in a statement next day, "then he is an unmitigated liar. In all my negotiations with him, over three years in private and in public, I rejected and spurned every demand, request, suggestion he made to change the Labrador boundary by even one inch. I did so in Jack-blunt, categorical fashion . . . . I rejected . . . all his crazy demands or proposals . . . . Before his face and behind his back, in secret and in public, I told him in blunt terms that even a child would understand that there would be nothing doing to change the boundary." The purpose of Pigeon's visit to Newfoundland "had nothing to do with changing the boundary." His government, Joey said, had worked hard to get the Churchill developed, "but that water will run through all eternity without being developed rather than change one single inch of the boundary . . . . No power under God will change us in this."

In the face of such vehemence, Lesage backed down at a press conference the following day. He had recognized, he said, that any attempt to recover part of Labrador by legal means was doomed because Quebec had accepted the imposed boundary for too long: Duplessis had in effect recognized the Privy Council decision by not demanding mining royalties from the Iron Ore Company for minerals it was extracting east of the disputed boundary, and even before that the line had received tacit approval by Quebec, since such agencies as the provincial police and the education department had at no time since 1927 attempted to extend their jurisdiction into what the Privy Council had decided was Newfoundland territory.

Realizing that the only way to recover the territory was "to commit an act of aggression," he had begun negotiating to obtain rights to the headwaters of the five southward-flowing rivers, and he had used the phrase "boundary negotiations" because these rivers crossed the boundary; the negotiations had still been in progress when they were interrupted by the election campaign.

It was the last engagement in what had been an extraordinary war of words, but it apparently revived Joey's impatience at the continued delay in reaching an agreement with Quebec. Early in September, he told McParland by phone that he was considering asking the federal government to intervene by declaring the project to be in the national interest. Well aware of the explosive consequences this could have, McParland persuaded him to hold off until September 23, by which time, he thought, a decision might have been reached in Quebec City. And on September 18, McParland and Henry Borden flew to St. John's, told the Premier in person they were encouraged by the trend of the negotiations, and asked him not to pursue his plan to enlist Ottawa's aid.

McParland was able to tell Joey that Roland Giroux now seemed to be in favour of the deal. Giroux had told him a couple of weeks earlier that he realized it would relieve Hydro-Québec of the necessity to raise several hundred million dollars on the U.S. capital market, at a time when lenders were already "loaded with Hydro bonds" and Johnson was trying not to increase the province's debt. Also, he understood how important it was for Churchill Falls' financing to have an American customer for the power and had said he was in favour of an early approach by Hydro-Québec to the New England utilities.

A few days later, Giroux was more encouraging still: he told Borden and McParland the Premier would like to meet them.

From time to time during the negotiations, opponents of the Churchill Falls deal had raised the argument that nuclear power would soon be available at cheaper rates than even Churchill could offer. Among those who held this view was Jacques Parizeau, an economist who had joined the government as a financial adviser in Lesage's day and had been asked to stay on by Johnson. At the eleventh hour, during Pratte's last examination of the letter of intent, Parizeau (who would later join René Lévesque in the Parti Québecois) returned from an inter-provincial conference and told the Premier it might soon be possible to generate power in nuclear plants for as little as 2.5 mills. Johnson immediately asked Giroux, whom he had now appointed to the Hydro commission, whether this was so; Giroux asked Bob Boyd, who replied that there was no way at that time to estimate the cost of nuclear power with any accuracy, since the plants so far being built in Canada were subsidized by the federal government. The whole nuclear power business, Boyd said, was still too experimental for such factors as depreciation, which affected the price, to be properly worked out. But he was confident that no nuclear plant could ever produce power as cheaply as Churchill Falls.

When McParland and Borden went to see Johnson in Giroux's office on the morning of September 26, the Premier seemed to have accepted this advice and to be satisfied with the economics of the Churchill deal. He admitted, however, that there was political opposition to it and said he wanted to postpone making his decision. McParland and Borden protested that the repeated delays had already placed Brinco in a perilous financial position and impressed upon him the need for some concrete agreement if the company was to continue its program and not abandon the project entirely. Johnson promised to see what he could do, but he told McParland, who had mentioned Joey Smallwood's threat to ask for Ottawa's intervention, that this would "slam the door" on the deal altogether.

Next day, at a full-dress meeting in Quebec City, the Hydro commissioners and senior management put the case for the Churchill deal to the Premier, and that evening Giroux told McParland in a telephone call that the meeting had been a success and all that remained was for Johnson to win over the few members of the cabinet who were still against the agreement on nationalistic grounds.

On the morning of September 29, Giroux again told McParland all was well, that Johnson wanted a little more time to bring the cabinet dissidents into line, but that the decision would probably be announced by the middle of the following week. Joey Smallwood had by now had an order-in-council passed seeking Ottawa's intervention, and Giroux warned that if any news of it leaked out it would ruin the whole deal. That afternoon, the Dow-Jones ticker carried a brief announcement from Johnson's office promising a decision on Hydro-Québec's request for authority to sign the letter of intent "not later than October 6."

McParland drove out to the airport at 4 p.m. to meet Val Duncan, who had once again been summoned to Montreal in view of the expected developments. He gave him the good news on the way to Brinco's executive apartment, where a message was waiting from Joey Smallwood: he was in the Holiday Inn on Sherbrooke Street on his way to Bangkok for a vacation and wanted to see them. With Henry Borden, who was also staying at the apartment, they went over early in the evening and found Joey ensconced in a large penthouse suite with Les Curtis and two of his Newfoundland friends, Al Vardy and Arthur Lundrigan.

The Premier had a letter to Lester Pearson in his pocket, telling him of the order-in-council and asking the federal government to intervene to end the atmosphere of uncertainty surrounding the Churchill project. He was about to mail it, he said, but first he took McParland and the others into a bedroom and read it aloud to them.

When the Premier had finished reading, McParland in turn read him the notes he had made of his conversation with Daniel Johnson, and told him of the messages he had received since, including the assurance — and the warning — Giroux had given him that morning. He also read the Premier the news that had come over the Dow-Jones ticker a few hours before, and all three Brinco delegates pleaded with him not to send his letter to Ottawa.

Dubiously, Joey permitted himself to be persuaded to hold off for another week. But, he said, he was not going to fool around any longer: if Johnson had not fulfilled his promises by October 7, Churchill Falls would be taken out of the hands of Brinco and Quebec and would become a national project. And to underline the fact that he meant business he left the letter with Curtis to be mailed if Quebec's decision went against the scheme.

Relieved that they had once more managed to postpone, if not avert, disaster, Duncan, McParland and Borden returned to the Brinco apartment, where they had a few drinks before going out to dinner, in an atmosphere — as McParland described it in his diary — of "restrained jubilation."

On Tuesday the following week, October 4, McParland and Bob Boyd had lunch together at the Beaver Club and discussed a hunting trip they were planning and an idea they had for forming a bird-shooting club. But the conversation could not long avoid the main topic in both their minds. Boyd, a French-Canadian engineer who had joined Hydro soon after its formation in 1944 and risen through the ranks, had worked as hard as McParland in recent months to try to reach an agreement on the letter of intent. He now said he thought the odds that Johnson would sanction the deal were good. McParland said he certainly hoped so, but he also took the opportunity to press Boyd yet again on a matter Bill Mulholland was still insisting on: the importance of Hydro-Québec trying to find an American customer for some of the power.

Early next morning, Boyd called McParland and told him he had been summoned to Quebec City, where the Premier apparently planned to hold a press conference next day. A few minutes later, Val Duncan called from London to say he had heard from the Canadian High Commission there that Quebec had decided in favour of the deal. This rumour was at least more optimistic than those sweeping Montreal: Arthur Torrey called McParland in the afternoon to tell him Brinco shares had dropped from $5.75 to $5.

Early radio news broadcasts on the morning of October 6 said the Quebec cabinet was split on the Churchill deal and Brinco shares fell again, to $4. "Big panic," McParland noted laconically in his diary. Shortly before lunch, Joey Smallwood called from New Delhi and McParland told him there was no official news yet but things looked promising and he would get in touch with him when he arrived in Bangkok. In the afternoon, Gignac called and told McParland he had heard a rumour from Ottawa that the Quebec answer was "Yes." Evidently he was not the only one to hear that rumour, for by the close of trading Brinco stock had bounced back to $4.75.

At 6 p.m., Daniel Johnson finally put an end to all the rumours. The Quebec government, he told his press conference, had authorized Hydro-Québec to sign the agreement with Brinco for three main reasons: the province would need all the power by 1972; alternative sources such as the rivers emptying into James Bay or nuclear power were either too uncertain or too expensive; and the financing of other sources of power would weigh too heavily on the province's future borrowing programs.

Daniel Johnson had served his political apprenticeship at the feet of a master, Maurice Duplessis. "We are entering into this with great reluctance," he said, "and with a knife at our throat. I would have much preferred to have been able to announce the development of James Bay power, which is entirely within Quebec territory. Those whose carelessness and lack of foresight have contributed to placing before the government a decision to which there is no alternative will have to bear the full burden of their responsibilities."

Having thus begun the disarming of any potential political critics at the expense of Hydro-Québec, he then laid the groundwork for their eventual rout by announcing that the whole question of Quebec's territorial integrity and the Labrador boundary would be investigated by a royal commission.* Johnson had been told of the existence of the "gentlemen's agreement" on the five rivers, but he made no attempt to reopen the subject with Smallwood and nothing more was heard of it.

*The commission was headed by Professor Henri Dorion, a Laval University geographer who had written a book on the border controversy setting out Quebec's case against the Privy Council decision, and had suggested in 1964 that Quebec should nationalize the Iron Ore Company's railroad from Schefferville to Sept-Iles and impose a heavy tax

The atmosphere of jubilation in McParland's office that evening could hardly have been described as "restrained." Most of the staff had stayed late to hear the Premier's announcement and when it came over the radio Henry Borden helped to pour the champagne that had been laid in to celebrate the occasion. Somehow, amid the confusion, McParland managed to get off a series of cables announcing the decision to Duncan and the rest of the directors, past and present. To the message he sent Joey Smallwood, he added: "Do not burn Bangkok." Joey himself, when a *Time* reporter managed to reach him by phone, was for once lost for suitable words. Asked to comment on Quebec's decision, he could only reply: "Glory Allelujah!"

By the time the Montreal Stock Exchange opened next morning so many orders had come in overnight that trading in Brinco shares had to be delayed until twenty-five minutes after noon. It opened at around $6 — $2 up from the previous day's low — but after a few minutes it had to be suspended again to permit the exchange to match buy and sell orders. Five minutes before two, trading was resumed and before the exchange closed an hour and five minutes later 300,000 shares had changed hands, with a high of $6.25 recorded for the day.

The joy was not universal. Separatist Gilles Grégoire, leader of the short-lived political party, the Ralliement National, said Quebec had been forced into the Churchill Falls deal through "connivance" between "high finance" and the federal government. And Réal Caouette, leader of the Créditiste party, said Daniel Johnson had no right to make a forty-year commitment on behalf of the province. "This means," he added, "our children will still be bickering over the ownership of Labrador forty years from now."

Nevertheless, at 10.45 a.m. on October 13, a Brinco party consisting of Borden, McParland, Bud Manning and Mike Nicholson arrived at Hydro-Québec's headquarters and was escorted with due ceremony to Jean-Claude Lessard's office on the twenty-second floor. There, as tele-

---

on the iron ore it carried, to force the mining companies to put pressure on the Newfoundland government to agree to a change in the border. The Dorion Commission handed in its report to the government in 1971 and while it was not published, press reports at the time said it had concluded that because successive Quebec governments since 1927 had recognized the border administratively the Privy Council decision was "legally unassailable." A prime opportunity to negotiate a change in the border, the commission said, had been lost by the Liberal government of Jean Lesage during the Churchill Falls negotiations.

vision cameramen and newspaper photographers jostled for vantage points, the letter of intent, those twenty-one pages whose every word had undergone more searching scrutiny during the past three years than any other document with the possible exception of the Dead Sea Scrolls, was finally signed — by Jean-Claude Lessard and Jean-Paul Gignac for Hydro-Québec and Don McParland and Bud Manning for Brinco.

October 13, coincidentally, was Lessard's birthday. It was also the date Henry Borden had chosen back in June in a pool held by the Brinco directors on the most likely date for the signing of the letter. Borden was the only one remotely close to the actual day; all the rest had picked much earlier dates. Said Borden philosophically: "You can't do things that quickly."

III
The Builders

Canada remains as it has always been — a land of vivid
character; a land for men and women who are not ashamed
to dream and not hesitant to pursue their dreams; a land of
enthusiasm; a land of achievement. The Churchill Falls
project represents for every Canadian in every part of Canada
one of those proud achievements in our history; it is a strong
beat of the country's adventurous heart.

Pierre Elliott Trudeau

EIGHTEEN

The big push begins

There is a medieval tale about a traveller who meets three stone-cutters working beside a road. He asks the first man what he is doing. "I am cutting stone," the man replies, no doubt wondering why the traveller can't see that for himself. The second man, asked what *he* is doing, displays more imagination: "I am cutting a corner stone." he replies. The third man's eyes light up when he is asked the same question and he replies: "I am helping to build a cathedral."

For the Churchill Falls project, Don McParland wanted cathedral-builders — and the scale of the job ahead demanded them. The first hydro-electric power station in the world went into operation on the Fox River at Appleton, Wisconsin, in 1882, within the lifetime of many still alive in 1966. Its water-wheel was forty-two inches in diameter and the head of water which drove it was ten feet. Its two generators provided twenty-five kilowatts of electricity to light some of Thomas Edison's new-fangled incandescent lamps.

Each of the eleven* water-wheels at Churchill Falls (technically, they are vertical-shaft Francis turbines) is 19 feet across and weighs 85 tons. Each is spun to a speed of 216 m.p.h. at its rim by a tumbling column of water 20 feet wide, pouring down a penstock, or concrete-lined tunnel, bored through the rock from the forebay of the reservoir more than a thousand feet above. Each water-wheel drives a generator producing 648,000 horse power, almost 485,000 kilowatts. From the top of its generator to the foot of its turbine, each of the eleven units is as tall as a nine-storey building and its rotating parts weigh 850 tons. And all that throbbing machinery is housed in the largest underground power station in the world, built in a cavern bigger than any cathedral hollowed out of the rock near Big Hill.

*The eleventh unit was added to the original plan at Hydro-Québec's request in 1967, bringing the plant's capacity up to more than seven million horse power.

Had a reincarnated John McLean climbed Big Hill in the fall of 1966 he would have found the landscape unchanged, still dominated by the endless rocks and the tattered black spruce trees, their branches short and sparse as though afraid to push too far out from the shelter of the trunk into the paralyzing cold of the Labrador winter. Fifteen miles to the west, albeit almost lost in the immensity of the wilderness, there were now signs of the hand of man: the gravelled road snaking in from the railway, the Twin Falls plant and its little airstrip, and the steel bridge across the river above the falls. But the bridge at this time led nowhere, and the first task was obviously to build the road to link it to the power site.

Within two weeks of the signing of the letter of intent, Contract No. 12001 for the completion of the access road and construction of the first camp buildings was awarded to a company set up as a joint venture by two contractors, Dufresne and Mannix. And by the middle of November, a month after the signing, the first fill for the road had been trucked into place.

This prompt resumption of work was made possible by the extraordinary thoroughness of the Churchill project's planning, which never entirely ceased through all the years of uncertainty. Ironically, the dragged-out negotiations and repeated delays, frustrating though they certainly were at the time, may have contributed to the efficiency which eventually enabled the project to survive near-disaster and yet be completed not only ahead of schedule but within the budgeted cost. At any rate, McParland used the time well, to gather crucial information and analyze it minutely. He was always hungry for "data," and the more he had, the firmer his plans — and hence the company's costs — could be. He did not get as much money as he wanted during the lean years, but he got a lot and he used it wisely, building up a fund of information that later proved invaluable.

The Acres Canadian Bechtel organization began to come together again some months before the letter of intent was signed, by which time the concept of the development had been worked out in such detail that models of the proposed turbines were already being tested. By now, also, McParland had received several possible construction schedules from Dick Phillips' schedulers and estimators, whose special task it was to build the project on paper: to decide how long it would take to do the engineering design, prepare blueprints, draw up specifications and put the work out to bids; to assess which firms were best able to manufacture equipment or build dykes and control structures, and how long their respective tasks would occupy them; to predict how long it would take to ship materials and machinery to the site, in what sequence, and how long it would take to complete the electrical and mechanical installations; and, by no means least, to estimate how much these myriad operations would cost.

Obviously, such detailed planning is only as good as the information upon which it is based, so that an estimator assessing a factory's ability to fabricate a piece of machinery will want to know, among other things, where it proposes to buy its metal; he will then visit the metal supplier, and might discover that one of the ingredients of the metal to be used is nickel; in that case, he will want to know whether the supplier has an assured source of nickel, or whether perhaps there is a shortage of nickel on the market, or a labour contract is about to expire, which might mean a strike and an interruption in supplies. In the words of Canadian Bechtel's Sid Blair: "We follow the job right back to the ore."

It was this kind of organized attention to detail that McParland had admired in the Bechtel group, for it matched his own dedication to planning. An engineer who walked into his office in the early years was impressed to see on his wall a chart listing fifteen major decisions he had to make, and the dates by which he must make them. This was a legacy of his early days with the Rio group, when as chief engineer he suffered through a nightmare experience with one of the uranium properties Rio had taken over. Because the initial construction estimate had been unrealistic and controls on spending were inadequate, the project floundered from one crisis to another. But since the entire job had been delegated to an outside company, McParland could only stand by helplessly watching the situation go from bad to worse. Eventually, the final cost of the mine exceeded the estimate by $22 million, a sum large enough to imperil the parent company's existence until Val Duncan tightened belts all round and managed to raise enough new capital to weather the storm.

This experience convinced McParland that the owner of a project must always have a good organization to manage the spending of his money by others. He must ensure right at the outset that the estimate for a job includes a thorough analysis of every possible cost, based on exhaustive preliminary studies, to serve as a measure of performance as the work progresses. The estimate must periodically be re-examined, particularly during the design phase, to forestall the temptation to design a Cadillac when a Chevrolet would serve equally well. The owner should also supervise the work in progress to make sure he gets what he wants and has specified. And above all, costs must be reported and approved as they are incurred, to limit the risk of over-runs.

Thus, in a sense, McParland considered Acres Canadian Bechtel to be an extension — though more than usually autonomous — of his own management team. The agreement with Churchill Falls required ACB to provide the overall general management of the project: to collect and analyze all the necessary engineering data and make up budgets and construction schedules; to prepare all the layouts, plans, blueprints and specifications; to break down the job into its component parts and call for and evaluate bids from contractors capable of handling the work; and to supervise the performance of the work in the field. ACB's own activities were directed by a policy board formed by the parent organization and composed initially of John Kiely and Sid Blair, representing Bechtel, and Norm Simpson and Hugh Rynard, for Acres. The board met once a month, either in Montreal or on site, to hear reports from the various ACB managers, review any major decisions they had made, determine policy to deal with any problem that had arisen, and agree on recommendations to be made to Churchill Falls.

As the agreement stipulated, ACB worked under "the direction and control" of Churchill Falls, but in practice there was a continuing exchange of ideas along the way. McParland often attended the board's meetings, and even when he skipped them because of pressure of other business he was aware, through his constant contact with Fred Ressegieu, of what was likely to be discussed and decided. He was, in Blair's words "a great cooperator," and Kiely, whose experience and thoroughness set the pattern for ACB's operations, admired his capacity for making a quick decision whenever some problem arose which demanded his ruling.

Fortunately, Kiely and McParland, though approaching them from different angles, usually agreed on the main requirements of the job. For instance, in the early days Kiely suggested that the work should be broken down into packages which could be handled by medium-sized contractors, rather than depending entirely on one large contractor; then, if any contractor ran into difficulties there would be others who could be enlisted to finish the job. Also, he held that "you can't put all the mystery on the contractor." In other words, as many risks on a job as possible should be eliminated, and where they could not be eliminated they should be shouldered by the owner, rather than the contractor. This, he said, was the way to get tight bidding.

This recommendation coincided neatly with McParland's own thinking. He had, of course, a contractual obligation to have as much work as possible done by Newfoundland and Quebec companies. But he also wanted to distribute the benefits of the construction job, not only from the point of view of earnings but of the experience to be gained, throughout as wide a segment of Canadian industry as he could. And in the interests of the coming financing it was obviously desirable to break down the risks inherent in the project into manageable pieces and spread them around as much as possible.

More than eighty major construction contracts were ultimately awarded to fifty or so different companies, and as many of them as possible were let on a fixed-price basis. The contract for the turbines and generators, as one example, fixed approximately $65 million of the project's costs. In some cases — on the dykes, for instance — unit price contracts were awarded, with the contractor being asked to quote a price for excavating a cubic yard of rock, say, or placing a cubic yard of concrete or a ton of structural steel. The ACB estimators would include in a contract the quantities they felt were involved, but the contractors would be paid for the actual number of units done in practice, which would be checked by the ACB inspection staff as the work proceeded.

It was realized early that one of the major imponderables facing contractors would be how much they should include in their bids to cover the cost of transporting their material and equipment to such a remote site, a field of expertise foreign to most of them. To remove this particular element of "mystery" from their shoulders (and possibly unduly heavy charges from their bids), Churchill Falls undertook to organize and pay for all transportation to the site from stipulated shipping points at Montreal and St. John's. This not only enabled economies of scale such as the ability to charter ships to carry full loads, but also gave ACB control of priorities, so that machinery or equipment could be delivered to the site in the order in which it was needed. To further purge bids of those uncertain factors known as "contingency," contractors were assured that they could buy such commodities as cement, fuel oil and gasoline on site at fixed prices, and Churchill Falls assumed responsibility for the housing and feeding of the whole work force.

To organize and supervise all this varied work, ACB built up a substantial staff, much larger than McParland's own. While it fluctuated according to the demands of the moment, at its peak it comprised 531 non-manual workers: engineers, technicians and managers. From time

to time, also, ACB called on its parent organizations and outside consultants for specialist help; Gray Thomson, for instance, used twenty-two
consulting firms in the design of the project.

Churchill Falls' own staff parallelled the higher echelons of ACB's.
As general manager, Fred Ressegieu reported to McParland. His manager
of construction, J. Herbert Jackson, a widely experienced field man
Canadian Bechtel had wooed away from Ontario Hydro, worked closely
with Harold Snyder, and so on down through the various levels.

In building up his own staff, McParland naturally turned first to
men who had been through the fire with him at Rio Algom. Harold
Snyder, of course, had gone with him as his right-hand man at the
beginning, and the circumstances of their association typified McParland's
approach to the hiring of his assistants. Years earlier, when he was plant
superintendent at one of the Rio mines, he had designed a concrete
portal for a mine tunnel. Snyder, as the contractor's superintendent, was
responsible for its construction, but he considered there was not enough
reinforcing steel in the design and sent a messenger to McParland to
announce that he would not build it. Snyder recalls that McParland in
those days was "regarded as pretty much of a terror," and when he was
summoned to his office he expected fireworks. Instead, McParland
acknowledged the error without any embarrassment, seemed grateful
it had been discovered, and told Snyder it was being corrected. And
soon afterward he invited him to join Rio.

Back in 1963, McParland had also planned to take with him to Brinco
Vince Steepe, a red-haired young paymaster at one of the Rio mines
who, though he learned his accountancy on the job rather than at university, had proved adept at juggling the logistical complications of construction work without antagonizing the engineers he worked with.
The 1964 breakdown in the negotiations with Quebec postponed Steepe's
move but as soon as the letter of intent was signed McParland sent for
him and he ultimately became comptroller of Churchill Falls. For two
men whose varying talents he had noticed on his travels, McParland
cast his net wider: Elmer Squires was a Newfoundlander who had
handled labour relations for Bowaters and Wabush Mines and knew
the Labrador scene; and P.A.T. "Pat" Keeping was an Englishman
who had trained as a chemist before gravitating to Rio's planning staff
in London.

For the key post of Vice-President, Finance, Val Duncan had already
suggested Eric G. Lambert, a burly, imperturbable Scot whose capacity
for hard work and imaginative approach as a trouble-shooter had been

demonstrated during yet another crisis survived by the Rio uranium properties during their early years. In those days, each of the seven mines in the group had a contract to supply uranium to the government's purchasing body, Eldorado, which in turn had virtually identical contracts with the U.S. Atomic Energy Commission and Britain's Atomic Energy Authority. When the U.S. and Britain announced in October 1959 that they would not exercise their renewal options with Eldorado, the Canadian uranium-mining industry faced disaster.

While at that time he held only a subordinate position within the organization, Lambert devised an ingenious "stretch-out" program of production and sales for the company's seven mines which managed to keep some of them operating and salvage many of the miners' jobs. Later, feeling his efforts had been insufficiently recognized, he left to become Vice-President, Finance, of Canada Wire and Cable Co., but he readily agreed to renew his association with McParland when the time came.

Among Lambert's many contributions to the company's efficiency was his policy of having costs reported to and controlled by the engineers who were making the decisions. This called for close collaboration between engineers and accountants, which extended to the top of the organization, Lambert and McParland working as a team to keep the project on schedule and within budget.

Among those who welcomed Lambert's appointment was Bill Mulholland, who had worked with him on some financing for the Rio group early in his career at Morgan Stanley. Mulholland felt that Brinco's financial planning had so far taken a potentially suicidal back seat to the preparations for the construction job. He was still worried by the rate at which money was being spent and new contracts worth millions of dollars were being entered into while there was still no assurance that the project could be financed. And it seemed nothing was being done to line up an American customer for some of the power: months had gone by without any talks between Hydro-Québec and Con Ed, and despite his efforts no approach had yet been made to the New England utilities. Senator Fayette still seemed to be in touch with Jean-Claude Lessard but Mulholland had no confidence in the Vermont scheme.

He received some encouragement soon after the letter of intent was signed when he was summoned to Quebec City to see Premier Johnson, who appeared to have a policy of meeting those involved in the Brinco deal privately to size them up and decide for himself whether he could trust them. They met in Roland Giroux's suite at the Château Frontenac and after a few jocular remarks about Mulholland's Irish name (Johnson himself was of Irish descent on his father's side), the Premier told Mulholland Hydro-Québec had asked the government for formal approval in advance of a resale to the United States. This posed a problem for him, in that the government's acceptance of the Churchill deal had been justified to the electors on the basis of the cheapness of the power and the province's pressing need for it; it would be difficult politically for him now to concede that some of this allegedly vital power must be sold to the Americans to finance the project.

Mulholland said he appreciated this difficulty, and in fact it would be unwise from a business point of view for the government to approve a resale in advance, because this might suggest to potential U.S. customers that their cooperation was essential to the project's success, thereby enhancing their bargaining position. But in view of the importance to all concerned of the Churchill deal, would it not be possible for Hydro-Québec, in private, to pursue purely commercial inquiries in the United States? Then, if it were able to negotiate a deal on favourable terms, it should be able to justify them to the government when the time came to grant the necessary formal approvals. Johnson welcomed this as a solution to his problem and went on to ask Mulholland about a report he had seen that Senator Fayette had been indicted by a federal grand jury. Mulholland replied that the charge involved the alleged sale of a postmastership.* Disgusted, Johnson told Giroux to make sure that the Vermont negotiations went no further. But he agreed that Hydro-Québec should sound out the New England utilities to see what terms could be arranged for the sale of some of the power.

Mulholland lost no time calling Howard Cadwell of Western Massachusetts and arranging a meeting in Boston on December 22 at which Boyd, deGuise and McParland met representatives of the New England companies. It was now almost a year since Mulholland had initiated this contact and in the interim the controversy over the Vermont scheme had suggested to some of the New Englanders that the import of Canadian power was fraught with political complications. But their interest was reawakened when Boyd said the negotiations with both Con Ed and the Vermont group had been suspended, and assured them

*Fayette was fined $300 when he was found guilty of accepting $3,000 from a county sheriff in an attempt to influence the appointment of a postmaster. He denied that the money was a payment for influence-peddling and claimed it was a contribution to Democratic party funds.

Hydro-Québec was willing to enter into the various commitments involved in establishing a link between the Quebec and New England systems — an attractive prospect to the New Englanders, whose geographical position leaves them somewhat isolated on the fringe of the U.S. national power grid. After a day of talks, it was agreed that both sides should set up technical committees to investigate each other's systems.

By this time, the work of preparing the site was well under way, despite the bitter Labrador winter. When the men broke off to celebrate Christmas, three camps were almost finished: one for twenty-five men, at Esker, where the access road starts out from the railway; one on the west side of the river near the bridge, to house a hundred men; and the third, half that size, at Mount Hyde Lake, midway along the new stretch of road from the bridge to the power site.

Those early camps were spartan compared to the ones which would be set up later to accommodate the more than fifty thousand men who worked on the project at one time or another. But John McGowan, project manager for Bona Vista Food Services, the Newfoundland company which would feed this army of workers through the years, managed to serve not one but two Christmas dinners: roast turkey and all the trimmings, plus a cold buffet and lashings of puddings and pies, at midday and again in the evening.

The access road was completed in February 1967, and machines began to clear and level the ground for the first streets in Main Camp, a mile from the powerhouse site. Don McParland was well acquainted with bunkhouses and ramshackle mining towns. One day he took David Morgan-Grenville out to lunch and told him that if the design of the town site were left to the engineers it would inevitably take second place to the project itself. He wanted top-quality men for what he was determined would be a top-quality job and so he proposed to offer them a model community to which they would not mind taking their families; a place where the housing, school, hospital and recreation facilities would match those of other towns further south in which they might choose to live. And he asked Morgan-Grenville to take on the supervision of what was henceforth to be called "management services."

A philosophy was thus developed of providing the permanent facilities which would ultimately be needed right at the start of construction — or at least, where temporary buildings had to be used, of designing them so that they could be incorporated into the permanent structures to be built later. While the first Churchill Falls hospital was little more than a glorified first-aid post in a trailer, it was sited where it could be used as extra ward space when the permanent hospital replaced it. The school operated in trailers at first, until its substantial modern quarters were ready, and then the trailers served as overflow classrooms during the peak construction years. And from the beginning, with the aim of attracting good teachers as well as assuring parents that their children's education would not suffer during their stay in the north, the school budget provided the same funds per student as were allocated in Montreal and other cities in the south.

For those supervisors and permanent employees who had their families with them, comfortable modern houses were eventually built. But most of the labour force, of course, lived in the camps, where the standard accommodation was a far cry from the customary log bunkhouse. The men lived in clusters of three well-heated trailers set down side by side and linked by corridors. The two outer trailers housed ten men each, two to a room, and the centre unit contained washrooms and showers, clothes washers and dryers. Janitors were provided so that men coming off shift found their rooms cleaned and their beds made. For this accommodation, similar to that in a small-town motel, and for their meals (which consisted largely of steaks, with second and third helpings quite usual) the men paid $2 a day.

Offices, too, were established in linked trailer units. The first trailers began to arrive on site in February, and during the following month the nucleus of what would ultimately be Bell Telephone's second-largest mobile system in Canada arrived: a telephone and teletype service tied in to Bell's continental network. In the peak construction year, there were 1,336 telephones and 540 mobile radio units on the site. These mobile radios were vital not only to the work but to the personal safety of men travelling what ultimately became more than three hundred miles of isolated roads: a breakdown in a blizzard with the thermometer well below zero could easily be fatal if there was no way to summon help.

During that same month, March 1967, Churchill Falls and Hydro-Québec agreed that the power would be delivered into the Quebec grid by alternating current, at 735 kilovolts (735,000 volts). The highest transmission voltage envisaged anywhere in the world at that time, this was a pioneering achievement of Hydro-Québec's engineers which involved liaison with manufacturers to improve the design and performance of such equipment as transformers, reactors and circuit-breakers, and research into such arcane matters as how far apart the conductors, or cables, which carry the power should be spaced. The advantage of extra-high-voltage transmission is economic. Just as you can force more oil or gas through a pipeline by increasing the pressure, you can carry more power on a transmission line by increasing the voltage: in fact, doubling the "pressure," or voltage, of a line multiplies its power-carrying capacity four times. Had Brinco tried to develop the falls with the technology existing in the mid-fifties it would probably have needed a prohibitively expensive dozen or more rows of transmission towers to bring the power out. With 735-KV transmission, only three rows of towers are needed and the route they follow from the falls to Point "A" was chosen during 1967. It turned out to be 126 miles long.

The beginning of 1967 also brought to the helm of Brinco a man whose name and towering figure were familiar to all Canadians. When the time came for Henry Borden's retirement, as arranged, after the signing of the letter of intent, someone pointed out that Donald Gordon was about to retire as chairman of the Canadian National Railways. A man of legendary vitality, Gordon had let it be known among his friends that he had no intention of vegetating in his retirement. Late in 1966, over a lunch of Nova Scotia lobster in Gordon's private railroad car, Val Duncan persuaded him to become president of Brinco and chairman of Churchill Falls.

Brought to Canada from Aberdeenshire by his parents when he was thirteen, Gordon worked for a dollar a day in a Toronto bakery before joining the Bank of Nova Scotia at the age of fourteen. He studied banking from correspondence courses and quickly rose through the ranks to the executive level. In 1935 he was made Secretary of the newly formed Bank of Canada and three years later became its Deputy Governor. During the war he was at first chairman of the Foreign Exchange Control Board and later head of the Wartime Prices and Trade Board. He became chairman and president of CN in 1950, at the age of forty-nine, and revolutionized its operations during a career in which his clashes with parliamentary committees often enlivened news columns.

A giant of a man, both physically and figuratively, Gordon could, in the words of the famous song, "rant and roar" like any true Newfoundlander. But his sometimes fearsome bluffness was accompanied by a sense of fairness and a crystalline integrity which inspired not only affection in his subordinates but a confidence among the business community which was to be a priceless asset to Brinco. His arrival on board was marked by a "get-acquainted" party at the office which was expected to be both decorous and brief. Hours later, after he had charmed all the secretaries and caused most of the men to call home and say in slurred voices that they would be late for dinner, Gordon had won a new following of devoted admirers. Often in the months ahead, when McParland and Lambert returned to the office tired and perhaps dispirited after a tough day of negotiations, he would pour them a tumblerful of his native spirit, tell them a couple of off-colour stories, his repertoire of which seemed inexhaustible, and then quietly advance a possible new approach to whatever problem had arisen that day. And of problems, during 1967, there was no noticeable shortage.

Gordon used to tell his friends, who could never quite decide whether or not he was joking, that he had thought when he agreed to head Brinco that the project's financing was all arranged. While he wanted to remain active, he certainly never dreamt that the presidency of Brinco would make so many demands on his considerable stamina. "He used to call me a skunk for talking him into it," Val Duncan recalls.

Gordon arrived at Brinco during yet another of the corporation's periodic crises. McParland was wrestling with the problems posed by Acres Canadian Bechtel's latest estimate of the cost of building the project, delivered to him in December 1966. This increased the expected bill for the work by a horrifying $89 million and McParland was having almost daily meetings with Fred Ressegieu and his aides at ACB in an attempt to whittle down the figure before approving the estimate.

He gave Bill Mulholland the bad news at a somewhat strained meeting in New York in February. Most of the increase, he said, was attributable to inflation: an extra $55 million had had to be set aside to cope with escalating costs. But there was also the unfortunate matter of "Heartbreak Ridge." This, as he explained it, was a ridge that had been discovered across the proposed reservoir which threatened to reduce its potential storage capacity by 20 per cent. To compensate for it, an extra $32 million would have to be spent to raise the dykes. Happily, the re-estimate had reduced the likely cost of the material from which the dykes would be built by $5 million, but that still left a net increase of $27 million in dyke costs. With these and other increases (including an extra $4 million for freight charges), the expected total capital cost of the project was now $800 million.

Mulholland's senior partners at Morgan Stanley were now becoming even more nervous about Brinco's exposed situation than he was himself. A total of $20 million in shareholders' funds had been spent on the project so far and contracts worth a further $3 million had been awarded. The company's immediate requirements were covered by a $10 million "bridging" credit granted by the Bank of Montreal in February; but after that the position seemed cloudy, to say the least.

Bridge financing is a well-recognized mechanism by which banks tide companies over those temporarily awkward but not unusual circumstances in which they must spend money before they have it. Bankers are understanding on these occasions, but quite naturally they like to know when they advance their loans how they are going to be repaid.

When the Bank of Montreal made its first $10 million credit available to Churchill Falls, the company pointed out that this would be only the first instalment of the bridging it would need: the total amount might be as much as $30 million. This was no mean sum for a Canadian bank, but the prospect was viewed with equanimity. Donald Gordon's standing in the financial community; Eric Lambert's meticulous preparation of any presentation he was called upon to make; Don McParland's breezy mastery of the complex engineering involved — all of these combined with the bank's long association with the Churchill project and its internationally known backers to inspire confidence in the company's assurance that the loan would be retired before the end of the year by a new share issue. Another meeting was arranged for May, at which the bank would approve the granting of the extra $20 million credit — assuming, of course, that the company could by then demonstrate that enough progress had been made with its financing to justify the borrowing and satisfy the bank that the extra money would be repaid.

It was now almost six months since the letter of intent had been signed, and Churchill Falls had not yet begun to negotiate with Hydro-Québec on the details of the final, binding contract; it had not even decided on the latest estimate of the cost of building the project. Any prospect of arranging the major financing was thus as far away as ever. The Morgan Stanley partners, conscious of the danger that the whole project might still collapse, were ready to go to Val Duncan and ask for changes in the Brinco management. Mulholland persuaded them to hold off until he had talked things over in Montreal, where a series of crucial meetings took place between April 12 and 14.

NINETEEN

Joey turns the first sod —
and lays down the law

As he familiarized himself with Churchill Falls' financial position, Eric Lambert began to share Bill Mulholland's misgivings about the shaky state of affairs. His searching eye for a balance sheet was accompanied by a grain of Scottish caution which occasionally conflicted with Don McParland's "damn-the-torpedoes" style. At Lambert's request, Mulholland agreed to have dinner with him and McParland on the evening of April 12, before his meeting with Donald Gordon arranged for the next morning. With banker-like restraint, Mulholland wrote later that "the course of the discussion was not entirely smooth." In fact, the atmosphere, as well as the topic under discussion, could best be described as electric. The dinner began at 7:30 p.m., and as the air became increasingly full of sparks the three men repaired to the privacy of McParland's home, where they argued until 2 a.m.

The main thrust of Mulholland's remarks is easily summarized. Progress had been too slow all round. Churchill Falls' commitments would soon outrun its resources and the project was still in no shape to be financed. Under the circumstances, borrowing more money without any clear idea of how it would be paid back could be disastrous. Since it was unlikely that the problems in the way of the financing could be resolved quickly, Churchill Falls should either reduce the commitments it proposed to undertake or find some other way of raising funds than bank loans.

McParland's resentment of this criticism was hardly appeased by the fact that his own vice-president of finance appeared to agree with most of it — Lambert had in fact already communicated his anxiety to Donald Gordon. Mulholland recalls the occasion as the only one on which he and McParland had a full-blown row. But during the next two days, he developed his case. Until Churchill Falls accepted the latest ACB cost estimate, there was no prospect of Hydro-Québec's approving it. Without that approval, there could be no negotiations on the final contract, no hope of winning Hydro's agreement to the increase in the price of power made necessary by the continued delays, and no chance of a contract with a U.S. customer. Furthermore, nothing seemed to have been done to raise another problem he had been stressing for months: the need for a completion guarantee. Before the U.S. lenders would put up the bonds to finance the project, he explained, they would have to be satisfied beyond all doubt that the plant would be completed successfully, no matter what difficulties or extra costs the company might encounter along the way; and the only organization capable of providing that assurance was Hydro-Québec.

Mulholland urged the company to prepare a specific timetable for action to resolve all this unfinished business before a worse crisis arose. Several technical decisions ought to be made at once: on the most economic size for the reservoir, for instance. Also, would Hydro-Québec definitely need the power by the envisaged first delivery date of May 1972, and was a field program during 1967 absolutely necessary to meet that date? In any case, current expenditures should be cut to a minimum and, since Hydro-Québec had contributed to the delays, it should be asked to underwrite any further spending which did prove necessary. The company should also explore the possibility of bringing another partner into Churchill Falls to assume part of Brinco's 68 per cent interest. When this point was raised, Donald Gordon said he thought Canadian Pacific might be interested.*

It was a trying two days, but the mere definition of the problems, the charting of the shoals still ahead, proved a useful, if chastening, experience for all concerned. By the time it was over, McParland had assured Mulholland that he appreciated his criticism. "If you're concerned," he told him, "then so am I." And he promised that within a week he would have a specific written plan of campaign drawn up for further discussion.

On his return to New York, Mulholland recommended to his partners

---

*Gordon did in fact make an informal approach to Canadian Pacific later. Ian D. Sinclair, its current chairman, recalls two conversations with him on the subject late in 1967 or early in 1968. In the first, Gordon talked about an investment in general terms and outlined the corporation's future as he saw it. In the second, he became specific and suggested that Canadian Pacific Investments put $50 million into Brinco in the form of fixed-income securities. Sinclair told him he was not interested in fixed-income securities for the restructuring of CPI's portfolio which he realized was necessary. Gordon did not pursue the matter by suggesting that CP purchase equity and become a partner in Brinco.

that while Morgan Stanley should continue to give advice wherever it could, it should not attempt to set up the company's project for it. However, he warned them that "we must not undertake the financing of the project and fail," adding: "The statement is often made that this project is going to go ahead regardless, that there is too much momentum, governmental and otherwise, for it to be stopped now. There is probably a good deal of truth in this, but it doesn't necessarily follow that the interests of the company will be automatically protected in the process. In other words, this inevitability which is said to exist does not justify recklessness or carelessness."

McParland's thoroughness and the incisive way he made decisions had already become legendary among his own staff and the senior men at Acres Canadian Bechtel. During the next few days he had them all in and galvanized them into action to supply him with the information he needed to draw up the timetable he had promised Mulholland, which included a schedule for the further negotiations with Hydro-Québec and a critical-path plan for the new financing the company needed.

The wave of activity that followed more than justified Mulholland's hope that by reading the riot act in such unequivocal fashion he would spark a program of organized action to speed up the negotiations. His feelings about the completion guarantee were the same as those about the desirability of securing a U.S. customer: publicly, he always insisted it was an essential prerequisite of the financing, but privately he recognized he might not get it; in which case, he was determined to equip himself with every possible argument to demonstrate that the project could not fail.

Two steps taken as a result of his criticism eventually provided him with a formidable arsenal of these arguments. First, a control committee was formed, consisting of McParland, Lambert and Mulholland himself, which met every week and supervised numerous mathematical and technical studies which bolstered his case. Second, McParland established a task force which during the summer of 1967 was to carry out probably the most exhaustive analysis ever made of a major construction project and produce a monumental report known thereafter as the "five-foot shelf" — sixteen closely packed volumes covering every conceivable aspect of the development. Gavin Warnock, a vice-president of Acres, and Ken Wolfe, Bechtel's chief estimator from San Francisco, were asked to head this task force and at the beginning of May McParland gave them a sheaf of foolscap sheets defining in detail the "input" he wanted in each volume of the study.

268

Expo '67 created accommodation problems for anyone visiting Montreal that summer, but Warnock and Wolfe took over an unoccupied set of offices at 1980 Sherbrooke Street, rented desks, hired temporary secretaries and crowded the various specialists whose talents were drawn on during the next three months into company apartments. More than fifty experts from all over North America eventually contributed to the report — engineers, estimators, schedulers, economists, nuclear-power consultants — and their studies encompassed regional economic surveys, assessments of the project's likely effect on eastern Canada and the United States, and on Labrador and Newfoundland, analyses of competing forms of energy that might appear in the future, and detailed financial projections designed to show that the element of risk in the project had been reduced to its absolute minimum.

But before this work had even begun, McParland received a disquieting intimation that the project's momentum might be flagging. On April 28 he took his timetable to Hydro-Québec and told Bob Boyd it required that they open negotiations on the final price of the power by mid-May and agree to it by May 30. Consequently, Hydro-Québec would have to approve Churchill's final capital-cost estimate within a couple of weeks.

The target date for the offering of the first mortgage bonds in the United States, he said, was some time after August 1; he hoped it would be before the end of September, so that by the end of the year the company could "view the successful conclusion of our senior financing with some confidence." Any delay in fixing the price of the power would upset this financial timetable and would have "most serious consequences."

McParland also explained Churchill Falls' financial situation, saying that by the end of 1967, the company would have outstanding loans of between $25 and $30 million (over and above the $20 million it had already spent), and its forward commitments into 1968 would be "of the order of $75 million." If anything happened to delay the financing, he warned Boyd, the company would either have to postpone the 1972 date for first power or ask Hydro-Québec to match its expenditures.

Boyd's response both surprised and disturbed McParland. Hydro must have complete confidence by September that the project was financed and that the 1972 deadline for power could be met, he said. Otherwise it would have to initiate alternative plans to safeguard its 1972 requirements; in fact, it had already awarded a contract for the engineering design of a thermal plant to be sited at Salaberry, near

Montreal, and if the Churchill project was not financed by September it would have to start building this "backstop" plant.

McParland protested that there was virtually no prospect of the financing being lined up so soon, and that letting bids for thermal equipment at that time could be interpreted as a lack of confidence in Churchill. Boyd did not think so, because the Salaberry plant could be treated as peaking capacity, which would ultimately be required in any case. He explained that as much as Hydro would like to avoid spending perhaps $150 million on this plant, it was beginning to despair of ever reaching an agreement with the Americans, and he realized the effect this could have on Churchill's financing plans: the whole project might collapse. Hydro could hardly be expected to help with the bridge financing for Churchill at the very time when it was spending money to protect itself in case the project had to be abandoned. However, he agreed to try to bring the negotiations with the New England utilities to a head.

The New Englanders and Hydro-Québec had by now held a series of amicable meetings and had discussed various methods of delivering the power into the New England system. But the tie between the systems, however it was achieved, promised to cost at least $130 million. And to recoup this investment, the New Englanders wanted a longer contract than Hydro-Québec felt it could enter into. Also, while substantive negotiations on the price of the power had not yet begun, the New Englanders were still talking in terms of four mills per kilowatt-hour. Howard Cadwell recalls that they had just brought in the Millpond nuclear plant at New London, Connecticut, at a price only slightly above that, which they thought would henceforth be the cost of nuclear generation. (Their hopes were sadly disappointed: current nuclear costs in the United States range from eight mills all the way up to twenty and more.) Hydro-Québec felt it was going to have to get 5.2 mills to make the deal economic.

After his dismaying meeting with Boyd, McParland asked Morgan Stanley for a formal opinion on the prospect of financing the development in the United States if all the power had to be sold in Canada, and it was now his turn to become impatient: Bill Mulholland assured him in May that the opinion was "in the pipeline," but by mid-June he was still waiting for it. Neither had he received the latest profitability studies from the Morgan Stanley computer team. McParland had felt for some time that the company was too dependent on its financial advisers, so he decided Churchill Falls should have its own computer program, and

Pat Keeping, with the help of his former colleagues of Rio's consulting wing in London, devised the complex equations which enabled not only the profitability studies but various other calculations which became necessary as the project developed to be fed into a computer at McGill University. Often, as the negotiations with Hydro-Québec became more and more complicated, Keeping would return from a day of meetings, tell the computer operator to make some key changes in the program, and by next morning a whole new set of calculations would be on McParland's breakfast table.

But this system, naturally, took some time to evolve and in the meantime, McParland, lacking the profitability studies, could not begin his price negotiations with Hydro-Québec. His carefully prepared timetable was now in ribbons and the work of translating the letter of intent into a firm contract had still not begun.

Far from the financing being in place by September, it now seemed unlikely that it could be arranged, even if all went well, before the middle of 1968. If the construction work was to continue without interruption — which it must to meet Hydro-Québec's deadline — the company now needed not the $20 million it had contemplated borrowing from the bank in May but $45 million, to carry it through until June 1968. The May meeting, with the bank's concurrence, was postponed and the Brinco management sat down with furrowed brows to puzzle out the next step.

Bank bridging was now out of the question: with so many uncertainties still unresolved, the bank could not be expected to advance the extra $20 million, let alone $45 million. And if the deal fell through, even the repayment of the outstanding $10 million would strain Brinco's resources severely; to have to repay a much larger amount could, in the words of Eric Lambert's assessment of the situation, "bankrupt Churchill Falls and imperil Brinco." Hydro-Québec had refused to finance the 1967 program, and even if a new partner could be persuaded to join Churchill Falls it was unlikely that arrangements could be made in time to be of any help, nor would this course raise all the money the company needed to solve its problems.

The only other way out was a new equity financing. Much discussion took place about the form this should take. Lambert pointed out that if a new issue of Brinco shares were made it would be the corporation's third speculative issue in five years; furthermore, the amount of money needed could hardly be raised in one bite: six million shares of Brinco at the current market price would raise only $24 million, which would make yet another issue necessary within six or nine months.

And so Arthur Torrey suggested that the public should be given its first opportunity to buy shares directly in Churchill Falls. He pointed out that for the ordinary investor this would be the best way to participate in the venture anyway, since Churchill Falls would be the most productive arm of Brinco. There was also a feeling that the broadening of the company's ownership would increase its Canadian flavour and identity.*

After much calculation, Torrey suggested $15 as an appropriate price for the shares, based on what the company could be expected to earn during the life of the contract. It was agreed to raise $37½ million in the first place, to cover requirements until early in 1968. If sufficient progress had been made by then to reassure the bank, the rest of the money needed before the senior financing could be borrowed in a new bridging loan; failing that, another issue could be made. Torrey agreed to put together a group to handle the underwriting as usual and September 27 was chosen as the date for marketing the issue.

Don McParland was only too pleased to leave the details of this offering to the financial people. He had his hands full with a variety of key engineering decisions he had to make so that Dick Phillips and his staff could complete the master project schedule, a wall-sized chart spelling out the exact sequence of every operation entailed in the construction job. While the detailed engineering had to wait until the financing provided the funds to pay for it, ACB's "building on paper," the breakdown of the project into its component parts and the visualization of how they must all mesh together, was so meticulous that the master schedule, ready by the end of 1967, proved firm enough to govern the job to its end yet flexible enough to cope with some horrendous problems still in store.

On site that summer, the build-up of men and materials continued without hitch. The Twin Falls airstrip had been upgraded and daily flights by twin-engined DC-3s began on May 1. A temporary "mess hall" in trailers, capable of feeding six hundred men, was now in

*It was around this time that the long-standing, and long-criticized, arrangement by which some of Brinco's shares carried ten votes instead of one was ended. Since most of the Founders' shares were held in England, Eddy de Rothschild went the rounds of the City persuading their holders it was in the best interests of the corporation for all shares to have an equal number of votes. All agreed to give up their privileged position; they were compensated by the issuance of one free share for each twenty Founders' shares converted back into common shares.

operation. But most of the work was still road-building, to provide access to the area of the power complex. One road was being pushed down the edge of the plateau to what would eventually be the opening of the mile-long tunnel which would take the men and machines into the heart of the rock where the powerhouse excavation could begin. Another was descending further down the hill to the river bank, where the twin tailrace tunnels would be driven in below water level. Yet others were taking shape to link the various work sites on the surface.

During the summer of 1967, also, an agreement was negotiated which was to have a major influence on the ultimate success of the project. From the beginning, it had been realized that one of the worst potential causes of construction delays — and hence possibly uncontrollable cost over-runs — was labour strife. Long before the letter of intent was signed, computer simulations had been carried out to try to estimate how much damage a strike would cause; and it was clear that, because of the short construction season, an astutely timed work stoppage could be calamitous. McParland and his friends at ACB discussed various methods of averting this danger, and of ensuring that the company would always be able to obtain the skilled technicians it would need during the eight years the job was expected to last. The idea of purchasing insurance against strikes was investigated, unsuccessfully (though the company *was* able to buy insurance against loss of profits, from a consortium of U.S., Canadian and British companies led by the worldwide Marsh and McClennan Company). And in the fall of 1966 McParland went to see Carl Goldenberg, a Montreal lawyer (and later senator) who was recognized as one of the country's foremost labour negotiators (and who had, coincidentally, represented Newfoundland in constitutional and financial dealings with Ottawa for many years).

Eventually it was agreed that an attempt should be made to secure a project agreement, covering all contractors and unions on the job. This was not an original idea — similar agreements had operated on previous projects such as the St. Lawrence Seaway — but with so many contractors and unions involved it was no easy matter to arrange. Happily, Goldenberg was impressed by McParland's obviously sincere desire to reach an agreement fair to all concerned, and he agreed to act as an impartial adviser. Thanks to his skill and many contacts within the union movement, the agreement, signed that August, proved triumphantly successful.

As a condition of their bids, Churchill Falls contractors had to agree to join the employers' association and delegate to it their authority to negotiate and administer labour contracts. At the peak there were as many as sixty members of the association. On their part, the fifteen unions on the job — representing all employees from ironworkers to waitresses — formed the Allied Construction Council, with power to bargain for them all. The eight-year agreement outlawed strikes and lockouts and set up a procedure for the settlement of grievances which stipulated that unresolved disputes would be referred to final and binding arbitration. The plant was completed with only one case going to arbitration, and that was an amicable "dispute" in which both sides had difficulty interpreting a clause governing wage premiums and asked for its resolution by a third party. In practice, even though the peak work force numbered more than six thousand men, most disputes were settled on the spot. The nearest approach to a strike was in the early years, when a man was fired and a small group of his friends demanded he be reinstated; sixty-five men downed tools for a shift and a half but returned to work when their union leaders, who happened to be on site for a regular meeting, investigated the situation and supported the contractor.

Partly responsible for this excellent record was an unusual feature of the contract governing pay. The initial wage rates were set somewhat higher than those ruling in St. John's, though not as high as those in Montreal, and to meet the unions' wishes, the men were promised plenty of overtime. Contractors were expected to schedule jobs so that their men could count on a minimum of sixty hours' work every week, with anything over the normal work week paid for at overtime rates. In practice, those who wanted to were often able to work even longer hours and one electrician was reported to have made $26,000 in a year — an astronomical wage in those pre-inflation days. The agreement provided for twice-yearly wage increases of 15 cents an hour for the first three years and 10 cents an hour thereafter. Its unusual feature was that it also guaranteed a yearly adjustment equivalent to the average wage increases granted to each craft during the previous year in ten major cities across Canada. As another incentive to the work force, men who stayed on site three months were given a one-way air ticket home, with a return ticket if they had decided to come back for another three-month stay on the job. While the labour turnover was high on some jobs, many of the trained men stayed on as long as their jobs lasted.

The agreement not only succeeded in its aim of protecting the project against interruption by labour troubles but also had the effect of raising wage rates in Newfoundland and, in a sense, of completing the organization of the labour movement there: more than twelve thousand Newfoundlanders worked at Churchill Falls at one time or another and returned to the island as union members.

But the vexed issue of whether Newfoundlanders or Quebecers had priority for jobs arose several times in the early days. It caused a flurry of excitement the day after the signing of the letter of intent when Jean-Claude Lessard, who for some reason seemed to have overlooked the qualifying clause covering the company's obligations to Newfoundland, announced that the letter of intent gave preference to Quebec labour and materials. "These very explicit clauses," he said, "were inserted by Hydro-Québec into the letter of intent and their application will be implemented by liaison committees. . . ." Joey Smallwood, returning to St. John's from his Far Eastern holiday a few days later, indignantly denied Lessard's statement. But he need not have bothered, because Daniel Johnson himself corrected it in a television interview the same evening: the Hydro president's statement, he said, was "inexplicable and unexplained."

As it turned out, Newfoundlanders made up about 70 per cent of the work force over the years. But even though some men were trained to operate heavy equipment and fill other technical jobs at special schools opened by the province, with Churchill Falls' support, Newfoundland was unable to supply enough men in some specialized fields, and even on occasion labourers, to keep up with manpower requirements, and there was a strong Quebec representation on site.

So much so that Joey Smallwood, arriving to preside at the groundbreaking ceremony on July 17, 1967, noticed it immediately; he was not, as they say, amused. "Two things put the devil into me," he told the author years later in explanation of the extraordinary outburst that followed. First, as he came down the steps of the plane he saw that the yellow buses waiting to carry the 150 visiting dignitaries to the site of the ceremony bore signs in French. It was clearly cheaper to bring in buses from Quebec on the railroad than to ship them all the way from Newfoundland to Sept-Iles, but Joey could not see why buses on Newfoundland territory should not be Newfoundland buses. Then, moments before the ceremony began, he discovered that Tom Burgess, a union organizer who had been elected to the Newfoundland Legislature from a Labrador riding, had no seat on the platform. Even though Burgess had fallen out with Joey and crossed the floor of the House, the Premier held Brinco guilty of a slight on a member of the House of Assembly. He had a sore throat that day, but the fact was not evident to his embarrassed hosts as they listened in astonishment to the speech with which he chose to celebrate the realization of his long-cherished dream.

He began conventionally enough, by saying that three great things had happened to the province since its discovery five hundred years before: the coming of Confederation, the coming of the university, and the coming of Churchill Falls — and it was a moot point whether the university or the Churchill project ranked second in importance to Confederation. He paid tribute to the twelve men "without whom there could have been no Brinco and no Churchill Falls project,"* and acknowledged by name the contribution of those of them who were present at the ceremony: the federal Minister of Trade and Commerce, Robert H. Winters, Edmund de Rothschild, Henry Borden, Don McParland and Donald Gordon.

As the Premier went on, he began to gather momentum like the river foaming down the chute above the nearby falls. His voice rose and he said Newfoundland had been "entirely, completely selfish" in its determination to have the falls developed: "We were not thinking of the welfare of Canada as a whole; still less were we thinking of the needs or the welfare of the people of the Empire State of New York; and even less were we thinking of the good of mankind in general." Then, as his hosts glanced nervously at each other — and at the Hydro-Québec contingent of Jean-Claude Lessard and Bob Boyd — he raised his voice to a shout and went on: "This is *our* land. This is *our* province. This is *our* river. This is *our* waterfall. And we will forever make sure that it will be developed, and when developed will operate, primarily, chiefly and mainly for the benefit of the people of Newfoundland. Let there be no mistake about that."

The Minister of Energy, Mines and Natural Resources, Jean-Luc Pépin, who was also on hand, had said in a brief speech that all the Churchill Falls power would be going to Quebec. Joey corrected him:

*The list, in Joey's order: Sir Winston Churchill, Lord Beaverbrook, Lord Leathers, Sir Eric Bowater, Anthony de Rothschild, Edmund de Rothschild, Peter Hobbs, A. W. Southam, Robert H. Winters, Henry Borden, D. J. McParland and Donald Gordon. To celebrate the occasion, Joey had brought over Sir Winston's grandson and namesake, Winston Spencer Churchill, author and broadcaster, who observed the proceedings with interest, if not astonishment.

"That is almost, but not entirely, true; about 90 per cent of it will go to Quebec, and 10 per cent of it will stay in this province. *All* the power from the Lower Churchill — 100 per cent of it — will stay in this province. . . ."

The other great benefit to Newfoundland from both projects would be employment, but here he had a warning for Brinco: "There are one or two problems. You would not expect me to come here today, in the presence and in the hearing of hundreds of workers on this job, and fail to speak of these problems. . . ." In short, there was some discontent among the workers. There was bound to be discontent among workers living in the bush away from their families, but it would be very foolish to just shrug it off. When the government gave Brinco the rights to develop the falls — and only the government could have given them those rights — there had been one condition: that "all the work on this job — *all* of it — shall be done by Newfoundlanders, so far as Newfoundland is able to produce the men." Brinco had no choice; it was the law of the land. But if Newfoundland was unable to provide the workers, then "Quebec comes second, and all others come third, fourth, fifth, tenth or twentieth."

His voice rose to a shout again: "Number one is Newfoundland. Number two is Quebec. And number one is ahead of number two — and don't you forget it. . . ."

It had been arranged that after his speech the Premier would detonate a series of explosive charges on a nearby hill, their sole though unpublicized purpose being to symbolize, rather than begin, the underground blasting, which was still a couple of months away. Joey ended his remarks by looking at the remote-control detonating switch and muttering, though in a voice loud enough to be heard over the loudspeakers: "I'm supposed to turn this handpiece and blow the bloody place up". Bursts of laughter interrupted him and he waited for them to subside before going on: "I don't know what to blow up . . . whether it's the platform . . . ." More laughter greeted this sally, some of it perhaps a little strained.

The ceremony ended with the Premier turning the first sod with the gold-plated shovel he customarily used for this purpose. This time, to his apparent distaste, the "sod" was a carefully arranged chunk of caribou moss, grass being an exotic plant which was not imported to Churchill Falls until the permanent town was built.

After that, the Premier handed out souvenirs to selected guests.

Donald Gordon received a polished lump of Labradorite,* surmounted by a miniature replica of the famous shovel and bearing a gold plate on which was engraved a representation of the falls. "May I ask you to accept this," he said to Gordon, who towered above him like some giant Labrador bear, "from the people and government of Newfoundland, as a symbol of the great affection and respect they have for you — knowing as we do that you will protect the government and people of Newfoundland to the last drop of your blood."

There were many unusual aspects of the Churchill Falls project; all in all, its ground-breaking fitted the pattern.

---

*A semi-precious stone which Brinco had long ago found within its concession area and for a while had tried unsuccessfully to promote as an attractive material for facing buildings.

TWENTY

An issue collapses,
and disaster looms anew

On August 14, 1967, Donald Gordon and Don McParland lunched with Premier Daniel Johnson at the Bonaventure Hotel in Montreal in an atmosphere Gordon described later as "very cordial." By now, all attempts to sell some of the power in the United States had been abandoned, the realization having finally sunk in that Quebec would need it all itself. Bob Boyd and Yvon deGuise had recently visited Boston for a meeting at which the New Englanders, assuming that the technical aspects of the deal were agreed, had expected to get down to negotiations on the price of the power. Instead, Boyd and deGuise apologized and told them Quebec could not enter into a long-term contract because of its own needs. This complicated the financing plan but Morgan Stanley had finally delivered its opinion to Gordon that the project could be financed even without an American customer, though the sum raised might not be as large as had originally been expected.

Premier Johnson told Gordon and McParland he had instructed Hydro-Québec to open negotiations on the contract. Business activity in Canada in 1967 had been slowed almost to a standstill by federal measures designed to dampen the inflationary boom of the previous year. Ottawa had then begun to relax its tight-money policy to encourage a new round of expansion but, partly because of the inflationary influence of the Vietnam war in the United States, interest rates and bond yields remained high and money scarce. The economic climate in Quebec was further depressed by the end of the boom occasioned by the building of Expo '67 and rumours that capital was fleeing the province because of the rising tide of separatist sentiment. Johnson told Gordon and McParland he wanted Hydro-Québec to take the Churchill power, rather than borrow $400 million or more to develop its own power for 1972; this would leave more room in the reluctant money markets for other provincial requirements. He wanted the contract drawn up as soon as possible, and seemed pleased to hear that Churchill Falls had set a target date of October 15 for its signature. To make up the possible deficiency in the U.S. financing, Gordon had been considering ways of reducing the project's capital cost, and he was contemplating asking the federal government to build the Labrador section of the transmission line, as it had recently agreed to subsidize the Nelson power project in Manitoba. Johnson said he had no objection to this, provided any federal assistance was confined to Newfoundland. He also made it clear that he understood the contract would have to incorporate guarantees to satisfy the potential lenders.

It was an encouraging conversation and McParland returned to his office beaming. At last, he thought, he could get down to the final negotiating which, with the Premier's backing, would no doubt go smoothly enough. Then Bill Mulholland could tie up his end and it would be full steam ahead with the biggest and best damned power plant anyone ever built.

Incredibly, it was only two days before this latest mood of optimism was shattered by a disturbing new threat, this time in a telephone call from Gordon Pushie in Newfoundland. During the months following the signing of the letter of intent, the legislation covering financial and other arrangements between the province and the company (there were five bills in all) had been piloted through the House of Assembly without undue complications and incorporated in an agreement which now awaited only the Premier's signature. But Joey had apparently been brooding about his experience at the sod-turning a month earlier. "He won't sign anything," Pushie told Gordon. "No conditions — just a flat refusal to sign under any circumstances."

The problem, Pushie explained, was that Joey had lost faith in the corporation's bona fides. He felt the project had really become a joint venture with Quebec and had lost its Newfoundland identification. So he intended to pass legislation requiring the corporation to operate its headquarters in Newfoundland; requiring all foremen on the job to speak English; and requiring all contractors to register with the Newfoundland government before doing business in the province.

Gordon asked Pushie to arrange for the Premier to call him so that he could make an appointment to see him. Smallwood called later, said he was about to leave for Montreal to visit Expo '67 and agreed to see Gordon there the following Sunday.

Gordon and Bud Manning stayed late at the office on Friday evening preparing a press release with the headline: "Smallwood Reneges — Churchill Project Closes Down." This said the Premier had "categorically refused to authorize the execution of an agreement" which had been passed by the Newfoundland Legislature and was essential to the project's viability. As a result, the seven hundred men on site and several hundred others connected directly or indirectly with the project would have to find other work within a few days, and contracts worth more than $50 million awarded by the company in good faith would have to be cancelled. And the release ended ominously: "Mr. Gordon reserved comment on whether legal action would be instituted pending consultation with counsel."

As it happened, Gordon did not have to show Smallwood the release, though he told him forcefully that the project would inevitably have to be abandoned if he did not sign the agreement. The Premier grumbled that, perhaps because they had come to office within the past five years or so, the current Brinco management seemed to pay altogether too much attention to Quebec's role in the Churchill Falls project; somehow the feeling appeared to have grown up that Quebec and Newfoundland should share its benefits — the jobs created, the contracts awarded for services and materials, and even the language spoken on site. This had to stop: Quebec had no rights in Labrador and Churchill Falls would be a Newfoundland town.

Gordon's friends could not decide afterward whether he charmed or terrorized the Premier into changing his mind: his wrath could be a fearful thing to behold. At any rate, he managed to convince Joey that the corporation was still well aware of its responsibility to Newfoundland. Joey accepted his assurance and agreed to sign the agreement and permit the project to continue; and yet another crisis passed into history.

That fall, the first explosive charges signalled the start of the power-house excavation, an operation which would later be compared to that of a mine working at a rate of three thousand tons a day for three years. By this time there were 745 workers on the job and thirty families living in the temporary town site, including those of the camp doctor and the teachers for the school, which opened on September 11 with sixteen pupils and twenty more expected imminently.

Those first permanent residents soon became familiar with the flora and fauna of Labrador: the caribou moss, partridge berry and Labrador tea; the otters which could occasionally be seen frolicking down hillside runs into the rivers and lakes; the bears that sometimes wandered through camp; and the more populous bird life, ranging upward in size from sparrows and whisky jays, through ptarmigan and ravens, to the rare and majestic bald eagle. During the summer, the fishermen on site made their first acquaintance with the huge pike and trout to be had in local lakes and streams; and one and all suffered a less welcome introduction to the twin scourges of the north, the black fly and the mosquito. And with the first frosts, the weekly *Churchill Falls News,* launched by Brinco's newly established public relations department to keep workers and their families abreast of project developments, ran a series of sketches of the tracks made in the snow by animals that might be encountered away from the town site: squirrels, rabbits, weasels, mink, muskrats, wolves, bears and, occasionally, caribou.

Unfortunately, the scene of well-ordered progress on site by no means accurately reflected the true state of the corporation's affairs. Churchill Falls was still, as one of its directors once described it, like a car without a motor. And September brought its builders the most alarming intimation yet that putting a motor in it and getting it on the road was going to be a trickier operation than they had expected.

Throughout the summer, preparations had gone forward in great secrecy for the first public issue of Churchill Falls shares. When Donald Gordon mentioned this possibility to Val Duncan in a letter at the end of May, Duncan expressed concern that, first, it might not raise all the money needed, and second, that Rio Algom would not be able to afford enough new shares to maintain its percentage holding in the company. But the planning went on. For one thing, a public issue appeared to be the only answer to the pressing financial problem. It was also thought that broadening the corporation's ownership might protect it against the periodic threats of nationalization — or, if they were carried out, improve the takeover terms — and to some extent de-fuse any allegation that the deal would put unconscionable profits into the coffers of that only vaguely perceived but widely resented entity sinisterly known as "high finance." Furthermore, while the new issue would reduce Brinco's holding in Churchill Falls from 68 per cent to less than 50 per cent, there was a disposition among management to accept this — perhaps even to welcome it — on the grounds that the diffusion of ownership would Canadianize a project whose British connection had sometimes been more of an embarrassment than an asset.

Probably because of this, the house of Rothschild was not brought into the original planning and, indeed, for the first time since Brinco's formation, its name did not appear on the preliminary prospectus for the offering prepared by Pitfield's and filed with the Ontario Securities Commission early in September. As is customary on these occasions, such details as the number of shares being offered and their price were

282

represented in the document merely by large black dots, known in the trade as "bullets". In the absence of the final contract with Hydro-Québec, the prospectus, while it outlined the arrangements set forth in the letter of intent, also lacked information on two major aspects of the deal that might have been expected to interest potential investors: the price to be paid for the power, and how it was proposed to assure the major financing.

Nevertheless, the offering was reported in the financial pages of Canadian newspapers and in London, where the news both surprised and annoyed Eddy de Rothschild, neither he nor Val Duncan having been told that the prospectus had been filed. Bill Mulholland had warned both Donald Gordon and Eric Lambert it was a mistake to leave Rothschilds out of the underwriting group, if only because the absence of that familiar name would inevitably suggest they lacked confidence in the issue. He had also voiced his conviction that the issue could be successfully sold only if Arthur Torrey could persuade all the leading Canadian investment houses to support it.

Eddy de Rothschild was present at the fifty-third meeting of the Churchill Falls board of directors on Friday, September 22, which discussed and approved the final wording of the prospectus, then adjourned until the following Wednesday, the day chosen for the marketing of the issue. But Eddy apparently had a premonition that all was not well. At around that time, an emissary from Rothschilds approached Ian Steers, the London partner of Wood Gundy, and asked if his firm, widely considered the leading investment house in Canada, would be willing to talk over the Churchill financing with Rothschilds. Wood Gundy had already been invited by Torrey to support the Churchill underwriting. After discussion among themselves, the partners had decided that since the contract with Hydro-Québec was not yet signed, and in any case no dividends could be expected for at least eight years, they could not recommend the shares to their clients, and they had declined to join the group Torrey was trying to put together. However, they agreed to discuss the matter with Rothschilds.

On September 25, William P. Wilder, president of Wood Gundy, and J. Ross LeMesurier, one of the senior partners, flew from Toronto to Montreal to meet Philip Shelbourne, a Rothschild partner who had flown in from London. After hearing their views, an agitated Shelbourne telephoned Donald Gordon and urged him to see them right away. Wilder and LeMesurier then rocked Gordon with the bad news that they considered the issue too speculative to be sold. They advised him that Brinco should carry things one step further, put up the $37½ million itself, and wait until the project's future was assured before inviting the public to back it.

Gordon immediately summoned Arthur Torrey, and to his dismay Torrey confirmed that even though Rothschilds had agreed to back the issue by taking as much as $7 million worth of the shares (the maximum the Bank of England would permit), other Canadian investment houses shared Wood Gundy's misgivings and he had been unable to secure enough support to guarantee that the whole offering could be placed. Gordon and Torrey were friends of long standing, but this bombshell, coming right on the eve of the issue, led to an exchange that it would be understatement to describe as acrimonious.

Obviously, to go ahead with the issue and have it fail would be a disastrous — if not fatal — blow to the whole project, and it was a sombre group that gathered at 9.30 a.m. on Wednesday for the resumption of the meeting of the Churchill Falls board, which it had been expected the week before would be a mere formality. Gordon opened the meeting and then immediately adjourned it again until 2.30 that same afternoon when, in the restrained language of the minutes, he "explained that for technical reasons, there would be a delay in executing the final prospectus and the underwriting agreement." He apologized for the inconvenience caused, particularly to out-of-town directors, and the meeting was once again adjourned, this time until October 2.

Gordon, with the aid of Bill Mulholland, then attempted to persuade Wood Gundy to put its muscle behind the issue. Would they try to form an underwriting group, he asked, if they were placed in charge of it? Wood Gundy continued to insist that no one could successfully sell an issue with so many doubts attaching to it. However, they agreed to study the problem of the project's financing as a whole and give whatever advice they could, provided they were not committed in advance to the public issue as a solution.

The October 2 meeting opened only to be adjourned again immediately, the frantic activity which had been going on since the previous week having not yet produced a way out of the impasse. Before the next resumption, which was set for October 16, an unusually subdued Donald Gordon and his lieutenants paid a call on the Bank of Montreal, where they outlined their proposed rescue operation to J. Leonard Walker, the bank's Chief General Manager,* and George N. Scott, its General

*And later, until his death in 1973, its president.

Manager, Credit. The public issue would not now be made, Gordon said. Instead, the existing partners in Churchill Falls proposed to take up the two and a half million shares themselves. This would cost the corporation $21 million which, Gordon said, would be raised by a Brinco rights issue early in 1968.

In the meantime, Brinco would like the bank to extend it a line of credit for the $21 million, to assure its partners it would be able to take up its portion of the share issue when the time came; it would also like the outstanding $10 million Churchill Falls credit increased by $2 million to take care of immediate necessities.

Walker and Scott could not promise anything on the $21 million credit to Brinco: a sum that size, of course, would have to be approved by the bank's board of directors. But they could, and did, advance the extra $2 million to Churchill Falls right away. And they told their visitors they were sure the board would examine their request sympathetically.

Lambert explained the new plan to the fifth session of the marathon fifty-third meeting of the board on October 16, and said the Bank of Montreal board was meeting to consider it the following day. If, as all hoped, it was approved, the $12 million Churchill Falls owed the bank would be paid back with part of the $16½ million which would be subscribed to the private issue by Hydro-Québec, Newfoundland (which wanted to increase its percentage holding in the company), and Rio Algom. And at the new projected rate of expenditure, enough funds would be assured to carry the project through to April 1968. Relieved, the board gave the plan its blessing and finally wound up the meeting which had begun almost a month before.

As helpful as ever, the bank added its support to the plan the next day, the arrangements proceeded as agreed, and with the new subscriptions to Churchill Falls the percentage holdings of its partners became: Brinco, 63.3 per cent, Hydro-Québec, 16.3 per cent; Rio Algom, 10.4 per cent; and Newfoundland, 10 per cent.

With Churchill Falls' solvency assured, at least until the next crisis, its management could now turn its full attention to the negotiations on the power contract, which had begun in August. During the next ten months, the letter of intent was to be completely rewritten, and so the apparently endless process of drafting and redrafting was resumed. The evolving versions of the final agreement, often drawn up by one side or the other over the weekend to meet a deadline, make a stack of files too high to stand comfortably on a desk. But while the bargaining was as determined as ever, there was a growing cooperation between the bargainers.

Hydro-Québec was now fully convinced not only that it needed all the power, but that it could neither produce it for itself nor buy it elsewhere at anything approaching the Churchill price. Furthermore — and this was probably every bit as important — as the months of discussion had dragged on into years, the Hydro negotiators had gained a confidence in Brinco's ability to get the job done that they had not felt in 1963 or 1964. Mutual confidence is essential to any successful deal. It can take a long time to develop, and it does not depend only on the calibre of the top men in an organization, but on their support troops also. Hydro-Québec was about to place a large number of its eggs in Churchill Falls' basket, and it would not have done so had not McParland and Mulholland been able to convince them of the efficiency of their organizations. Once this had been achieved, Hydro put its considerable weight behind the project by giving guarantees that were more far-reaching than any envisaged in the letter of intent. In return — a concession that was naturally not publicized — Churchill Falls agreed to measures which, had its financing fallen through or its operation been less successful than it turned out to be, could have resulted in Hydro taking over the entire project.

One of the first matters discussed when the negotiations resumed was the take-or-pay provision of the contract, and the way Hydro-Québec's initial reluctance to accept this was overcome reflected the growing spirit of cooperation and trust between the two sides. On his part, McParland realized that, since the Churchill output would amount to a third of its system's total capacity, Hydro must be given some operating flexibility. Hydro was now confident that the water — and hence the power — existed in the quantity that Churchill said it did. And so Hydro was offered, and gladly accepted, the right to have the plant operated to suit its own requirements, subject to limitations imposed by such things as safety factors and reservoir levels.

The peak flow of a northern river — during, say, the spring run-off or after a succession of wet years — is forty or more times its lowest flow, during the winter or after a long dry spell. The purpose of forming a reservoir, of course, is to even out the flow by storing the water and releasing it at a controlled rate. By efficient operation, it is possible to use virtually all the water that flows down the river. In effect, the power contract gave Hydro control of the reservoir. For example, in the spring Hydro must use the complete output of its large Beauharnois plant on the St. Lawrence River or lose some of the water, since it is a "run-of-river" plant without a reservoir. With Beauharnois running flat out, Hydro might not need all the Churchill output and might ask for part of the plant to be shut down, causing the water to rise in the reservoir — conceivably, if it were already high, making some of it overflow down the spillway provided for that purpose. In return for the right to vary the Churchill plant's output to fit in with its overall requirements, Hydro-Québec undertook to pay for any water spilled in the process.

When the contract negotiations resumed, Daniel Johnson asked his friend Jean-Paul Cardinal, a Montreal lawyer, to supervise the legal aspects of the deal. Cardinal's partner, Marcel Lajeunesse, took part in many of the drafting sessions on the Quebec side — and he soon noticed something that puzzled him about a clause in the letter of intent: the agreement that each increase of ¼ per cent in the rate of interest Churchill Falls had to pay on its bonds would increase the price of the power by .075 of a mill. To Lajeunesse, this seemed like comparing apples with bananas: he could not see how the increase in the mill rate bore any direct relationship to the higher interest charges.

Hydro-Québec eventually came to believe that this arrangement would increase Churchill's profits by as much as $120 million over the life of the contract. The Churchill negotiators tried to point out that this was not so, and that what appeared to be a large increase in the gross number of dollars involved was actually only a reflection of the fact that a dollar paid out thirty or forty years hence would be worth less in real terms than a 1968 dollar. All agreed, however, that it was a complicated equation and Churchill raised no objection when the Hydro negotiators suggested a solution: Hydro would continue to shoulder the extra interest charges, which it admitted had arisen because of the delays in reaching the agreement, but the payment would be taken out of the mill rate and made separately. The negotiations on the price of the power proceeded henceforth on the assumption that Churchill would be paying 5½ per cent on its first mortgage bonds, the figure ruling at the time of the original offer. Any interest above that rate would be paid directly by Hydro-Québec, and in return Hydro would have the right to approve the interest rate at which the bonds were ultimately sold.

The new arrangement eliminated some of the continual reworking of figures which had complicated the effort to reach a final agreement on the price of the power, but the search for a formula to express the price in the contract remained fiendishly complex. Eventually, a "base rate" was set, declining in stages from a figure of 2.7734 mills per kilowatt-hour for the first five years to 2.3787 mills for the last fifteen years of the contract. In addition, Churchill Falls granted a twenty-five-year extension of the contract at two mills which, notwithstanding the rosy predictions often made for nuclear power, seemed certain to be the cheapest power available anywhere in the world during the first quarter of the next century.

Infinitesimally exact as these figures appear to be, the final mill rate was not known until early in 1975, some months after the power plant was completed and all eleven units were on stream. This was because Hydro-Québec agreed in the contract to share any escalation in the final capital cost of building the plant, up to a total of $900 million (after which Churchill Falls was to have borne any increased costs alone). When all the bills were paid and the final capital cost was computed, it turned out to be almost exactly $900 million. When the adjustments envisaged in the contract were made, the final mill rate became 2.9645 mills per kilowatt-hour for the first five years of the contract, declining to 2.5426 mills for the last fifteen years. The extra interest charges shouldered by Hydro added about half a mill to that figure. The transmission lines needed to take the power from Point "A" into the Quebec grid were built as part of the huge Manic-Outardes project and their cost was not separated out, but Hydro-Québec estimates it at approximately $200 million, which would add a further two mills to the eventual price of the power.

As the negotiations wound their tortuous course through the winter and into the spring of 1968, with the signature of the power contract still seemingly only a distant vision, Churchill Falls once again found itself in dire financial straits. Early in the year, a draft prospectus had been drawn up and actually printed for the issue of Brinco shares with which it had been intended to repay the $21 million loan from the Bank of Montreal. But once again Wood Gundy advised against going to the public for money before the contract had been signed and the major financing was in place.

By the early summer of 1968, almost all the money brought in by the previous fall's equity issue had been spent to keep the construction work on schedule. Outwardly, the company managed to preserve a confident front. Construction work was going forward as planned and the work force continued to be built up; the contract negotiations were progressing, if slowly; and in the New Year the company had moved into plush quarters on the top floors of a new glass tower on Westmount Square.

But, in fact, that summer there was barely enough money in the till to meet the payroll and the company was virtually bankrupt; at one time, the situation was so desperate that all company officers who could authorize the payment of bills were sent out of town on one pretext or another so that creditors could be kept waiting without causing a general panic.

Something had to be done quickly and it was decided to make another equity issue in Churchill Falls, to raise $25 million. With its $21 million loan still outstanding, Brinco obviously could not find enough money to "follow its interest" and retain its 63 per cent share of Churchill Falls. But Hydro-Québec agreed to buy $15 million worth of the offering, increasing its holding in the company to 25 per cent; Newfoundland and Rio Algom followed their interests; and once again, Brinco approached the long-suffering Bank of Montreal for a further $5 million credit, to enable it at least to buy enough shares to prevent its holding from falling below 55 per cent.

To safeguard Hydro-Québec's investment against the obvious risk that the project might collapse for lack of financing, Lajeunesse suggested this latest share purchase should be conditional on the acceptance by Brinco of a *dation en paiment,* or "taking in payment" clause. Under Quebec law, this is a clause which permits a lender to repossess a property he has sold if the buyer does not keep up the mortgage payments. It was discovered no such provision existed in Newfoundland law, so after much debate Brinco signed an undertaking known as Voting Trust Agreement No. 1, which had pretty much the same effect; under it Brinco agreed that if it could not raise at least $515 million in financing by December 15, 1968, control of the project would pass to Hydro-Québec. Brinco actually handed over to a trustee, Trust General of Canada, enough of its Churchill Falls shares to give Hydro majority control of the company if the financing failed. This agreement naturally caused some agonizing at Morgan Stanley.

As a further safeguard to Hydro, Churchill Falls enacted a new company by-law, No. 13, which imposed stringent limitations on its freedom of action. It bound itself, for instance, not to incur debt for any purpose other than construction of the Churchill Falls project: in other words, not to engage in any other business. It also agreed not to increase its capital stock or sell any more shares to anyone other than Hydro, without Hydro's permission. Also — since if the project collapsed Hydro would presumably not wish to keep on the men who had failed to carry it through — By-law No. 13 prevented the company from employing senior officers or consultants on any contract which could not be cancelled by a simple six months' notice.

While this might sound like a hard bargain, the guarantees that ultimately went along with it, by satisfying the lenders that the project had sound backing, helped to ensure that the voting trust agreement would not be triggered and the shares would not have to change hands.

It was in 1968, also, that Hydro-Québec undertook another commitment which helped Mulholland over an unexpected early hurdle in his financing plan. The latest ACB estimate of the actual cost of building the plant, which was delivered in January and remained the official project budget throughout, was $665,644,000. But with all the other administrative, financing and interest charges, the full price tag was now expected to exceed a billion dollars. In his financing plan, Mulholland earmarked $1,073 million for the project, though it was hoped not all this sum would actually be spent. He planned to raise the largest portion of it with an issue of $500 million worth of first mortgage bonds to lending institutions in the United States. At the prevailing exchange rate, this would bring in $540 million in Canadian funds. A further $50 million was to be raised by the sale of first mortgage bonds to Canadian institutions. These bonds, as their name implies, give their holders first call on the assets of the company if it gets into difficulties, but they do not carry votes like common shares. The rest of the money needed was to include: $83 million in shareholders' equity (the amount that would be invested by the time the senior financing was available); $150 million in earnings from the first generating units as they came on stream (which it was planned to plough back into the project); and a $150 million loan from a consortium of Canadian banks. That left $100 million, which Mulholland planned to raise in Canada by an issue of debentures — bonds without the lien on the property carried by the first mortgage bonds. To make these debentures attractive to investors, both financial institutions and the public, he proposed that a number of free common shares be attached to each $1,000 bond.

Wood Gundy agreed with the main outline of this plan, but expressed reservations about the debentures, wondering whether they could be sold before the major financing was assured. Surprised, Mulholland said Morgan Stanley would be only too pleased to take $30 million of them: he considered them a more attractive investment than the first mortgage bonds, since in addition to their free shares they would carry a higher interest rate. But Wood Gundy remained doubtful. Among the many suggestions its partners considered were that the debentures should carry warrants — in effect an option to buy shares over a certain period — or that they be made fully convertible into common shares over a number of years. Brinco rejected this feature out of hand, since it would have diluted the equity to the point at which it would have lost control of Churchill.

Wood Gundy was also concerned about the security of the debentures and suggested that they should carry the right to declare the project in default if it got into difficulties. While the holders of first mortgage bonds have the right to step in and take over a project in an emergency, in practice they prefer to waive that right if at all possible and give the management a chance — albeit under stringent supervision — to work out its difficulties and complete the project, thereby safeguarding their investment. And Mulholland knew they would never agree to give the holders of any form of junior securities the opportunity to usurp their privilege and declare a default: in other words, to put the company out of business, leaving the main investors, conceivably, with nothing more to show for their money than a huge hole in the ground in Labrador. Besides, Mulholland argued, the security of the debentures would be as solid as that of the senior bonds, in that it would be based on the contract with Hydro-Québec.

In the event, the suggestion that the holders of junior bonds should be able to declare a default proved just as outrageous to Hydro-Québec as it would have been to the holders of the first mortgage bonds. Hydro realized that the main investors would insist on a lien on the project in return for their half a billion dollars, but it had no intention of entrusting the future of the scheme to yet another group whose interest would be less than its own. The need for money was urgent, though, and the debenture issue was an important part of Mulholland's financing plan. If it fell through, something else would have to replace it.

One Friday evening, when the problem was on the table at a meeting in the Hydro offices on Dorchester Boulevard, Bob Boyd had to leave early to pick up his wife, who had been shopping in town. Driving home to St. Hilaire, on the South Shore, he was unnaturally silent, turning the problem over in his mind. Suddenly, he startled his wife by bursting out, in the manner of Archimedes, "I've got it!"

As soon as he got home, Boyd called Jean-Paul Cardinal and suggested that Hydro-Québec buy the $100 million issue itself. The ten bonus shares attached to each $1,000 bond, he explained, would increase Hydro's equity in the company, and since it looked as though Hydro was going to have to give some guarantees for the financing anyway, it was in its own interest to make sure it succeeded. Besides, if the worst came to the worst, Hydro would inherit the entire project.

Cardinal thought the plan sounded feasible, but when he raised it with the Premier, Johnson responded dubiously. "It sounds like a lot of money," he said, and suggested Cardinal talk it over with Giroux, who eventually agreed to it in principle, if the details could be worked out satisfactorily.

As the plan developed, it was agreed that the general mortgage bonds, as they now became known — they were in effect a second mortgage — would be offered to all the Churchill shareholders. But Brinco could not afford to take up its share, and neither could Newfoundland. Joey Smallwood was disappointed when Donald Gordon and McParland told him about the plan, and explained that it would increase Quebec's equity in the company to 34.2 per cent. "Is this what it comes to after all these efforts down through the years," he said, "it ends with Quebec owning the damn thing?" Gordon assured him this was not true, that Brinco would still have control of the company and the development, but that the bonds were essential both to continue the work and to ensure the success of the financing. Joey had to agree that Newfoundland could not buy any of the bonds itself and so, sadly, he gave his approval.

The arrangement did not come into effect, of course, until after the power contract had been agreed and the commitments had been received for the main financing. And once again, to protect Hydro's interest, a second voting trust agreement was drawn up — which is still in effect — designed to give Hydro control of the project in case of any default by Churchill Falls.

While this transaction was not, strictly speaking, part of the power-contract negotiations, it is an indication of how closely interrelated the various commitments and guarantees by each side were becoming as the deal moved closer to realization. Hydro's agreement to share the currency exchange risk was set down in the letter of intent and incorporated in the contract as planned. And as the negotiations progressed, it also undertook to advance funds if Churchill ever found itself unable to meet its mortgage payments, or if it needed money to repair damage to the plant. Both these guarantees were also accompanied by provisions which, had they come into play, would have increased Hydro's equity in the company, perhaps to the point of giving it control.

The explanation for many of these unusual features of the contract, of course, was the fact that the price of the power was to be fixed for such a long period. Hydro, by pledging money it would probably never have to spend, obtained a great deal of inflation-proof power without adding to its burden of capital debt; on its part, Churchill Falls naturally sought guarantees to share the risk of unforeseen cost increases which another company would normally compensate for by raising the price of its product.

But the guarantee that Bill Mulholland most needed proved to be the most difficult to obtain: the firm undertaking that the plant would be completed and put into operation come hell or high water. Don McParland, anticipating Hydro's likely reaction, hesitated to broach the subject. By now, the negotiations had become frozen into a sort of rigid pattern: the political complications were such that no one wanted to introduce new concepts that might prompt second thoughts in Quebec City; the Hydro negotiators, in particular, wanted to be able to say if asked that no changes of substance had been introduced into the agreement. Mulholland was adamant, however. The company's word that the project would be completed successfully was just not enough. That assurance could only be given by an organization with the resources of Hydro-Québec, whose undertakings were backed by the whole weight of the provincial government.

So McParland was ultimately prevailed upon to raise the matter with Hydro. As he had expected, his reception was less than enthusiastic. Yvon deGuise recalls: "It was a little delicate on our part . . . to undertake to finish the plant at any cost when we had just seen the St. Lawrence Seaway costs, which went up more than 40 per cent over what had been planned. And our own costs on the Outardes were about forty per cent above the estimates. Supposing the ceiling of the underground power house had fallen down and it had meant starting the work all over again somewhere else. I don't know that at double the price it would have been a good deal as far as we were concerned. The idea of having absolutely no limitation on what it might cost to finish the work was the point that was worrying many people."

As Dr. Johnson said: "When a man knows he is to be hanged in a fortnight, it concentrates his mind wonderfully." Churchill Falls' travail had now lasted almost fifteen years, not a mere fortnight, and the dire consequences of failure — the prospect that all the money poured into the project so far might be lost and Hydro would inherit the whole thing — had concentrated the company's energies on efficiency and a determination to prove that nothing had been overlooked to ensure success. The evidence was there for Hydro to see, particularly in the voluminous product of the 1967 task force's labour. This, and the smooth progress of the work on site, reassured Hydro-Québec, though only after months of discussion and after intervention at the highest level.

Roland Giroux, representing the Premier, paid several visits to the Morgan Stanley offices in New York to investigate the situation, and finally, over lunch at the Brussels restaurant, Mulholland managed to convince him the completion guarantee was essential. Giroux reported back to Daniel Johnson, and the Premier decided to visit New York to look into the matter for himself. Fortunately, he was impressed by Morgan Stanley's explanation of the problem — and in turn, over lunch in the company's dining room, he impressed the New York bankers with his wit and charm. Later, chatting with the senior partner, Henry S. Morgan, the Premier noticed on his wall a framed quotation from Shakespeare's Henry VI: "The first thing we do, let's kill all the lawyers." A lawyer himself, Johnson chuckled appreciatively, and Morgan later sent him a duplicate of the quotation for his own office.

Before he left New York, Johnson told Mulholland not to worry about the completion guarantee: when the time came, he would authorize Hydro-Québec to enter into whatever commitment was necessary. Shortly thereafter, one of those situations arose which cause businessmen occasionally to echo the sentiment expressed in the Shakespeare quotation.

Institutional lenders — life insurance companies, fire and casualty companies, pension funds — are governed by legal investment statutes stipulating the form their investments may take. What is a legal investment for one type of company may be barred to another, so investment bankers must make sure the bonds they are offering a lender satisfy whatever legal requirements affect him. And one of the factors affecting the legality of a bond, of course, is the soundness of the credit behind it.

The $500 million Mulholland was seeking amounted to the largest private bond issue ever marketed in the United States. Since it was obviously a far larger sum than any single investor would take up, he had to ensure that his bonds would meet the legal requirements of as wide a range of lenders as possible. One way of doing this would have been to qualify them under the statutes permitting investment in bonds "rated" by two or more recognized bond-rating agencies. Quebec government bonds are rated in the United States, as are those of Hydro-Québec, so that if Mulholland could somehow say his bonds represented their credit his task would be considerably easier.

The lawyers thus began to investigate the validity of an undertaking made by Hydro-Québec. Did it amount to a legal guarantee? Did it commit the Quebec government? They unearthed what appeared to be a contradiction between the Quebec Finance Act and the Hydro-Québec Act. Section 28 of the latter made provision for the government to guarantee financial obligations assumed by Hydro. But sections 30 and 31 of the Finance Act, which the lawyers considered to take precedence, stipulated that "no contract obliging Her Majesty to pay a sum of money" was valid unless an appropriation covering it had been made in advance during the year the payment fell due.

The Morgan Stanley and Brinco lawyers considered that these sections could not only nullify Hydro's contract with Churchill, which was to be for forty years, but that they made the guarantees on all the other Hydro-Québec bonds already sold in the United States invalid.

This alarming supposition was communicated to Jean-Paul Cardinal, who lost no time raising it with the government. And John Tennant, a Montreal lawyer who had been helping to frame the power contract on the Brinco side, was summoned to Quebec City. The only plane he could get arrived at 8 a.m. and Tennant's appointment with the Attorney General was not until noon. It was a fine sunny day and he spent the interval dozing on a park bench. After he had explained the doubts that had arisen, he was asked to return at 4:30 p.m., so he spent the afternoon, too, sitting on park benches. By the end of the day he had a fierce sunburn; but the government had acknowledged that the doubts might be well-founded and showed him draft legislation which eventually resolved the contradiction and enabled Hydro-Québec to enter into the contract legally.

Mulholland's need to make the bonds attractive to as many lenders as possible led to another representation by Brinco to the federal government on an aspect of Canadian tax policy. Some of the lenders he planned to approach, such as pension funds and charitable institutions, being exempt from United States tax, could also claim exemption from the 15 per cent withholding tax Canada would otherwise levy on the interest to be paid to them on their bonds. Other lenders, such as some of the life insurance companies, would be able to use the Canadian tax credit to reduce their U.S. tax payments, and so would be unaffected by it. But some of the companies Mulholland meant to approach were, for a variety of reasons, not paying enough U.S. tax to make the Canadian credit any use to them. Naturally, to compensate for the tax they would be paying in Canada, these companies would demand a higher interest rate on their bonds. And, since a preferential rate could not be offered to one group of lenders, the interest on all the bonds would have to be higher, thus increasing the price Hydro-Québec would have to pay for the power. Since Hydro-Québec's own bonds were exempt from the withholding tax, Churchill Falls said in a brief to Ottawa, there seemed to be a case for exempting the Churchill Falls bonds also, thereby bringing down the cost of power to Quebec consumers.

Donald Gordon, Eric Lambert and Mulholland went to Ottawa on April 25, 1968, to put their case to the government. During the morning, they explained it to Louis Rasminsky, Governor of the Bank of Canada, who seemed sympathetic, and after a friendly meeting escorted them on a guided tour of the bank, including the gold vaults. In the afternoon, they repeated their presentation to the recently appointed Minister of Finance, Edgar J. Benson, and his Deputy Minister, Robert B. Bryce. Benson promised to speak to the Prime Minister that same evening and have the matter discussed by the cabinet the following week. And on April 30 the government announced an order-in-council exempting the Churchill bonds from the tax. Donald Gordon was so pleasantly surprised at this speedy response that he called Benson and congratulated him. "It reminds me of the way we used to do things when I was in Ottawa," he told him.

One by one, the remaining points at issue were being resolved and by the end of May a master draft of the contract had been drawn up. Early in June, Hydro-Québec, satisfied at last that all its conditions had been met, sent it to Daniel Johnson. And on July 10, 1968 — fifteen years after Brinco's formation and almost five years after the talks on the letter of intent had begun — the government authorized Hydro-Québec to sign the contract. There was, of course, one condition: that Churchill Falls complete its financing arrangements successfully.

TWENTY-ONE

Agreement at last

Even looking back on the bewildering multiplicity of interlocking arrangements which had to be made during those desperate years of 1967 and 1968, each one in some way dependent on all the others, it is difficult to see how Brinco managed to escape the financial disaster that was never further away than just around the next corner. The less reverent might describe it as one of the most remarkable financial tight-wire acts of all time.

Despite Morgan Stanley's continuing forebodings, Churchill Falls went on spending money at an ever-increasing pace during the 1967 and 1968 construction seasons. Between April 1967, and August 31 1968, for instance, direct project expenditures totalled $57.3 million — almost a million dollars a week on average. By that time, a cumulative total of $77.7 million had been ploughed into the project. Not all of this money was provided by Brinco, of course; some came from Hydro-Québec and the other partners. But the bulky figure of Donald Gordon became a familiar sight in the halls of the Bank of Montreal, where he would turn up regularly to see G. Arnold Hart, its chairman, for what they both came to call "comfort sessions." One day, Gordon told Hart reassuringly not to worry about Brinco's huge outstanding loan. "*We're* not worried, Donald," Hart told him. "It's *your* problem to pay it back."

Without the Bank of Montreal's support through the years, which seemed at times to be based on no collateral more substantial than its own faith in the Churchill project and in the integrity and ability of its management, Brinco might well have foundered more than once. But banks, of course, are not quite as carefree in the dispensation of their depositors' funds as Hart's jocular remark to Gordon might suggest. The bank understood why Brinco had been unable to make an offering of shares in the early part of 1968; but by June, when it learned that the corporation wanted to increase its loan by $5 million, it had become under-standably uneasy. The Quebec government had still not approved the power contract, so the senior financing was as far away as ever; money was still tight and interest rates high, so that the climate was hardly promising for either a share issue or the main financing; and under the voting trust arrangement Brinco had just agreed to place a large number of its Churchill Falls shares — part of its collateral — in trust, and risked losing control of the project.

"The bank," as Gordon wrote to Val Duncan, "points out that we have presented no plan that will assure them of our ability to pay off the loan over the next few months, or, for that matter at any specified date."

Under the circumstances, this was a reasonable complaint. Nevertheless, the bank agreed to advance the first $300,000 of the extra $5 million, which Brinco needed immediately to make its first subscription to the latest Churchill Falls share issue. But it insisted that before it could part with the next instalment of $1.8 million, a month hence, it must have some firm indication of how it was proposed to pay back not only this $5 million but the earlier $21 million.

"This brings me," Gordon wrote to Duncan, "to the RTZ situation. If we were able to inform the bank that a positive deal was in progress and outline how it was being accomplished, then I believe we could get them to ride along for at least a reasonable period. But, this would have to be very convincing and [would] probably need a letter from you outlining what is in play, and how it is to be accomplished."

What was in play, in fact, was an operation that very few within either Brinco in Montreal or Rio Tinto-Zinc in London yet knew anything at all about; and the complex series of transactions by which it was to be accomplished was still being worked out in the utmost secrecy: whenever any of its details had to be committed to paper, Brinco was always referred to by the perhaps not impenetrable code name of "Bunker," Churchill Falls as "Cigar" and Rio Tinto as "Tonic."

After the collapse of the public issue in Churchill shares in 1967, while they were wrestling with their mounting financial problems, Gordon and McParland had asked Val Duncan to take over Brinco. Rio Tinto seemed the logical choice as the "big brother" it had often been suggested the corporation needed. It was the largest single shareholder; ever since Bob Winters' arrival and the management contract, it had been in effective control of the corporation; and Val Duncan had become more and more involved with its affairs: during the negotiations with Hydro-Québec his presence at all the most crucial meetings clearly established him as the guiding genius on the Brinco side.

But Duncan turned them down. For one thing, it would have meant

Rio launching a huge share issue to finance an investment that would not return any dividends for at least eight years. Even more important, he realized that British exchange restrictions would prevent Rio from exporting the millions of dollars the deal would require.

Later, as Brinco's fortunes plunged from bad to worse, Duncan began to see a possible solution to this last problem. The powerful Bethlehem Steel Corporation in the United States, which had already cooperated with Rio on a mining operation in Malaya, had been seeking further participation in some of Duncan's ventures. Here, it seemed, might be the source of hard currency needed if Rio was to take over and restore Brinco's position.

But before he approached the Bethlehem management, Duncan needed for his board of directors Morgan Stanley's assurance that the Churchill project could be financed. Don McParland was deputed to pass on this request to Bill Mulholland. Unable to find him in New York, he eventually tracked him down late at night — at Churchill Falls, where he was showing potential lenders around the site. Sir Mark Turner was in New York, McParland said, and by next morning he must have a letter on the financing to take back to London. To the astonishment of the long-distance operator at Sept-Iles, Mulholland spent the rest of the night on the telephone to another Morgan Stanley partner in New York, Frank Petito, and while at least one other partner expressed strong objections to any commitment being given at this stage, a suitably worded letter was ready for Turner in the morning. The assurances it contained satisfied the Rio board and Duncan was able to approach Bethlehem, which agreed in principle to the scheme he proposed.

Duncan was away from London when Gordon asked for the letter to reassure Arnold Hart at the "comfort session" arranged for early in July, so Sir Mark Turner wrote instead. His letter spoke of "the interest which RTZ has in increasing its stake in Brinco and if possible obtaining, through a controlling interest in that company, a controlling position in Churchill Falls." And it dropped the intriguing hint that "we have recently been courted by quite a number of substantial U.S. industrial companies with suggestions for close cooperation and even a merger of interests. . . . We have already taken active steps to find such a partner and will pursue our investigations vigorously. . . ."

Gordon showed Hart this letter and told him that while he could not give him any more details, he could pledge his word that there was a good prospect of a new injection of equity capital into Brinco which would more than take care of its $26 million loan. Gordon's word was not taken lightly anywhere, and supported by Turner's letter it was more than enough for Hart, and for the bank's board of directors. The new loan was approved in full.

The mechanics of the scheme by which Rio was to purchase control of Brinco were worked out by the Rio planning staff in London and one Thursday, Harry W. Macdonell, a senior partner in the Toronto law firm of Fasken and Calvin who had acted for Rio in Canada since leaving law school in 1956, was summoned to Montreal to hear its details. Macdonell was due to leave next day for Cape Cod, where he had rented a house for a month's vacation. He had done the same thing the year before, but had ended up spending most of the month in New York on business. This time, his wife had laid down the law: this was to be no busman's holiday. But McParland was so insistent that Macdonell arranged for an articling student to take his wife and children to the airport next day and promised to join them on the Cape from Montreal on Saturday morning.

It took McParland two hours to explain the proposed transaction, with the aid of a blackboard, and Macdonell's first reaction was that someone had chosen an incredibly complicated way of doing something relatively simple. But he reserved comment until he had had time to think it over. He spent that weekend on the beach with his wife and children but his mind was elsewhere. And by 4 p.m. on Saturday he called McParland, having realized there were at least two grave flaws in the proposal.

In outline, the plan was that Rio, using dollars paid by Bethlehem for a part-interest in Rio Tinto-Zinc, should set up a new holding company in which Bethlehem would buy a 20 per cent interest. The holding company would then assemble the shares needed to give it control of Brinco in a number of ways: by taking a two-year option on a large number of treasury shares at one price; by buying Rio Algom's Churchill shares and selling them to Brinco at another price; and by rounding up the rest of the shares it needed for control from two sources — the Founder shareholders (again at two prices, since some of the shares they had held since the early days were not subject to exchange controls and were thus worth more than the ordinary shares) and on the open market. Macdonell realized that the exchange of Rio Algom's Churchill shares for Brinco shares at a higher price would involve Rio Tinto-Zinc in a heavy taxable gain. Also, if any hint of the plan leaked out, the price of the shares which would have to be bought on the open market would immediately sky-rocket.

300

Once again, Marie Macdonell's hope for an uninterrupted vacation was disappointed. Fascinated by the problems involved in the takeover operation, Macdonell discussed it in New York with Sam Harris and Bob Sonneman, Bethlehem's corporate lawyer and secretary, who told him that the complexity of the proposed arrangements, and the offering prices envisaged for the shares, might create difficulties under the Securities Act and the tax legislation in the United States. Macdonell then flew to London, where, after more discussions, he suggested a simpler transaction to Ray Robinson, Rio's executive director. Rio, he said, should make an immediate offer to Brinco to purchase 4.7 million treasury shares, for a cash payment large enough to allow Brinco itself to buy back Rio Algom's Churchill shares; that way there would be no taxable gain. And the offer should be made conditional upon Rio's managing to buy enough extra shares from the Founder shareholders to give it 51 per cent of the corporation, thus eliminating the risk of buying shares on the open market. The offer should also be conditional on Brinco agreeing to make a rights offering, underwritten by Rio and Bethlehem, which would raise the rest of the money needed to pay off the bank loans and continue the construction work.

Robinson liked the sound of the revised proposal, but pointed out one drawback: Val Duncan had told Bethlehem the whole operation would cost it $50 million; if the other shareholders did not take up their rights and Rio and Bethlehem had to buy them, the scheme could cost Bethlehem as much as $72 million. Macdonell communicated this news to Sonneman, who promptly responded: "That's no problem. I couldn't understand why you didn't plan it that way in the first place."

Once agreed, the operation was accomplished quickly (the contracts between Rio and Bethlehem were drawn up within two weeks) but though the deal was announced to the public in August the various transactions involved extended to the end of the year. Bethlehem bought three and a half million shares of Rio Tinto-Zinc, giving it an approximate 3½ per cent interest in the company, and since the dollars realized on the sale by Rio were immediately reinvested in the dollar area, there was no objection by the British Treasury. The new holding company set up by Rio and Bethlehem, which eventually acquired approximately 50 per cent of Brinco, was named Thornwood Investments, the name being chosen by the simple expedient of looking through the Toronto telephone book for a street name which had not yet been used by any other company.

To the intense relief of Gordon, McParland and everyone else, the deal at last put an end to the long series of financial troubles which had plagued Brinco. Thornwood paid $18.8 million for its 4.7 million shares, plus a further $12.8 million for 3.2 million shares not taken up in the rights offering, made in November. With the proceeds of the offering, Brinco received $42.3 million worth of new capital, which it used to buy Rio Algom's shareholding in Churchill Falls — assuring it of a controlling interest of 56.96 per cent — and to pay off its $26 million bank loan. But in September, before the various transactions were completed, the bank's "total exposure," as the banking phrase has it, had risen to $45 million. The Brinco loan had by this time been reduced to $20 million, but after the announcement of the Thornwood deal the bank had opened a $25 million line of credit for Churchill Falls. Toward the end of the year, after the Quebec government had approved the power contract, Hydro-Québec subscribed for the first $25 million worth of its general mortgage bonds, which enabled Churchill to retire this latest credit. And by Christmas, 1968, Gordon's comfort sessions with Arnold Hart were no longer necessary.

Fortunately, few hints of Brinco's ongoing financial vicissitudes had filtered through to the lenders, and with the Quebec government's approval of the power contract in July, Bill Mulholland was at last able to begin putting the finishing touches to his financing strategy. While the Thornwood deal was about to restore Brinco's corporate health, Mulholland's approach to the lenders was still crucial: because of the various contract provisions, if he failed to pull it off successfully the Churchill Falls company would lose its project and Brinco the jewel from its crown.

An investment banker can be described as a financial architect, and the measure of his success is how well the structure he creates, the deal, serves the interests of the project he is trying to finance and the lenders whose money will go into it. He needs a wide range of expertise — in accounting, statistics, economics, corporate law — and it helps if he has a capacity for sustained work. Mulholland's working style amazed, and sometimes infuriated, his colleagues. He would wander in to the office around 10 a.m., after everyone else was hard at work, and spend the rest of the day on the telephone. Around 6 p.m., he would summon his assistants, chat for an hour or two, apparently inconsequentially but in reality thinking aloud, and then keep them furiously busy until perhaps midnight. Early in his career at Morgan Stanley, he quit to take a job in his home town of Albany, where he expected to be under less pressure and to have more time for his outdoor hobbies. He was back within a year, having found it insufferably frustrating to work in an office where an executive was considered eccentric if he stayed at his desk until 5 p.m.

By the summer of 1968, Mulholland, and Ed Vollmers before him, had been laying the stonework for their particular cathedral for almost ten years, ever since the early days of Twin Falls. In fact, before Eric Lambert's arrival, Morgan Stanley seemed in effect to be acting as Brinco's financial department. And, since they were well aware of the project's tortured history, of how it had been beset throughout by false starts and — worst of all for a businessman — political complications, some of Mulholland's partners in Morgan Stanley privately doubted that he would be able to pull off the financing. For the past two years the long-term bond market had been, in the words of one of them, "a shambles." In the summer of 1968, that term could fairly have been applied to the whole of Wall Street, if not to the country at large. It was a frightening, morale-sapping time for Americans: the year in which tiny North Korea captured their spy ship *Pueblo;* the year in which Martin Luther King and Robert Kennedy were murdered; the year a government commission on the civil disorders that were tearing the country apart reported that black violence was largely caused by white racism; the year in which their president, Lyndon Johnson, evidently felt himself so defeated by events that he refused to run for re-election.

The confusion was reflected, even magnified, on Wall Street. Some of the gloss was beginning to fade from the so-called glamour issues that had powered the tremendous stock-market boom of the middle 1960s. It was becoming apparent that there was less mutuality of interest than had been imagined between the entrepreneurial managers of some of the more spectacular mutual funds and the small investors whose savings they handled. But none of this dampened the tremendous speculative surge of 1968, when Americans plunged into the stock market in greater numbers than ever before. Such great numbers, in fact, that brokers' back offices could not handle the flood of transactions and lost track of securities worth at various times between $3 and $4 billion. Even closing the market every Wednesday failed to enable back-office staffs to catch up and bring some order out of the chaos, and several brokerage firms eventually went under in the flood.

The long-term bond market, by its nature, was more orderly, but by no means immune from fluctuations. Bond interest rates in 1930 had been around 5 to $5\frac{1}{2}$ per cent. Partly because of the depression, and consequent government intervention in the management of the economy, they went down to the point at which the Second World War was financed at $2\frac{1}{2}$

per cent. After the war, they began to rise again: the first Twin Falls bonds were sold at 5⅝ per cent. By early 1968, the rate was up to the unprecedented figure of 8 per cent. But that summer, the money market was what the professionals call "rather soft": demand for money was down and it seemed as if interest rates might begin to decline.

This was encouraging for Mulholland, but he faced other problems. For one thing, the United States was becoming concerned about its balance of payments position, and there were doubts whether the export of the huge amount of capital he was seeking would be approved. Also, the insurance companies whose money he needed were facing a "run on the bank": policy-holders, feeling the pinch of the prevailing high interest rates, were taking advantage of the clause in their policies permitting them to borrow against them, usually at a rate of interest much lower than current levels. This practice tends to unbalance the inflow and out-flow of insurance companies' funds and they are inclined to rein in their horses and take a look around to see what is happening before resuming the normal pace of their operations.

Mulholland was reasonably sanguine about the first of these hurdles. He had made a point through the years of keeping the Federal Reserve Bank informed of the progress of the Churchill deal and had in the process built up a file there which he hoped would give it some sort of priority or "grandfather" status. The main concern of the U.S. Treasury was that Canada not be used by Americans to bypass regulations enacted to cope with the balance-of-payments crisis, and this had led to an exchange of letters between the Treasury and the Canadian Minister of Finance, Mitchell Sharp, clarifying the position, from which Mulholland correctly assumed the United States would not put any impediments in the way of the Churchill financing.

As to the second point, he had taken up where Ed Vollmers had left off in "massaging" the two huge insurance companies he knew he must have in if the financing were to succeed: the Metropolitan Life Insurance Company and the Prudential Insurance Company of America. The Met had bought all the bonds for the Twin development, and Mulholland had taken care ever since then to keep its vice-chairman, George Jenkins, up to date on the Churchill progress. In fact, even Jenkins' predecessor as head of the bond department had had a coloured photograph of Churchill Falls on his wall. And in June, when the preparations for the financing had begun to intensify, Mulholland had taken a party of executives from both companies up to Churchill for an inspection visit, leavened by a spot of fishing.

304

Banteringly — though in reality he was utterly serious — he had long told both companies that when the time came he would need $150 million from each of them. The Met and the Pru in those days each invested close to $2 billion every year, but this was a large amount for them to allot to one project, particularly a far-off project to be built by what to them was an untried company. And yet it was vital that Mulholland get their support; the $500 million he planned to raise would be the largest private bond issue ever placed in the United States up to that time, but there is a "bandwagon" tendency in the financing business and once the Met and the Pru were committed the twenty or so other insurance companies whose support he needed would rally round much more readily.

First, though, the key issue of the interest rate on the bonds had to be settled with Quebec. This was a matter of considerable concern to the Quebec government — and not only because of Hydro-Québec's agreement to pay any interest charges above 5½ per cent. On August 5, Mulholland, McParland and Lambert met with the full Hydro commission and Marcel Casavan, Quebec's Deputy Minister of Finance. Casavan explained that the province was worried about the effect on the market for future provincial government and Hydro-Québec issues if the Churchill bonds had to be offered at 8 per cent or even more. Privately, Mulholland thought he could place them at 7¾ per cent, and he agreed to try to do so, though he felt obliged for the record to warn Casavan he might have to go higher than that.

This feeling was even more marked at Morgan Stanley, where most of the partners when the matter was discussed thought the rate should be 8 per cent, or even 8¼, and that by trying for less Mulholland was running a grave risk of wrecking the deal. One partner was so nervous about Mulholland's approach that he threw up his hands and announced he would have nothing more to do with it.

But on August 21, Mulholland and two of his partners from the sales department, Sam Payne and Bill Sword, made their "bond-offering presentation" to the Pru in the morning and the Met in the afternoon.

Mulholland made virtually the same pitch to both companies. Effortlessly and convincingly, he outlined the Churchill development: the ideal topography of the Labrador plateau, which made the power so cheap; the exceptionally thorough planning, which virtually ruled out the risk of failure; Quebec's mounting power needs and the backing given to the project by Hydro-Québec. He was also able to assure both companies that Canada's leading lender, the Sun Life Assurance Company of

Canada, was solidly behind the project, considering it of such importance to both Quebec and the rest of the country that it was planning to take up part of both the U.S. and Canadian bond issues.

Each company was also given a two-volume "offering memorandum," the writing of which had occupied Mulholland's lieutenant, Jim Smith, for the better part of a year. This spelled out in exhaustive detail the history of the Churchill Falls company and its project; the money spent and progress made so far, with engineering drawings and construction estimates for the project's completion; the power contract and the various agreements associated with it. And, even though Hydro-Québec's completion guarantee now made them largely just the icing on the cake, the potential lenders also received copies of the sixteen volumes of supporting data produced by the 1967 task force.

By the end of the day, both of Mulholland's chief quarries had agreed to consider the case he had made and get back to him. George Jenkins and his colleagues at the Met took only a week to study the impressive mass of documentation and summoned Mulholland and his partners to another meeting on August 29. To no one's surprise, they started out by challenging some details of the plan, such as the sinking-fund provisions and the commitment fee. The separatist movement in Quebec came in for some apprehensive comment, and it was also suggested that since the bonds did not carry the actual guarantee of the province they were not equal in quality to Hydro-Québec bonds. Nonetheless, Jenkins agreed to take $150 million worth of them — but only at 8 per cent.

Mulholland assured Jenkins that the technical points the Met had raised could be settled to everyone's satisfaction. As to the separatist problem, he referred them to a voluminous report the company had had prepared which concluded it was no threat to its plans. And the guarantee behind the bonds was cast-iron: it was unthinkable that Hydro-Québec would be permitted to jeopardize the province's power supply by defaulting in its payments to Churchill Falls. The ultimate source of funds to service the debt was the payment by millions of Quebecers of their hydro bills, and since the government would obviously not permit the lights to go out across the province, all in all he thought it could be argued that the Churchill bonds were as good as, if not better than, those issued or guaranteed by the province itself.

On the interest rate, he pointed out that there were a number of interested parties to the deal, including certain governments, so he had no flexibility to change that. But in any case, he had considered it very carefully and was convinced that 7¾ per cent was fair, and even generous, under the circumstances.

It was agreed that the Met officials would think this over and they would all meet again on September 6. When he got back to his office, Mulholland called Donald Gordon in Montreal and told him he now had a firm offer for $150 million worth of the bonds at 8 per cent, but he recommended the company turn it down. Gordon gasped. Surely, he protested, that would be taking an awful gamble? After all, $150 million was a large sum. . . . Mulholland repeated that he thought he could get the money at 7¾ per cent. Lesser men might have sought the comfort of a few committee meetings to bolster their resolution before making such a key decision, but Gordon hesitated only a few moments, then authorized Mulholland to hold out for the lower rate.

Everything hinged now on the September 6 meeting. Mulholland knew — and he knew George Jenkins knew — that it was one thing to sell $150 million worth of bonds at 7¾ per cent, quite another to place the unprecedented sum of half a billion dollars at that figure. And with the range of the dickering now established at 7¾ per cent to 8 per cent, the penalty for his failure would be to move the whole range higher: next time around, if there was one, 8 per cent would be the rock-bottom figure in the range.

He began the September 6 meeting by recapitulating all the Churchill project's virtues and then went on to compare it with other investments the Met might make in the current unsettled market, concluding — he hoped persuasively — that there could be none better. He also turned the discussion to an unusual aspect of the proposed deal which had caused him and the Churchill Falls planners endless soul-searching and which might have caused the lenders hesitation, though in retrospect it probably helped to swing the deal. This was the long "commitment" period — four years — over which the half a billion dollars was to be borrowed.

Obviously, with the interest on such a sum amounting to millions of dollars a year, it would have been ruinously extravagant for the company to have borrowed more than it could spend at any one time and left it sitting idle in the bank. And so it was proposed that the bond issue should be "taken down" at quarterly intervals over the four-year period.*

*There were sixteen bond "draw-downs," or "closings," between July 1969, and July 1973, for sums varying from $11 million to more than

Mulholland stressed the advantages of this long take-down period to the lenders, pointing out that the commitment fee the company would pay to make sure the money would be available would in effect increase the interest rate. Also, he said, the Met would have the assurance that its money would be usefully employed at the 7¾ rate for the next four years, regardless of what happened to the market during that period.

At that time (as indeed at any other), no one could predict with certainty what would happen to interest rates in the months ahead. Though it turned out to be only a brief interval of calm between the storms for borrowers, there were those who thought that summer's decline in interest rates might continue. But even more important than this, probably, was the fact that George Jenkins had been thoroughly sold on the Churchill project through the years. It was, after all, the project of the decade. Lenders like to be associated with important and prestigious ventures — even feel a responsibility to support them — and Jenkins had seen for himself on the ground, and liked, the way McParland and his team operated.

At any rate, he agreed to take the bonds at 7¾ per cent, provided Mulholland could persuade the rest of the lenders his rate was justified. In effect, he was saying: "Okay, I'm a sport, too. I'm not convinced you can swing this, but if you can, good luck to you. We both know what's going to happen if you don't."

Of course, Jenkins told Mulholland as they wound up the meeting, since the Met was the first to commit itself and would be taking such

---

$50 million. Each necessitated the presence in Montreal of large numbers of lawyers and accountants from the various companies concerned. In view of the size of the cheques that changed hands on each occasion, the proceedings were conducted with considerable care. But accidents will happen. Once a typist evidently confused the destination to which she was supposed to send the cheque with the name of its payee, since it turned up at the closing ceremony made out to "Fifth Floor Boardroom, Royal Trust." On another occasion, a messenger was given a package containing cheques for several million dollars to be delivered to the board room, but was not informed of the urgency of his mission. While the dozens of waiting lawyers stood around fretting, a search for the messenger discovered him quietly enjoying a beer in a nearby tavern, his despatch case on the table beside him. When the cheques had been examined by all concerned at a closing, the Churchill Falls representatives endorsed them over to the Royal Trust for deposit at the Bank of Montreal. Only when the company later produced appropriate auditors' certificates that it had incurred "bondable expenditures" could it draw the money.

a large amount of the bonds, it would expect the "lead position" among the bond-holders, precedence being as highly prized on these occasions as at a royal wedding.

The Pru, the other keystone in the financing, took a little longer to consider the terms of the offering but it, too, eventually accepted the 7¾ per cent rate — though before it committed itself Mulholland had to return to Jenkins and persuade him, "for the good of the project," to share the coveted lead position.

The $300 million now in the bag strengthened Morgan Stanley's hand when it approached the other lenders, and the response to the offering was so enthusiastic that the Met and the Pru were ultimately asked to take only $125 million each.

Mulholland could not have been more fortunate in his timing. By October, interest rates were on the way up again, to the point at which the project could probably never have been financed. A year or so later, at least one top-rated U.S. bond issue could only be sold at a 9¼ per cent interest rate, and as inflation roared on through the early seventies like a forest fire out of control, the bond market went even more hay-wire. Telephone bonds with the highest Triple-A rating sold for 10 per cent in 1974, and the interest on a lesser-rated issue such as Churchill Falls could have been as high as 11½ per cent — in the unlikely event that it could have been sold at all.

On September 25, Mulholland flew to northeastern Quebec, one of four hundred guests invited by Hydro-Québec to the ceremonies marking the completion of the great Manic-5 dam. He was aboard the last plane to land that night, and when he arrived at the huge reception, which was still in full swing although it was nearly midnight, he met Daniel Johnson, who had stayed up to greet the late arrivals. Johnson had had a heart attack three months earlier and had just returned to his office after a long convalescence in Bermuda. He took Mulholland over to a side of the room away from the other guests and asked him how the Churchill financing was going. Mulholland had not yet got all the commitments he needed, but by now he knew where they were going to come from. "We're home free — it's done," he told the Premier.

"That's wonderful," Johnson said. Then he shook Mulholland's hand and walked around among the guests, saying goodnight. Next morning, his private secretary, Paul Chouinard, found him dead in his bed; he had suffered another heart attack in his sleep.

The sale of the $50 million "Series B" first mortgage bonds, while not the largest issue made in Canada to that time, was a large sum for a new construction project. Wood Gundy, which made the offering in consultation with Morgan Stanley, found some buyers reluctant because the 7⅞ per cent interest rate did not amount to the full differential of half a per cent customary between issues in the United States and Canada, where interest rates are traditionally higher. And one potential lender refused to buy the bonds at any price because, he said, the project would "dry up" a waterfall. But eventually the issue was bought by thirty-one Canadian insurance companies and pension funds. (There are twenty-one bond-holders in the U.S.) The Sun Life took $13 million worth of the U.S. issue, and $9 million of the Series "B" bonds in Canada, making it the largest single Canadian investor in the bonds. The Caisse de Depôt et lacement du Québec, the Quebec government's pension fund, took $14½ million worth of the Canadian bonds.

Only one more step in the financing remained to be negotiated: the $150 million loan which would be required from Canadian banks in the later stages of the construction work. That this money would be needed had been recognized from the beginning, and the preliminary approach had been made to the Bank of Montreal while the negotiations on the letter of intent were still in their early stages. Bill Mulholland recalls that when Len Walker at the bank first heard the magnitude of the sum envisaged he blanched and then blurted out: "That may not seem like a lot of money to you guys from New York City, but it's a *hell* of a lot of money in Canada!" Nevertheless, he agreed that the bank would take the lead position in trying to form a consortium to include the five nation-wide chartered banks and the Quebec-based Banque Canadienne Nationale and Banque Provinciale du Canada, to advance what would be the largest loan ever granted to a Canadian company.

Beginning early in 1968, Brinco and Bank of Montreal officials met regularly in an attempt to draft a document that was by no means simple: a loan agreement meeting all the varying requirements of all the parties, and tied in with all the other documentation, such as the power contract and the first mortgage trust deed. Once again, the lawyers had a field day. In the later stages of the drafting, almost daily meetings were held at the bank and much midnight oil was burned.

But by the end of September the draft agreement was ready and on October 29 Donald Gordon gathered the presidents of the seven banks together in the Brinco board room.

He presented each of them with a draft copy of the proposed loan agreement and a set of the sixteen volumes of facts and figures compiled by the task force, and treated them to an enthusiastic review of the project's progress — so enthusiastic, in fact, that it seemed he expected them to sign up there and then.

Senior officials of all the banks met to discuss the loan a few days later, and once again the thorough preparations paid off: they reached what George Scott, of the Bank of Montreal, described as "quite substantial agreement." And on December 16, Arnold Hart assured Gordon formally that the $150 million loan 'was "in place" and would be signed as soon as all the other agreements had been completed.

The only task outstanding now was to tidy up the many technicalities, draft the numerous interlocking agreements in legal language and have all the documents printed "for execution." This process went on all through the winter and the following spring, rising to a crescendo in the early days of May 1969. Tons of paper were eaten up preparing the documents and their many copies. The bond purchase agreement to be signed by each of the fifty-two lenders extended to sixty pages of closely packed legal terminology; there were 226 pages in the first mortgage trust deed; 146 in the general mortgage trust deed. Then there were the many copies of the power contract and the supplementary agreements between Hydro-Québec and the Churchill Falls company; the collateral agreements with Newfoundland on such matters as the Upper Churchill lease and the tax rebate; and the loan agreement between the banks and the company.

Human nature being what it is, the morning of Friday, May 9 — three days before the date chosen for the signing ceremonies — found a large group of lawyers and their assistants gathered in New York amid a stack of paper, dickering over the position of commas and, at the last minute, whether or not the title "vice-president" should have a hyphen. All day long, documents were rushed back and forth to the printers for proof corrections and it was two a.m. before the lawyers called it a day. Jim Smith, supervising the traffic to and from the printers for Morgan Stanley, snatched perhaps an hour of sleep before the session resumed at nine on Saturday morning. This time, as the deadline moved nearer, the lawyers kept working until five a.m. on Sunday, then resumed before noon. About four, Smith and a colleague, Bruce Bochman, left for the printers, where they were joined shortly before midnight by Don McParland and Eric Lambert, who had flown in from Montreal to put the company's signatures on the bond purchase agreements, which were still not yet bound into folders.

For the legal record, all the documents had to be signed simultaneously, the day chosen for this being Thursday, May 15. But in practice, with fifty-two lenders scattered all across the continent and many other associated papers to be signed, the actual signatures had to be obtained in advance and the documents held in escrow until the appointed time. On Monday morning, emissaries from Morgan Stanley set off with boxes of documents in three rented planes, and by commercial airlines, to round up the lenders' signatures. One young man found himself plucked from an office in which he customarily supervised the duplicating machines, to be given a parcel of papers and a first-class airline ticket to Los Angeles. There, after a taxi ride to the offices of the Pacific Mutual Life Insurance Company in Newport Beach, he waited while the required two vice-presidents signed his precious papers, and then headed straight back on the next flight to New York, where he delivered them to Jim Smith, the most unusual day's work of his life satisfactorily accomplished. The rented jets carried Morgan Stanley men to Hartford, Connecticut, and Boston; Montreal and Quebec City; Toronto and Winnipeg; from where they fanned out in rented cars in search of signatures.

Meanwhile, in Montreal, as cameras rolled and cabinet ministers looked on, representatives of the company and Hydro-Québec signed the power contract, the indispensable foundation of the deal and the culmination of so many years of work by so many people. It bound Churchill Falls to supply, and Hydro-Québec to buy, electricity worth $5 billion.

On Tuesday morning, as those couriers who had not reached Montreal the night before began winging in and delivering their prizes to the offices of the Royal Trust, the bank consortium agreement was signed. On Wednesday, there was another signing ceremony for the benefit of the cameras in the Brinco board room, with Joey Smallwood beaming his approval. On Thursday, the whole thing came together in the offices of the Royal Trust; the last signatures were put in place on the trust deed, and the deal was at last a reality.

One distinguished and well-loved figure was missing from his place at the various board room tables where all these complicated transactions had been completed: on the evening of Friday, May 1, Donald Gordon had worked late with his young colleagues and then headed home for a weekend's respite from the exertion of the job he had merely intended to give him an interest during his retirement. More tired than usual, he went to bed early and died in his sleep, the victim of a heart attack at the age of sixty-seven.

TWENTY-TWO

Flight into tragedy

To the people of the new town of Churchill Falls, the signing of all these papers must have seemed a mere formality. Notwithstanding the political and financial complications far away to the south, the mammoth construction job that would finally put Churchill's bridle on the Falls had now been gathering momentum for almost three years. The work force had grown to forty-five hundred men and the signs of their activity were everywhere; the roar of trucks and tractors and bulldozers seldom ceased and new supplies and equipment lumbered in daily along the dusty road from Esker. The town itself, which now included several hundred women and children among its residents, was beginning to take on a settled look. The recreation centre at Main Camp, with its thriving tavern, and the main mess hall, capable of serving eleven hundred workers at a sitting, were already popular institutions. The permanent school would not be ready until the fall; nor would the Town Centre, where stores, a hotel, bank, theatre, cinema, curling rink and swimming pool were all being built under the same roof. But families were beginning to move from the trailers into the new split-levels and apartments, and the fully equipped twenty-four-bed hospital operated for the company by the International Grenfell Association had been open for some months.

By the time the power contract was signed, $150 million had already been spent on the project and contracts committing the company to a further $240 million in expenditures had been awarded to contractors and manufacturers. These were incredible sums, considering that the whole venture could have collapsed right up to the moment all those signatures were in place on all those documents. Yet such was the size of the job ahead, the work had scarcely begun.

The underground excavation, started in the fall of 1967, was still only half-finished. There was more than a year to go before the last explosive charge would complete the honeycomb of tunnels and chambers blasted out of the rock on the rim of the plateau. While it was planned to produce the first commercial power from Units 1 and 2 by May 1, 1972, the schedule allowed a comfortable three more years, until 1975, for the installation of the rest of the eleven generating units. But even the first kilowatt could not be produced until the water that still poured unimpeded off the plateau into the Atlantic was collected and controlled by the forty miles of dykes and the great concrete towers and steel gates of the control structures. Since the dykes could not be built in winter, when the ground was frozen solid, this left only three brief summer seasons for the herculean labour of moving the 26 million cubic yards of rock and glacial debris that would go into them.

This year, 1969, was therefore scheduled to be the first of the three peak construction years, and the contractors assigned to build the eighty-eight dykes were beginning to mobilize their men and equipment. The men were being flown in; their huge machines were being shipped to Sept-Iles and railroaded to Esker, from where the trucks were driven and the bulldozers transported to the site — until May 10.

On that day (ironically, just as the lawyers in New York were putting the final touches to the contracts), the Churchill Falls project encountered the latest in the seemingly endless series of setbacks that had dogged it since its early days: the Quebec North Shore and Labrador Railway, its vital lifeline from the outside world, was closed by a strike of Iron Ore Company and Wabush Mines employees.

Marooned on the dock at Sept-Iles when the railroad issued its embargo against shipments was much of the material required for the coming season's work on the dykes and the powerhouse excavation, including several dozen heavy trucks belonging to one of the dyke contractors, Miron Company. Plainly, if the tie-up lasted more than a few days, it could spell disaster for Churchill's carefully planned master project schedule.

Jim Hayward, traffic manager for ACB, and later Churchill Falls, had been warned that there might be a strike a month earlier and had gone to Sept-Iles to take precautions. By accelerating delivery schedules, he had managed to get some of the more urgent shipments away from the dock before the railroad stopped running. He also had extra fuel tanks installed at Esker and sent in enough diesel fuel and gasoline to keep the wheels turning for ten weeks. Altogether, he managed to get 5,400 tons of cargo shipped north in the two weeks before the strike began. But when the last train pulled out, more than 1,300 tons of vital consignments, including those trucks, were still stranded on the dock.

The railroad employees themselves were not on strike — they did not

314

walk out until two months later — but they refused to cross the picket lines set up around the rail terminal on the Iron Ore Company's dock. There was, however, another point on the line, Mile 9, where Hayward thought it might be possible to load trains if the material could be trucked there from the dock. With Lionel Watson, ACB dock supervisor, he drove to Mile 9 to take a look around. They found half a dozen determined-looking "woodsmen" apparently cutting trees in the bush but actually contemplating them with what Hayward took to be altogether too much interest. "These guys aren't bush workers," Watson said out of the side of his mouth. "They're all strikers." Hayward feigned innocence and asked the men if there were any likely fishing spots in the neighbourhood. It was quite obvious nothing was going to be loaded on to any trains at Mile 9.

As so often in the history of the north, there was only one answer: aircraft. Quebecair and Eastern Provincial Airways, which were by now providing daily service into Churchill's almost-completed new airport, had promised to make freight-carrying planes available if the strike materialized. But Air Canada's six thousand machinists had just walked off their jobs and regional carriers had their hands full serving its routes.

Quebecair could spare only one C-46 transport plane, but Hayward cast around and managed to charter a British-built Argosy freighter from Universal Airlines in Detroit.

On May 15, the Argosy launched an airlift that was to last three months, flying into Churchill with more than eleven tons of truck parts and caterpillar tracks for bulldozers. The C-46 took off soon afterward and by the end of the day the two planes had moved in more than eighty-one tons of freight. With spare crews and maintenance mechanics, and carrying their own return fuel on each flight, they flew virtually round the clock for the next two weeks. Often, the pilots did not turn off their motors on the Churchill strip, since the unloading crews worked so quickly. But Hayward soon realized he needed bigger planes and started telephoning all over the continent in search of a Hercules, a four-engined freighter with doors in its tail and a payload of more than twenty-two tons. The only Hercules owned by a Canadian company at that time was committed to the North Slope oil development in Alaska, but he managed to track down another in Florida. About three weeks after the strike began, it made its first approach to the Churchill airport. The pilot set his huge plane down somewhat gingerly, and on his return to Sept-Iles indignantly hauled Hayward out of his office to look at a series of dents in his fuselage.

The new strip was 5,500 feet long, capable of taking modern jets and a considerable improvement on the old 4,000-foot strip at Twin. But it was not yet paved, and when the Hercules reversed its turbo-prop engines on landing it blew away the layer of compacted dust on the strip and threw up the stones beneath, which rattled like hail on its fuselage, to the consternation of its pilot. In colourful terms, he told Hayward there was no way he was going back in to that blankety-blank place.

Hayward promised that every available grader in Churchill Falls would be assigned to repair the strip forthwith and, dubiously, the pilot agreed to go in again later to see what kind of a job they had made of it. He was apparently satisfied, for during the next week his Hercules, with two crews, flew in the Miron trucks and other urgent cargoes. But under the heavy wear the strip deteriorated again and the pilot decided the toll on his fuselage — and his nerves — was just too much; he returned to the more salubrious climate of Florida, taking his plane with him. Luckily, another Hercules was found in Alaska and ferried to Sept-Iles at a cost of $20,000. Its pilot, apparently more blasé about the rigours of northern flying, stayed on until the end of the airlift.

The strikers permitted occasional trains to head north with specified cargoes such as food, cigarettes and medical supplies, but by July shortages had developed on site and the company had to charter an F-27 aircraft which ultimately flew in forty tons of food. The stockpiled fuel also began to give out toward the end of June and extra planes were chartered to take in diesel oil and gasoline. Altogether, the various planes used on the airlift made almost twelve hundred round trips, carrying 12,000 tons of vitally needed freight and 650,000 gallons of fuel.

The worst moment was suffered by the crew of a DC-4 assigned to fly in three tons of explosives needed to keep the powerhouse excavation abreast of schedule. When its pilot began to let down for his landing he discovered his undercarriage was jammed. He radioed Sept-Iles and warned the air control officer there he was returning, and that he was "bringing in a flying bomb." Fortunately, the crew managed to winch the wheels down by hand and the plane landed safely.

While the airlift succeeded in its aim of averting a complete shutdown of operations, which would have been fatal to the all-important schedule, the railroad stoppage nevertheless played havoc with what was to have been the first full year of dyke construction. Fortunately, the underground blasting and excavation continued throughout the summer without too much disruption: in one week of June, enough rock was removed from the powerhouse area to fill 2,800 35-ton trucks. But when October put an end to dyke-building for the season (nineteen inches of snow fell during the month and the temperature dropped to two degrees above zero), the engineers realized they faced a monumental problem. Less than four and a half million cubic yards of fill had been packed into the embankments, instead of the target figure of ten million cubic yards. That left more than twenty million cubic yards to be put in place during the next two seasons. So even before construction ended for the year the planners in Montreal were reviewing contracts and work schedules, estimating how many extra men would be required to make up the lost time and planning an expansion of the camp to house them.

It was an anxious time for Don McParland who, already chairman and president of Churchill Falls, had also become president of Brinco after Donald Gordon's death. But during the summer and fall of 1969, after the successful conclusion of the negotiations with Hydro-Québec, he did manage to get away more often to enjoy his favourite sports of fishing and hunting and indulge his latest enthusiasm; he had bought a racing yacht and that summer was applying himself to mastering the intricacies of sailing with the same intensity and competitive spirit he brought to all his activities. He liked to think of himself as a small-town boy who had made good and Carl Goldenberg, lunching with him once in the Beaver Club, asked him how it felt to be carried around in a chauffeur-driven limousine. McParland grinned and replied: "I laugh at myself sometimes — when I'm alone." While he was proud of his success, he was still as much at home partying with his employees and their friends as mingling with business leaders at more formal gatherings, and the miners he sometimes chatted with on his visits to the site were invariably impressed to find an executive in suit coat and tie who knew as much about the technicalities of their trade as they did.

At forty, as the $75,000 a year head of the largest civil engineering project in North America and a director of a growing number of companies (in addition to Brinco and its subsidiaries, his directorships now included Rio Tinto-Zinc, Power Corporation and the Bank of Montreal), McParland was becoming known to a wider audience and there was a rising demand for his services as a public speaker.

On Monday, November 10, he was due to address a luncheon meeting of the Canadian Club of Montreal. On the previous Friday evening, the federal government released the White Paper on tax reform which had been anxiously awaited by the business world ever since the report of the Carter Royal Commission on Taxation three years earlier. McParland worked all weekend to rewrite his speech and became the first nationally-known business leader to comment on Ottawa's proposals. He reminded his audience that last time he had addressed them he had spoken of the Churchill Falls project as a prime example of cooperation between governments and private interests. "Churchill Falls is not being built with taxpayers' money," he said. "No government, provincial or federal, has diverted revenues taken from the Canadian taxpayer to support uneconomic power for political or for regional reasons. Churchill Falls is a viable commercial undertaking, selling a commodity — electricity — in a competitive market, in a businesslike fashion, to a sophisticated and responsible buyer, who had alternate choices available."

This business approach to the development of Canada's resources, he went on, seemed to make sense. It should be the government's role in a free enterprise society to create an environment in which private enterprise could do its job economically and responsibly. But the White Paper's proposals seemed likely to lessen, rather than increase, the incentives for investment in Canada's development. Even with the incentives the White Paper proposed to remove, Canada had never been able to attract enough money to do all the things it really needed to do.

The White Paper, McParland concluded, was not so much a paper on tax reform as a paper on the redistribution of Canada's wealth. "No one would want to dispute the paper's stated objective of increasing the wealth of less well-to-do Canadians," he said. "What the White Paper does not tell us is what the impact on the Canadian economy will be as a result of this proposed redistribution. Effectively, the principle is to take a dollar from the man most likely to invest it, and put it in the hands of a man who will almost certainly spend it on consumer goods. Is the resulting impact likely to be inflationary? There is some evidence to support that this is a likely probability. . . ."

Though McParland had had only the weekend to assess the White Paper, his speech articulated what businessmen all over the country were thinking and expressed views that would be put to Ottawa in succeeding years in dozens of other speeches, briefs and private conversations.

Later in the afternoon, he left Montreal in Churchill Falls' new DH-125 executive jet for Sept-Iles, where he was to make a very different sort of speech that evening. He had been invited to be the 1969 Distinguished Lecturer of an organization for which he had a particular fondness, the Canadian Institute of Mining and Metallurgy, and characteristically had resolved to visit as many of its smaller branches across the country as he could, where speakers, whether distinguished or not, were often hard to come by. At home as always among engineers, he delivered a practical speech, without any oratorical flourishes, outlining the various mining methods used in the Churchill powerhouse and their relative merits; the vital importance of detailed planning before any construction job was begun; and the equal importance to its successful completion of strict management controls and error-proof communications, not only electronically, on site, but among the people involved at all levels of the work.

Next morning, McParland flew on to Churchill Falls for one of his periodic inspection visits and for an afternoon conference to be attended by the brass and senior on-site managers and engineers. The Churchill Falls representatives at this meeting included McParland, Eric Lambert, Harold Snyder and Bill Bradford, a Montreal accountant who had joined the company two years before as project controller. The Acres Canadian Bechtel team was headed by Fred Ressegieu and Herb Jackson, by now his assistant general manager. It was the kind of day for which Labrador is notorious: damp and coldly grey, with clouds pressing low on the hills and fog swirling among the trees. The site was unusually quiet, Armistice Day still being a holiday in Newfoundland, and the atmosphere of the town that fall was unsettling: a mixture of annoyance at the delays of the past season, anxiety that the lost time might not be made up, and yet a sort of frustrated eagerness to get on with the job.

McParland's confidence and breezy manner revived some flagging spirits as he listened attentively to reports, issued orders in his customarily crisp fashion and went on to preside over the afternoon meeting, whose order of business included an item that seemed impossibly remote to some of the men there: the ultimate transformation of Churchill Falls from a construction job to an operating power plant.

The conference began at 3:30 p.m. McParland, who was to deliver his speech again that evening to the Wabush-Labrador City chapter of the CIMM, wound up the proceedings soon after five and the party drove out to the airport, pausing briefly on the way to inspect a spacious VIP lodge which had just been completed to McParland's design on the cliffs overlooking the river gorge a short way from town. At the airport, pilot Jim MacLeod and co-pilot Robin Elley had the DH-125 ready for takeoff. The weather was no better than it had been all day, but as a pilot himself McParland could see it would not prevent their departure. He and his executive assistant, John Lethbridge, were to be dropped off at Wabush. The plane was then to fly on to Montreal with the others: Lambert, Ressegieu, Jackson and Arthur J. Cantle, ACB's on-site assistant manager of construction. Harold Snyder was originally to have travelled with McParland, but since the Dutch ambassador to Canada was visiting the site he remained behind to be his host at an informal dinner in the hotel.

The jet took off at 6 p.m. Half an hour later, airport manager Harry Swiggum, who was dining with Snyder and the Dutch ambassador, was summoned to the telephone in the hotel dining room to receive a message from Bob Sharples, the Department of Transport weather observer at the airport, among whose duties was relaying instructions to incoming and outgoing aircraft from the air traffic control centre at Moncton, which directs traffic movements at both the Churchill strip and Wabush.

White-faced, Swiggum returned to the table, apologized to the Dutch ambassador and asked Snyder to step outside the room for a moment. There he gave him the message he had just received: Sharples had overheard the operator in the Wabush tower reporting to Moncton on the hot line that he had suddenly lost voice communication with a DH-125 which had been coming in for a landing. At the same moment, a flash had been reported several miles beyond the runway.

Snyder had worked closely with McParland and Lambert ever since those testing days at Rio Algom. He knew only too well what their loss would mean to the company. But more than that, they were his friends. And he knew the others on the plane almost as well. As Swiggum drove him to the airport, he had that stunned, half-awake feeling of unreality that overtakes people at such a time.

After talking to Sharples himself, Snyder picked up the phone and, his voice shaking, gave the news — fragmentary as it still was — to Gerry La Fontaine, a former Canadian Press reporter who had lived at Churchill Falls since 1967 as the on-site public relations man. As soon as Snyder hung up, La Fontaine glanced at the clock, realized it was after office hours in Montreal and called his boss, David Willock, at his home. Willock was still on his way home, so La Fontaine told his wife: "Gloria, please have him phone me as soon as he gets in. It couldn't possibly be more urgent."

By the time Willock returned the call, fifteen minutes or so later, La Fontaine knew the worst had happened: the Royal Canadian Mounted Police detachment at Wabush was now satisfied that the Churchill Falls jet had crashed and no one could possibly have survived.

There followed a night that all concerned remember with horror. Willock drove straight back to the office, his first concern being to break the tragic news to the men's families before it was broadcast on radio

320

or television, a task shouldered by the dead men's friends within the companies. As the news bulletins began to come over the radio, other members of the staff and some of the local directors converged on the office, talking in stunned whispers and anxious to do anything they could to help, though knowing nothing could. Willock spent the rest of the night tracking down and breaking the news to the various out-of-town directors and their associates at Hydro-Québec, the Bank of Montreal, Morgan Stanley in New York, Rio Tinto in London, Bechtel in San Francisco. Sir Val Duncan — he had been knighted the year before for his services to British industry — was in South Africa. When he heard the news, he took the first available flight to London and, after meeting Sir Mark Turner at the airport, switched planes and flew straight on to Montreal. Bill Mulholland had returned to his office after a dinner engagement in New York when Willock reached him. He went home for some shirts and was on the first flight to Montreal next morning. John Kiely, who was fishing for marlin from a boat off the coast of Mexico, was told the news by radiophone from his office, promptly gave orders for Bechtel's executive jet to pick him up at the nearest airport at first light next morning, and was in Montreal that evening.

Willock could not reach Henry Borden, who was on the evening train from Toronto to Montreal, where he was to attend a meeting of the Bell Telephone Company's board of directors next day. Keith Laidley, a Brinco lawyer, went to Central Station to meet him, but the first face Borden recognized when he came into the concourse was that of Robert Scrivener, president of Bell. "My God, Bob, is anything wrong at home?" Borden gasped, unaccustomed to being met at the station. "Not at home, Henry," Scrivener replied, "but I think you'd better come over here and sit down."

Borden sat on a bench in Central Station battling tears for several minutes after Scrivener had broken the news; during the years he had worked with Don McParland he had not only come to admire his ability but had developed almost a father's affection for him. Then he rose wearily and Laidley drove him to the company apartment where, like so many other Brinco people that night, he found himself unable to sleep.

It was morning before the police at Wabush were able to examine the crash site properly, fog and rain having hampered their efforts the night before. While trying to make an instrument landing, the plane had flown into the side of a mountain, the Smallwood mine, which was being stripped of its iron ore in thirty-foot open-pit terraces. Wreckage was strewn over several terraces and the only recognizable parts of the jet remaining were its tail and wingtips. It appeared to have hit the mountainside only a hundred feet or so below its crest. Its crew and passengers had obviously been killed outright, at the moment when the tower lost contact with them.*

The weather over Labrador on November 12 was worse than it had been the day before. Early in the morning, Snyder, La Fontaine, Swiggum and Bloss Sutherland, of ACB's administrative staff, took off for Wabush in a Jet Ranger helicopter. After skimming the trees for about ten miles, trying to pick his way through the fog, pilot Dave Wilson told them, "Look, there's no way we can get through." They returned to the airport, picked up Swiggum's car and set off down the road to Esker. The fog was so thick there were no other vehicles on the road and driving was such a strain that the men took turns at the wheel. At Esker, they boarded a southbound train for Wabush, where they arrived at ten that night. After the melancholy task of identification, the bodies were sealed in coffins and next day, since the weather was so bad that aircraft were still unable to land at Wabush, Snyder accompanied them on the long and

---

*There were two navigational beacons at Wabush: WK, to the north of the runway, and WZ, south of it. The procedure for an approach using the northern beacon, which called for aircraft to land from north to south, had been officially cancelled more than six months earlier, though some pilots had continued to use it. The currently approved approach, using the WZ beacon, called for aircraft to land on the runway from the south. A Department of Transport inquiry into the crash found that Elley, the co-pilot of the Churchill jet, had received and acknowledged clearance for the cancelled approach procedure, on the WK beacon, but that the plane had apparently tried to land from the south, using the currently approved procedure but on the WK beacon instead of the WZ beacon. The inquiry report stated: "Flying the approved approach procedure on the WK beacon, rather than on the WZ, resulted in a six-mile northward displacement of the approach pattern. Having crossed over a beacon that the pilot apparently assumed incorrectly to be south of the field, he was now flying at his minimum approach altitude expecting to see the runway ahead. Routine transmissions from the aircraft were heard moments before the impact. The aircraft crashed 5.5 miles north of the WK beacon into the rock face of a lighted open-pit mine . . . ." In an action for damages brought against the crown, the federal court held in 1974 that the pilot of the Churchill jet was entirely to blame for the crash. "Although the air traffic controller on duty should not have given a WK clearance," the judgment said, "it was not reasonably foreseeable that the pilot would thereafter execute a WZ approach on the WK beacon." The judgment was appealed but at the time of writing the appeal had not yet been heard.

lonely journey by rail to Sept-Iles, where an Iron Ore Company DC-3 waited to fly them to Montreal.

The day after the crash, considerable dismay was caused in Montreal by a statement issued by Dr. Fred Rowe, Newfoundland's Minister of Education and acting Premier in the absence of Joey Smallwood on vacation in Panama. The crash, Rowe said, was "one of the most serious blows that could have happened." The loss of McParland alone would have been enough to create large problems for the Churchill project, but the loss of "the tremendous amount of knowledge carried in the heads" of those who had died with him, "would not be easy to replace."

While this fear was an obvious one, no one wanted to put it in words at this critical moment. To restore morale, Henry Borden gathered the employees together that afternoon, assured them the project would go on and appealed for their continued efforts to make it a success. And a statement was issued to the press saying the company was fortunate to have "management in depth" and a board meeting would be held as soon as possible to discuss new appointments.

On the morning of November 14, three days after the crash, the executive committees of Brinco and Churchill Falls held a joint meeting at which it was agreed that to maintain confidence in the project Sir Val Duncan would temporarily assume all of McParland's posts until a successor was chosen.

That afternoon, as the bells tolled over the narrow, rain-drenched streets of old Montreal, the families, friends and business associates of the dead men, more than two thousand in all, crowded into the magnificent church of Nôtre Dame for a moving ecumenical memorial service requested by the widows and hastily arranged by Father Peter Timmins, a member of the famous mining family and a friend of McParland's. The altar was hidden by a cascade of white carnations which, though the effect had not been intended, reminded the mourners of the turbulent waters of Churchill Falls. The forty-five-minute service included prayers by clergymen of several denominations and readings by John Kiely and Sir Val Duncan, whose grief at the loss of friends was sharpened by the fact that he had privately chosen McParland to be his eventual successor at the head of the whole Rio Tinto-Zinc group.

As a further memorial to the dead men, permanent facilities in Churchill Falls were named after them. The main street leading into town is Ressegieu Drive. The three main residential streets are Jackson, Lethbridge and Cantle avenues. The children attend the Eric G. Lambert school. And visiting dignitaries and executives stay in that comfortable lodge with its awe-inspiring view of the river now known as McParland House.

On May 7, 1970, in the presence of their families, a plaque bearing the names of the dead men was unveiled in the Town Centre. Addressing his remarks to the children, Sir Val Duncan said the plaque was not their fathers' memorial. For that, he directed them to the words of the Latin inscription on St. Paul's Cathedral in London, celebrating the achievements of its builder, Sir Christopher Wren: *Si monumentum requiris, circumspice.* Or, in English: "If you want a monument, look around you."

TWENTY-THREE

A vintage year saves the day

Few companies can ever have faced a more critical set of circumstances than those which confronted Brinco at the beginning of 1970. As if the sudden loss of its top management was not enough, the company found itself in a position where, in the words of one executive who lived through it, "everything seemed to be coming out of the sky at once."

The disruptions of the 1969 work season threatened to banish the vitally important master project schedule into the realm of wishful thinking. On top of that, the company faced about $30 million worth of claims from contractors who contended that their schedules, too, had been irreparably damaged, to the point of completely changing their terms of work. If the big push needed to make up lost time was to have any chance of success, these claims would have to be dealt with to the contractors' satisfaction. Otherwise, it looked as if some of them, at least, would not put their men back to work at the start of the coming season. The loss of another all-too-brief above-ground construction season would magnify into at least a year's delay in completion of the project, and a consequent steep escalation of costs. The ultimate penalty for a cost overrun was only too well known at the higher levels of the company: the loss of the project and all the money invested in it.

But the shareholders' investment was also imperilled from a totally different direction. In his speech just before his death, Don McParland had criticized the government's White Paper on tax reform in general terms. Neither he, nor Eric Lambert, who had helped him to write it, had spotted that some of its fine print threatened to be utterly disastrous for the Churchill Falls company. On the very day of the plane crash, November 11, his department prepared a memorandum for Eric Lambert that he was fated never to read. It was the first warning that if several of the government's proposals were enacted into law they would virtually wipe out Brinco shareholders' return on their investment.

Clearly, a daunting volume of work awaited whoever took over the reins from the dead men: preventing a collapse of morale and a possible complete breakdown of the job; restoring the field work to schedule; examining and settling contractors' claims; and assessing the full impact of the White Paper's proposals and devising a strategy to protect the company's interests.

It was vital that strong hands be restored to the tiller as soon as possible. That this could be done so quickly is the best testimony to the strength and resilience of the Churchill project's planning, and the mutual confidence and team spirit which had been built up among all those concerned with it.

When news of the plane crash interrupted John Kiely's marlin-fishing expedition, he immediately told his office to track down George Saul, a thirty-year Bechtel construction veteran who had worked on hydro and nuclear power projects and mining operations around the world. Saul, a senior executive who had been in on the early Churchill planning and the assignment of men to ACB, was visiting a job in Oklahoma. He flew to Montreal the day after the crash and left right away for Churchill Falls to take temporary charge and reassure the ACB orgnization and those contractors still on site that there would be no let-up in the work.

It was to be four months before Saul could return to his duties in San Francisco, and by that time Bechtel had reached into its wide resources of management talent for two men well-suited to fill the gap at the head of ACB. Named to replace Ressegieu as general manager was Steven V. White, special assistant to the president, Steve Bechtel, Jr. White's whole career had been spent in administration; his last post before joining Bechtel had been as director of the contracts division of the U.S. Atomic Energy Commission's operations in Chicago, a background that was to be useful in the strenuous negotiations ahead on the Churchill contracts. To head the organization on site, as manager of construction, Bechtel appointed a tough, self-confident Scot, Joe Anderson, who had designed hydro-electric projects during five years at Bechtel headquarters in San Francisco, as well as supervised their construction in Turkey and on the Columbia River in the United States.

On the Churchill Falls side, the continuity of the construction job was assured by the steady presence of Harold Snyder, now vice-president as well as project manager, and Sir Val Duncan's task was to find the right man to take overall charge of the whole group of Brinco companies and guide them through all the difficulties ahead. He discussed this problem with Sir Mark Turner and Sam Harris immediately after the crash and they agreed that the logical choice was Bill Mulholland; he had amply demonstrated his analytical mind and understanding of finance, and no one else knew as much about so many aspects of the corporation's activities. But he was one of the foremost men in his field on Wall Street and the move would entail considerable financial sacrifice. Nonetheless, Duncan undertook to apply his formidable powers of persuasion and asked him to take over. Through the years, a strong bond had developed between Don McParland and Mulholland, and perhaps the challenge of an entirely new career was too much to resist: he moved his wife, Nancy, and their eight children to Montreal and became president of both Brinco and Churchill Falls.

Mulholland was no stranger to long hours, and he was under no illusions about the magnitude of the task he was shouldering, but even so he was not fully prepared for the situation he encountered when he took over early in January. Bud Manning had resigned to join the Royal Trust, his assistant had left shortly thereafter for another post, and Brinco was virtually bereft of its entire legal department. With so many delicate problems pending, this was obviously intolerable and Mulholland turned to Harry Macdonell for help. The prospect of extending his horizons into the executive field appealed to Macdonell and he resigned his Toronto law partnership to become vice-president of Brinco and Churchill Falls.

The changes at the top were completed at Brinco's annual general meeting the following May, when Henry Borden, whose term of duty had extended long past its originally intended limit, finally retired as chairman and was replaced by Robert D. Mulholland, vice-chairman of the Bank of Montreal. No relation to Bill Mulholland, "Pete," as he is known, had become familiar with the corporation's affairs during his years as an executive of the bank.

As a tax specialist, Harry Macdonell had done a thorough analysis of the White Paper on tax reform for Rio Tinto-Zinc before he even joined Brinco. When he came to examine how its proposals would affect his new company, he was appalled. In its desire to make a fundamental change in the corporation-tax structure, the government (he hoped inadvertently) proposed to go back on several key assurances given by previous governments, without which the Churchill deal could never have been arranged. For instance, the effect of one proposal would have been to abrogate the Public Utilities Income Tax Transfer Act, at least insofar as it concerned Churchill Falls. The White Paper said that because of the rebate of corporation taxes to the provinces under the PUITTA legislation, private utilities would be deemed not to have paid any tax. Their shareholders would therefore not be granted any credits for taxes paid by the company. This threatened to be catastrophic for Brinco's profitability, since while Newfoundland was to return half of the rebate to Churchill Falls, that money would not be available to shareholders; all of it would go to Hydro-Québec, to bring the price of the power down to the agreed rate. Normally, a company faced with new taxes could raise the price of its product. This option, of course, was not open to Churchill. In effect, Brinco shareholders were being taxed on income which had already been fully taxed.

Another provision of the White Paper would have eliminated approximately $100 million of capital cost allowances Churchill could have legitimately claimed under the existing legislation during the first thirty-five years of the contract. The effect of this, also, would have been disastrous: Churchill Falls was contractually forbidden to pay any dividends until 1977 — no less than twenty-three years after the first investment had been made in the project — and if this section of the White Paper was adopted it would delay payment of dividends for many more years.

Mulholland and Macdonell visited Ottawa several times during 1970 to complain about these inequities to Finance Minister Edgar Benson and his aides, and appeared before both House and Senate committees considering the proposed legislation. In essence, their case was that shareholders should not be penalized retroactively for investments made in good faith under the tax laws ruling at the time. The effect of the proposals, they pointed out, would be not only to wipe out the profitability of the Churchill project, but to discourage investors from participating in any similar ventures in the future.

Eventually, the government recognized the validity of the company's case and dropped the relevant clauses from the ultimate legislation. But preparing the company's arguments and briefs called for the burning of much midnight oil at One Westmount Square when many other problems also had to be dealt with. At around this time, for instance, the government decreed that copper producers must sell their output to domestic consumers at a price much below that ruling on the world market. This deprived the Whales Back mine of substantial profits it might otherwise have made, and once again necessitated the preparation of representations to the government.

While all these high-level negotiations were going on, the company also had to replan and reschedule the 1970 construction work. There was no time to pause for regrouping: the planning had to be done on the run, so to speak. To accomplish this, tight financial controls were essential. After the plane crash, Eric Lambert's job in effect was divided between Bill Bradford, as controller, and Robert C. Berry, who had joined Brinco as vice-president, finance, from Peat, Marwick. Under their direction, the cost reports — at a time when the company was spending from $25 to $30 million a month — were available within seven days of the end of each month. This avoided the pitfall so common to construction projects in which management, forced to rely on out-of-date cost reports, focuses its attention on problems that have already changed, and takes remedial action to correct situations that no longer exist. Under this system, problems tend to go rapidly from bad to worse and costs spiral right out of court.

With so many contractors' claims pending, of course, Churchill Falls had to bear extra expenses during 1970, but the contingency reserves set aside in the budget proved equal to the demand. In the early months of 1970, Steve White and the ACB staff put in long hours examining claims and recommending settlements to Churchill Falls. The guiding principle adopted within the company was that there was little point in quibbling over a claim if in the process no work was accomplished during the coming season. But naturally all claims had to be examined for authenticity, and even though much knowledge perished with the men killed in the air crash, the accurate records kept at lower levels often proved helpful in assessing claims. In general, settlements were designed to give contractors an incentive to complete their jobs on time. Some work was rearranged in the interest of greater efficiency and it was recognized that some contractors, particularly those building the all-important dykes, needed more money to provide more equipment and labour for the extra task ahead. Considerable amounts were offered as bonuses for early completion of jobs and some contracts were renegotiated on a target-cost basis, so that if a contractor finished his work for less than the estimated cost he would be awarded the lion's share of the saving.

Brinco had now vastly outgrown its shoestring beginnings, but it speaks well for its handful of pioneers that the work now swinging into high gear followed very closely the plans for the Channel Scheme formulated in the early fifties. Apart from the realization that the site had an even greater potential than had been thought at first, the changes which had to be made as the scheme progressed were comparatively minor. For instance, the larger-scale drilling sanctioned by McParland after the 1963 Acres report disclosed a major fault in the rock structure in the area where it was proposed to site the powerhouse; had blasting gone ahead there it could have led to expensive work to shore up the fractured rock, and even more costly construction delays. But when the location was moved a mere thousand feet, to the other side of the hill, the powerhouse was actually built in what turned out to be the most solid piece of rock in the area.

The way the water was eventually stored and conducted to the powerhouse intake also remained essentially the same as in the original plan, though modifications had to be made as a result of some unpleasant shocks encountered as the project developed. Before the hundreds of lakes in the area were deepened and merged into the project's two reservoirs, the Churchill's two main tributaries, the Ashuanipi and the Atikonak, flowed into it from the northwest and from the south. The Ashuanipi, which drains an area of thirteen thousand square miles, rises in a lake of the same name west of the Quebec North Shore and Labrador railroad and about fifty miles south of Esker. From there it flows north, parallelling the railroad, to a point south of Schefferville, where it passes through the Menihek power station, which supplies the Schefferville mines. From Menihek it runs into Petitsikapau Lake, then doubles back and flows southeast into Sandgirt Lake, thence into Lobstick Lake, source of the Churchill.

The Atikonak, which drains an area of almost nine thousand square miles, rises in Lac Joseph, about sixty miles southeast of Churchill Falls. From there it runs east into Atikonak Lake and then north into Ossokmanuan, which has two natural outlets to the Churchill, one discharging east down the Unknown River and the other north through Gabbro Lake into Sandgirt.

As the various stages of the Twin Falls plant were built, the Atikonak's northward route into the Churchill was blocked by a series of dykes which sealed off Gabbro Lake from Sandgirt, and which also carried the access road from Esker to Churchill Falls. The Atikonak's water was stored in the Ossokmanuan reservoir and the huge steel gates of the Ossokmanuan control structure released it down the Unknown River as needed to power the Twin plant. Since the Unknown joins the Churchill below the falls, all the Atikonak's water would have been lost to the Churchill power station if provision for its recapture had not been made during the Twin Falls negotiations. When the time came for the Churchill plant to take over from Twin, the original dykes were breached and the new Gabbro control structure directed the water from Ossokmanuan reservoir back into Sandgirt.

Between them, the Ashuanipi and the Atikonak drain an area of almost 22,000 square miles. But just to the east of Lobstick Lake there was another area of more than four thousand square miles which drained into the Atlantic down two smaller rivers to the north of the Churchill: the Kanairiktok and the Naskaupi. The water from this drainage basin — which contained the biggest lake in the area, Michikamau — was ultimately diverted into the main reservoir by a series of dykes at Sail and Orma lakes that blocked its former outlets to the Kanairiktok and the Naskaupi.

The total catchment area of the Churchill project is therefore almost 27,000 square miles, only slightly smaller than the entire province of New Brunswick. At first it was contemplated that 1,085 billion cubic feet of the water originating in this area would have to be stored for the efficient operation of the power station. Since the Ossokmanuan reservoir stores 100 billion cubic feet, that meant the main reservoir would have to hold 985 billion cubic feet. But 1964 and 1965 turned out to be dry years and it was decided more storage was needed to avoid the danger of "bottoming" the reservoir: that is, running short of water to operate the plant. The storage figure was then set at a total of 1,200 billion cubic feet, with 1,100 billion of that in the main reservoir.

In 1963, when the planners were still using the sketchy one-mile-to-an-inch maps which were the only ones then available from Ottawa, it was thought that the main reservoir would back up the water along the Ashuanipi into Petitsikapau Lake and perhaps as far back as the Menihek dam. Serious consideration was given to whether it would, in fact, be possible to back water up against the dam. But in 1965 the federal Department of Mines and Technical Surveys did some more work to improve the maps; and by the spring of 1966 it was clear that at least some of the levels along the Ashuanipi were wrong and the reservoir might be smaller than expected.

The ACB engineers consequently thought it would be wise to do some more measuring of levels during the summer of 1966 and Churchill Falls — even though it was not yet certain the power could be sold — sanctioned the additional expense. It soon emerged that the maps of Petitsikapau Lake and the Ashuanipi were wrong by up to forty feet; in other words, the lake bed was as much as forty feet higher than the maps showed it to be. Since water does not flow uphill, the reservoir was plainly going to be smaller than had been anticipated: far from holding 1,100 billion cubic feet it would hold only 820 billion, unless the dykes were raised to deepen it. Hence the extra $27 million set aside for dyke-building in the 1966 cost re-estimate and Don McParland's "Heartbreak Ridge" session with Bill Mulholland in New York early in 1967.

Still further shocks were in store. While this 1966 survey work was going on, Charlie Atkinson, a sandy-haired Englishman with a Newcastle burr who was in charge of the storage aspects of the project for Acres, made his first visit to the site. As he flew over the miles of lakes and marsh and rock, he did not like what he saw. All the drawings and maps he had been working with showed nice big lakes with no apparent restrictions on the free flow of the water. But where the blue areas on his map indicated open lakes perhaps a hundred miles across, the cold Labrador water was so clear that from the air Atkinson could see islands, ridges and channels scattered all over them beneath the surface.

The original cost estimate had included $3.8 million for the excavation of a channel to permit the waters of the Michikamau system to pass freely into Lobstick as the level of the main reservoir was drawn down. But Atkinson now discovered that the whole area around both ends of the proposed channel was full of other underwater features that might interfere with the flow of water and would thus have to be removed, at extra expense, or compensated for by raising the dykes to deepen the reservoir — again at extra expense.

Back in Montreal, he voiced these misgivings, amid cries of disbelief. He was insistent, however, and in 1967 a full field program was launched to plumb the lakes with echo-sounders and make yet another check of elevations around them. One of the parties engaged on this work, using benchmarks established by a Newfoundland firm commissioned to do surveys in 1964 and 1966, was astonished to come across a stream which, if the benchmarks were correct, was burbling merrily uphill. When they reported this phenomenon to Atkinson, he assumed their readings were incorrect and had them do the job over again. The stream apparently still ran uphill.

And eventually, to everyone's horror, it was realized that the prospective reservoir was on a tilt.

The 1966 survey parties had run a line of levels right across the main reservoir from Lobstick in the west to Orma and Sail lakes in the east — work, of course, which had to be done in the winter when the lakes were frozen. No one could ever discover why (perhaps their instruments sank slightly in the snow each time they took a reading) but the elevations they established at Lobstick were about two feet out and the error magnified as they headed east, so that the ground at Orma was actually seven feet higher than had been thought. This meant that the reservoir could not be filled to its projected level unless the Lobstick dykes were considerably raised. Fortunately, from the point of view of costs, the Orma and Sail dykes would not need to be as high as had originally been expected.

Raising a dyke, of course, is not a simple matter of dumping a few more truckloads of fill on its crest. Since they are built of rocks, gravel and glacial till (the dust-like debris left by retreating glaciers), they may be hundreds of feet wide at their base, tapering to road-width at their crest. And if their height is to be increased, they must be redesigned with a wider base, at the consequent cost of much more material.

When he came to make the final decision on the size of the main reservoir, Don McParland had to balance the extra cost of raising the dykes against the earnings that could be expected from the extra water impounded, and reach a happy economic medium. But he also had to be sure the reservoir would be sufficiently large that a succession of dry years would not leave him without enough water to spin the turbines. To do this, he really needed accurate records of the yearly rain and snow fall in the catchment area over a much longer period than actually existed. So once again it was decided to use the only standard of comparison available, the flow records of the Outardes River in nearby Quebec. The Churchill Falls and ACB engineers constructed a remarkable computer program which projected the Outardes figures forward for five thousand years.

With the aid of this electronic prognostication, McParland decided in 1967 that the main reservoir would be built to hold 1,000 billion cubic feet of water which, with the Ossokmanuan reservoir, gave a total storage of 1,100 billion cubic feet. Once this figure was settled, the ACB engineers collated all the conflicting data which had now been accumulated on elevations around the reservoir and settled on the best levels they could establish theoretically. And it was decided that in places the dykes would have to be up to eight feet higher than the original plan had stipulated.

In 1969 the Geodetic Survey of Canada spent a year making what is known as a "precise-level survey" from Esker to the falls and on to Sail Lake, a total distance of 265 miles. The ultimate in accuracy, precise-level surveys are made with ultra-sophisticated equipment. The rods on which sightings are taken, for instance, are made of a special alloy with a low coefficient of expansion, so they are unaffected by either heat or cold, and they are calibrated in millimeters. The bubble in the surveyor's level is more accurate than those in ordinary equipment and a sunshade above it prevents it being distorted by the sun. Inside the telescope in the level are three bars, which take three readings on each rod. The longest sight taken is two hundred feet and each sight is checked both backwards and forwards. Elevations are set to within a thousandth of a foot, and before they are published they are corrected to compensate for the flattening of the earth at the poles, a refinement that scarcely concerns the average surveyor.

Fifty-five thousand miles of precise-level lines criss-cross Canada, with benchmarks (brass pins set in bedrock or firm ground) every two miles along them. And when the benchmarks were established in the Churchill Falls area, the calculations on which the reservoir was ultimately based were found to be accurate to within a few inches.*

The decision to raise the dykes eliminated the need for the Michikamau channel, and as the work progressed another modification — or rather, addition — to the initial plan was found necessary in the forebay, the "channel" part of the Channel Scheme. The flow of water out of the main reservoir is controlled by the Lobstick control structure, built on what, until it was submerged, was a ten-acre island. The structure consists of three steel gates 63 feet high, 45 feet wide and thick enough (four feet) to enable a man to work inside them. The gates are supported by tall concrete towers and lifted hydraulically from above. Like the rest of the gates in the other control structures, they are heated electrically to ensure their operation in the coldest weather and under normal circumstances are operated by remote control from the power station.

The Lobstick gates release the water into the Churchill River through a series of lakes and rapids, its natural course, where it falls sixty-five feet in thirty-five miles until it reaches Jacopie Lake. There another gated structure five miles before the falls, the Jacopie spillway, with its flanking dykes straddling the river, diverts the water into the twin forebay, formed by linking the lakes in a shallow valley running parallel to, and north of, the river. The spillway also performs another function: if the water in the main reservoir should ever rise to danger level it would open to

*Such was the difficulty of establishing levels in that remote country, the Desbarats survey carried out for the Newfoundland government in 1947 was found in 1963 to have placed the whole area sixteen and a half feet lower than it actually is. Later surveys suggested the error might be only thirteen and a half feet, but since it was consistent it made no practical difference to the levels used in establishing the reservoir.

permit the flood to run harmlessly away down the river's normal course.

Originally, it was planned to have one forebay, running east from Jacopie all the way to the powerhouse intake. But a ridge was found in the channel leading out of the lake which threatened to cause trouble during the winter because of a natural phenomenon occurring in very cold climates. Unless an ice cover forms above the water — which it does not do with the kind of fast flow passing through the Jacopie channel — the water can become super-cooled to a fraction below its normal freezing point of 32 degrees Fahrenheit, generating ice crystals, known as frazil ice, without actually freezing solid. When this happens, there is a danger that a slight change in conditions will form a solid mass of ice very quickly. At first, it was planned to excavate and deepen the channel to prevent its becoming blocked by ice — which would not only have caused a flood upstream but would have cut off the supply of water to the turbines. When the ridge was discovered it was decided that a more certain, and only slightly more expensive, way to avoid the risk of an ice jam would be to raise the forebay dykes and insert another control structure into the scheme, the Whitefish structure, which not only deepens but slows down the water, enabling an ice cover to form. The effect of Whitefish was to divide the forebay into two, the eastern section, containing the intake, being fourteen and a half feet below the level of the western section.

The splitting of the forebay necessitated one other change in the original plan: the addition of a sixth control structure, another spillway east of the powerhouse intake. Its function is simple, but no less vital for that: the intake sits above the town site and if for any reason the east forebay ever reached flood level the water could overflow the dykes and pour down on the town. To prevent that, the east forebay spillway would be opened and the floodwaters would be released into the river down a valley east of the town site and power station.

The building of the five new structures (Ossokmanuan had been installed earlier for Twin) went hand in hand with the construction of the dykes, and fortunately 1970 was a beautiful summer, so that the work force, which rose during the year to its peak level of 6,245 men, suffered few of the interruptions considered normal in Labrador's capricious climate.

The 1970 work was also helped along by a new administrative set-up introduced in the light of the experience gained so far. During the early years, the construction managers of both Churchill Falls and ACB had been based in Montreal. Though they made frequent visits to the site, often they were not there at the same time and sometimes decisions needed by the men on the spot had to await their arrival. The first step to remedy this failing was taken when Joe Anderson replaced Herb Jackson as ACB's top construction man and instead of working out of Montreal moved in to the site. What proved to be a crucial reorganization was completed after Harold Snyder became executive vice-president of Churchill Falls and his chief lieutenant, Dick Boivin, replaced him as project manager.

Boivin was born in the hard-rock country of Northern Ontario and one of his first jobs was as resident engineer and general foreman on the QNS&L railroad. Since then, he had supervised dozens of construction jobs on projects as various as the Montreal Metro and power stations in New Zealand and Australia. When Snyder hired him as assistant construction manager in mid-1968 he was project manager of the Tehachipi discharge tunnels, a series of penstocks being bored through the Sierra Mountains to supply Los Angeles with water from northern California.

Short but stocky, Boivin is a tobacco-chewing outdoorsman who loves fishing and hunting. He had never before sat behind a desk at head office, and he didn't like it. His philosophy is reflected by the fact that his correspondence for several years sat in a few slim file folders on a bookshelf beside his desk. "If you're writing a letter," he once said, "you're not working."

Believing that a construction boss's place is in the hole with the men doing the job, Boivin had recommended in his report for 1968 that both Churchill and ACB should have more senior men on site. He therefore welcomed the decision early in 1970 to transfer him to Churchill, and moved in with his wife and family and probably the most exotic bird ever seen in Labrador: their mynah. He got along well with Joe Anderson and henceforth decisions were made on the spot; and the new resident project manager soon became famous — or notorious — for his fanatical dedication to the master project schedule.

The Churchill planners constantly compared the actual progress of the job against the master schedule by computer, a process that was sometimes able to predict delays before they actually happened, enabling something to be done about them before they got out of hand. And the computer's pronouncements were carefully plotted on huge charts in Boivin's office. Contractors, of course, had similar schedules and Rudy Scarabelli, project manager for Spino Construction, a contractor on the tailrace tunnels, went so far as to prepare a weekly chart for his foremen, showing them where they were supposed to be and where they actually were. After a period during which the tunnelling had fallen a little behind, Scarabelli was pleased to be able to produce a chart on which the curve of actual progress coincided with the curve of progress required by the schedule. That evening, he met Boivin at a party. "What do you think of Spino now? We're right on schedule," he said triumphantly. "Bullshit," snorted Boivin. "You're two days behind."

At the end of his construction report for 1969, Boivin had described that year as "rough" but forecast that the year 1970 would be "a vintage one." And so it turned out to be. By July, as the dykes were rapidly taking shape up on the plateau, the last explosive charge was detonated underground. In less than three years, more than 2,300,000 cubic yards of rock had been removed from the powerhouse complex.

When this work began in the fall of 1967, the drilling and blasting crews drove into the heart of the mountain from two different directions. From the surface, in the area of the intake, they started sinking a 22-foot-wide elevator shaft almost a thousand feet straight down to where the east end of the powerhouse would ultimately be. Eventually, this would house a double deck elevator capable of carrying sixty men or 12,000 pounds of freight. And from the side of the mountain overlooking the river, work began on a pilot tunnel, 12 feet by 12, for the main access tunnel, leading a mile into the rock to the west end of the power-house. This two-lane tunnel, in which trucks kept to the left, so that their drivers could get as close as possible to the rock wall without hitting it, was eventually enlarged to be 33 feet wide and 28 feet high. Larger still are the two tailrace tunnels, lower down the mountain; in fact, their portals are below the level of the river, so that a coffer dam had to be built to permit their construction. Each of these twin tunnels, which conduct the water back into the river after it has turned the turbines, is more than a mile long, 45 feet wide and 60 feet high.

As these tunnels pushed into the rock, the drilling crews worked perched on "jumbo" steel rigs 24 feet high and 12 feet wide and each equipped with nine drills mounted on pneumatic booms. Having drilled the rock face and packed it with their explosive charges, the men would retreat to a safe distance, the charges would be detonated and then mechanical shovels would move in to scoop the shattered rock into giant off-highway trucks with six wheels each six feet in diameter. This work, of course, went on regardless of the weather outside, though the drills need a supply of water and air and there were occasional difficulties with frozen water lines. Ventilating the tunnels also presented some problems when the air brought in from outside had a temperature of perhaps forty degrees below zero. Spino, on its tailrace-tunnel job, used two one-hundred-horsepower fans and a sixty-inch airline for ventilation, and in winter the heater used to warm the air ate up six hundred gallons of fuel a day.

In July 1968, as the access tunnel neared the powerhouse area, the largest single construction contract of the project was awarded to Churchill Constructors, a joint venture linking several Canadian companies and headed by the Montreal-based Atlas Construction Company. Worth $46.8 million, this covered the main civil work on the powerhouse: construction of the powerhouse itself and the two other large caverns associated with it; tunnelling of the eleven penstocks to conduct the water from the intake down to the turbines; most of the concrete work in the underground complex; the installation of miles of embedded conduits and piping; and the erection of two electrically operated overhead cranes in the powerhouse, each with a capacity of four hundred tons.

Churchill Constructors ultimately spent $10 million on equipment: drilling rigs and compressors to drive the drills, power shovels and mechanical loaders, 35-ton dump trucks, even a crushing plant to make aggregate for concrete — which had to be broken down and flown in to the site during the airlift, then rebuilt on the spot.

Even before CCJV, as it became known, had mobilized all this equipment and the men needed to operate it, and before the main chambers had begun to be hollowed out of the rock, Prime Minister Pierre Elliott Trudeau paid his first visit to the site. "Bigger than the catacombs," was his verdict, "and I suspect . . . a lot more useful."

CCJV began its work by pushing two pilot tunnels through the rock from the access tunnel: one along the top of what would eventually be the powerhouse, to link with the elevator shaft at its eastern end, and the other into the area from which the penstocks could be excavated from the bottom up, since it is cheaper to blast the rock and let it fall to the bottom of the hole than to begin from the top and have to haul the muck to the surface. Since all this tunnelling had to be extremely accurate — the penstocks, of course, had to emerge at the right place in the intake structure — laser beams were used to keep the drillers on the right track. Penstock No. 1, which broke through to the surface in May 1969, emerged within two inches of where it was supposed to be.

When the plant was being designed, it was realized that the penstocks could be vertical. But by slanting them down at an angle of fifty-eight degrees, the engineers were able to site the powerhouse closer to the river, thus reducing building costs by shortening the much larger access and tailrace tunnels. Each penstock is 1,380 feet long. Its inclined section, 20 feet in diameter, is lined with concrete, to reduce friction and prevent the water from gradually penetrating and breaking up the rock, and its last horizontal section, 170 feet long and 14½ feet wide, is lined with steel, for the same purpose.

Originally, it had been thought that the roof of the powerhouse would have to be concreted, for strength. But the pilot tunnel revealed that the rock was so good — it had no major faults — that it was possible to switch to the much cheaper procedure of strengthening it with rock bolts, steel rods 15 to 25 feet long driven into the arched roof in carefully calculated patterns. Then a false ceiling of stainless steel was installed, from which the powerhouse lighting was suspended. When completed, the powerhouse was 972 feet long, up to 81 feet wide and 154 feet high — more than five times the size of the concourse of Central Station in Montreal.

Between the powerhouse and the river is another cavern almost as large — 763 feet long, 40 to 64 feet wide and 148 feet high. This is the surge chamber, which collects the water after it has spun the turbines, directs it into the two tailrace tunnels and protects the powerhouse against surges of water resulting from fluctuations in its flow through the turbines. When Churchill Constructors began to excavate this chamber, the geologists suspected there was a rock fault between it and the powerhouse, and the work was delayed for a time while one-hundred-foot bolts were driven into the rock to strengthen it.

Some slippage in the contractor's work cycle occurred, but by accelerating activities elsewhere and hiring more men the contract was kept abreast of schedule.

The third major underground chamber — the transformer gallery, which is 856 feet long, 50 feet wide and 39 feet high — was another change made in the original plan as the project developed. The transformers, which step up the electricity from the 15,000 volts produced by the generators to the transmission level of 735,000 volts, each contain thousands of gallons of oil, partly for insulation and partly as a coolant. McParland feared that if they were installed underground there was a danger that fire could destroy the powerhouse, so it was proposed to take each generator's output up to transformers on the surface by cable through eleven tunnels each ten feet wide. This raised a variety of technical problems; for one thing, to take a unit out of service for maintenance would have meant interrupting the current at the 735-kv level and no circuit-breaker capable of doing that had yet been developed. So McParland was persuaded that in the interest of reliability it was better (and no more expensive) to go to "two-stage" transformation, stepping up the generators' output to 230 kv underground and then combining the output of two units into each 735-kv transformer on the surface, which meant only six cable shafts were required.

To complete all this underground excavation on time, Churchill Constructors employed an average work force of 625 hourly-paid workers, and such was the labour turnover on the job that a total of 4,300 men had to be hired to maintain that figure. But on a good day, as much as 22,000 tons of rock was hauled out of the mountain and by the end of 1970 the echoing caves were beginning to look like a power station. The overhead cranes were in operation, and the concreting and mechanical and electrical work involved in the installation of the first four generating units was well under way.

On the surface, the fine summer had extended into a mild fall which permitted a welcome extra month's work. The Lobstick gates were being installed, the structural steel was rising in the 58-acre switchyard, the intake structure for the eleven penstocks was nearing completion, as was the control and administration building.

And above all, when work ended for the season the dyke-builders had moved the remarkable total of sixteen million cubic yards of fill into position — almost four times the production of the year before. That left only six million yards to be completed during 1971, a quantity described by a well-satisfied Dick Boivin as "peanuts."

The railroad stoppage and its aftermath had cost Churchill Falls at least $15 million. But the master project schedule had proved more than equal to the task in hand: it had been so skilfully assembled and so strictly adhered to that the dislocations of 1969 were taken in stride and the vintage year Boivin had predicted not only made up all the lost time — in some areas, the project had even forged ahead of schedule.

TWENTY-FOUR

First power!

One of the by-products of the Churchill project was that, in addition to creating hundreds of jobs in factories in the south, it gave Canadian manufacturers valuable experience in the design and fabrication of large and sophisticated electrical generating machinery. Economic factors had dictated the choice of the largest possible units, and while the turbine runners, for instance, were not the biggest ever built, the combination of the size of the units and the weight of their rotating parts, their unprecedented output and the high head with which they were to be used, made them, in the words of one manufacturer, "somewhat heroic." The Acres engineers who laid down the specifications for them, while admitting they were "pushing the state of the art," considered them to be a relatively reasonable extrapolation on current practice, but their manufacture was to create some problems. Don McParland anticipated this and felt that if such critical equipment were put out to bid in the conventional way, competition between manufacturers might lead to the cutting of corners at the expense of reliability. Also, as he had done in the case of Acres and Bechtel, he wanted to benefit from as many combined talents as possible. And so a consortium of Canadian companies was invited to build the turbine runners, generators and transformers.

Back in 1964, English Electric, which then had a manufacturing plant in Scarborough, Ontario, had negotiated a consortium agreement with Canadian General Electric and Dominion Engineering Works, of Montreal, intending to share the work on Churchill. When the negotiations with Quebec broke down that July, the consortium's plans were put on ice. But in May 1965, after the talks resumed, Paul de Laszlo, English Electric's representative on the Brinco board for many years, wrote to Bob Winters saying that since the company had now sold its Scarborough plant, the equipment it expected to build would have to be manufactured at its Netherton plant in England.

On May 28, 1965, even before the question of preference for Quebec labour and materials had become an issue in the negotiations, Winters replied to de Laszlo saying: "I don't think we can assume that . . . the five water-wheels in question will automatically come from your plant in Netherton. Even though you and I might deplore it, nationalist feelings run fairly high, with protectionist overtones, in both our countries. When Quebec is involved, this is especially true . . . . You would have to demonstrate that water-wheels produced in Netherton would have significant economic advantages over water-wheels produced here in Canada . . . ."

As a Founder shareholder of Brinco, English Electric, which had supplied some of the machinery for Twin, felt disappointed and perhaps cheated that it lost out on the much larger contract for Churchill. But the clauses in the agreement specifying preference for Newfoundland and Quebec made its exclusion unavoidable. The new consortium formed later, the Churchill Falls (Machinery) Consortium, linked Canadian General Electric and Dominion Engineering with Marine Industries, of Sorel. The Quebec government owned a major interest in Marine Industries, and the company had established a department to build equipment for the Manic project under licence to a French company, Neyrpic, part of the internationally known Alsthom group.

These three companies shared the manufacture of the Churchill machinery, using their own designs but working to general specifications laid down by ACB. In this way, more than 90 per cent of the machinery was manufactured in Canada and the pooling of technical information among the companies not only benefited their own engineers but made available to Churchill Falls the latest refinements of both North American and European technology. The huge shafts linking turbines and generators (the bolts attaching them weigh 350 lbs. each) were forged in England; the turbine runners were cast in Canada, after models of them had been tested here, in France and in Scotland; and the governors to control the speed of the turbines were designed and built in the United States.

Marine Industries chose to manufacture its turbine runners entirely in stainless steel, to give the necessary resistance to cavitation, or pitting of the blades by the action of the water. One of the runners, with a casting weight of 145 tons and a finished weight of 80 tons, was the largest stainless-steel casting in the world up to that time. But the first runner cast had seventeen cracks around its band; for a while the ACB engineers contemplated rejecting it, until a technique was evolved for repairing it by welding. The company had even worse luck with its second runner, which turned out to be unusable. There was a crack in the crown and one blade of the third runner cast, but once again it was repaired by welding and thereafter Marine Industries encountered no more problems.

Dominion Engineering decided to use a standard carbon-steel casting for its runners and coat them with stainless steel by welding. The first castings were satisfactory, apart from the usual defects such as slight cracks and imperfections in the metal. But because of the difficulty of working inside the thirteen turbine blades, it proved costly to repair these defects by welding on more steel or gouging it out in spots and refilling them. So a new but expensive technique was adopted: after casting, the runners were cut into fifteen pieces, each of which was upgraded by welding before the whole wheel was welded back together again.

When each runner was in place in the powerhouse, it was enclosed in a spiral steel scroll case, shaped like a snail's shell, which directs the water from the penstock on to the turbine blades. As each scroll case was installed, it was embedded in tons of concrete for stability. By the beginning of 1971 the scroll cases for Units 1 and 2 were in place and the rest of the machinery needed to put the plant on line — the generators, transformers, circuit-breakers, cables, transmission towers and a host of other items — was in various stages of manufacture or shipment to the site.

Immense logistical problems were involved in gathering together and then transporting all the material and equipment needed from factories in Montreal, Sorel, Peterborough, Hamilton, Guelph and even the United States and Europe, by ship to Sept-Iles, up the railroad to Esker and from there by road to the site. To eliminate bottlenecks and make sure each item would be delivered to where it was required at the right time, a computer program was developed which enabled the whereabouts of any item shipped to be checked daily.

The heaviest single items shipped in to the site were the transformers, the largest of which weigh 224 tons. They had to be built to an unusual design so that they would pass through the tunnel at Mile 12 on the railroad and since the heaviest lift that had gone into Labrador previously was a 125-ton diesel locomotive, special equipment had to be built to handle them. A $1.3 million crane with a lifting capacity of 250 tons was built in Wisconsin for the Sept-Iles dock. The weight of the crane itself and its load was more than the capacity of the dock and it had to be set so far back from the edge that it was fitted with a 175-foot boom to swing out over ships' holds. A 250-ton railroad car was built, and a 250-ton gantry crane to unload it at Esker.

But perhaps the most remarkable piece of equipment was a 200-foot-long transporter designed to trundle the transformers along the road from Esker. It consisted of a low-slung float, designed and built in France, and two 700-horsepower diesel tractors built in Chicago, one at the front and one at the rear, to push or brake according to conditions. The tractors, 15 feet high and with wheels more than 7 feet in diameter, each burned 15 gallons of diesel fuel per mile. Loaded, this 26-wheel goliath rumbled along at two and a half miles an hour, and each trip in took three days. So that other traffic would not be held up any longer than absolutely necessary, the transporter pulled off the road every few miles into specially built sidings where it was thoroughly inspected before resuming its journey.

Another, rather more conventional, vehicle which rendered yeoman service to the project was the helicopter. At the peak of construction, the company owned five of them, and others were operated by some of the contractors. Their uses ranged from setting down surveying parties in remote areas to ferrying engineers and inspectors around the building sites, thus saving thousands of man-hours of driving over rough roads; the Sail Lake dykes, for instance, are 120 miles northeast of the town, the Lobstick control structure is 80 miles away to the northwest, and the 710-foot cleared right-of-way for the transmission line extends 126 miles to the southwest.

The helicopter's "maid-of-all-work" capability was demonstrated when the time came to string the transmission lines across the mile-wide gorge of the river. Three rows of transmission towers carry the thirty-six power lines (more properly called "sub-conductors") connecting the plant with the Quebec grid at Point "A", which for some reason was later christened "Seahorse." The sub-conductors, slightly more than an inch thick, consist of aluminum strands woven around a steel core, for strength. The towers in a row stand three or four to the mile, and each supports twelve sub-conductors, grouped in three "bundles," or "phases." The spacing of the sub-conductors is critical. There must be 45 feet between each "phase" on a tower, and the four sub-conductors of which it consists are held 18 inches apart in a square pattern by aluminum spacers.

Most of the five thousand or so miles of sub-conductor used on the line weighs slightly more than a pound a foot; but to span the gorge, stronger — and thus heavier — cables were needed, weighing almost two pounds to a foot. Since the distance between the towers on the north

344

and south banks is about six thousand feet, the weight of each length of sub-conductor strung between them is more than five tons. To string thirty-six cables of this weight across a gorge a thousand feet deep without damaging them by scraping them against the ground or some other obstacle might have been expected to call for considerable ingenuity. But the way it was done could hardly have been simpler: a helicopter first flew across to the south bank carrying the end of a half-inch nylon rope wound on a spool set on the north bank; the rope was then used to pull across a three-eighth steel wire; that wire was used to winch across a thicker one, which in turn pulled across a cable strong enough to haul the heavy sub-conductor over without damaging it.

It is so important not to damage conductors as they are being installed that anything coming into contact with them, such as pulleys or clamps, was coated with plastic. Even a slight nick or scratch — engineers prefer the term "discontinuity" — can cause electricity to leak out of a cable. In fact, there is always some leakage along a transmission line, particularly in damp weather, when it is sometimes possible to see a blue glow around the line, and even to hear the leakage as a quite noticeable hum. An American company once ran into so much trouble with leakage from a line in a populated area that it was faced with damage suits alleging noise pollution.

Most of the work of erecting the transmission towers and stringing the conductors could only be done during the winter, when the swamp and muskeg along the route was frozen solid, enabling the men and machines to get into areas which in summer are inaccessible.

The design chosen for the towers was unusual, but not unprecedented: they are V-shaped, standing on one footing and supported by four inch-thick guy wires. One advantage of this design is that V-shaped towers weigh 30 per cent less than conventional towers, which meant a considerable saving in transportation costs. Also, having only one base, they were easier to site in rough terrain than conventional towers, which need four footings.

Conventional four-legged towers were used on the Twin Falls line, built ten years earlier, and experience showed that some of them were damaged by the irregular heaving action of frost on their foundations. So the base for a Churchill tower was a pit 9 feet deep, in which was sunk a platform 10 feet by 12 built of 12-inch steel beams. The twin arms of the tower were lowered into place on a double steel pillar resting on the platform, and the pits were filled with gravel to combat the action of the frost. The guy wires are held by steel anchor bars sunk

12 feet into rock or 100 feet where only earth was available. Their tension is measured periodically by a device resembling a tuning fork and they can be loosened if the tower is forced upward by heaving.

The conductors themselves were strung in their "phases," four at a time, from reels weighing five tons and holding about 10,000 feet of cable. The degree to which they sag between towers was carefully measured: it is not merely the result of the weight of the cable. The conductors must not be too taut, otherwise the whole line might be brought down by the dangerous "piano-wire" vibrations that could be set up in high winds. Neither must they sag too much: there must be a minimum clearance of 40 feet above the ground, or anything that might go under the line, to prevent a charge of electricity from jumping over.

While it is not unknown for a vehicle or load to receive an electric charge when passing too close to a transmission line, no accident of this sort took place during construction of the Churchill line. But one of the first deaths on the project occurred when a radio aerial on a mobile office being hauled to a new site touched an overhead power line and a man inside the office was electrocuted. Stringent safety precautions were enforced throughout the building of the project and full-time safety supervisors monitored each aspect of the job. Even during the design stage, efforts were made to create a hazard-free environment; for example, refuge stations were excavated between the main underground chambers, with steel doors to protect the workers against fire. But no amount of care can altogether eliminate construction accidents, and thirteen men were killed during the life of the project. Nevertheless, its safety record was 20 per cent better than the North American average.

By the middle of 1971, the complex electrical installations in the switchyard had been completed, the last conductor had been strung across the river gorge and the first two transmission lines were well on the way to completion. Down in the powerhouse, the first two generating units, due to start supplying power to the Quebec system the following May, were being assembled on schedule. And the last loads of fill were being packed into place in the dykes — though there were some anxious moments that summer when one of them sprang what at first seemed to be a dangerous leak.

The eighty-eight dykes built to plug the low spots on the rim of the Labrador "saucer" range in height from four feet to 90 feet above the original ground. The shortest is less than 200 feet long and the longest, in the Sail Lake area, stretches four miles. No one had ever tried to build so many earth dykes on a single project, or under such sub-arctic conditions; to have followed the usual procedure of designing each one after its site had been excavated would have been impossibly costly and time-consuming. So a "catalogue" of possible designs, or cross-sections, was prepared in advance, to suit various foundations and make use of whatever gravel or rock was most easily available close by. In all, fifty-three different cross-sections were used, as many as six going into one dyke.

The muskeg or boulder fields where dykes were to be built had to be excavated down to bedrock or a firm foundation of glacial till. The ACB engineers would then examine the foundation, select the cross-section best suited to it, and the contractor could begin building the dyke without delay. Generally, the central core of a dyke consists of the dust-like glacial till which, when compacted with heavy rollers and held in place by either a mixture of sand and gravel or broken rock, is almost watertight. All dykes are protected from the action of waves by a layer of rocks, called "rip-rap," on their upstream sides. And since some water always seeps through them, they have drains of processed sand and gravel with outlets on the downstream side.

All the dykes are inspected constantly from helicopters and, more closely, by inspectors on regular ground patrol who take readings from piezometers, perforated pipes set in the dykes to measure the water levels inside them. At 11:30 a.m. on August 10, 1971, a surveillance heli-copter reported a patch of muddy water on the downstream side of dyke GJ-11A, flanking the Jacopie spillway. At 8:45 p.m. that evening, a team of investigators despatched in response to the helicopter's sighting came across a sinkhole 10 feet in diameter near the crest of the 70-foot dyke and another subsidence in the rip rap on its upstream bank. Within a couple of hours, as its sides continued to cave in, the first hole had doubled in size and cracks were appearing in the road along the top of the dyke. It was obvious that the till in the core of the dyke was being washed out — a dire emergency, since once this washing process begins the till offers little resistance to it.

Joe Anderson was in Montreal for a series of meetings and had just sat down to dinner with his wife in the Bonaventure Hotel when Harold Snyder reached him by telephone at 10 p.m. and told him he had ordered the Churchill jet to stand by to fly him back to the site right away. Anderson did not need to have the gravity of the situation explained to him. The reservoir was being filled in preparation for the test rolls of the first two generating units later that fall. If the dyke collapsed, the avalanche of water spilling through it could flood the nearby Bridge camp. Orders had already been given to open the Jacopie gates and lower the water level in the west forebay to take the pressure off the damaged dyke. But this could not be done too quickly without risking damage elsewhere in the forebay: the suction created by water receding too rapidly might pull down other dykes. Also, lower down the river, the coffer dam at the entrance to the tailrace tunnels was being removed and if too much water was suddenly released down the river the resulting flood might surge into the tunnels and possibly even inundate the power-house.

When Anderson reached the site at 3 a.m., he was relieved to find that the worst was over. As soon as the holes were discovered, every available bulldozer and truck within reach of the spot had been mobilized and by midnight they were feverishly dumping fill from a nearby stock-pile into the holes. Also, emergency work had begun to raise the level of the coffer dam and the Jacopie gates had been opened to permit the water to drain away at the rate of 85,000 cubic feet per second — far more than the average flow over the falls but well within the gates' capacity: in a test during 1973, 145,000 cubic feet per second were spilled through Jacopie without mishap.

These measures averted disaster and the damaged dyke soon began to heal itself, as it had been designed to do. But the work of reinforcing it went on around the clock for the next thirty-six hours. Then it became more important to discover what had gone wrong, because of the im-plications for the other eighty-seven dykes.

From the early days of the project, ACB had been advised by a board of consultants consisting of some of the continent's foremost authorities on soils and dams and on civil engineering in general and hydro-electric installations in particular. The board held regular week-long meetings, which usually included visits to the site, to review every major decision the ACB engineers had made since the last meeting and offer advice on what they proposed to do next. As soon as the dyke subsidence was reported to him, Steve White set out to locate Wallace L. Chadwick, a leading member of the board who had spent a lifetime in hydro-electric construction and is a member of the U.S. committee on the International Commission on High Dams. Chadwick was advising on a lawsuit in Little Rock, Arkansas, but he immediately took off for Churchill Falls, where he was joined by three other consultants: F. B. Slichter, chief of the civil works division of the U.S. Army's Corps of Engineers for many years; Ralph B. Peck, professor of soils and foundations at the University of Illinois and author of several highly regarded textbooks;

and George Bertram, another former U.S. Army specialist in soils and foundations.

With the benefit of their advice, and behind the protection of a hastily erected coffer dam, the dyke was dismantled five feet at a time and minutely examined. No fault was found with its design or construction, though the bedrock on which it was based was found to contain unsuspected fissures. After the usual procedure of sealing these with "dental" concrete to make a firm base had been repeated, the dyke was rebuilt satisfactorily before the end of the season and gave no further trouble. On occasion since then excessive water flows through drains have been detected in other dykes and repairs or modifications have had to be made to them: this is considered normal and provision was made in the Churchill planning for continuous maintenance work on the dyke system.

A symbolic milestone for the project had been reached earlier that summer, on July 1, when Premier Smallwood had pressed a button to close the 250-ton centre gate of the Lobstick structure and start the filling of the main reservoir which, it was announced during the ceremony, would henceforth be known as the Smallwood Reservoir. When the reservoir finally reached its maximum level of 1,551 feet, in the fall of 1973, it covered an area of 2,200 square miles and thus became the third-largest man-made body of water in the world, after the Volta reservoir in Ghana and the V.I. Lenin reservoir in the Soviet Union.

It was almost exactly four years since the Premier had turned the caribou-moss sod to launch the project, and an altogether happier occasion: in addition to congratulating the thousands of Newfoundlanders who had helped to build the development he paid a graceful tribute to the part played in its success by Quebec. And among the guests of honour when he dined in the main mess hall on the night before the ceremony was Natasha, daughter of a local couple, Mr. and Mrs. Douglas Harvey. Born in the Churchill Falls hospital only fifteen months earlier, Natasha was perhaps too young to realize that the triumphant little man in the horn-rimmed spectacles bouncing around shaking hands with the workers was her great-grandfather.

On his two-day visit to the site, Joey also inspected the Orma and Sail dykes from a helicopter and visited the newest bush camp to be established in central Labrador, at Seal Lake, 120 miles northeast of the town, where Brinex had recently begun to explore a 300-square-mile area for minerals in cooperation with its latest joint-venture partner, the Bethlehem Steel Corporation.

And before he left for home, thrilled with the realization of what not so long ago had been only his dream, the Premier had one more announcement for the press: Churchill Falls had agreed to complete another of his cherished projects — a trans-Labrador road. The company, of course, had built the original 113-mile road from Esker to Churchill Falls; the province had then extended it 55 miles east in the direction of Goose Bay, and had started building another road west from Goose Bay to join it. Churchill Falls now undertook to complete the link, and before one of the dyke contractors, Mannix, removed its equipment from the site it was awarded a further contract to close the 55-mile gap. The work was completed in November, and for the first time Goose Bay — which is on tidewater even though its shipping season is a short one — had overland access to the heart of Labrador.

It is still impossible to foresee the benefits this road will ultimately bring to the economy of Labrador and the province of which it is a part, and perhaps even to the rest of eastern Canada. Certainly, more changes lie ahead for the land Jacques Cartier spurned as God's gift to Cain. But while the passing of another wilderness may be mourned by more than mere traditionalists and enthusiasts for what is loosely termed "the ecology," human hands have yet to make more than a comparatively puny imprint on the vastness of Labrador. And at Churchill Falls, a determined effort was made to avoid the disastrous short-sightedness man has often displayed by pursuing his own immediate needs without heed for the impact of his activities on the environment he shares with the other creatures of nature.

From the beginning, every Churchill Falls work camp, large or small, was equipped with a sewage-treatment system, so that the Churchill, unlike so many rivers in more populated areas of Canada, remains unpolluted by human waste. And in its program for controlling black flies and mosquitoes, the company abandoned DDT for less persistent insecticides long before its use was banned elsewhere in Canada. From the early years, also, cooperation in conservation programs and research was invited from the federal and provincial governments and universities, particularly Newfoundland's own Memorial University. Fishing and hunting in the project area have always been closely monitored to ensure provincial regulations are observed and the *Churchill Falls News,* in addition to publishing frequent and informative articles on Labrador flora and fauna, gently tried to wean outdoorsmen from guns to cameras by offering a weekly cash prize for the best wildlife photograph. Naturally, since not everyone is a conservationist, it was not wholly successful:

Hugh Boyd, an ACB cost engineer, once discovered a pair of ospreys nesting at the top of a dead tree near the airport and spent many evenings trying to win a prize with a photograph of them against the moon; he was enraged one night when he returned and found someone had shot both birds.

Before Churchill Falls began its operations, scientific knowledge of the various elements of the Labrador plateau's environment, and their inter-relationship, was sadly lacking, and one of the first aims of the company's conservation program was to encourage its acquisition so that mistakes could be avoided or corrective action taken if any appeared to have been made. Everyone knew, of course, that the water in the area was both plentiful and pure; but no scientific studies had been done on its chemical and biological characteristics — the minerals it contains, in what proportions, and its capacity for sustaining plant and animal life. So Churchill Falls retained Sheppard T. Powell Associates, a Canadian environmental consulting firm experienced in water resources management, which set up eighteen control stations throughout the reservoir area and upstream and downstream of it to take regular water samples which will enable scientists to judge the eventual effects of the flooding.

Other scientists from governments and universities set up programs to study the area's fish, small and large mammals, trees and other vegetation — even its prehistory. Between 1967 and 1969, Donald MacLeod, an archeologist then with the National Museum of Man in Ottawa, travelled hundreds of miles by canoe and on foot exploring the area about to be flooded. He found ancient camp sites where he was able to unearth chipped stones and two cracked caribou bones which had obviously been used as tools. Carbon-dating of the bones established them as being no more than a thousand years old. MacLeod was able to find no earlier signs of human life — which is perhaps not surprising since the area was covered by the remains of the continental glacier until six thousand years ago. He concluded that no permanent settlements ever existed in the interior of Labrador, probably because the small family groups of Indians had to keep moving all year round to wrest a living from their inhospitable surroundings: MacLeod estimated that the area would have supported only one person per ten square miles, at a time when the native people living in the Toronto area were settled in villages holding as many as two thousand.

As the number of research projects mounted, the company formed a committee known as the Conservation Coordination Group, which met regularly to consider the various reports and initiate action on them when

351

necessary. It included the company's outside scientific adviser and consultant, Dr. Allen S. West, professor of zoology at Queen's University, Kingston. West has been studying black flies and mosquitoes in northern Quebec and Labrador for almost twenty years, and his association with the company began when he was asked to organize a fly-control program for it during the building of the Twin Falls project.

As anyone who has worked or even fished in the North knows, the tiny black fly is a menace to man quite out of proportion to its size. Only a few of the more than a hundred species known to occur in Canada bite man, but two of these, rejoicing in the names of *Prosimulium hirtipes* and *Simulium venustum,* make the coming of summer an occasion to be dreaded, rather than welcomed, in Labrador.

Black flies breed only in running water, where their larvae, anchored to rocks or logs by silken threads, need a constant flow of water around them to supply them with oxygen. The white-water streams around Churchill Falls are ideal breeding-grounds and the control program includes aerial spraying of streams in the project area with methoxychlor. In large enough doses, this is poisonous to fish, but it breaks down within the fish's body in from thirty to sixty days and does not accumulate from season to season like DDT. Also, the concentrations used are carefully measured to avoid damage to fish and so far no evidence has been found that they have been harmed. After the aerial spraying, known breeding grounds in the immediate area of the town are visited by graduate students employed during the summer to check its effectiveness. If any larvae remain, the students treat the streams with another chemical called Abate, which is considered by federal authorities to be even safer than methoxychlor.

This program also controls mosquitoes, the largest breed of which in Labrador winters over in the caribou moss in its adult stage and emerges full-blown in the spring hungry for its meal of blood.

While a careless control program could be a hazard to fish life, the overall effect of the Churchill project is almost certain to be a large increase in the fish population. Some of the first water-quality studies revealed that because of their rocky beds and lack of vegetation, many of the lakes in the area lacked nutrients and were virtually barren of fish. But as the submerged vegetation in a flooded area decays it releases chemical compounds into the water which promote the growth of unicellular plants and the minute forms of animal life that feed on them, which in turn provide food for fish.

Old-timers agree that the best fishing at Churchill Falls for the past ten years has been in the Ossokmanuan reservoir. To test this empirical view is one of the objectives of the conservation program, and to further the scientific work the Smallwood Reservoir has its own fishing fleet: a 40-foot tuna boat named the *Pennywell* which was transported from Newfoundland's Conception Bay to the site by ship, train and truck. Its crew of graduate biology students spends each summer netting fish — lake trout, speckled trout, pike, *ounaniche,* or land-locked salmon, whitefish and suckers — to discover, by measuring and weighing them and examining their scales, what types, ages and sizes of fish the reservoir holds now. Continuing examinations in future years will disclose whether their numbers and size do increase as expected.

Some concern was expressed in the early days that the Orma dykes, by depriving the Naskaupi river of almost half its watershed, might impair its potential as a salmon stream. But the Naskaupi has never been regarded as a good salmon river: a study by the federal Department of Fisheries a few years ago estimated its salmon population to be five thousand, when it seemed as though it should support perhaps forty thousand. One theory for the disparity was that the fish had trouble beating upstream against several very rough and fast stretches of rapids. After the Orma dykes were completed, the department made another survey of the river and found the reduced flow had caused no obstruction to the free passage of fish anywhere along its length. In fact, there are hopes that by somewhat taming the rapids, the slower flow might result in increased salmon production in future years.

During the two and a half years it took to fill the reservoir, many small mammals (mostly various species of mice and voles) were undoubtedly drowned, but biologists who studied the situation in advance concluded there was no chance of any species facing extinction. The biologists recommended that flooding should be carried out during the summer, to give displaced animals a chance to establish new burrows before they were overtaken by the bitter winter. This advice was followed, so that some of the larger animals, from mink and marten to beaver and porcupines, were probably able to retreat to new quarters as the water advanced.

A weekly search was conducted by helicopter for any larger animals such as caribou or bear which might be marooned on islands, and plans were made to capture them by netting, or quietening them with tranquilizer darts, and then ferry them to safety aboard the good ship *Pennywell*. But no marooned animals were ever detected. The only two herds of caribou known to be in the general vicinity were well outside the reservoir area, though they occasionally crossed it. One herd traditionally migrated across the Esker road, calving north of it and going south in the winter; but even before the reservoir was filled their movements indicated that they were starting to calf south of the road, perhaps because of all the activity north of it.

The flooding also submerged some marshy areas which had traditionally been used as nesting grounds by migratory waterfowl, chiefly ducks, but a survey done by the Canadian Wildlife Service concluded that the area was not a major nesting site. How the birds adapt to the new conditions will not be known for several years.

The most conspicuous scar the project has inflicted on the environment is an unfortunate one which might have been considered intolerable in an inhabited area. Much of the 947 square miles flooded to create the reservoir was bog and open barrenland, but more than half of it was classed as forest. Estimates of the cost of completely clearing the land before flooding were astronomical, amounting to many millions of dollars. A Memorial University study found only 1 per cent of the trees to have any commercial value, and then only if there had been a road to get them out to Goose Bay, which did not exist at that time. Consequently, it was decided to confine the "cosmetic surgery" to particularly visible areas around the townsite. Elsewhere, the tops of drowned trees protrude from the water, making sections of the reservoir look like gigantic beaver ponds.

Esthetically unpleasing as this scene may be (though few will ever see it), it is a small price to pay for such a huge quantity of electricity. Hydro-electric power is the cleanest and most economical source of energy available to a society which has only lately come to appreciate the finite limits on its galloping consumption of the various fuels upon which its functioning depends. It has been estimated that to produce Churchill Falls' annual output of electricity, oil-fired thermal power stations would have to consume more than 57 million barrels of oil a year — the equivalent of a medium-sized tanker-load every day. Coal-fired power stations would have to burn 25 million tons of coal a year, polluting the atmosphere with 500,000 tons of sulphur dioxide in the process.

Countries without hydro-electric resources might well envy Canada. But large hydro-electric projects often exact a high cost in the dislocation of human lives. The Volta River scheme in Ghana, for instance, displaced 65,000 people, who had to be resettled in fifty new villages. In contrast, the Churchill Falls project did not deprive a single person of

354

his home or his livelihood — the few trappers who still eked out a marginal existence on the Labrador plateau all now work for the company in some capacity.

And they were as enthusiastic as everyone else connected with Brinco when, on December 6, 1971, almost five months ahead of schedule, Unit 1 of the Churchill Falls power station began to supply power to the Quebec system, to be followed only nine days later by Unit 2.

TWENTY-FIVE

The property of the people

In mid-June, 1972, the Churchill Falls airport had its most hectic three days since the crucial airlift mounted three years earlier. The circumstances were happier, the rush of traffic being occasioned by the project's official inauguration. But the Labrador weather lived up to its reputation for hostility and the eight hundred guests from the upper reaches of government, industry, and international business and finance, fresh from balmier climes, were given at least a glimpse of what it is like to live and work in the north.

The guests began to arrive on Thursday, June 15, a day on which the thermometer never rose above 46 degrees and almost half an inch of rain turned the site into a quagmire, though it failed to melt the ice which still lingered in hollows and on the lakes. Worst of all, fog and low clouds frustrated attempts to land by several of the fourteen chartered airliners and forty-one executive jets involved in the operation. An armed forces mobile radar unit and an instrument-rated air traffic controller from Moncton had been imported to reinforce the airport staff — a fortunate precaution, since two-thirds of the 220 landings and take-offs registered during the airlift had to be made on instruments.

A typically unnerving experience was shared by the passengers aboard an Air Canada DC-9 which unfortunately carried some of the widows of the men killed in the Churchill Falls jet in 1969. The plane took off from Montreal soon after noon and made a couple of unsuccessful passes over Churchill before being diverted to Sept-Iles. After some hours on the ground, the pilot was told the weather at Churchill was clearing, but by the time he reached there it had closed in again. After circling in vain seeking an opening in the murk, he returned to Montreal, where he landed at 2 a.m. Friday after ten hours in the air. Buses took the passengers to hastily booked hotel rooms, where they tried to snatch a few hours' sleep before taking off again early next morning, this time managing to land in time for the inaugural ceremony.

Touring the site after their arrival, those visitors who managed to get in on the first day found a settled community whose residents were cheerfully making the adjustments necessary to life in such an isolated area. Gardeners, for instance, refused to be deterred by the short growing season and the sparse and excessively acid soil. Armed with plenty of lime and fertilizer they would try to transplant, say, a particularly pretty mountain ash from the bush to their front yard; but when the time came to replace the earth around its roots they would find they had picked so many rocks out of it there was not enough left to fill the hole. The Town Centre, with its movie shows, dances, curling, swimming and other recreational activities, provided residents with perhaps fuller social lives than they could have led in small towns elsewhere in Canada — though not quite so full as one American visitor apparently expected: he stepped from the plane into the gray Labrador drizzle carrying two tennis rackets.

Above ground, most of the construction work had now finished. But the visitors were escorted on tours of the powerhouse, where the job of installing the rest of the machinery continued against the background throbbing of the two units already supplying power. The man chosen to run Churchill Falls as an operating power station, John Beaver, had arrived on site so recently that he found himself somewhat at a loss when asked to give visitors directions. A former chief from the Ojibway Indian reserve at Alderville, on the south shore of Rice Lake seventy-five miles east of Toronto, Beaver flew a Spitfire in the Battle of Britain and went to Queen's University after the war on a veteran's grant. After graduating in electrical engineering, he joined Ontario Hydro and was operations manager of its huge northeastern region when he was appointed vice-president and general manager of operations of Churchill Falls.

The guests invited to the inauguration included many of those who had pioneered in the corporation's earliest days and the atmosphere was that of a huge family reunion. Bill Southam was among those over from England, renewing old friendships and doubtless fighting some of the old battles again in recollection. Bertie Gardner, unhappily, could not attend: frail now and almost totally blind, he had only a few more months to live. Eric Webb, as erect as when he dragged his sled into Antarctica sixty years earlier, made a hit with the younger engineers who had designed and built what he had only envisaged; and after his inspection of the powerhouse he was overheard excitedly discussing the quality of the rock with his old colleague, Dick Heartz, first president of the Hamilton Falls company.

On Friday morning, visitors touring the site could hear aircraft still

357

circling trying to find their way down through the fog and drizzle. Between 9 a.m. and noon, planes landed or took off every four minutes as the rest of the guests arrived. The weather was even colder than it had been the day before, and a fifteen-mile-an-hour wind blowing unimpeded down from the Arctic chilled the hundreds of onlookers in the blue-painted wooden stands erected for the inaugural ceremony on top of the intake structure, above the town and the great gorge of the river.

Bill Mulholland opened the proceedings promptly at noon with a brief welcoming speech and the next speaker, Premier Frank D. Moores of Newfoundland, won a spontaneous round of applause with a graceful tribute to a man whose absence from the dais had occasioned some surprise. "Through all the years," Moores said, "from the days when there was no Brinco to this day when the project is a reality, there was one presence whose influence was undeniable. When many people felt the project would never come about there was one man who fought and fought hard to keep that spark alive. He succeeded, and the province of Newfoundland today benefits."

That man, of course, was Joseph Roberts Smallwood, whose long, often stormy but never dull reign over Newfoundland had recently been ended by Frank Moores' Progressive Conservatives. The cheers that greeted the new Premier's mention of his name demonstrated that Joey had not forfeited the affection of all the people he had led for almost a generation. But he had turned down the invitation to celebrate the fruition of his long-held dream for Grand Falls, pleading a prior engagement in Britain, where he had launched a tanker named after him by John Shaheen, the American entrepreneur and architect of another of Joey's cherished projects which everyone had said would never materialize, the oil refinery at Come-by-Chance. Instead, Joey sent his successor a telegram, which Moores read out, saying that "on this historic day I join you in spirit, side by side with all Newfoundlanders, wherever they may be. It is a proud and a happy moment for all of us."

Premier Moores described Churchill Falls as "proof of what can be achieved when private enterprise works in cooperation with governments," and added: "Long before the first physical work was done on this site, there were a group of men, most of them world-known financiers and bankers, who took the initiatives that made even the idea of a hydro-electric project in this sub-Arctic region possible. They were the men who were willing to put their money on the line for something that had never been tried before and which carried an element of real risk." He praised by name some of those men who shared the platform with him — and some, like Don McParland and Donald Gordon, whose absence on this day so saddened their colleagues.

The Premier also looked forward to the eventual harnessing of the millions of horse power remaining in the Lower Churchill, though in terms which suggested that the negotiations ahead would be no easier than those that had gone before: "It is our hope and desire that the lower river development will tie more closely to developments that this government has in mind for Labrador and the province in general." This apparent warning of heavy weather ahead passed unremarked at the time, though in retrospect it seems to have been echoed in the Premier's closing words: "I would like to say, as representative of the host province, we are pleased with our tenant and we hope we will be able to continue to develop the proper landlord-tenant relationship. We hold other properties and the tenant seeks to expand. In this world of supply and demand I am sure agreements profitable to both the tenant and the landlord will be made."

Appropriately, Prime Minister Trudeau placed the project in a national context. The endeavours of Canadians, he said, had often matched in scope and grandeur the size of their country. So it was with Churchill Falls. But Churchill was more than simply a construction achievement. It was a reminder that "Canada, wisely developed and carefully conserved, can provide a standard of living and a quality of life as rich and as satisfying as is found anywhere in the world. There is evidence here that man can employ — not exploit — the resources of the world for his benefit, without causing harm to the environment or destroying the life styles of others . . . . Churchill Falls is testimony of man's desire to see the remote, to explore the hidden, to achieve the difficult . . . . This is Canada — this excitement, this opportunity, this self-confidence, this accomplishment. It has never been a land for the faint of heart. Nor is it now. Canada remains as it has always been — a land of vivid character; a land for men and women who are not ashamed to dream and not hesitant to pursue their dreams; a land of enthusiasm; a land of achievement. The Churchill Falls project represents for every Canadian in every part of Canada one of those proud achievements in our history; it is a strong beat of the country's adventurous heart."

The framers of Brinco's Principal Agreement had started out with the preamble: "Whereas it is desirable to promote the industrial and economic development of Newfoundland and Labrador . . . ." From that phrase, in less than twenty years, had flowed the construction of this huge power station and the planting of a modern town in this ancient wilderness. Those who had been part of the Brinco adventure listened to the Prime Minister's stirring words with a satisfying sense of accomplishment: from Val Duncan and Eddy de Rothschild, who had been in since the beginning, to all the others, far too numerous to mention, who had brought their talents and enthusiasm to the job along the way.

As it happened, the satisfaction was not shared by all who heard the Prime Minister that day. But it would be a little while yet before this was made painfully apparent.

A few months before the inauguration, soon after Premier Moores had formed his first administration, a Brinco party headed by Bill Mulholland and Harry Macdonell called on him for a "get-acquainted" meeting. In preparation for that meeting, the corporation had drawn up an approximate balance sheet listing the benefits Newfoundland could expect from its operations. It predicted that over the forty-year life of the Churchill Falls contract the province would receive $530 million in corporate income taxes, rental payments and horse-power royalties. This amounted to roughly 34 per cent of the profits the Churchill company itself could expect. The $84 million in dividends to be derived from its Churchill Falls shareholding would increase the province's receipts to $614 million, or 43 per cent of the company's profits. And to this should be added $73 million in various forms from other Brinco activities.

Also, the 12,000 Newfoundlanders employed at Churchill up to that time had earned — and presumably spent within the province — approximately $67 million. Contracts worth $64 million had been award-ed to Newfoundland contractors and more than $19 million had been spent in the province on such commodities as aluminum conductor, cement, steel, paint and beer. At no cost to the provincial treasury, Labrador had been provided with almost three hundred miles of all-weather roads, a new town and one of the best airports in the whole North. And by having the falls developed by private investors, the province had avoided increasing its indebtedness by a billion dollars. Such a large sum, in the unlikely event that the province could have borrowed it, would have been enough to have doubled the provincial debt as it stood at the time of Joey Smallwood's defeat.*

*The economic and technological spin-off for the rest of the country is incalculable, but it was obviously substantial. For instance, more than 90 per cent of the equipment used on the project was manufactured in Canada. The turbine-generators and transformers provided more than seven million man-hours of work for the three companies involved in

Confident that if anything these figures were on the conservative side, Brinco's management was just as astonished as everyone else when, less than two weeks after the inauguration, Newfoundland's Minister of Economic Development, John C. Crosbie, told the House that far from benefiting from the Churchill development the province would actually lose money because of it. There were no dissenting voices when he called this situation "absolutely incredible." It arose out of the federal government's intricate formula for equalizing revenue among the provinces. At the risk of over-simplification, this in effect balances a province's revenues from a number of sources against the national average, on a per capita basis, so that a province receiving less than the national average from, say, its retail sales tax, receives an equalization payment to make up its deficit. In most categories, as a traditional "have-not" province, Newfoundland qualifies for equalization payments. But one of the categories is revenues received from water-power rentals. This meant, the Newfoundland government now realized, that a dollar would be deducted from its equalization payment for every dollar it received in water-power rentals and royalties, thus wiping out the revenue that was at last beginning to come in from Churchill Falls.

Even worse than that, the federal government had decided early in 1972 to add payments made under the Public Utilities Income Tax Transfer Act (PUITTA) to the list of revenue categories for equalization purposes. Since Newfoundland had agreed to pass on to the company half of the corporation-tax rebate it would receive under PUITTA, to bring the price of the power down to a level acceptable to Hydro-Québec, it was now faced with the dismaying prospect of losing more in equalization than it would be receiving under PUITTA — the prospect, in fact, of paying the government a dollar and a half for every dollar it received.

Once again, as with its original proposals for tax reform, the federal government was abrogating the provisions of PUITTA, taking away with one hand what it had given with the other. With his experience in tax matters, Harry Macdonell, who had become president of Churchill Falls when Bill Mulholland moved up to the chairmanship the day

the machinery consortium and their suppliers. And in 1973 one of them, Canadian General Electric — bidding against United States, Soviet and Japanese competition — won a $57.8 million contract to build three generating units even bigger than Churchill's for the Grand Coulee power project on the Columbia River in the State of Washington.

before the inauguration, doubted that this was intentional. So the company cooperated with Newfoundland in representations to Ottawa and both submitted briefs on the subject which ultimately resulted in the regulations being changed. The province continued to make payments under the water-power rental category of the equalization formula, which, since Churchill Falls gave it roughly 20 per cent of the hydro-electric generating capacity of the whole country, it acknowledged was only fair. But the PUITTA payments were placed in the "miscellaneous revenue" category, exempting them from the equalization levy and restoring Newfoundland to equal footing with those provinces whose power is generated by crown corporations.

While the episode ended satisfactorily for Newfoundland, it had some disturbing implications for Brinco. John Crosbie had been a minister in the Liberal government until 1968, when he had clashed with Joey Smallwood and crossed the floor of the House. Before joining the Conservatives formally, he had returned to the Liberal fold long enough to challenge Joey, unsuccessfully, for the party leadership. The enmity between the two men was well publicized, and Crosbie's speech disclosing the equalization problem suggested that his disapproval of his former leader extended to all his works.

Brinco had hitherto escaped virtually unscathed from the mounting hail of fire the Conservatives had directed against Joey's development schemes. And the company could hardly be blamed for the vagaries of the federal equalization formula. But Crosbie made it clear that he, and presumably the new government, was dissatisfied, if not with Brinco, certainly with the deal that had been made with Hydro-Québec. The government, he said, had been amazed to discover that the power contract gave preference to Quebec labour and materials. This was an old charge, of course, but the clause he referred to was over-ruled by another stipulating the company's prior obligation to Newfoundland, and this had been made clear publicly on several occasions. For instance, the rap on the knuckles Daniel Johnson administered to Jean-Claude Lessard for making the same assertion had been well-publicized at the time of the signing of the contract. And Brinco people found it difficult to believe that Crosbie, who was a member of the House at the time, had either overlooked the incident or forgotten it in the interim.

The minister also professed to be surprised that Newfoundland would have to pay the same price as Hydro-Québec for any power it bought under the recapture arrangement. If the Lower Churchill were to be developed, he added, it would be on completely different terms. It was one of the province's last great resources and the government would not "barter it cheaply away."

To Harry Macdonell and others within Brinco, this statement smelt strongly of nationalization. A more specific indication that this might be in the wind came a few months later, in the Newfoundland brief to Ottawa on the equalization issue. "The present Federal-Provincial Fiscal Arrangements Act," this said, "contains a strong bias towards nationalization of the Upper Churchill development and makes it impossible to develop the Lower Churchill without full public ownership." Coming from a Conservative government, this could have been taken as mere rhetoric designed to underline the strength of the province's case. But even before Joey Smallwood's defeat there had been a government edict which it did not take too much imagination to see as the thin end of the wedge of nationalization.

In the fall of 1970, hearing that the Iron Ore Company planned a $300 million expansion of its operations at Labrador City, the Churchill Falls company wrote to its president, Bill Bennett, asking him how much new power he would require. Bennett replied that he would need an extra 60 megawatts (80,000 horse power) beginning August 1, 1972. In the power contract with Hydro-Québec, Churchill Falls had reserved 225 megawatts to supply Twin Falls' customers when that plant was closed down, but this extra requirement would have to come from the 300 megawatts set aside for recapture by Newfoundland.

Under the Twin Falls contract, the Iron Ore Company and Wabush Mines had committed themselves to take or pay for 280,000 horse power at a price that averaged out to 4.32 mills per kilowatt-hour. Any power they took above that guaranteed minimum, up to the 307,000 horse power rated capacity of the Twin plant, cost them only 2 mills. And Bennett apparently expected that this 2-mill rate would apply to *any* extra power he needed, including the new 60-megawatt load. He was both surprised and annoyed when the company quoted him a price of 4 mills which, he was quick to complain, was considerably more than Hydro-Québec was paying for the same power.

The company explained that one of the conditions in the trust deed covering its first mortgage bonds was that it must not sell recaptured power on terms any less advantageous than those in the contract with Hydro-Québec. This meant that the price for recaptured power must include not only the mill rate agreed in the contract but an extra half a mill to make up for the other financial commitments Hydro had shouldered, including its payment of part of the company's bond interest.

Also, the price must include a component to compensate the company for the corporation tax it would have to pay on the sale of recaptured power, since the Newfoundland government had decreed originally that the PUITTA rebate would apply only on power sold to Hydro-Québec. The company had pointed out to Premier Smallwood at the time that this would penalize Newfoundland customers for recaptured power, but for some reason the legislation had never been changed.

Relations between the Iron Ore Company and Brinco, never exactly easy, became even more strained as the dispute dragged on. At one point, Bennett complained to Joey, protesting that a Newfoundland customer ought not to be asked to pay more for its power than a Quebec customer. Joey apparently agreed with him (even though one reason for the higher price was the tax the government would be retaining) because in September, 1971, he wrote to Bill Mulholland formally requesting the recapture of 65,000 horse power (the IOC's scaled-down requirement) and expressing the government's belief that its price should be "substantially less" than that offered to any other purchaser (in other words Hydro-Québec).

Perhaps the Premier was by now weary of the year-old dispute and had decided to teach both parties to it a lesson. At any rate, he also announced in his letter that the power would be bought by the Newfoundland and Labrador Power Commission and re-sold by that body to the Iron Ore Company — presumably at a profit.

The threat implicit in the entry of this government commission into the field elicited a prompt reply from Bill Mulholland explaining the company's position, assuring the Premier there was no impediment in the way of Churchill Falls supplying all the Iron Ore Company's needs, and requesting an appointment to discuss "the other very important matters dealt with in your letter."

There was no comfort in Joey's brisk reply. He was, he confessed, "somewhat perplexed" by Mulholland's request for an appointment.

> I am, of course, happy to see you at any time, and to discuss any point you wish to raise. At the same time, I am not clear that any of the statements made by me require further discussion. My letter conveyed to you a decision by the government of this Province, the decision being that we wish, through our Power Commission, to be the agency which purchases from you and sells to consumers any power produced by you at Churchill Falls which is to be sold for consumption in Labrador. This is a decision by the Government that does not

seem to require further discussion. What we would appreciate is confirmation by you that your company are prepared to help to implement this decision.

The Conservatives showed no sign of wishing to overturn this arrangement when they took office. In fact, the dispute over the price of the recaptured power, which was still unresolved, coupled with the belated discovery of the bizarre workings of the equalization formula, apparently contributed to a disenchantment with the Upper Churchill deal that mounted steadily throughout the summer of 1972. The bloom was certainly off the rose by September 28, when Harry Macdonell headed a Brinco delegation which called on Premier Moores in St. John's to put forward the company's plans for the development of the Lower Churchill.

It had been realized from the beginning that there were other potential power sites on the Churchill River and Don McParland had commissioned a preliminary investigation of them as early as 1967. By 1972, the company had spent $3 million on studies which showed that a development at Gull Island, about 150 miles downstream from the falls, could produce 1,800 megawatts, roughly a third of the output of Churchill Falls. Because the site lacked Churchill Falls' ideal combination of high head and a natural reservoir structure, the Premier was told, the Gull Island project would require an earth-fill dam 3,800 feet long and rising 317 feet from the river bed. This would give 40 billion cubic feet of water storage — a mere pond compared to the Churchill Falls reservoir, so that the efficient operation of the plant would always depend to a great extent on how the Churchill Falls plant was operated.

At this time, Quebec was still acknowledged to be the only possible customer for the power, and the proposed development included the construction of two transmission lines to the Hydro-Québec delivery point and a tie line to Churchill Falls. The total bill for it, Macdonell told the Premier, was estimated to be $550 million. This was more than half the cost of the Churchill Falls development for only a third of the power, because of the less efficient site and the way construction and interest costs had risen. For these same reasons, the mill rate for the power would probably have to be 6 or 7 mills, more than double the Churchill Falls rate.

The Premier was obviously not overly impressed by the plan for, after the meeting, he told the press Brinco would be presenting further proposals later. In the meantime, he sounded a warning note: "Besides Brinco and Quebec," he said, "another company is interested in developing the Lower Churchill." He declined to name this other company but it was variously rumoured to be owned by either John Shaheen or the well-known Atlantic provinces oil magnate K. C. Irving.

The succeeding weeks did nothing to improve relations between the government and the company, and Mulholland and Macdonell bridled in December when John Crosbie, now Minister of Finance, asked for the reports compiled so far on the Lower Churchill. This was an unusual request, to say the least, in the light of the government's admission that it was discussing the Lower Churchill with another potential developer. Having spent $3 million on the reports, the company naturally considered them proprietary material. And since the government apparently did not feel Brinco was entitled to any priority — notwithstanding the rights granted to it in the Principal Agreement, its performance on the Upper Churchill and its large investment in Gull Island — the company was understandably reluctant to part with reports that would be invaluable to a potential competitor.

The battle lines were drawn in January 1973, at a meeting between Crosbie and a Brinco party, again headed by Harry Macdonell, at which the minister laid down no fewer than eighteen conditions for the Gull Island development. Macdonell described them in a follow-up letter to Crosbie as "highly onerous." Without saying so at the time, he considered they all but ruled out any development of Gull Island.

The government, Crosbie said, had no intention of passing on any portion of the PUITTA rebate (the vital link in the Churchill Falls deal) to the company developing Gull Island. Nor would it grant any exemption from the provincial sales tax or gasoline tax during the con-struction period. (These exemptions had been granted by the Smallwood government in return for the company's shouldering expenses for roads and other services at Churchill Falls, such as schools and hospitals, which would normally have been the responsibility of the government.) Crosbie also told Macdonell the province must receive, free, a one-third share of the equity of the company carrying out the Gull Island development, in return for which it would give up its 8 per cent rental and 50-cent horse power royalty — a condition admittedly inspired by the working of the equalization formula. The developing company must agree to build a transmission line to take some of the power to the Goose Bay—Happy Valley area, about sixty miles away, and Goose Bay must be used as the port for the project. Furthermore, no lease would be granted until the negotiations on the price of recaptured power from the Upper Churchill were "brought to a successful conclusion." And the Gull Island contract must also include a clause for the recapture of 300 megawatts, at a price which "should not exceed the generating station busbar cost."

Macdonell gave the company's reaction to the government's conditions at another meeting in Crosbie's office on February 1. Once again, he tried to explain that the PUITTA rebate was essential, that Hydro-Québec had refused to enter any deal that would have meant it paying federal corporation tax, and would be no more inclined to pay an additional tax to Newfoundland. (The company's consistent view that the PUITTA rebate would be indispensable to the new development also had been demonstrated as early as 1967, when the Smallwood government passed legislation approving a draft lease to the Lower Churchill; the company did not take it up, partly because it did not guarantee the PUITTA rebate.)

Macdonell told Crosbie the withholding of the rebate would subject the Gull development to a tax rate of 49 per cent, more than double that borne by Churchill Falls. By also asking for one-third of the equity in the new company, the government was claiming 64 per cent of the profits to be expected from the deal. And by removing the exemptions from the provincial sales and gasoline taxes it was imposing an estimated $32 million down payment on the Gull Island developer.

By now, almost three years after the dispute with the Iron Ore Company had begun, Macdonell was beginning to despair of ever making the company's point on the price of the power recaptured from the Hydro-Québec contract, but he repeated it once again: if it were not for the tax burden, which was not imposed on the sale to Hydro-Québec, the province would have a substantial block of Churchill Falls power available to it at the same price Hydro-Québec was paying, without ever having assumed any of the guarantees or financial expenditures incurred by Hydro.

As for the condition that the Gull developer should build a transmission line to Goose Bay, that seemed reasonable enough. The company would also examine the dock and road facilities at Goose Bay to assess its suitability as the port for the project. And there should certainly be no difficulty negotiating the recapture of some of the Gull power. But, Macdonell reminded the minister, the twin restraints of geography and long-distance transmission technology meant that the project required the cooperation of Quebec, either in buying the power itself or permitting it to be transported through the province to other customers, which historically it had always refused to do. And the combination of conditions stipulated by the government threatened to make the project so expensive that the mill rate would be such that Hydro-Québec might well turn to some other alternative, such as a nuclear plant.

It was not an encouraging meeting, and the clear implication of Macdonell's comments was that unless the government modified its stand it was going to be difficult for him to justify committing any more of the shareholders' funds to the project. Nevertheless, the company agreed to re-work its calculations on the basis of the figures supplied by the government, in preparation for another meeting.

So far the discussions, unpromising though they seemed, had at least been conducted in private. But on March 30, in his budget speech, Crosbie told the House that the returns to the province from Gull Island would have to be substantially greater than those from Churchill Falls. And, he announced, three of the government's conditions for the development were "non-negotiable": namely, there would be no PUITTA rebate; the project would not be exempt from sales and gasoline taxes; and a transmission line must be built to Goose Bay.

Bill Mulholland laboured long and hard composing his speech for the annual meeting of Brinco on April 12. There were divided views as to whether he should make a public reply to the minister at all, and in the event the speech he delivered was considerably shorter than the one originally prepared. He repeated the case against the government's conditions which had already been made to Crosbie and pointed out that both the province and the company must keep their demands and expectations in line with the buyer's ability to pay. "If either the company or the province sets unreasonable or unacceptable conditions," he said, "then the price will not be right. And if the price is not right, then there will be no buyer. If there is no buyer, there can be no project."

A passage omitted from the original speech made much the same point — a point worth repeating since it continued to divide the company and the government to the end: "Power cannot be made cheap by decree. The costs of generation and transmission are governed more by the laws of physics than by the statements of cabinet ministers or company presidents. There is a price above which Gull Island power cannot be sold. It will take the earnest and determined efforts of both the province and the company developing the site to make it possible to determine, and to meet, that price."

In the normal course of economic and commercial events, the validity of that statement is self-evident. In the government's view, as events were to demonstrate, there were other factors transcending normal economic or commercial considerations.

Macdonell met Crosbie again on April 24. The government had supplied the company with calculations claiming to demonstrate that if it charged 8 mills for the power it could meet all the government's conditions and still make a return of 15 per cent on its equity. Macdonell pointed out an omission that Brinco's financial department had discovered with some surprise: the government calculations assumed that investors would be content to receive no return on their money during the four or five years it would take to build the plant and get it into production. According to Brinco's calculation, Macdonell said, the power would have to be sold for 12 mills to meet the government's conditions, and at that price there was no possible customer in sight.

Having recently consulted Roland Giroux, president of Hydro-Québec, Macdonell passed on to Crosbie the commission's latest position: it had no immediate need of the Gull power, but if the price was right it would consider a deal. And, in Macdonell's view, Hydro-Québec would expect a price of less than 8 mills.

Once again, the meeting ended inconclusively, and soon afterward the government informed the company it had commissioned a preliminary study of the feasibility of keeping the Gull power in the province, using some of it in Labrador and transmitting the rest to the island by way of submarine cables beneath the Strait of Belle Isle. The U.S. economic and engineering consulting firm engaged to carry out this study, H. Zinder and Associates, reported by the early summer that this scheme was "both economically viable and socially desirable." And on July 30, Premier Moores told a press conference the government had decided to go ahead with the Gull project without Quebec as a customer. "It is the intention of the provincial government," he said, "to use power created from the Lower Churchill within this province only. It is clear to us that this position is in the best interests of all Newfoundlanders."

The scheme naturally recalled Joey's ill-fated experience with his "Anglo-Saxon route" but the Premier said that technological advances in Scandinavia and the Soviet Union made the underwater crossing of the Strait of Belle Isle more feasible than it would have been in the early sixties. He forecast that the power would be on stream by 1978 or 1979 if construction work began during the following year, 1974, and announced that further feasibility studies would be carried out by Zinder and another company, Teshmont Consultants, of Winnipeg,* Moores pre-

*Formed in 1966 for the huge Nelson River hydro-electric project in Manitoba, Teshmont is a joint venture linking Templeton Engineering, of Winnipeg, Shawinigan Engineering and Montreal Engineering.

dicted the energy shortage in the United States would reach crisis proportions within the next few years and added: "Regardless of any change in the cost of other forms of energy, such as thermal and nuclear power, we will have a stability in this province that few parts of the world could depend on with the same reliability."

On behalf of Brinco, Harry Macdonell promised any help the company could give to the studies, but he was not optimistic. When the idea that Gull Island power might be transmitted into the Island grid had arisen at the first meeting between Moores and the company, early in 1972, Macdonell had said that to the extent that it was economic and feasible, the power should be used within the province. But the technical difficulties involved in transmitting it across the Strait of Belle Isle, plus the huge increase in demand that would be necessary if the output were to be used on the island, were such that he was not convinced the scheme was either economic *or* feasible.

Huge icebergs jostle each other through the Strait of Belle Isle every spring, and the Brinco engineers were convinced that cables lying unprotected on the sea bottom would be damaged or cut by their grinding action. The only alternative was an eleven-mile tunnel beneath the sea bed, but so little was known about the geology under the strait that it was difficult to make a firm estimate of its eventual cost because of the risk that cave-ins or other unforeseen problems might lead to horrendous overruns. This, coupled with the need for almost seven hundred miles of transmission line across the rugged country between Gull Island and St. John's, was likely to raise the cost of the power beyond anything the customers would pay — even if enough customers could be found, and of this Brinco had grave doubts. Using all of Gull's potential output of 1,800 megawatts on the island would call for a threefold increase in the demand for electricity, since the island's total consumption at that time, industrial, commercial and residential, was less than 800 megawatts. So the position seemed to be that even if the scheme proved physically possible, the price of the power in St. John's would probably be too high to attract customers. And without firm customers, the project could not be financed.

Nevertheless, Brinco cooperated in the new study, supplying Teshmont with the cost estimates it had developed through the years and other relevant data. The Teshmont-Zinder report, when it was submitted to the government in February 1974, turned out to be markedly more optimistic than Brinco had been. It said that the Gull project was technically feasible, that there were "excellent prospects" of new

370

industries being established in Newfoundland, and that forecasts indicated the full output of the plant could be absorbed on the island between 1986 and 1988. The total cost of the power station and transmission lines was estimated to be almost $1.2 billion, a considerable portion of which, the report said, would probably be met by the federal government financing the transmission, as it had done on the Nelson project. The cost of supplying customers on the island would therefore average 14.1 mills per kilowatt-hour.

Premier Moores and an official party which included Crosbie and Leo Barry, Minister of Mines and Energy, visited Montreal on February 27 to discuss these conclusions with the Brinco management. The company had received a copy of the summary volume of the report a few days earlier, but the two volumes of back-up data had been delivered only that morning. So Macdonell reserved his judgment on them for a later date. He did, however, tell the Premier that the company had serious reservations about the sets of figures purporting to show how much cheaper it would be if the scheme were carried out by the government rather than a private company. Because the calculations seemed to be based on different formulas, he said, the comparison they were supposed to provide was a distorted one. For instance, while the figures for the private company included a component for corporation tax, it was not taken into account in the comparison that most of this tax would ultimately be returned to the province. In short, the figures obviously showed a bias toward public ownership.

Macdonell did not know how right he was. The whole meeting, in fact, was merely an academic exercise, because by now the die had been cast and the company's days were numbered. The more the government had reflected on the Churchill Falls deal, the more dissatisfied it had become with it. And the Premier eventually became convinced that the interests of Brinco's shareholders conflicted with the interests of the province. The corporation seemed to be adamant that the only way to develop Gull was by selling the power to Hydro-Québec. "From the private point of view," Moores told the author, "it makes more sense to put the Gull power into an eastern grid. But from our point of view, it would have been almost a dereliction of duty to do that."

And so in July 1973, he had asked the province's financial advisers, the Toronto investment firm of Burns Bros. and Denton, to make a financial assessment of the effects of nationalizing all or any of the province's electrical utilities, and the province's ability to raise the financing required to do so. The Burns report, presented in November, analyzed various possibilities open to the government and while it did not make any recommendations as such, its message was clear: the government should take over Brinco by making a cash offer of $6.75 per share to all shareholders. Moores and his colleagues took a few weeks to mull over the report. Then, in mid-February 1974, assured by the Bank of Nova Scotia that the required funds would be forthcoming, the government set the machinery for the takeover in motion, in great secrecy. The February 27 meeting on the Teshmont-Zinder report was therefore a mere formality.

Less than two weeks later, just before midday on Monday, March 11, Frank Moores paid an unexpected visit to Sir Val Duncan in his London office. An hour or so later, John Crosbie called on Bill Mulholland in Montreal. Unlike Duncan, Mulholland had been forewarned of the reason for the visits: just before Crosbie walked in he had received a telephone call from Michel Bélanger, president of the Montreal Stock Exchange, who told him that the previous evening the Newfoundland government had asked him to suspend trading in Brinco shares when the market opened that day because the government planned to make an offer for them. By the time Mulholland had reached Duncan with this bombshell, Duncan had already heard the news from Frank Moores: that the government intended to buy Brinco, it hoped voluntarily; but if the company objected, the Premier wanted Duncan to understand that the government had the power to enforce its wishes.

Duncan was taken aback as much by the tone of the ultimatum as by the government's intention, and deeply offended by the mistrust implicit in the government's unilateral approach to the stock exchanges. He told Moores it had been twenty years since he had first taken an interest in Brinco and he was disappointed that now that the many vicissitudes of the past had been overcome and Churchill Falls was virtually completed, the government was stepping in to take it over before its shareholders had received a penny in dividends.

As he listened to Moores' explanation for the move, Duncan decided the province's real objective was to repossess its water power. That could be done, he told the Premier, without the province taking over the whole of Brinco: Brinco could simply sell the government its shares in Churchill Falls and its remaining water rights, but retain its other interests and at least part of its identity. But there were 22,000 Brinco shareholders and Rio Tinto-Zinc would not be separated from them in the negotiations ahead. So he suggested that Moores return to Canada, where he and Sir Mark Turner would consult the Brinco management and directors before continuing the discussions. Moores agreed, and next day he with his party, and Duncan with his, flew the Atlantic as the only occupants of a more than usually silent first-class cabin.

In Montreal, meanwhile, Bill Mulholland had also told Crosbie he thought the government could attain its objective without in effect destroying Brinco. This point became one of the major issues between the company and the government in the strenuous negotiations that occupied the next two and a half weeks. The company could never quite understand why the government wanted the whole of Brinco. One reason the government advanced publicly was that it hoped to preserve the talented and experienced Brinco team intact to run Churchill Falls and carry out new ventures, including Gull. But quite early in the negotiations it became clear, at least within the company, that many of the senior members of the staff had no more intention of working for a nationalized concern than they had of emigrating to Siberia. Perhaps a more influential reason was that Brinco was a company incorporated in Newfoundland, which clearly gave the government the power to expropriate it, whereas Churchill Falls was incorporated federally, making provincial action at least doubtful.

The other major issue of the negotiations, of course, was the price of $6.75 that the government offered for the shares. This was $1.50 more than they had been trading at when they were taken off the market, but the company argued that their quoted price was far below their true eventual value because the company had never paid a dividend, and investors who had held the shares for many years without return had done so confident that the company's ultimate dividend policy would repay their patience.

On the Newfoundland side, the negotiations involved at various times the Premier himself, John Crosbie, Leo Barry and Industrial Development Minister C. William Doody, supported by advisers from the power commission and government departments. The tenor of the many meetings held was seldom smooth, and occasionally rancorous. During a series of discussions on Wednesday, March 13, the government turned down Duncan's suggestion that it buy Brinco's 57 per cent holding in the Churchill Falls company, and its remaining water rights, for $200 million. It also rejected a complicated alternative plan which would have transferred Brinco's staff and all its non-hydro assets to its Brinex subsidiary before the government takeover. And Moores warned Duncan that if the company did not agree to his terms by 3.30 p.m. Friday, he would initiate expropriation legislation.

More proposals and counter-proposals were exchanged without any progress in meetings on Thursday and Friday morning, and as Moores' deadline approached the company requested and was given an extension until 6.30 p.m. Then Paul Desmarais, chairman of the Power Corporation, from his vantage point as a friend of Frank Moores and a director of Brinco, arranged a private meeting between Duncan and the Premier. To reach the Premier's suite in the Ritz-Carlton Hotel unobserved by the journalists camped in the lobby, Duncan slipped in through the hotel's back door — and in trying to find the service elevator temporarily lost himself among the redolences of the Ritz's excellent kitchens.

In private the two principals seem to have found the beginning of a rapport that was sadly absent from full meetings of the negotiators. They managed to agree on a compromise solution restoring all Labrador water power to the government but permitting Brinco to remain in private hands as an ongoing concern, retaining all its non-hydro assets and its staff, who would complete the Churchill Falls project and manage the development of Gull Island on a contract basis. This agreement foundered at another series of meetings on Saturday, apparently because Moores' aides had assumed Brinco would retain only those members of its staff directly involved in its mineral exploration and investment program.

There was no more contact between the two sides until nearly midnight on Monday, March 18, when the government submitted a revised offer raising the price it was prepared to pay for the Brinco shares to $7.07 but voicing its belief that Brinco was "not divisible" and insisting that its terms be accepted by midnight Wednesday. The Premier and his party then returned to Newfoundland to await developments. The Brinco board considered the new terms, concluded that even the new price was not high enough and decided it could not advise the company's shareholders to accept the offer. Moores was so informed on Wednesday evening, but the company again put forward a counter-proposal: that the government buy Churchill Falls and the water rights for $164 million. That sum worked out to the government's original offer for Brinco shares of $6.75 per share, but the company undertook to offer dissatisfied shareholders the opportunity to cash in their Brinco shares at the government's new price of $7.07.

Moores rejected this counter-offer within the hour, in a telex message which also announced that he would introduce expropriation legislation to the House next day. The mood prevailing at One Westmount Square at this time hovered somewhere between resignation and acute depression, with a simmering of revolt thrown in. Some employees, distrustful of the government's intentions, tried to form an association to protect their interests in the event of a government takeover. Many of those in the upper echelons of management had already received offers of new positions, and Mulholland, Macdonell and John Beaver feared that some key employees, particularly among the operating personnel up on site, would just walk away from their jobs if the nationalization went through. On Thursday morning, they sent a message to Moores warning him of their fears and strongly suggesting that a cabinet minister go to Churchill Falls within 24 hours to explain the government's position and try to reassure the employees.

On Thursday afternoon, Premier Moores told the House the government had reluctantly decided to vest all the shares of Brinco in the province. This was not a decision made on the spur of the moment but a "well-planned, thoroughly researched move which will prove to be of incalculable benefit for future generations of Newfoundlanders." A nation or region with its own sources of primary energy had a distinct advantage when it came to economic development, particularly in the light of the world energy crisis, and the government intended to establish a comprehensively planned approach to the development of the province and its resources. "The resources of Newfoundland are the property of our people," the Premier said. "It follows that control over these resources must rest with the people's government."

Clearly implying that Brinco had been dragging its feet on the Lower Churchill project, he said the government was determined to have Gull Island developed and have the power brought to the island. It had been assured that the projected costs of the development could be fully recovered from anticipated revenue "based on competitive rates that will attract new industry." Building the project in the most economic way — namely, all at once — would mean it would supply more energy than the province could use in the immediate future, but it was hoped to sell that energy to Quebec on a short-term basis. It was important for the government to be in a position to deal directly with other provinces, and the decision to acquire Brinco "should in no way be interpreted as being indicative of any nationalization policy on the part of my government. Indeed, we are of the firm opinion that government ownership of Brinco is a necessary and fundamental step toward ensuring that this province will continue to be able to attract private enterprise in the future."

That, it seemed, was the end. In fact, the expropriation bill was introduced to the House next morning. But at almost the same time as Moores was speaking, Crosbie called Bill Mulholland, thanked him for his warning about the restlessness at Churchill Falls and told him his colleague Bill Doody was preparing to leave for the site as soon as transportation was available. Then, to Mulholland's astonishment, he said he thought there was still room for an agreement along the lines suggested by the company and would he, Mulholland, and Sir Val Duncan, consider coming to St. John's for further discussions? Mulholland let out a whoop as he put down the phone and told a startled group of executives who had been sitting moodily in his office: "There's the greatest shoestring catch in history." From now on, he figured, it would be just a question of setting a price for the Churchill Falls company and the water rights.

Moores smiled as he discussed the episode with the author months later. "We introduced the legislation to identify what we *could* do, if we had to," he said. "But we had no aspirations to nationalize mines or cement factories."

Duncan and Mulholland flew to St. John's on Friday, for more meetings — including another private session between Duncan and Moores at the Premier's home at the weekend — at which misunderstandings were apparently resolved and bygones permitted to remain bygones. And on Thursday, March 28, the Premier told the House that the province and the company had reached "an amicable negotiated position" under which the province would buy the Churchill Falls company and all Brinco's remaining water rights in Labrador for $160 million. Brinco agreed to "use its best efforts" to complete the Churchill project, to carry on the current program for the development of Gull Island for the rest of 1974 and, at the government's request, to submit a proposal for the continued management of the Gull project. The Premier said the agreement would enable Brinco to "retain its corporate viability" and provide the cash for its expansion into other fields.

Henceforth, obviously, it would be quite a different company from the one its shareholders had originally invested in, so it was agreed that all shareholders would be given the opportunity to sell back their shares to the company at $7.07, the price the government had offered. The majority shareholders, Rio Tinto-Zinc, Bethlehem Steel and the Marubeni Corporation and Fuji Bank (Japanese companies which had bought a 5 per cent share of Brinco in 1973) announced that they would not take up the cash offer for their shares, thus ensuring Brinco's continued existence.

The many documents involved in the sale were signed in Montreal on June 27 and the government handed a bank draft for $160 million to Brinco. After the traumatic division of the hitherto closely knit Brinco and Churchill Falls staffs, the new Churchill Falls company completed installation of the plant independently of Brinco. The eleventh and last unit began supplying power on September 25, 1974, eighteen months ahead of schedule and almost two full years before the company's obligations under the power contract.

John Beaver, appointed president of the new company by the government, now had a headquarters staff of about a hundred in Montreal and a little over two hundred employees on site to man the power station and airport and perform maintenance work, including inspection of the dykes. Counting families, and those employed in the hospital, school and Town Centre, the permanent population of Churchill Falls settled down at around one thousand.

As discussions on Gull Island continued, the Newfoundland and Labrador Power Commission disagreed with the extent of the control Brinco felt it needed if it were to manage the project and so the company withdrew from the scheme entirely, finally ending its involvement with the hydro-electric power resources of Newfoundland and Labrador.

The other assets it had retained still included the mineral rights to 20,000 square miles of Labrador and 4,500 square miles on the island, the rest of the original concession area having been surrendered at intervals as envisaged in the Principal Agreement. By mid-1975, the many joint venture exploration projects carried out by Brinex with various partners — in other parts of Canada as well as Newfoundland — had resulted in only one mine. Originally forecast to produce 4 million tons of ore grading $1\frac{1}{2}$ per cent copper, the Whales Back mine actually produced 4.2 million tons grading less than 1 per cent. It cost Brinex $8.5 million in capital expenditure to open it and $16.6 million in operating costs during its lifetime. The $10 million profit it produced fell more than $2 million short of matching the amount of shareholders' funds spent on mineral exploration up to the time it closed, its ore played out, just before the Churchill Falls inauguration in 1972.

Brinco still held its rights to the Kitts and Michelin uranium deposits which, in view of the sharp rise in the price of uranium, formed an important company asset. Brinex geologists, having identified several "lead-zinc targets" on the west coast of Newfoundland, were conducting further investigation into their possibilities. And Brinex retained, until 1979, its exclusive right to explore for oil and gas in an area of almost

6,000 square miles in western Newfoundland, 1,200 square miles of which is under water in bays and inlets.

The Brinex concession area on the Port-au-Port peninsula of western Newfoundland contained a large deposit of high-quality limestone suitable for the manufacture of cement — the largest such deposit known to exist on the eastern Canadian seaboard. In 1974, after joint feasibility studies by Brinex and Lehigh Portland Cement Company of Allentown, Pennsylvania, it was hoped to build a $100 million plant there, with the substantial capacity of a million tons a year. Lehigh dropped out, however, early in 1975 for several reasons: the fall in the number of construction starts in the United States because of the recession; increased shipping charges caused by mounting fuel costs; and its own growing capital requirements at home. At the time of writing, Brinco was continuing to investigate the proposed project with another partner, Lake Ontario Portland Cement.

Ironically, perhaps, the assets remaining in Brinco's hands did not include those with which Eric Bowater had attempted to dazzle his dubious friends when he was trying to enlist them in the consortium: the exploitation of the Labrador spruce stands was never deemed commercially feasible and the timber rights were returned to the government in the late sixties.

For the rest, Brinco's surviving assets were outside Newfoundland. And — in a parallel that recalled the company's early years in the wilderness — the most publicized of them was in a sense also the least tangible, since it consisted only of knowledge: knowledge painstakingly acquired and stored partly in the formal language of highly confidential reports, partly in the heads of men with the confidence to dream big dreams.

While the British government lost interest in the late fifties in the proposal to build a uranium-enrichment plant to use some of the Hamilton Falls power, the idea never entirely died within Brinco. It was revived by Don McParland in the late sixties, as more and more countries around the world turned to nuclear power for the generation of electricity. The Canadian system of nuclear power generation uses natural uranium, more than 99 per cent of which consists largely of the isotope U-238, with the remainder — about 0.72 per cent — being the fissionable isotope U-235. Elsewhere in the world, most nuclear power plants use uranium in which the U-235 has been concentrated, or enriched, to 3 per cent of the whole. The concentration process is so complex and expensive that only the major powers have so far built enrichment plants, as government projects.

378

This government involvement, and the obvious danger of nuclear technology being applied to the construction of nuclear weapons, had resulted in some key details of the enrichment process being shrouded in official secrecy. But the Brinco team set about learning as much as possible about it and concluded it would be within the corporation's capability to build and operate a plant. Bill Mulholland announced in March 1971, that it would like to do so, and said the project would cost at least a billion dollars. "The limited availability of enrichment capacity in the free world will result in a critical shortage of enriched fuel within a few years," he told a meeting of the Empire Club in Toronto. "It would appear therefore that steps should be taken at once to augment existing free world enriching capacity."

The company believed Canada was the most suitable site for a new enrichment plant but a final conclusion could not be made without further studies of the various possible enrichment techniques, which would require official sanction. Brinco had therefore asked the Canadian government for its approval of its plans and the diplomatic support it would need to gain the technological assistance of the United States authorities (which the corporation had already been promised informally).

Brinco's initiative did not meet with universal approval. Some critics feared the effect of an enrichment plant on the environment; others protested that Canada should not export energy, in the form of either enriched uranium or the immense amount of electricity the plant would consume; still others wondered about the effect on Canada's own efforts to sell its Candu-type reactors abroad if the country began to produce fuel for competing systems. It was more than two years later, in August 1973, that Ottawa issued a none-too-enthusiastic statement saying the construction of an enrichment plant on Canadian territory would be acceptable and the government would, provided a long list of conditions were met, give companies hoping to build one the diplomatic support they would need in their negotiations with the Americans. The Americans, in turn, had their own list of conditions, and as this book went to press Brinco was considering the effect of all the various conditions on its plans before deciding whether to go any further with a project in the enrichment field.

Apart from this ambitious undertaking, which would in its own way be as much of a challenge for a private company as was the building of Churchill Falls, the rest of Brinco's pending projects were in the mining and mineral-exploration fields. Between April 1972 and December 1974, the company spent almost $5 million to build a pilot plant and evaluate the possibilities of one of the largest known undeveloped asbestos deposits in the world, fifty miles north of Amos in northern Quebec. Having bought control of the company owning the deposit, Abitibi Asbestos Mining Company, Brinco in mid-1975 was still evaluating its commercial potential. If the decision to go into production were made, it would be one of the biggest asbestos operations in Quebec, and hence in the world.

The company also had investments in other mining companies with various interests in Quebec, British Columbia, the Yukon Territory and the State of Washington, and in September 1974, after long negotiations, the directors agreed to merge Brinco with Rio Tinto-Zinc's Canadian mining arm, Rio Algom. The merger terms gave Brinco shareholders the option of becoming shareholders in the merged company or, if they wanted to cash in their shares, assured them of not less than $8.27 per share — $1.20 more than the price offered by the Newfoundland government, which neither the company nor its financial advisers, Morgan Stanley and Wood Gundy, had ever considered adequate.*

The method by which the merger was to be achieved was a complicated one but in effect it valued one Rio Algom share at $24.33 in terms of Brinco's assets. Gordon Ball, a partner in the Toronto firm of Martens, Ball, Albrecht Securities, decided this placed too high a value on Brinco and organized a campaign against the proposed merger, claiming it would be unfair to Rio Algom's minority shareholders, diluting their earnings by as much as 26 per cent. Whether or not this would have been the case, Ball was not alone in considering that the terms of the merger favoured Brinco's shareholders. Some commentators pointed out that Brinco would bring Rio Algom a considerable amount of cash which it could use for expansion at a time when raising money was both difficult and expensive (and in mid-1975, to finance the expansion of its uranium-mining operation at Elliot Lake, Rio Algom did go to the market to raise $75 million by an offering of debentures and an issue of rights to shareholders). By the beginning of December, Rio Algom's market price had fallen from $26 to $19.75. It was possible to hold that this was a normal market decline, but in the face of it, and in view of

*The share purchase offer remained open until March 31, 1975, by which time minority shareholders had cashed in a total of 9,946,389 shares. This left Rio Tinto-Zinc and Bethlehem Steel in control of 83 per cent of Brinco and Marubeni Corporation and Fuji Bank with 8 per cent. Heads bloody but unbowed, enough private shareholders retained their faith in Brinco to hold on to 1,347,065 shares, or 9 per cent of the total.

several other factors, the wise course was considered to be to call off the merger. A brief statement attributed the decision to "market conditions."

Unfortunately, the idea of the merger had proved no more appealing to the Brinco staff than it had to Gordon Ball. Employees who seemed likely to be displaced by it were assured of generous severance terms at the outset, and Rio Algom offered to absorb as many key personnel as it could with offers of new posts. But there is a limit to the number of new chairs that can be squeezed into an executive suite. By the time the merger was called off some members of the Brinco team whose names will be familiar to readers of this book — and others no less important whose names have not even been mentioned, merely because there were so many of them — had accepted the attractive offers in other organizations that almost all of them had received when it first seemed the company was about to be nationalized. Bill Mulholland accepted Arnold Hart's invitation to become president of the Bank of Montreal. Harry Macdonell agreed to replace him as president of Brinco long enough to shepherd the company through its latest crisis, then returned to the practice of law in Toronto. Harold Snyder became head of the newly created Centre for Cold Ocean Resources Engineering at Memorial University in St. John's, where he would coordinate and supervise research into the technology needed to harvest valuable resources in cold ocean areas. Dick Boivin was invited to become general manager of Spino Construction, one of the Churchill Falls contractors which had gone on to even bigger things since, and took a hand-picked team of his favourite men with him.

Wherever graduates of Brinco went they carried with them a reputation for drive and efficiency. Those who remained with the company retained the tradition and the taste for challenge. During the summer of 1975, the corporation seemed to pause for a period of readjustment, assessing its options under the interim presidency of Nick Crossley, a California engineer and Rio Tinto-Zinc consultant who had become familiar with its activities during the crisis days that followed the air crash of 1969. In September, the directors announced the appointment as president and chief executive officer of Donald Robins De Laporte, a geologist and mining engineer who had joined one of the corporation's founder shareholders, Falconbridge, in 1956 and became vice-president of its western minerals division and president of several of its most important subsidiaries. As this book went to press, a suitable encore for Churchill Falls had still to be decided, but surmounting obstacles and surviving crises had become a way of life for Brinco during its twenty-two-year history, and it seemed unlikely that the story had ended.

Index

227n, 246
Peat, Marwick, Mitchell and
  Company, 28, 101, 329
Peck, Ralph B., 348
Pekans River, 95, 103
Pépin, Jean-Luc, 276
Petito, Frank, 299
Petitsikapau Lake, 330, 331
Petroleum and natural gas rights,
  24, 58, 377
Phillips, Dick, 189, 254, 272
Photographic Survey
  Corporation, 29
Pickands Mather and Company, 99,
  100, 102-106, 110,
  113, 114
Pickersgill, Jack, 180, 191, 216, 217,
  219, 223, 224
Pigeon, Louis-Philippe, 226,
  235, 244
Piloski, Murray, 73, 76
Pitfield, W. C. and Company,
  31, 94, 282
Plowden, Sir Eric, 78
Pointe Noire, 160, 178
Potvin, L. E., 79
Poulin, Noella, 218
Powell, Ray E., 65-67
Powell, Sheppard T., Associates, 351
Power Corporation of Canada, 88,
  317, 374
Pratte, Yves, 235, 236, 241-43, 245
Preece, Cardew and Rider, 197,
  200, 204, 205, 207, 209
Principal Agreement, 24, 33, 37,
  58, 59, 86, 98, 111n, 169, 198,
  204, 359, 366, 377
Privy Council ruling on Labrador
  boundary, 132, 133, 185, 186,
  244, 248n, 249n
Project labour agreement, 273-75
Prudential Insurance Company of
  America, 304, 305, 309
Public Utilities Income Tax
  Transfer Act (PUITTA), 226,
  327, 361, 362, 364, 366-68
Pushie, Gordon F., 17, 100, 127,
  205, 208, 209, 211, 223, 234, 280

Quebec North Shore and Labrador
  Railway, 19, 50, 69, 93, 114,
  314, 330
Quebecair, 315

Rasminsky, Louis, 296
Rebate of corporation tax, 183, 210,
  215, 216, 219, 220, 224, 226,
  233-35, 311, 327, 361
Reid, Angus, 30
Rental on profits, 23, 24, 360,
  361, 366
Ressegieu, Fred E., 165, 189, 240,
  256, 258, 264, 319, 326
Retty, Dr. J. A., 92
Riley, Daniel A., 209
Rio Algom Mines Ltd., 137, 139,
  158, 161-63, 169, 192, 227, 236,
  237, 240, 255, 258, 259, 282,
  285, 289, 300-302, 320, 380, 381
Rio Tinto-Zinc Corporation Ltd.
  (formerly Rio Tinto Company
  Ltd.), 13, 14, 17, 18, 20, 27, 60,
  101, 137, 138, 161,
  161n, 163, 164, 192, 271,
  298-301, 317, 321, 323, 327, 372,
  376, 380, 380n
Robertson, R. Gordon, 192
Robinson, Ray, 301
Roderick, Stan, 52
Romaine River, 132, 143, 223
Rothermere, Lord, 15
Rothschild, N. M. and Sons, 14, 16,
  24, 28, 35, 86, 282-84
Rowe, Dr. Fred, 323
Roy, Leo, 124, 125
Royal Bank of Canada, 33, 34, 130
Royal Securities, 94
Royal Trust, 308n, 312, 327
Royalties, 24, 169, 170, 360, 361, 366
Rynard, Hugh, 155, 189, 256

Sandys, Duncan, 8, 10
Sail Lake, 331-33, 344, 346
St. Augustine River, 143
St. Laurent, Louis, 3, 89, 134
St. Paul River, 143
Sandgirt Lake, 330
Saul, George, 326
Sauvé, Paul, 119, 124
Scarabelli, Rudy, 336, 337
Schefferville, 40, 41 50, 56, 93, 103,
  126-28, 140, 180, 248n, 330
Scott Falls, 93
Scott, George N., 284, 285, 311
Scott, Sir Hilary, 24, 26, 98, 138
Scrivener, Robert, 321
Seal Lake, 349

390

Seewer, P. W., 17, 19
Sept-Iles, 19, 50, 61, 64, 66, 79, 83,
    84, 103, 114, 122, 126, 127,
    160, 248n, 299, 301, 314-16, 318,
    323, 343, 356
Shaheen, John, 358, 366
Share issues, 85, 86, 145, 204, 205,
    271, 272, 282-85, 288, 289,
    298, 302
Sharp, Mitchell, 304
Sharples, Bob, 320
Shawinigan Engineering Company,
    55, 56, 79, 86, 94, 95, 97, 109,
    124, 138, 142, 152, 168,
    169, 178, 199, 369n
Shawinigan Water and Power
Company, 55, 68, 79-81, 142, 152
Shawmont, 199
Shelbourne, Philip, 283
Sherwin, John, 114
Simon, Sir John, K. C., 132
Simpson, C. Norman, 165
Sinclair, Ian D., 267n
Slichter, F. B., 348
Smallwood, Joseph Roberts, 3, 7-17,
    19-25, 30, 31, 35-37, 43, 58, 59,
    69-71, 74-76, 78, 86-90, 90n, 96,
    98, 99, 101, 103-105, 110, 111,
    120-22, 125-28, 134, 134n, 135,
    136, 136n, 139, 140, 142-45,
    150-54, 157, 160, 161, 168-70,
    172, 177-79, 182-84, 184n, 185,
    186, 186n, 192, 195, 197-200,
    203-11, 213-26, 227n, 228, 231-37,
    244-49, 275, 276, 276n, 277, 278,
    280, 281, 292, 312, 323, 349, 350,
    358, 360, 362-64, 366, 367, 369
Smallwood reservoir, 349, 353
Smith, Jim, 159, 191, 306, 311, 312
Smith, H. Greville, 105, 113, 114,
    119, 121, 123, 136-38, 140, 158
Smith, Victor H., 94, 97, 98, 100,
    102, 103, 106, 110, 119, 149, 162
Smith, W. R., 44
Snyder, Harold, 240, 258, 319, 320,
    322, 326, 336, 347, 381
Sogemines, 31, 67
Sonneman, Bob, 301
Southam, Alexander William, 26-31,
    35-37, 49-62, 65, 66, 68-70, 74-76,
    78, 80-82, 82n, 83, 86-88, 90,
    94-97, 100-105, 111, 119-21, 123,
    125-27, 134-38, 140-42, 147-50,

152-54, 155, 157, 162, 198, 276n,
    357
Southern Newfoundland Power
    and Development Ltd., 88, 90,
    91, 197, 198
Spino Construction Ltd., 336,
    338, 381
Squires, Elmer, 258
Squires, Sir Richard, 133
Stairs, Denis, 49-52, 55
Steel Company of Canada Ltd., 105
Steepe, Vince, 258
Steers, Ian, 283
Stephenson, Sir William, 14
Stokes-Rees, Commander R. H.
    (Rosie), 53, 54
Strait of Belle Isle, 130, 180, 197,
    211, 223, 369, 370
Stuart, Ron, 81
Suez Canal Company, 86, 161
Sun Life Assurance Company of
    Canada, 305, 310
Sutherland, Bloss, 322
Swiggum, Harry, 320, 322
Sword, Bill, 305

Taché, J. E., 130
Taku River, 142n
Taschereau, Alexandre, 131,
    132, 135
Tax on private utilities, 80, 141,
    176, 177, 183, 201, 203, 204, 209,
    210, 214, 225, 234, 242, 360
Tax, withholding, 295, 296
Templeton Engineering, 369n
Tennant, John, 295
Teshmont Consultants Ltd., 369,
    369n, 370
Teshmont-Zinder report, 370, 372
Thibaudeau, Wilfrid, 46, 48
Thomas Falls, 93
Thompson, Joe, 95, 103
Thomson, Gary, 189, 258
Thornwood Investments Ltd.,
    301, 302
Timber, 9, 13, 18, 19, 23, 24, 33,
    49, 87, 231, 378
Timmins, Father Peter, 323
Timmins, Jules, 21, 92, 94, 96, 103
Topographical Survey of Canada, 29
Torrey, Arthur S., 94, 95, 100, 147,
    148, 224, 241, 248, 272, 283, 284
Tourigny, Emile, 78